Body of Text

SUNY series in Medieval Middle East History
Jere Bacharach, editor

Body of Text

The Emergence of the Sunnī Law of Ritual Purity

Marion Holmes Katz

State University of New York Press

Published by
State University of New York Press, Albany

Printed in the United States of America

For information, address State University of New York Press,
90 State Street, Suite 700, Albany, NY 12207

Production by Marilyn P. Semerad
Marketing by Anne M. Valentine

Library of Congress Cataloging-in-Publication Data

Katz, Marion Holmes, 1967–
Body of text : the emergence of the Sunni law of ritual purity / Marion Holmes Katz.
p. cm. — (SUNY series in medieval Middle East history)
Based on the author's thesis (doctoral)—University of Chicago.
Includes bibliographical references (p.) and index.
ISBN 0-7914-5381-2 (alk. paper)—ISBN 0-7914-5382-0 (pbk. : alk. paper)
1. Purity, Ritual—Islam. 2. Islam—Customs and practices. I. Title. II. Series.

BP184.4.K37 2002
297.3'8—dc21 2001049803

10 9 8 7 6 5 4 3 2 1

Contents

Acknowledgments

This book is based on my doctoral dissertation, written under the supervision of Professors Wadad Kadi, Fred Donner, and Robert Dankoff of the Department of Near Eastern Languages and Civilizations, University of Chicago. They have been models of deep learning and reliable kindness as well as sources of valuable criticism. Without their erudition and their patience, this work could not have been written. I also have a debt of gratitude to Professor Frank Reynolds and the members of the Institute for the Advanced Study of Religion at the University of Chicago Divinity School, 1995–96, who critiqued chapter 1 and provided a stimulating environment for the early stages of my project. My colleagues at the Department of Religion, Franklin and Marshall College, 1996–97, and at Mount Holyoke, from 1997 until the present, also provided valuable advice and support. Finally, my thanks go to the members of my family, Adria, Stanley, and Derek Katz. I can never express my gratitude to you.

The following quotations from previously printed works are reprinted here with the permission of their publishers. Quotations from Mary Douglas, *Purity and Danger: An Analysis of the Concepts of Pollution and Taboo* (Routledge, 1966) reprinted by permission of Routledge. Quotations from Julie Marcus, *A World of Difference: Islam and Gender Hierarchy in Turkey* (London, Atlantic Highland, N.J., U.S.A.: Zed, 1992) reprinted by permission of Zed Books Ltd. Quotation from Howard Eilber-Schwartz, *The Savage in Judaism* (Bloomington and Indianapolis: Indiana University Press, 1990) reprinted by permission of Indiana University Press. Quotation from P. Hershman, "Hair, Sex and Dirt (*Man*, n.s. 9 [1974]) reprinted by permission of Blackwell Publishers. Quotations from Carol Delaney, "Mortal Flow: Menstruation in Turkish Village Society," in Thomas Buckley and Alma Gottlieb, *Blood Magic: Explorations in the Anthropology of Menstruation*, © 1988 The Regents of the University of California, reprinted by permission of the University of California Press. Quotation from Jack Goody, *The Domestication of the Savage Mind* (Cambridge, Cambridge University Press, 1977), reprinted with the permission of Cambridge University Press. Quotations from Mary Boyce, "Padyab and Nerang: Two Pahlavi Terms Further Considered," *Bulletin of the School of Oriental and African Studies* 54 (1991), pp. 281–91, reprinted with the permission of Oxford University Press. Quotation from Peter Brown, *The Body and Society: Men, Women and Sexual Renunciation in Early Christianity* (New York: Columbia University Press, 1988), reprinted with permission of Columbia University Press. Quotation from Sherry Ortner, "Is Male to Female as Nature is to Culture?" in Michelle Zimbalist Rosaldo and Louise Lamphere, eds., *Woman, Culture, and Society* (Stanford, California: Stanford University Press, 1974), © 1974 by the Board of Trustees of the Leland Stanford Junior University, reprinted with permission of Stanford University Press. Quotation from Geraldine Brooks, *Nine Parts of Desire* (New York: Anchor Books, Doubleday, 1995), reprinted with permission of Doubleday, a division of Random House, Inc.

Introduction

The Comprehensiveness of the Law

> Someone said to [the Prophet Muḥammad's Companion] Salmān, "Your Prophet has taught you everything, even how to defecate!" [Salmān] said, "Yes, he has! He has forbidden us to face in the direction of Mecca (*al-qibla*) when defecating or urinating, to cleanse ourselves after defecation or urination (*an nastanjiya*) with the right hand, to cleanse ourselves with less than three stones, or to cleanse ourselves with a piece of dung or a bone."
>
> —Muslim ibn al-Ḥajjāj, *Ṣaḥīḥ Muslim bi-sharḥ al-imām Muḥyī l-Dīn al-Nawawī*

It is a truism that Islamic law (the Sharīʿa) is a comprehensive system encompassing all aspects of life. Not limiting itself to public or enforceable norms, it provides guidance for the most intimate and the most apparently trivial details of the believer's private conduct. The Sharīʿa's unflinching attention to the least sublime aspects of human existence has often, as the above anecdote suggests, been met with the incomprehension of outside observers. Its exhaustive examination of the minutiae of the believer's biological functions, up to and including the details of elimination and sexual behavior, has provoked the mirth of seventh-century pagans and twentieth-century Americans alike.[1] The classical Islamic sources themselves, however, consistently insist that false modesty should not prevent thorough inquiry into this area of the law. "God is not ashamed of the truth [Qurʾān 33:53]," an Anṣārī woman declares to the Prophet in an early report; "how should I wash myself after menstruation?"[2] "How praiseworthy are the women of the Anṣār," the Prophet's wife ʿĀʾisha is supposed to have said, remembering this event: "shame did not prevent them from informing themselves about their religion (*lam yakun yamnaʿuhunnaʾl-ḥayāʾ an yatafaqqahna fīʾl-dīn*)."[3] Like a growing number of other studies, this work takes as its premise that Islamic legal discourse on the body, its healthy functioning, and its various discontents is meaningful and that analysis of this discourse reveals an important aspect of Muslims' understanding of the human experience.

I will begin by giving a brief outline of the system of ritual purity in Islamic law, as it has been known to Sunnī Muslims since approximately the fourth century A.H./tenth century C.E. The Islamic system of ritual purity (*ṭahāra*) recognizes three types of impurity. Two of these forms of pollution affect the human person. Someone who is affected by either of these forms of impurity may not engage in acts of worship without performing the appropriate ablutions. Contact with sacred objects and places is also limited: one should be in a state of purity to touch a copy of the Qurʾān, and persons who are in a state of major pollution should not tarry in (or, according to other opinions, should not enter) the mosque. Minor impurity is caused by urination, defecation, farting, sleep, or other loss of consciousness, and skin-to-skin contact with members of the opposite sex.[4] Some jurists also hold that it is caused by vomiting or bleeding. Minor impurity necessitates the minor ablutions known in Arabic as *wuḍūʾ*, which involve washing the face and hands, wiping the head, and washing the feet. These ablutions are strictly symbolic, in the sense that they do not cleanse the parts of the body physically involved in the polluting act.[5] Major impurity, or *janāba*, is caused by sexual activity and requires washing of the entire body. Neither the major nor the minor form of personal pollution is contagious; one can enter these states of impurity only by having the relevant bodily functions oneself, and not by coming into contact with another person in a state of pollution. The third type of pollution recognized by Islamic law, technically designated by the Arabic term *najāsa*, refers to substances or beings that are inherently impure. Something that is substantively impure, or *najis*, can never be rendered pure; it is essentially and unalterably defiling.[6] However, it is not contagiously impure.[7] A person with such a substance on his body must remove the substance before he can perform acts of worship requiring purity. However, he suffers no pollution of his person. He is not generally required to perform any prescribed ablutions beyond the physical removal of the offending substance; nor is the impurity of the substance communicated to him so that he in turn defiles other things or people. The main impure substances recognized by most schools of Islamic law are blood, bodily wastes (of humans and some animals), alcohol, carrion (that is, the dead bodies of animals that have not been ritually slaughtered), and the living or dead bodies of pigs and dogs.

This work deals with the process by which the basic lineaments of this system were developed by the Sunnī Muslim community. The term "Sunnī" is anachronistic for much of the period covered by this study, and should not be understood to imply that the early figures discussed here understood themselves as members of a distinct and self-conscious religious community clearly demarcated from other sects. Some of them, indeed, displayed a loyalty to the Prophet's cousin and son-in-law, ʿAlī ibn abī Ṭālib, and his family that led contemporaries to refer to them as "Shīʿī" (that is, "partisans" of ʿAlī).

However, all of the major sources referred to here became part of the emerging Sunnī tradition, and all share the fundamental assumption that distinguishes Sunnī tradition compilations from those of the Imāmī Shī'ites: that the example of the Prophet is transmitted by the community as a whole, and through ordinary modes of communication, rather than exclusively and esoterically by the Prophet's direct descendants through 'Alī. The Imāmī tradition has elaborated a highly distinct understanding of the Islamic law of ritual purity, one which will not be examined here. The Imāmī material is far too rich, and the distinctive challenges posed by the nature of the Imāmī sources too divergent, to allow inclusion in this study.

The Historical Background

Islam was born into a world in which all of the major religious traditions subjected their followers to strictures of purity. Jews, Zoroastrians, and Christians alike surrounded bodily functions—eating, sexual intercourse, elimination—with prohibitions and counteracted the pollutions thus incurred by rites of purification before engaging in ritual activities or entering sacred spaces. Similar avoidances and ablutions were practiced in Ancient Greece and thus formed part of the Hellenistic heritage of the Middle East.[8]

By the time of the rise of Islam in the seventh century C.E., the rabbinic Jews of Palestine and 'Irāq had essentially closed the Talmudic canon, enshrining a form of Jewish practice in which the daily life of the common believer was constrained by a complex body of purity law. Exacting rules of food purity regulated the ingress of substances into the body; the law also prescribed avoidances and ablutions for certain kinds of bodily flux. Menstruating women, and those who had recently given birth, were regarded as contagiously impure and observed rules of sexual avoidance until purified by complete immersion. Many Jews also believed it obligatory to perform ablutions before prayer or Torah study if they had engaged in sexual intercourse. Distinctively, Jewish law stipulated that most pollutions could not be reversed by appropriate ablutions as soon as they had been incurred; depending on the degree of defilement, the affected person was required to wait either until sundown or for a full week before purification was performed. The stipulation that purification occur by full immersion in "living water" also imposed unusually stringent requirements; specially constructed ritual baths had long been indispensable features of Jewish communities everywhere. While the avoidance and counteraction of corpse pollution (which could be communicated by mere "overshadowing," without physical contact with a dead body) had been a central feature of biblical and Mishnaic law, the destruction of the Temple and residence in the Diaspora made these features of the law largely obsolete.[9]

Zoroastrian purity law was, if anything, more exacting than that developed in the Jewish Halakha. Zoroastrian purity practices were distinctive in that they sought to protect not only sacred activities and places but the pure elements of fire, water, and earth from pollution. This element of Zoroastrian belief gave rise to practices, such as the exposure of human corpses (which was based on the impossibility of interring the dead in the pure earth), which were both odd and offensive in the sight of neighboring religious communities. However, Zoroastrians also followed a number of purity strictures which focused on the human body and which strongly resembled those of other religious traditions in the region. A simple form of ablution, involving the washing of the extremities, was performed by the adult Zoroastrian upon arising, at the beginning of each of the five watches of the day, before eating or engaging in religious ritual, and after urination or defecation.[10] All substances emitted by or separated from the body—urine, feces, saliva, breath, blood, semen, hair—were considered polluting.[11] Sexual intercourse and seminal emission caused ritual defilement, and men and women were required to purify themselves by ritual bathing.[12] Menstruating women were regarded as contagiously impure, and performed ritual ablutions after the cessation of the menstrual flow. Similarly, marital intercourse was forbidden for forty days after childbirth.[13] Zoroastrians divided the animal world into Ahuric creatures, which were beneficial and pure, and Daēvic creatures, which were harmful and polluting. Most edible animals were considered Ahuric, and all Ahuric animals were permitted as food, with the exception of the dog and the cock—two animals which were the object of religious reverence among Zoroastrians.[14] Daēvic animals were primarily insects, reptiles, and beasts of prey; domestic cats and elephants were also included in this category. Meat was rendered permissible for consumption by ritual slaughter, and carrion (that is, the flesh of animals that had died of natural causes or been improperly slaughtered) was considered highly polluting.[15]

Ritual purity is not a concept ordinarily associated with Christian practice. Indeed, the radical rejection of Jewish purity strictures, or their displacement into the realm of metaphor, is as deeply rooted in the Christian tradition as the documents of the New Testament.[16] Nevertheless, purity practices seem to have been deeply entrenched in the lifeways of what became the Christian world. There is ample evidence that, although Christians never developed a "law of purity" comparable in complexity, uniformity, or authority to the Jewish and Zoroastrian strictures, many early medieval Christians followed purity practices that paralleled the major elements of the ritual law of neighboring religious communities. Evidence of these practices is to be found in handbooks of penance, which included, among the many other infractions of which a priest or layperson might be guilty, a wide variety of purity violations. These offenses fall into two major categories: sexual pollution (associated with sexual intercourse, menstruation, and childbirth) and the consumption of forbidden foodstuffs. The opinions attributed to Theodore of Tarsus (archbishop of Canterbury, 668–90 C.E.), should suffice to indicate the degree to which a prominent Christian living shortly after the lifetime of the Prophet Muḥammad embraced the concept of ritual purity. He stipulates that menstruating women may neither enter a church nor partake of communion; women are similarly barred from the church during a forty-day period of pollution following childbirth.[17] Married couples are to observe three nights of sexual abstinence before taking communion, and to wash themselves before entering a church if they have engaged in relations.[18] Carrion includes those animals which have been killed by birds or beasts or strangled in nets.[19] Carrion may not be consumed, but its skin, wool, and horns may be put to nonsacred uses.[20] Fish are exempted from the rules regarding carrion.[21]

A basic set of roughly analogous purity strictures apparently formed part of pre-Islamic pagan Arabic tradition. Pre-Islamic poetry invokes the impurity of menstrual blood, using it as a metaphor for the defiling power of the unavenged blood of a tribesman. Women performed ablutions at the end of their menstrual periods; their blood polluted water, and thus they were given access to the waterhole last, after the more prestigious (and purer) male tribal warriors had cleansed themselves.[22] Menstrual pollution was, of course, a ritual disability; an early Muslim source notes that "the menstruating women were not allowed to come near the idols or touch them."[23] Later Muslims also believed that pre-Islamic Arabs had avoided intercourse with women during their menstrual periods.[24] Sexual intercourse was considered polluting and was followed by ablutions.[25] Sacred places and objects could be defiled (and thus deconsecrated) with various impure substances including blood, human waste, and carrion (particularly, if this is not an Islamic anachronism, that of dogs).[26]

Similar purity strictures also formed part of the religious heritage of pre-Islamic South Arabia, a highly distinct cultural area. Surviving South Arabian inscriptions installed to commemorate the expiation of various sins include several which mention offenses against the rules of ritual purity. Recorded transgressions include having relations with a menstruating woman or one who has recently given birth, failing to perform ablutions after sexual relations or after contact with menstruating women, and entering the temple with soiled clothes.[27]

In light of all of these data, it is unsurprising that early Orientalist scholars of Islam saw the Islamic law of ritual purity largely as a derivative offshoot of earlier religious traditions. Opinion was, however, divided on the identity of the tradition to which Islamic conceptions of purity could best be traced. In a 1914 article, A. J. Wensinck offered a detailed comparison of the relevant provisions of Islamic and Jewish law, arguing that the parallels were so extensive and precise as to exclude any possibility of accidental convergence.[28]

Although the parallels between the Jewish and Islamic laws of purity are, as Wensinck noted, extensive and occasionally striking, his arguments are ultimately less rigorous than impressionistic. Many of Wensinck's parallels are either broad enough to open the possibility that a given practice represents a general, interconfessional trend rather than a distinctively Jewish precedent or obvious enough to suggest independent yet parallel development. The conclusion that a large amount of water cannot be polluted by mere contact with impure matter, or that pollution does not travel upstream in flowing water, suggests common sense more than authoritative precedent. Furthermore, adopting the same ad hoc procedure as Wensinck, it would be possible to suggest just as convincingly that Muslim purity law was drawn primarily from Christian sources. The strictures attributed to Theodore of Tarsus provide more than one parallel fully as striking as those cited by Wensinck; thus, Muslim jurists similarly exempted fish from the ban on carrion and allowed the utilization of the hides of animals that had not been properly slaughtered.[29] Despite a number of major (and symbolically potent) differences of opinion, such as the permissibility of pork, a combination of common sense and interconfessional contact guaranteed that all of the major religious groupings encountered by the early Muslim community shared a certain number of commonalities with the emergent Islamic law.

Another hypothesis about the origins of the Islamic law of ritual purity was presented by Ignaz Goldziher in an impressionistic yet insightful lecture entitled simply *"Islamisme et parsisme."* Goldziher suggested that the Islamic law of purity as a whole was grounded in Zoroastrian tradition. Speaking in highly general terms, he argued that Islamic purity practices were generally *either* continuations *or* deliberate and polemical reversals of those established in Zoroastrianism. Muslims had been influenced by Persian ideas, but naturally did not wish to engage in "servile" copying. The remaining strictures which could not be related to the Zoroastrian example, either positively or negatively, were to be regarded as "survivals of ancient pagan taboos."[30]

Without giving any general account of the parallels between the Zoroastrian and Islamic laws of purity, Goldziher offers two examples of polemical reversals of Zoroastrian conceptions: the Muslim rejection of the idea (present in both Zoroastrianism and Judaism) that human corpses defile and the Muslim belief that dogs are impure (which contrasted sharply with Zoroastrian veneration of dogs).[31]

Despite the apparently vague nature of Goldziher's knowledge of Zoroastrian practice, some aspects of his argument have subsequently proved convincing to the leading authorities in Zoroastrian studies. Although they differ over some details of the ritual, both Jamsheed Choksy and Mary Boyce have noted that the Zoroastrian purification ritual of *pādyāb-kustī* bears a striking resemblance to the Islamic *wuḍūʾ* ablutions. Indeed, the parallelism between the two rites is self-evident from the following description of the *pādyāb* ritual, drawn from a modern Zoroastrian source:

> When people rise from sleep at daybreak, they should first apply something (*chīz-ī*) to their hands, and then wash their hands and face with clean water, thus: the hands should be washed from the elbows to the tips of the fingers, thrice, and the face should be washed from behind the ears to under the chin and to the crown of the head. And he should wash the feet up to the knee, thrice, and recite the Avesta.[32]

Aside from a few differences of detail, for instance the washing of the feet up to the knees, this could almost be a description of the *wuḍū'* ablutions as prescribed by classical Islamic law. Not only are the individual elements of the ablutions very similar, but they are performed on a very similar list of occasions:

> It is enjoined that this ritual be performed early each morning on rising from sleep, prior to the religious act of eating, before ablutions, at the beginning of each of the five watches of the day, and after urination or excretion.[33]

Given the fact that, as will emerge from the remainder of this work, the definition of the details of the *wuḍū'* ablutions and the occasions for their performance constitute the most detailed, distinctive, and controversial element of the Islamic law of ritual purity, this parallelism with Zoroastrian practice is highly provocative. The central problem in interpreting the significance of this parallelism is posed by the difficulty of dating the Zoroastrian rituals. The Zoroastrian texts providing the details of the relevant rites postdate the rise of Islam by many centuries.[34] Nevertheless, Boyce concludes that it "appears to have been the case" that "the Zoroastrian *kustī* rite [also known as *pādyāb*] . . . created a pattern for the Muslim *wuḍū'*."[35] She bases this conclusion on the convergence of the Iranian and the Indian traditions of Zoroastrian practice:

> The closeness of the Persian and Parsi descriptions of rituals is striking, even allowing for the fact that Dastur Darab [her Parsi source], as a learned priest of Navsari . . . was familiar with the writings of his Irani predecessors; for the differences in ritual terminology, though slight, indicate an independent Parsi tradition. Clearly, therefore, the rituals described were firmly established throughout the Zoroastrian community well before the

> ancestors of the Parsis migrated to Gujarat and became in large measure separated from the Iranis. These rituals must therefore in their existing form have been at least a thousand years old before Dastur Darab [d. circa 1735 C.E.] recorded them in India. (In part they are evidently very much older.)[36]

Since, however, the ancestors of the Parsis are believed to have emigrated to the Indian subcontinent several centuries after the Muslim conquests, Boyce's chronological inference is not completely compelling.[37] Nevertheless, I believe that the adoption of the general outlines of a Zoroastrian ritual by the early Muslims is more likely than the opposite scenario for two reasons. One is that it seems inherently improbable that an old and well-established religious community with an entrenched priesthood would adopt a ritual from a parvenu religion, as Islam must then have appeared to Zoroastrians. Particularly given that the ancestors of the Parsis emigrated to India specifically to avoid suppression of their traditions in an Islamic state, it seems implausible that they would have been interested in adopting religious innovations from those whom they perceived as interlopers and oppressors. In contrast, it is not at all difficult to imagine a young and dynamic community of Muslims, including many converts from Zoroastrianism, adopting and transforming a ritual from the older tradition. Muslims could and did adopt many elements of preexisting faiths, which they then infused with the distinctive spiritual impulse of Islam.

Of course, it is very unlikely that Muslims would have adopted a ritual that they regarded as distinctively Zoroastrian. More probably, the basic elements of the *pādyāb* ritual—like a number of other purity practices—had become detached from their original confessional context to become part of what may be termed the ritual *koiné* of the late antique and early medieval Near East. Each individual confessional system was, from this point of view, merely a dialectical form of a broader language of purity that all contemporary inhabitants of the region probably understood to some extent.

According to the testimony of early Islamic sources, pre-Islamic pagan Arabs seem to have associated a basic set of purity practices relating to sexual intercourse, menstruation, and food avoidances with the practice of monotheism. The authenticity of reports about *ḥanīf*s, Arabs of the period immediately preceding the advent of the Prophet who allegedly adopted a generic Abrahamic monotheism, is of course open to question. Nevertheless, the content of descriptions of their conversion is suggestive. Ibn Isḥāq's biography of the Prophet reports of one such figure:

> As for Zayd ibn ʿAmr ibn Nufayl, he reserved judgment (*waqafa*) and did not convert to either Judaism or Christianity. He aban-

> doned the religion of his people and shunned idols, carrion, blood, and meat that was sacrificed to idols.[38]

Here, avoidance of blood, carrion, and animals sacrificed in the context of the pagan cult is second only to the rejection of idol-worship as a sign of monotheistic identification. Another such figure, Abū Qays ibn abī Anas, is said to have been

> a man who became an ascetic (*tarahhaba*) in the Time of Ignorance [i.e., before the advent of Islam]; he wore haircloth (*al-musūḥ*), abandoned idols, performed full ablutions from sexual pollution (*ightasala min al-janāba*), and avoided pollution through contact with menstruating women (*taṭahhara min al-ḥāʾiḍ min al-nisāʾ*). He almost became a Christian, but then held back. He went into a house of his and made it into a house of worship (*masjid*) which no menstruating woman (*ṭāmith*) or person in a state of sexual pollution (*junub*) was allowed to enter. He said, "I worship the God of Abraham."[39]

Muslims were always perfectly aware of basic commonalities between their own purity practices and those of their neighbors. Indeed, the Islamic master narrative in which successive prophets brought tidings of the same God encouraged the acceptance (or even the exaggeration) of continuities with the practice of previous monotheistic communities. Some medieval authors thus argued that *wuḍūʾ* had not originated with the own community, but was part of the broader monotheistic heritage. Ibn Ḥajar al-Haytamī (d. A.H. 974/1567 C.E.) writes of the *wuḍūʾ* ablutions,

> [*Wuḍūʾ*] was made obligatory [on Muslims], along with prayer, on the night of the Prophet's Night Journey. It was also commanded by God in the previous religious dispensations (*huwa min al-sharāʾiʿ al-qadīma*), as is indicated by well-authenticated *ḥadīth* reports. What is distinctive to us [i.e., the Muslims] (*alladhī min khaṣāʾiṣinā*) is either the specific way of performing it or the radiance of the head and extremities [appearing in the next life on Muslims who have performed *wuḍūʾ*] (*al-ghurra waʾl-taḥjīl*).[40]

However, Muslims were not interested in tracing their own purity practices back to the Zoroastrians. A description of the legislation of Zoroaster by the fourth century A.H./tenth century C.E. author al-Thaʿālibī[41] demonstrates that medieval Muslims were aware of (or emphasized) the differences between Zoroastrian and Muslim purity practices to the almost complete exclusion of the commonalities:

> [Zoroaster] venerated fire as a form of devotion to God, because it is from His light and is one of the greatest and most glorious of elements. He also commanded the veneration of water, which is the staff of existence and causes the world to flourish. He commanded that it be kept inviolate and that it not be used to remove impurities (*al-najāsāt*) or take off dirt except with the intermediation of a liquid such as that which is extracted from cows [*sic;* i.e., bull's urine], from grape vines, and from trees. He proscribed carrion and claimed that anything that issues forth from the interior of a human being, from any orifice, is impure (*najis*). For this reason, he established the practice of pursing the lips (*al-zamzama*) while eating as a precaution against spurtings (*bawādir*) of saliva, which would defile the food. He imposed three prayers in which they turn around with the revolution of the sun, one at sunrise, one when the sun is at its apex (*ʿinda intiṣāf al-shams*), and the third at sunset. He forbade eating and drinking from wooden and earthenware vessels, because they are susceptible to impurities. . . . He proscribed the touching of dead bodies and claimed that touching [a dead body] necessitates full ablutions (*al-ghusl*) because it has become impure through the departure of the pure spirit. He commanded the people to purify themselves once in every day and night, which according to him comprised washing the face and the hands.[42]

In fact, Islamic tradition seems to have a consistent tendency to elide the memory of Zoroastrian influence while emphasizing Jewish and Christian precedent—even when the practice involved would seem to be of Zoroastrian origin. For example, a widespread report from the tradition of the *asbāb al-nuzūl* (the "occasions of revelation," reports providing narrative settings for the revelation of individual passages of the Qurʾān) explains the historical background of the primary Qurʾānic reference to menstruation (verse 2:222) as follows:

> When a woman among them was menstruating, the Jews would not eat with her or live in the same house with her. The Prophet's Companions inquired [about this], and God revealed {They ask you about menstruation. Say: 'It is an indisposition. Keep aloof from women during their menstrual periods . . . "} [Qurʾān 2:222]. The Prophet said, "Do anything but have sexual intercourse [with them]." This reached the Jews, who said, "This man does not want to leave a single thing in which he does not contradict (*khālafa*) us!" Usayd ibn Ḥuḍayr and ʿAbbād ibn Bishr came and

> said, "O Prophet! The Jews say such and such. Can't we have sexual intercourse with them?" The Prophet's face changed so that we thought that he was angry with them.[43]

Now, while it is certainly the case that Islamic prohibitions on direct and indirect contact with menstruating women were less severe than those practiced by Jews—and some *ḥadīth* reports seem accurately to reflect practices documented in the Talmud—this particular tradition refers to a practice that exceeds ordinary Jewish strictures: the removal of menstruating women from their houses. The tradition is very explicit about this; in the version transmitted by Ibn Māja, the wording is: "they would not sit in the same house [with a menstruating woman]." This is, in fact, more likely a reference to a Zoroastrian practice; Zoroastrians relegated women to separate huts for the duration of their menstrual period.[44] In fact, a version of the tradition preserved by Jalāl al-Dīn al-Suyūṭī (d. 910–11/1505 C.E.) recognizes the provenance of this custom:

> [This passage of] the Qur'ān was revealed about menstruating women at a time when the Muslims were expelling them from their houses *as the Iranians do* (*ka-fi'l al-'ajam*). They asked the Prophet for a ruling on this, and God revealed {They ask you about menstruation. Say: "It is an indisposition. Keep aloof from women during their menstrual periods . . . "} [Qur'ān 2:222]. The believers thought that "keeping aloof" meant their leaving their houses, as they were doing, until he recited the end of the verse, and the believers understood what "keeping aloof" was, because God said, {Do not touch them until they are clean again}.[45]

How should we interpret the fact that Islamic tradition shifts the practice of sequestering menstruating women in separate huts from the Zoroastrians to the Jews? The answer clearly lies in the theological significance of Muslim successorship to the Jews as holders of the covenant, a position that demanded a complex mixture of continuity and opposition with respect to Jewish tradition. Zoroastrianism, unlike Judaism and Christianity, had no such role in Islamic salvation history. Although Zoroastrians were important historically, both as external influences and as converts to Islam, conscious memory of the Zoroastrian example had nothing to contribute to the theological self-understanding of the Muslim community.[46] Whatever the historical importance of the Zoroastrian contribution, therefore, it does little to illuminate Muslim understandings of the nature or importance of ritual purity.

As we have seen, one of the most influential early approaches to the study of the Islamic law of ritual purity among Western scholars was the search for the historical origins of individual purity practices in the traditions of other confessional communities. Another approach, inspired by early developments in the comparative study of religion, sought to understand some Islamic purity practices in the context of the belief in spirits which was then understood to dominate the earliest stages of religious development. This approach was pursued both by Julius Wellhausen (in his classic study *Reste arabischen Heidentums*) and by Ignaz Goldziher (in an article entitled "Wasser als Dämonen abwehrendes Mittel").[47] Wellhausen notes the connection among the *jinn* (disembodied spirits whose existence is recognized both by pre-Islamic Arab tradition and by the Qur'ān), places of burial,[48] and polluting bodily functions. He notes the practice of spitting to the left when relieving oneself, in hopes of warding off the *jinn*, who are known to hover to a person's left; similarly, the use of the left hand for lowly or polluting functions expresses contempt for them. Combining his ideas about "primitive" religion with the traditional search for origins, Wellhausen argues that such practices and the beliefs on which they are based are not authentically Arab at all. He speculates that "certain particularly characteristic customs" may have originated with the Essenes, passed through the Sabeans, and thus been transmitted to the Muslims.[49] Wellhausen's approach is more rigorous than Goldziher's in that he limits himself largely to cases in which the Arabic sources explicitly invoke fear of spirits as the rationale for specific purity practices; Goldziher, in contrast, infers such motivations primary from rough parallels with practices familiar from other cultural spheres. In most cases, he makes no claim that the practices in question are understood to have the meanings he proposes by those who practice or invoke them; the "original" purpose of the relevant practices is assumed to have been "forgotten" even before the time of the pre-Islamic poets.[50]

However, both authors' hypotheses regarding the apotropaic basis of certain Islamic purity beliefs are fundamentally limited by the larger theoretical framework in which they work. Goldziher and Wellhausen both base their comments on an evolutionary schema in which belief in spirits represents the central component of a primitive stage in the development of religion. Within this theoretical frame of reference, they are constrained to regard practices based on implicit or explicit apotropaic motives as "remnants" or "survivals" of the pre-Islamic past, even if the practices themselves are perpetuated by Muslims or, indeed, are known exclusively from Islamic sources. For Goldziher, as we have seen, many of the relevant practices are taken to have been vestigial and ill-understood for the entirety of the recorded Arab past, including the pagan period. As a result of this theoretical framework, neither author is able to give any account of the significance of the relevant practices within the religious world-views and the symbolic structures of the people who are actually known to have used them. Furthermore, both scholars are constrained by their approach to limit their analysis to peripheral elements of the Islamic law of purity; it does not allow them to enquire into more central and (in their view) more authentically "Islamic" elements of the law.

In fact, there are clear apotropaic elements in the law of ritual purity as understood by classical Islamic writers. One very obvious example of these elements is the formula (included in the sections devoted to ritual purity in a number of early sources) to be pronounced upon entering the privy (*al-khalāʾ*), that is, the secluded place used for urination and defecation: "O God, I take refuge with you from the vile ones (m. pl.) and the vile ones (f. pl.) (*allāhumma innī aʿūdhu bika min al-khubth waʾl-khabāʾith*)."[51] The commentator al-Qasṭallānī (d. A.H. 851/1448 C.E.) offers the classic interpretation of the invocation: "I take refuge with you and have recourse to you from male and female demons (*al-shayāṭīn*). . . . It is specifically used for the privy because demons frequent privies because God is not mentioned in them."[52]

This piece of lore reflects a strong yet complex connection between the concept of pollution and the presence of malign spirits. On one level, al-Qasṭallānī's second comment suggests that demons infest space that is desacralized by the absence of the invocation of God's name. Of course, it is precisely the filthiness of a place soiled by human wastes that prevents the invocation of God, thereby rendering it a fit haunt for demons. Here the relationship between pollution and demons would seem to be indirect: filth entails desacralization, which in turn attracts demons. However, al-Qasṭallānī's first comment suggests an even more intimate nexus between the concept of pollution and the indwelling of demons. This connection lies in the root *kh-b-th,* "to be vile." According to al-Qasṭallānī's (standard) gloss of the incantatory phrase "the vile ones (m. pl., *al-khubth*) and the vile ones (f. pl., *al-khabāʾith*)," the word refers specifically to demons. However, it is also the case that the root *kh-b-th* is the primary Qurʾānic root designating filthiness and ritual or moral impurity. *Kh-b-th* is the Qurʾānic opposite and counterpart of *ṭ-y-b,* "to be pure"; both can be used (literally or metaphorically) to refer to foods, actions, wealth, or people.[53] Thus, the root *kh-b-th* appears to refer *both* to that which is demonic *and* to that which is polluted or polluting—a highly significant combination. However, apotropaic motifs cannot elucidate the Islamic system of ritual purity as a whole. The demonic threat seems to be associated overwhelmingly with substantive impurity—what the classical legal tradition designates as *najāsa*—rather than to the states of pollution and the rites of purification applied to the human body.

Methodological Developments

While, as we have seen, scholars of the nineteenth and early twentieth centuries studied Islamic purity practices primarily in terms of "origins" and "survivals," the second half of the twentieth century saw a major theoretical shift towards the synchronic study of symbolic structures that transformed the study of ritual purity. The general theoretical trend that was to have the most fundamental and pervasive influence on the study of systems of ritual purity was rooted in the classical structuralism of Lévi-Strauss. Instead of pursuing individual ideas or practices backwards in time to their "origins" in other cultural groups or stages of religious development, an approach which (as discussed above) frequently led to the assumption that their meaning was vestigial or nonexistent in their present setting, scholars began to focus on the interrelationship between the various elements in a symbolic system. Central for the study of ritual purity was the Lévi-Straussian hypothesis that all symbolic structures can be reduced to binary oppositions ultimately resolving into the fundamental dichotomy between nature and culture.

At a basic level, this paradigm seems to fit the data of ritual purity very well. In the words of Louis Dumont,

> It can be seen that impurity corresponds to the organic aspect of man. Religion generally speaks in the name of universal order; but in this case, though unaware in this form of what it is doing, by proscribing impurity it in fact sets up an opposition between religious and social man on the one hand, and nature on the other.[54]

A corollary of this interpretation, in which rites of purity are seen to function as cultural responses to the irreducible residuum of the natural in human life, is that the fundamental raison d'être of these rites is the reassertion of control. From everyday bodily functions such as elimination to the final triumph of organic process at the moment of death, the events most widely regarded as polluting are either completely involuntary or (if, like elimination, performed at will) ultimately unavoidable. It is on this basis that Robert Parker explains the pollution associated with birth and death. The distinction between the "crucial transitions" in human life that are polluting (such as birth and death) and those that are not (such as marriage) is precisely the element of human control: "while marriage is a controlled event, birth and death intrude on human life at their own pleasure." Not only the timing of these events, but their nature as bodily experiences is chaotic; women in childbirth, like the dying, are in the throes of bodily events that neither they nor society can completely master. Thus, both require ritual responses in which personal and social control are reasserted.[55]

The most detailed and powerful elaboration of this general approach to the understanding of purity and pollution remains the pioneering work in the area, Mary Douglas's *Purity and Danger* (1966) and *Natural Symbols* (1970).

Douglas already articulates the idea that purity practices represe
imposition of control. However, she does not see this assertion c
function of a universal and undifferentiated symbolic opposition
ture and culture. Not all societies, she argues, have systems of ritual purity; not all of those who do have purity strictures of equal elaboration or intensity. Combining the structuralist tenet that rites of purity represent the assertion of cultural control over the functioning of the body with the Durkheimian axiom that religious rites are grounded in the representation of the body politic, Douglas argues that the nature and degree of purity strictures correspond to the nature and degree of the social strictures to which the individual is subject.

Douglas's approach, while sharing an emphasis on control, differs from that of the authors cited above in that she shifts the central focus of this control to the symbolic plane. She bases her analysis of the concept of pollution on the idea that "dirt is matter out of place." Defilement is produced by boundary violations, which can be either conceptual—failure to fit within a culturally accepted classificatory schema—or physical. Thus, polluting substances are fundamentally ambiguous; they fail to find a satisfactory or stable position on one side of some symbolically vital line of demarcation. For example, according to Douglas's now classic argument, the Hebrew Bible proscribes pigs and other animals because they fail to slot neatly into its classificatory schema, in which (among other things) ruminants have cleft hooves and fish have scales.[56] The boundary violations constituted by such taxonomic anomalies find their analog on the physical level in violations of the boundaries of the body: the bleeding, oozing, and elimination categorized in most systems of purity as polluting. Substances ejected from the body are, in this view, fundamentally ambiguous because they are neither fully part of, nor truly other than, the body. This idea has been elaborated by Edmund Leach, who argues that the repulsive quality of bodily exudations and wastes is grounded in early cognitive development:

> Such substances are ambiguous in the most fundamental way. The child's first and continuing problem is to determine the initial boundary. "What am I, as against the world?" "Where is the edge of me?" In this fundamental sense, faeces, urine, semen, and so forth, are both me and not me.[57]

The hypothesis that perceptions of pollution respond to failures of taxonomic control functions, in many cases, parallel to the hypothesis that pollution is to be equated with the loss of physical control. Robert Parker thus notes that birth and death are not merely "irruption[s] of the biological into social life" but, in their nature as points of transition, moments of ambiguity. Drawing on Van Gennep's concept of the rite of passage, Parker notes that newborns and corpses share a transitional quality, an anomalous condition of suspension on their way in or out of human society.[58]

Despite their pervasive influence on the study of ritual purity, however, Douglas's hypotheses have been subjected to sharp criticism in many subsequent studies. Parker, while noting (as quoted above) that human beings in certain life crises are both structurally ambiguous and associated with ideas of pollution, argues that such persons are not—as Douglas would argue—disturbing and thus polluting *because* they are ambiguous. Instead, they are regarded as ambiguous precisely because they are emotionally disturbing. "There is no intrinsic classificatory problem about the new-born baby," he notes; "he is alive enough when he enters the world. . . . Here, it is not the case that the logic of classifications has generated a misfit who therefore evokes a reaction of alarm; on the contrary, a disconcerting being has been declared a misfit by special manipulation of the classificatory processes."[59]

The anthropologist Jack Goody has similarly challenged Douglas's argument that purity taboos are grounded in cognitive dissonance generated by structural ambiguity. Discussing the work of Robert Horton, a student of African religion who adopts an approach very similar to Douglas's, Goody notes that in Horton's view

> incest is seen as flagrantly defying the established category system because it treats the mother, for example, as a wife and is therefore subject to a taboo. Equally, twins are dangerous because multiple births confuse the animal and the human world; the human corpse is polluting because it falls between the living and the dead, just as faeces and menstrual blood occupy the no-man's land between animate and inanimate.[60]

However, Goody argues, despite their initial plausibility these interpretations are far from compelling. In fact, he argues, these taboos cannot be traced to cognitive dissonance:

> Let us take incest. The argument is difficult to follow, for several reasons. Societies in West Africa often classify potential wives as "sisters" (this is indeed a feature of permitted cousin marriage and a Hawaiian terminology); nevertheless, men find no difficulty in sleeping with some and not with others. Equally, some "mothers" are accessible as sexual partners . . . If we look at systems of classification from the actor's standpoint, there is little problem in coping with overlapping categories; as we shall see, the Venn diagram is as relevant a model as the Table. Moreover, the whole discussion seems to rest upon a simplistic view of the relationship between linguistic acts and other social behavior.[61]

P. Hershman has extended the criticism that not everything that is anomalous is polluting (even in cultures that emphasize a concept of pollution) to emphasize the disjunction between the scholar's construction of a society's symbolic categories and that experienced by members of the society in question:

> It is the thesis of Leach and Douglas that where there is 'ambiguity' there is likely to be dirt and so taboo. This seems to me to be a big jump from a word like "ambiguity," which is a neutral observer's category with possible universal applications, to that of "dirt" which is an actor's category with emotive overtones implying a certain conception of things by people. The anthropologist, having derived the anomalies from his logical analysis of the categories of a culture, then proceeds to attribute emotional relationships by the actors to these so defined anomalies.[62]

Hershman applies this critique to a classical example from Douglas's interpretation of proscribed animals in Leviticus. In *Purity and Danger*, as we have seen, Douglas argues that pigs (and other proscribed animals) are impure because they are structurally anomalous; specifically, pigs violate the category distinctions established within the Hebrew Bible by chewing the cud without having parted hooves. In *Natural Symbols* she attempts to explain the fact that, while many animals are structurally anomalous with respect to the schema established in the Hebrew Bible, pigs have historically been regarded by Jews as uniquely repulsive and have been taken as an emblem of the system of prohibitions as a whole. Pigs have assumed a prominence that cannot be explained in purely structural terms, Douglas argues, because of the symbolic role they played in such early episodes of persecution as that associated with the Maccabean revolt.[63] Hershman argues that neither hypothesis tells us much about the ways in which the laws of *kashrut* are understood or experienced by Jews:

> It is certainly not true that in every generation Jewish children learn to reconstruct their environment so that the pig is always categorised as an anomaly, and that this socialisation process is reinforced by their being told the story of the Maccabees.[64]

Even a cursory survey of the literature on ritual purity suffices to support Hershman's contention that the anomalous nature of proscribed items is frequently an artifact of the scholar's construction of the symbolic structures in question, rather than that of the actors involved. It quickly emerges that a resourceful anthropologist can easily produce a structural argument according to which any given item identified as polluting is anomalous. Thus, in the passage quoted above, Goody cites Horton as arguing that African religious thought imposes taboos on twins because (presumably by resembling a "litter" of sorts) "multiple births confuse the animal and the human world." However, other scholars confronting the same data with the same theoretical axiom have produced completely different explanations of the supposedly anomalous nature of twins. Thus, John Burton writes: "Twin birth is an anomaly in Nuer society. Social placement is in large measure ascribed by age. Twins thus create for Nuer what Turner would call 'a source of classificatory embarrassment'."[65]

It is thus unclear whether the Africans who actually impose various taboos upon twins regard them as disturbing because they are like animals, because they cannot be satisfactorily ranked by age, or for some completely different reason. What these arguments do suggest is that the taboo nature of twins has here inspired a search for the structural anomaly they may be supposed to present, rather than vice versa. As suggested by Robert Parker in the case of corpses and newborns, twins are here "anomalous" because someone—either a group of Africans or a group of anthropologists—has chosen to regard them as such, rather than because they pose an inherent structural problem.

The Case of Islamic Law

Despite its inherent difficulties, the Douglasian approach has proved helpful in the interpretation of the Islamic law of ritual purity. A masterful application of Douglas's hypotheses to the Islamic data has been presented by Kevin Reinhart.[66] As at least one prominent medieval Islamic thinker explicitly recognized, Reinhart notes, the bodily emissions considered polluting in the Islamic system can all be interpreted as instances of matter crossing the boundaries of the body.[67] This is tantamount to a direct statement of Douglas's hypothesis that "dirt is matter out of place." However, Reinhart notes, not all such displaced substances are categorized by Islamic law as defiling. What of saliva, mucus, or sweat, none of which is regarded as impure? Reinhart hypothesizes that it is not transgression of the boundaries of the body per se that entails ritual impurity in the Islamic system, but the loss of bodily control that accompanies them. This hypothesis also accounts for the practice, considered commendable in some schools of Islamic law, of performing ablutions if one laughs raucously during prayer or indulges in intemperate speech. Here, Reinhart moves closer to the classic argument that purity practices are grounded in the dichotomy between nature and culture.

In light of this hypothesis, Reinhart interprets the minor ablutions that purify the believer after elimination as a symbolic sealing of the frontiers of

the body, a reappropriation of the person after the polluti
This is why the minor ablutions involve wiping or washing
rather than of the parts of the body physically involved in
A similar analysis of the Islamic data has been advanced
who concludes that in Islam, "Pollution law rests on three ... the primary distinction between inner and outer, on the need for control to maintain the division, and on the threat posed by flowing substances."[68]

I believe that Reinhart and Marcus are correct in their argument that Dougals's hypotheses elucidate some major elements of the Islamic law of ritual purity. Examples could be added; for instance, the idea that impurity arises from structural ambiguity also finds some support in early Arabic sources. The remarks of the litterateur al-Jāḥiẓ (d. A.H. 255/868–69 C.E.) regarding dogs, with the pig one of the two most polluting animals in the sight of Islamic law, are revealing in this respect:

> They are like composite creatures and patched-together (*mulaffaq*) animals, like mules (*al-baghl*) among beasts of burden and the *rā'ibī* among doves. It is neither a wild animal nor a domestic one (*lā sabu' wa-lā bahīma*), neither a human nor a spirit (*lā insīya wa-lā jinnīya*). They are of the *ḥinn*[69] rather than the *jinn*; they are riding animals (*maṭāyā*) of the spirits, and they are a kind of transformed being (*miskh*).[70]

The dichotomy between natural disorder and cultural control also finds support in several elements of Islamic law. It can be discerned in some of the laws concerning the purity status of various animals and the permissibility of eating them (two issues which are closely intertwined but not completely congruent). Muslims are forbidden to consume "all wild animals with canine teeth (*kull dhī nāb min al-sibā'*)."[71] This proscription seems to introduce two criteria: edible animals should be domestic (rather than "wild"), herbivorous (rather than a fanged beast of prey), or ideally, both. Although this is essentially a food prohibition rather than a statement about purity, at least some early Muslims seem to have regarded the two questions as inextricably connected. Thus, early traditions reflect concern that water holes where wild animals drank might be polluted (a fear that the traditions ultimately dispelled).[72] Mary Douglas has suggested that biblical food prohibitions in part reflect a preference for domesticated animals. Writing of "the herds of cattle, camels, sheep and goats which were the livelihood of the Israelites," she states:

> These animals were clean inasmuch as contact with them did not require purification before approaching the Temple. Livestock,

> like the inhabited land, received the blessing of God. Both land and livestock were fertile by the divine blessing, both were drawn into the divine order . . . Cattle were literally domesticated as slaves. They had to be brought into the social order in order to enjoy the blessing.[73]

Although Islamic laws relating to the symbolic incorporation of livestock order are less detailed than their Biblical counterparts, a similar basic tendency can be discerned in the prohibition of fanged "wild animals" (*sibāʿ*). Animals outside of the sphere of culture are under the suspicion of pollution.

The other criterion reflected in the tradition, the possession of "canine teeth," probably relates to the idea that fanged animals eat other animals; they are thus polluted and/or rendered unfit for consumption by consuming corpses. However, the fundamental taboo involved in the prohibition of carrion is not merely death, but death that is not subject to cultural control. Islamic law, after all, permits the consumption of meat. However, the meat must undergo "purification" (*dhakāt*) through appropriate slaughtering. *Natural* death, in contrast, renders the animal carrion and its meat ritually impure. While Muslims are permitted to consume the flesh of game animals that cannot literally be slaughtered in the prescribed manner—as they are not under the control of the hunter at the time of their death—death by the hunter's arrow is rendered equivalent to ritual slaughter by pronounciation of the *basmala* (the words "in the name of God") upon releasing the arrow or the dog. Similarly, according to a rule that was derived from Qurʾān 5:4,[74] it is permissible to eat game that has been brought down by a hunting dog—but only if the dog is trained. A dog that is untrained or disobedient to his master is, according to the wording of some early jurists, a "wild beast" (*sabuʿ*), and the meat that it has killed is not pure.[75]

That this distinction between the cultural sphere and the uncontrolled "wild" is not merely an artifact of structuralist thinking is demonstrated by early Islamic traditions relating to the purity status of domestic cats. This category distinction is one that was perceived by some early Muslims and used to generate new rulings. Thus, a tradition transmitted in a number of different versions recounts that a Companion of the Prophet allowed a cat to drink from his own water vessel and justified the action by remarking, "[The cat] is not ritually impure (*najis*); it is one of your servants (*min al-ṭawwāfīn ʿalaykum waʾl-ṭawwāfāt*)."[76] In other versions of the text, he remarks that "it is one of my dependents" or "the cat is among the goods of the household (*min matāʿ al-bayt*)."[77] The logic leading to the original suspicion that cats may be ritually polluting is not stated, but we may infer that it arose from the fact that cats both have fangs and are originally or potentially wild—although frequently dwelling with humans, they clearly do not fit into the same category as animals raised in herds. The logic of the various rebuttals of this assumption is very clear: cats are, in fact, pure because they are, in fact, domestic. They are variously equated to servants, family members, or household possessions; in any case, they are placed firmly within the sphere of culture.

Despite the helpfulness of the concepts of structural ambiguity and cultural control in understanding some aspects of the Islamic law of ritual purity, however, neither of these concepts explains the system as a whole. For instance, there are many things which Islamic jurists recognized to be ambiguous but did not categorize as impure. An example of this is the mouth, which one Islamic jurist has described as follows:

> Two different indices are competing with respect to the mouth (*al-fam tajādhaba fīhi dalīlān*); one of them indicates that it is exterior and the other indicates that it is interior, both *de facto* and *de jure* (*ḥaqīqatan wa-ḥukman*). As for [the mouth's] *de facto* [status], this is because when [a person] opens his mouth it is exterior and when he closes it, it is interior. As for [the mouth's] *de jure* [status], if a person who is fasting takes water into his mouth and swishes it around it does not invalidate his fast, just as if water were to flow over the exterior of his skin, so [the mouth] is exterior [in this respect]. If he swallows his saliva, this does not invalidate his fast either, just as if it moved from one part of his belly (*baṭn*) to another, so [the mouth] is interior [in this respect].[78]

If we assume, in Marcus's words, that in the Islamic law of purity "the first and most important distinction is that between inner and outer,"[79] the mouth should be a prime case of ambiguity and thus of pollution. However, according to Islam the mouth is in fact as pure as any other part of the body.

The problematic nature of the "control" hypothesis is also suggested by the fact that, Douglas's arguments having dominated the cross-cultural study of ritual purity for some time, precisely the same hypothesis has been used to "explain" systems of purity that are very different in their details from the Islamic case. A striking example of this phenomenon is provided by the arguments of Howard Eilberg-Schwartz regarding the underlying logic of the biblical law of ritual purity. Eilberg-Schwartz asks why, according to the Hebrew Bible, "semen contaminates a person only until evening, while the other fluids contaminate for seven days and have numerous other secondary effects which semen does not produce." He argues that there is a clear correlation between the potency of the pollution associated with a given bodily function and the degree to which it is subject to the conscious control

...ual. Presumably because engaging in sexual activity is (usually) ...y and controllable condition for emission of semen, he argues ...al discharge is more controllable and thus less polluting than ... and nonseminal discharges. Discharge of urine is even more controllable than that of semen, and thus even less polluting. "In other words," he concludes, "there is a direct relation between the controllability of a bodily fluid and its power to contaminate the body."[80]

This argument is both ingenious and plausible within the context of the Biblical rules Eilberg-Schwartz is confronting. It may well be that supporting evidence specific to the Biblical context could confirm a distinctive preoccupation with the element of control; Eilberg-Schwartz's contextually-specific work does suggest the extent to which (for instance) ejaculation was regarded as voluntary and controllable, rather than (in cases such as nocturnal emission) a disturbing exception to a man's conscious command of his own anatomy. However, insofar as recourse to the concept of "controllability" has become a reflexive strategy in interpretation of purity rules from diverse contexts, as I believe to some extent it has, it is highly problematic. The strategy is questionable because different systems of purity often present contradictory evaluations of the same bodily functions, and unless divergent attitudes towards the degree of control involved in these functions can be demonstrated, an identical criterion (controllability) must be manipulated to explain mutually contradictory data. The equation of pollution with loss of control cannot explain why urination pollutes in Islamic but not in biblical law. The fact that Reinhart and Eilberg-Schwartz are constrained to make opposite judgments about the same bodily function, one classifying urination as a loss of bodily control and the other arguing the opposite, is less a reflection of distinctively Jewish or Muslim experiences of urination than of the fact that they must fit the opposing legal evaluations of the purity status of urination into the same interpretive schema (impurity equals loss of control).

The idea that the Islamic law of ritual purity is based on the concept of control is further contradicted by the example of incontinence. In general, urination causes pollution and requires ablutions before prayer. However, if a person is incontinent and is afflicted by a constant trickle of urine that is not under his control, he is allowed to perform ablutions once and ignore the trickling that occurs after his ablutions, even if it continues throughout his prayers. If loss of control were the fundamental source of pollution, one would expect that incontinence would be even more polluting that ordinary urination. The fundamental problem is, after all, the loss of control over a bodily function that one usually performs voluntarily. However, Islamic jurists (guided by the systematic principle of "*ḍarūra*," necessity) make an exemption in this case to provide a normal prayer life for someone who would otherwise be chronically deprived of opportunities for worship.

Thus, the theme of the loss and reassertion of control is incapable of explaining the details of the system. Perhaps the fundamental problem with the idea that the loss and re-establishment of control is the underlying logic of the system of ritual purity is that the concept of "control" has itself not been adequately defined. Indeed, I am not convinced that there is a way of defining "loss of control" that would adequately explain the system of ritual purity by including all bodily functions considered to be polluting and excluding all those that are not.

As far as I can see, there are two basic understandings involved in the invocation of "loss of control" as the underlying cause of pollution in the Islamic system. Firstly, "loss of control" could be taken to mean "loss of composure." This understanding would arguably explain the polluting nature of sexual intercourse, an act in which (despite the note of dignity injected by such recommended Islamic practices as the pronunciation of the *basmala*) a person ordinarily abandons his gravitas to the throes of passion. This understanding of "control" would also explain some peripheral and controversial elements of the system of ritual purity, such as the minority opinions that one must renew one's ablutions after intemperate speech or after laughter during prayer. However, the interpretation of "control" to mean "composure" does not explain the majority of the basic and universally accepted features of the system. The concept of "control" in the sense of "composure" does not explain why urination, an act ordinarily performed by choice and in tranquillity, ruptures one's state of ritual purity while shedding tears of anguish does not.

An alternative interpretation of the concept of "control" would argue that it refers, not to a disturbance in one's emotional equalibrium caused by the momentary triumph of a baser passion, but to the ultimately unavoidable and involuntary nature of the bodily functions involved. This understanding obviously applies to menstruation, which is completely involuntary; it also applies to several other bodily functions categorized by the system as polluting. One may choose when to relieve oneself and perform the act itself with undisturbed poise, but the need to do so eventually is one over which the individual indeed has no control. This interpretation of the concept of control goes much further than the first in explaining the basic features of the system of ritual purity. Urination, defecation, and sleep are all acts which we may perform more or less at will, but which in the long run we are constrained to perform. However, even this second understanding of the concept of "control" is incapable of generating the system as a whole. Sexual intercourse, which is polluting, is a voluntary action which can be put off indefinitely or eschewed entirely (although, of course, in its affirmation of marriage Islamic law does not recommend such a course). The only sense in which it involves a "loss of control" is the first, that of a temporary triumph of the passions. Even the most basic features of the system as a whole can thus be generated only by an ad hoc combination of two analytically distinct conceptions of "control." Even less, of course, can this concept aid us in understanding the existence of fundamental differences of opinion among Muslim scholars—controversies in which they invoke many key concepts, but never that of "control."

In short, the concept of "control" does not stand up to the basic test for any hypothesis, the ability accurately to anticipate data other than those on which it was originally based. As suggested above, attempting to predict the categorization of an individual bodily function on the basis of the criterion of control is difficult because the concept itself is so ill-defined. By using the two distinct understandings of the concept suggested above, one could reach different conclusions about the purity status of the same bodily function. However, insofar as it is possible to define the results generated by the criterion of control, they prove to be inadequate to explain the actual positions of Islamic law.

Furthermore, the idea that the definition of the boundaries of the body and the preservation and ritual reestablishment of control underlies the Islamic law of ritual purity cannot explain the fact that, as we shall see, Islamic jurists differ over many features of the system. Had the individual provisions of the law all been generated by this central principle, it is difficult to understand why individual legal thinkers and established schools of law reached substantially different conclusions on many different issues related to the system. One would have to assume either that they were inconsistent in applying the criterion of control or that differences in opinion were simply peripheral and insignificant artifacts of the historical development of Islamic law. In fact, as I hope to demonstrate in the remainder of this work, Islamic jurists had significant and meaningful differences of opinion about individual issues because they pursued various different understandings of the underlying logic of the law of purity.

Approach to the Sources

At least since the middle of the twentieth century, western scholarly study of Islamic law has been dominated by an extremely skeptical stance towards the *ḥadīth* (the reports claiming to preserve the statements and actions of the Prophet Muḥammad) and towards the general picture of the early development of Islamic jurisprudence and substantive law presented by the classical Arabic sources. The most influential statement of the revisionist position was published by Joseph Schacht in 1950.[81] Endorsing and extending the observations of the Hungarian Islamicist Ignaz Goldziher, who argued in studies published at the end of the nineteenth century that the *ḥadīth* represented the evolving beliefs and debates of successive generations of Muslims rather than a literally historical picture of the life of the Prophet, Schacht advanced the thesis that few if any of the *ḥadīth* were actually authentic. The exclusive authority of the *sunna* (normative practice) of the Prophet, he argued, had been accepted only gradually and as the result of the polemical exertions of Muḥammad ibn Idrīs al-Shāfiʿī (d. A.H. 204/819–20 C.E.). The systematic demand for concrete texts documenting the *sunna* of the Prophet (that is, *ḥadīth*) and for chains of transmission indicating the provenance of these texts (*isnād*s) was similarly, according to Schacht, a belated innovation whose ultimate supremacy was owed largely to al-Shāfiʿī. In the earliest period, Schacht argues, Muslims followed various local forms of a continuous "living tradition" that was rooted largely in Umayyad-era popular and administrative practice. As demands for authoritative support of such preexisting practices were raised, reports were fabricated and attributed to prestigious early Muslims. As the intensity and sophistication of the legal debate increased, reports were attributed to progressively earlier and more august figures. While appeals to the opinions and practice of local notables had initially sufficed, reports were eventually attributed to the Companions of the Prophet and finally to the Prophet himself.

Schacht's theses pertain to the authenticity of individual reports alleging to preserve the statements and actions of figures who lived before the date of the earliest Islamic texts which are preserved in complete and continuous form. No complete legal texts are preserved from before the middle of the second century A.H./eighth century C.E. More recently, Norman Calder has extended Schacht's revisionist theses to argue that the ostensibly earliest Islamic legal texts are not, in fact, unitary works produced by the authors to whom they are attributed. Rather, Calder argues that they are composite works that developed organically over a period of centuries. Like Schacht, Calder inverts traditional Islamic chronologies, arguing that the elements attributed to the earliest figures (such as al-Shāfiʿī) are actually the latest elements of a given text.[82]

As will emerge from the argumentation of individual points in this work, I believe that the theses of Schacht and Calder are overgeneralized and should be approached as possible hypotheses whose plausibility must in each case be balanced against that of the chronology provided by the Arabic sources.[83] This study proceeds on the tentative methodological assumption that some of the earliest Islamic sources may be, broadly speaking, accurate. This assumption does not mean that individual reports about early figures are assumed to be literally true. In many cases, as will be clear from the individual arguments, individual reports emerge as discordant or anachronistic in the context of the overall debate over a given issue. I always attempt to proceed from a broad survey of the reported early opinions on a given subject, examining them for geographical, chronological, or ideological patterns. In many ways, this method resembles that advanced by Joseph Schacht.

Schacht, too, claims to evaluate the plausibility of individual traditions in light of their compatibility with an overall pattern of development. Schacht's argumentation, however, tends to be circular in that he asserts rather than demonstrates the chronological developments by which he judges individual traditions. Unlike Schacht, I do not assume that the use of Prophetic *ḥadīth* is chronologically later than that of traditions attributed to Companions of the Prophet or to early jurists. Neither, conversely, do I assume that individual *ḥadīth* are authentic or early. I attempt to fit any tradition, regardless of attribution, into the context of the logical progression and gradual refinement of legal thinking on a given topic.

Schacht, of course, claimed to do the same.[84] However, since he examined a vast array of individual traditions rather than studying a broad range of interrelated reports relating to a single, coherently structured area of legal thought, his judgments about the age or "sophistication" of an individual statement are frequently ad hoc and arbitrary. His data simply provide him with no overall picture of the development of legal thought in any given area; the overall framework in which he judges the chronological placement of the report is thus, in many cases, not the development of substantive law as witnessed by the early sources but the development of legal theory as posited by Schacht himself.

Both Schacht and Calder have attempted to construct "master narratives" that authoritatively structure the overall development of Islamic legal discourse. Like the classical Islamic narrative that they invert, both of these theses provide a coherent and unidirectional structure for the progression of legal thought. The classical tradition tells us that *ḥadīth* are earlier than traditions of the Companions; Schacht tells us that traditions of the Companions are older than *ḥadīth*. The classical tradition tells us that material attributed to al-Shāfiʿī in *Kitāb al-Umm* is older than that attributed to al-Rabīʿ; Calder tells us that material attributed to al-Rabīʿ is older than that attributed to al-Shāfiʿī. My position here is that it is, at least at this time, impossible for us to construct a master narrative (traditional or inverted) that will authoritatively explain the overall development of Islamic law. Instead, at least for the foreseeable future, it is necessary for us to conduct detailed investigations of the evidence relating to individual areas of Islamic law.

In order to conduct such a case study, however, it is unwise to rely heavily on the material which is generally considered most tenuous by secular Western scholars, the reports (*ḥadīth)* documenting actions and statements by the Prophet Muḥammad himself. After an initial examination of the relevant Qurʾānic texts, this study thus bases itself most importantly on statements attributed to early legal scholars (*fuqahāʾ*) in the *Muṣannaf*s of the Yemenī ʿAbd al-Razzāq al-Ṣanʿānī (d. A.H. 211 A.H./826 C.E.) and of the ʿIrāqī Ibn Abī Shayba (d. A.H. 235/849 C.E.). These compilations, I believe, offer a promising initial basis upon which to reconstruct a tentative picture of early juristic debates in a given subject area. One reason for this is that, unlike later works which enshrined the principle of the supremacy of the Prophetic *sunna* by keeping reports from lesser figures to a minimum, these books provide a wealth of information about the alleged opinions of scholars living in the generations after the Prophet's death. This format opens the prospect that, unlike in pure *ḥadīth* collections, meaningful differences of opinion can be openly articulated as individual points of view rather than appearing disguised as rival, tendentious versions of alleged statements or actions of the Prophet. Furthermore, recent work suggests that in the case of the *Muṣannaf* of ʿAbd al-Razzāq, at least, close examination of the text's structure of transmission lends credence to the statements of provenance attached to the individual reports. While no decisive proof is likely to be possible, Harald Motzki has demonstrated that the different strands of transmission within the text display distinctive traits whose systematic fabrication would have demanded implausible ingenuity from a forger. In addition, and perhaps even more compellingly, he has shown how the genre and content of many of the reports display trends in the development of juristic argumentation that are far from the idealizing back-projections often imputed to the Islamic sources.[85]

By starting out from a conditional acceptance of the overall accuracy of the testimony of the early sources, I hope to demonstrate that the broad picture of the development of the law of purity offered by these sources is highly plausible. Schacht states that his objective is "to replace the static picture of conflicting [regional and school] tendencies which has prevailed so far, by one showing the historical process."[86] By adopting a stance of conditional trust in the testimony of selected early Islamic sources, I hope to demonstrate that no such extreme revisionism as was proposed by Schacht is necessary to achieve precisely that objective. The early sources, as will emerge in the course of this study, do not present an idealized or static picture of the law of purity. Rather, they document lively debates reflecting uncertainty about the most fundamental dimensions of the structure and meaning of the law.

All of this does not, of courses, imply that any given report is necessarily true. This is a study of juristic debate, not (or at least, not directly) of the life and teachings of the Prophet or his Companions. Although the authoritative statements (from the Prophet, the Companions, and others) upon which early jurists sometimes relied may in many cases predate the known juristic debates, my focus is on the debates themselves rather than on the literal accuracy of these statements. The sources provide little information that would allow us to reconstruct juristic discussions of the period before the end of the first century A.H./eighth century C.E. Thus, with respect to *ḥadīth*, I will discuss only when, where, and by what groups the individual texts were circulated and deployed in juristic debate; the question of ultimate authenticity cannot be addressed on the basis of the approach used in this study.

Assume authenticity?

Chapter 1

Qur'ānic Rules of Purity and the Covenantal Community

The Biblical Example

"Defilement is never an isolated event," writes Mary Douglas in her classic study of the concept of pollution; consequently, "the only way in which pollution ideas make sense is in reference to a total structure of thought."[1] Despite reservations about the details of Douglas's argumentation, most scholars have embraced the central insight of her work: that purity practices must be understood to emerge from, and in turn to constitute, symbolic systems. Thus, rather than pursuing the origins and significance of individual purity practices as did earlier generations of scholars, it is necessary to elicit the underlying coherence of entire systems of purity.

At an even broader level, however, it is also necessary to address the place of ritual purity per se within the larger world-view of which it forms a part. Such an inquiry would ask, for instance, not merely how the prohibition of pigs fits into a complex of ideas about purity, but how the idea of purity fits into broader ideas about society and the self. Mary Douglas herself did so when she asked, among other things, why some groups had stringent rules of purity and others relatively few. Specifically, when addressing the nature of ritual purity in the nascent Islamic community, we will want to define the role of the motif of ritual purity within the symbolic system constituted by the Qur'ān as a whole. Systems of ritual purity are frequently treated as self-contained entities to be interpreted in relative isolation from other religious practices and beliefs. My assumption here will be that the inclusion of rules of purity in the Qur'ānic text is neither arbitrary nor gratuitous, and that there must be discernible linkages between the passages relating to ritual purity and the overall thematic structure of the text. To paraphrase Douglas, concepts of defilement and purification should not be regarded as isolated events.

In this chapter, I will examine the degree to which it is possible to elicit the symbolic context of the Qur'ānic rules of purity from cues within the Qur'ānic text. I do so against the background of an extensive dialogue about the relationship between the purity laws of the Hebrew Bible (most importantly, its extensive list of food prohibitions) and the other symbolic structures of the biblical text. This dialogue is significant for the interpretation of the Qur'ānic text as well, both because the hypotheses advanced on the basis of the biblical example are of general theoretical significance and because, as will emerge in the course of the discussion, the Qur'ānic treatment of the theme of ritual purity extensively and self-consciously invokes themes and concepts drawn from the biblical tradition.

The most recent phase of the debate over the interpretation of the biblical food prohibitions was, like so many other facets of the scholarly dialogue on ritual purity, initiated by Mary Douglas.[2] In her discussion of the "abominations of Leviticus" in her landmark work *Purity and Danger,* Mary Douglas interprets the list of unclean animals in terms of the central theological axiom presented within the text itself, the reiterated command that the Israelites "be holy, as I am holy." "Since each of the injunctions is prefaced by the command to be holy," she reasons, "so they must be explained by that command."[3] Beginning with the etymology defining the root meaning of the Hebrew word *qadōsh* ("holy") as "set apart," Douglas ultimately equates "holiness" with wholeness or completion. Any living creature or human activity with blurred boundaries, physical or conceptual, violates this ideal of bodily and taxonomic integrity, thus becoming unholy or impure.

In a later study, Douglas elaborates this theory to emphasize the isomorphism between the biblical text's classification of the animal kingdom and its classfication of human society: "A category which divides some humans from others, also divides their animals from others." Thus, for instance, both firstborn animals and firstborn sons are consecrated to the temple; both blemished animals and blemished human beings are excluded from the temple cult. This isomorphism is generated by the relationship to God that structures both human society and the animal world; both the Israelites and their flocks are "under the Covenant."[4]

Douglas's latter line of thought has been pursued by Jacob Milgrom, who proposes an even more direct relationship between the Priestly source's purity categories and its parallel structuring of the human and animal kingdoms. The food prohibitions of Leviticus, Milgrom argues, divide the animal kingdom into categories that can be represented as a series of concentric circles, each one of them successively smaller and associated with a higher degree of holiness. The largest, and least holy, circle comprises the animal kingdom as a whole. The middle circle includes those animals permitted to the Israelites as food. The third, smallest, and holiest of the circles comprises the limited set of animals appropriate for ritual sacrifice. These three circles correspond in their decreasing size and increasing degree of holiness to the most important categories in the division of human society, the outer circle including all of humanity, the middle circle all Israelites, and the inner circle the priests. Significantly, Milgrom argues that each of these divisions corresponds to a covenant described in the biblical text.[5] Milgrom adopts Douglas's terminology, speaking of the proscribed animals as "anomalies," while rejecting her understanding of the taxonomic principles involved. The rationale behind the criteria for clean and unclean animals emerges simply as the need to define a category of animals, similar to yet less restricted than the short roster of animals appropriate to sacrifice, corresponding to the middle grade of holiness—the grade corresponding to the Israelite people as a whole, between the profane level of "the nations" and the exalted level of the Temple cult.[6]

As discussed in the introduction, Douglas's equation of pollution with the violation of conceptual boundaries is highly problematic when generalized to a cross-cultural axiom. It is now clear that we cannot expect to reduce all purity taboos to cases of taxonomic ambiguity. It is questionable whether the schemata traced by Douglas can even be identified with the Hebrew Bible as a whole; the themes of categorization and separation fundamental to her thesis are typical of a specific strand within the text of Genesis, traditionally known as the "Priestly source."[7] (In fact, Douglas seems to be peripherally aware of this problem; she herself notes that "source criticism attributes Leviticus to the Priestly source, the dominant concern of whose authors was for order."[8]) More recently, Edwin Firmage has argued that the biblical food prohibitions reflect a priestly world-view assimilating the dietary practices of the individual Israelite to the sacrificial cult of the Temple. The underlying coherence of the system, he argues, lies not in a schematic categorization of the animal kingdom as a whole but in a single criterion: a given animal's resemblance, or lack thereof, to the animals recognized as appropriate for sacrifice. Firmage argues that the postdiluvian license to eat meat represents not (as commonly believed) a concession to human frailty, but an an enhancement of the status of human beings; this exaltation reaches its logical conclusion with the introduction of food prohibitions specifically. The dietary law obliges Israelites to "be concerned that the animals they raise for food and those that they hunt be like those that God 'eats' (in the form of sacrifices)," thus distinguishing them from their non-Israelite neighbors and allowing them to "enjoy unprecendented proximity" to God.[9]

[illegible]e differences of opinion relating to the biblical data, some [illegible] emerge. Douglas, Eilberg-Schwartz, and Firmage all agree [illegible]icance of the purity strictures that the Bible applies to the [illegible]et of Israelites is to be sought in a concept repetitively invoked by the biblical text itself, the concept of holiness. The idea of holiness is in turn grounded in another fundamental theological and sociological concept, that of the covenant.

The close relationship perceived by scholars between the purity scriptures of the Hebrew Bible and the concept of the covenant supports another axiom of Douglas's theory of ritual purity, the precept that there is a correspondence between ritual concern with the preservation of boundaries and sociopolitical concern with the the preservation of the boundaries of the group. Her interpretation of the food prohibitions of Leviticus focuses on the preservation of taxonomic boundaries, a position which (as we have seen) has been disputed by a number of other scholars. However, another form of boundary is indisputably involved: the boundary of the human body. As Douglas herself emphasizes, food prohibitions are fundamentally concerned with the regulation of the ingress of matter into the body. This concern with the integrity of bodily margins is also reflected in the association of concepts of pollution with bodily secretions and elimination, which violate the boundaries of the body in the opposite direction. As Douglas writes of the Israelite case, "The threatened boundaries of their body politic would be well mirrored in their care for the integrity, unity, and purity of the physical body."[10] The concept of the covenant is, of course, the primary theological concept delineating the boundaries of the Israelite community.

As we will see, the concept of covenant and the theme of community boundaries are highly relevant to the Qurʾānic treatment of ritual purity as well.[11]

The Qurʾānic Material: Sūrat al-Māʾida

The core of the Qurʾānic teaching on ritual purity is the description of the canonical ablutions and the situations in which they must be performed, which appears in its fullest form in verse 5:6:

> O believers! When you arise to pray, wash your faces and your hands up to the elbows; wipe your heads and [wash?] your feet up to the ankles. If you are sexually polluted, purify yourselves. If you are sick or traveling, or one of you has relieved himself [lit: "come from the privy"], or you have touched women, and you cannot find water, go to clean sand/dust and wipe your faces and hands with it. God does not desire to burden you, but He

> wishes to purify you and to complete his favor to you, that you may be grateful.[12]

This verse is a compact exposition of the rudiments of the Islamic law of ritual purity. It establishes that the believer must enter a special state of purity in order to perform his[13] prayers and describes the process of purification; it lists bodily functions that will cause him to enter a state of impurity and prescribes an alternate procedure for situations in which the normal ablutions cannot be performed.

Despite the fact that the verse leaves much unspecified in detail, it is remarkably comprehensive; it lays out the structure of causes of pollution and ritual remedies that is elaborated in the law of ritual purity as a whole. For this reason, it is reasonable to regard this verse as the founding Qur'ānic statement of the system of ritual purity as a whole. This is not to assert that this verse necessarily has chronological priority over all other verses that mention practices or concepts related to ritual purity, but that it is this verse that most centrally mandates and describes ritual purity within the Qur'ānic text. While it is natural to assume that purity strictures of some kind were observed before the promulgation of this passage (an assumption shared by most Islamic scholars), within the context of the Qur'ān it is this verse which allows such practices to be placed within a unified schema of ritual purity. Thus, understanding the significance of this verse is pivotal for our understanding of the Qur'ānic law of ritual purity overall.

While verse 5:6 is very informative with respect to the substance of the Qur'ānic law of ritual purity, it is much more reticent on the subject of its significance. In enjoining purity and identifying sources of impurity, it is remarkably neutral in language; although it states that they both entail ablutions, for instance, nothing in the verse explicitly suggests that there is anything particularly negative, perilous, or repulsive about either elimination or sexual intercourse. Only the final words of the verse seem to address the rationale of this set of injunctions: "God does not desire to burden you, but He wishes to purify you and to complete his blessing/favor upon you (*li-yutimma ni'matahu 'alaykum*), that you may be grateful."

At first reading, this formulation seems quite generic in the context of the Qur'ān. The statement that "God does not wish to burden you" is a commonplace in the Qur'ān, particularly in the context of special dispensations from general rules (compare verses 9:91, 22:78, 24:61, 33:37, 48:17); it can be assumed to refer to the simplicity of the rules in general and to the special provision for ablutions with dust in particular. The injunction to "be grateful" seems similarly general; gratitude is the constant stance of the believer, the opposite of the ingratitude (*kufr*) of the nonbeliever.[14] The statement that God "wishes to purify you and complete his favor (*ni'ma*) to you," however, has more distinctive associations. What is the "favor" that God will fulfill in connection with these observances?

A number of indices point to the conclusion that it is to be interpreted as God's covenant with the Muslims. This association is made explicitly in the following verse, which enjoins the believers to "Remember God's favor to you and the covenant (*mīthāq*) with which He bound you when you said: 'We hear and obey.' " Comparison with other passages of the Qur'ān suggests that the coordinating conjunction between *ni'ma* and *mīthāq* does not serve to link two heterogeneous or even completely distinct items; God's *ni'ma*, in these contexts, is specifically the beneficence He displays towards the people of His covenant (*mīthāq*). The Qur'ān certainly contains numerous references to God's *ni'ma* in the generic sense of any divine favor or benefaction, including all the wonders of creation as they conduce to the comfort and well-being of humanity; however, there are enough uses of the word in a specifically covenantal context to establish a distinct pattern, particularly within Sūrat al-Mā'ida (chapter 5) and in one of the chapters most closely associated with it both lexically and thematically, Sūrat al-Baqara (chapter 2).[15]

God's original *ni'ma* upon the Children of Israel is the Abrahamic covenant. Thus, verse 2:122–24 enjoins:

> O Children of Israel, remember the favor (*ni'ma*) that I have bestowed upon you, and that I have preferred you over all humankind. Beware of a day when no soul can benefit another, when no compensation will be accepted and no intercession will be of use, neither will anyone be aided. [Remember] when [*idh*] Abraham's Lord tested him with words, and he fulfilled (*atamma*) them, He said, "I will, indeed, make you a leader of humankind." [Abraham] said, "And my descendants?" [God] said, "My covenant (*'ahdī*) does not include evildoers."

Here, God's injunction to remember his favor (*ni'ma*) is followed by an account of the covenant of Abraham, an agreement that is sealed by the imposition of certain commandments.

The word *ni'ma* is also closely associated with the story of Moses and the events of the Exodus. Verses 2:47–48 open an extended sequence on this subject with the injunction,

> O Children of Israel! Remember the blessing/favor (*ni'ma*) that I have bestowed upon you, and that I have preferred you over all humankind. Beware of a day when no soul can benefit another, when no intercession will be accepted and no compensation will

> be received, neither will anyone be aided. [Remember] when [*idh]* We delivered you from Pharaoh's people,

This sequence, which is thematically cohesive up to about verse 70, culminates with the covenant at Sinai and its violation by the Israelites. The same linkage occurs in verses 5:20–21, which enjoin the People of the Book to

> [Remember] when Moses said to his people, "O people, remember how God blessed/favored you (*udhkurū niʿmat Allāh ʿalaykum*) by making prophets among you, making you kings, and giving you what none other among humankind have been given. O people, enter the Holy Land which God has assigned to you; do not turn back and return in ignominy."[16]

God's *niʿma* is thus associated with both of the major covenental events of Hebrew salvation history, the initial promise to Abraham (which is here clearly disengaged from his physical lineage and made conditional on obedience to God) and the communal affirmation at Mount Sinai. The association between the story of Moses and the concept of *niʿma* is close enough to prompt wordplay on the motif; it is surely not accidental when, in response to a plea for gratitude for his upbringing as an orphan in the royal household, Moses sarcastically asks Pharaoh in verse 26:22, "Is this a favor you are bestowing on me (*tilka niʿma tamunnuhā ʿalayya*), enslaving the Children of Israel?"[17] As we will see, this is a very significant context for the opening passage of Sūrat al-Mā᾽ida in general and verse 6 (the rules relating to ablution) in particular.

The linkage between *niʿma* and covenant is particularly constant in combination with other elements appearing with it in our passage: the preposition *ʿalā* (to, upon); the imperative of the verb *dhakara*, to remember; the verb *atamma*, to complete; and the idea of fear of God, expressed through any of a set of synonymous roots (*w-q-y, kh-w-f, r-h-b*). This complex finds almost complete expression in chapter 2 (al-Baqara), verse 40, which admonishes, "Children of Israel, remember the favor I have bestowed upon you (*udhkurū niʿmatī llatī anʿamtu ʿalaykum*). Be true to your covenant with Me, and I will be true to Mine to you (*awfū bi-ʿahdī ūfi bi-ʿahdikum*). Dread My power (*irhabūni*, rhyming with *ittaqūni* in the following verse)."

With respect to the verb "*atamma*," it may be appropriate in this context to translate it as "to fulfill" rather than "to perfect" or "to complete." This reading is supported by verse 2:124, which states that "his Lord put Abraham to the proof by enjoining on him certain commandments and Abraham fulfilled (*atamma*) them." The link between *ni'ma* as covenant and the verb "*atamma*" is reinforced by verse 12:6, where Jacob says to Joseph: " 'Your Lord will choose you; He will teach you to interpret sayings, and will perfect His favor to you and to the house of Jacob, as he perfected it to your forefathers Abraham and Isaac before you." I would argue that this statement could just as well be read "He will fulfill His covenant with you and with the house of Jacob, as He fulfilled [His covenant] with your fathers Abraham and Isaac before you."[18]

The connection between the theme of memory ("*udhkurū*") and that of covenant is an obvious one: just as the Israelites sealed their covenant with "your God who brought you out of Egypt," the Muslim community's sense of its covenantal relationship with God is based on the remembrance of God's salvific acts on its behalf. The links among *mīthāq*, *ni'ma*, and divine aid are articulated by verses 33:7–9:

> [Remember] when (*idh*) We took a covenant from the the prophets, from you, and from Noah, Abraham, Moses, and Jesus the son of Mary; We took a strict covenant from them, that [God] may ask the truthful about their truth—[God] has prepared a painful punishment for unbelievers! O believers, remember God's blessing/favor upon you (*udhkurū ni'mat Allāh 'alaykum*) when troops approached you and We sent a wind against them, and troops that you did not see. God has insight into all that you do.

Like the Israelites, who were delivered from the superior forces of Pharaoh by God's special favor, the Muslim community has enjoyed divine intervention in its conflict with the pagan Meccans. This close connection between the concept of the covenant and that of divine aid in battle with a superior foe creates the occasion for the final motif in this set, the admonition "Do not fear them; fear Me." The general idea is that one should not be deterred from fulfilling one's (covenantal) obligation to obey God's commandments by the fear of merely human opposition. The paradigmatic failure to observe this principle is that of the children of Israel, who refused to enter the Promised Land for fear of the race of giants that inhabited it (see verses 5:20–24). The Muslim community should not repeat this mistake in their conflict with the Meccans.

The linkage between the verse instituting the law of ritual purity and the idea of the covenantal community is reinforced by the context of the verse in Sūrat al-Mā'ida. Since the concept of context in the Qur'ān is a somewhat problematic one, it is appropriate to make a few remarks about it here. As is well known, the Qur'ān is not traditionally understood to have been revealed consecutively, nor is it believed to have always come down in long continuous sections. The order of the *sūra*s (chapters), insofar as it reflects the traditional chronology of revelation at all, is very roughly reverse chronological.[19] Within this schema, each individual chapter may or may not represent a single moment in the process of revelation. Frequently, the traditional data about the chronology of revelation state that various verses within a single chapter were revealed at different times, often some in Mecca and the others in Medina.[20] Whatever value we attribute to these data, which may well have been shaped by an effort to establish the early date of verses considered by later jurisprudence to be abrogated by other legislation,[21] the form of the text of the Qur'ān in itself strongly suggests discontinuity. The innumerable places where the text is at least superficially disjointed, the many abrupt shifts in subject matter or mode of address, recommend caution in the deployment of any concept of context.[22]

However, I would argue that in this case it is quite possible to detect an extended thematic context for the verses prescribing ablutions before prayer, one which allows us to reach some conclusions about the meaning of ablution (and, by extension, of ritual purity in general) within the Qur'ānic worldview. More specifically, I would argue that the beginning of Sūrat al-Mā'ida displays a degree of thematic unity that suggests that it is in some sense a cohesive whole.[23] In view of this overarching thematic unity, I will suggest, thematic context is a meaningful interpretive concept. Having made this case for Sūrat al-Mā'ida, I hope to demonstrate that a similar thematic coloring characterizes the other chapters and passages where references to rules of ritual purity occur.

The text of the opening passage of Sūrat al-Mā'ida runs as follows:

> [1] O believers, be true to your covenants. Permitted (*uḥillat*) to you are all domestic beasts, except those that are enumerated to you. Do not deem it permissible (*ghayr muḥillī*) to hunt when you are in a state of taboo/interdiction as pilgrims (*ḥurum*); indeed, God decrees as He wills. [2] O believers, do not profane (*tuḥillū*) God's prescribed rites, not the sacred month (*al-shahr al-ḥarām*), nor beasts that have been brought and garlanded for sacrifice, nor people who come to the Sacred House (*al-bayt al-ḥarām*) seeking the favor and satisfaction of their Lord. When you are freed of the taboos of pilgrimage (*idhā ḥalaltum*), you may hunt. Do not allow your anger against a group of people who have blocked you from access to the Sacred Mosque (*al-masjid al-ḥarām*) tempt you to transgress. Aid one another in right-doing and piety; do not aid one another in sin and transgression. Fear God; indeed, God's punishment is severe. [3] Forbidden to you (*ḥurrimat*

ʿ*alaykum*) are carrion, blood, the meat of pigs, and that which has been dedicated to [a deity] other than God; animals that have been strangled, bludgeoned to death, fallen from cliffs, or been gored to death; or those that have been [partially] eated by wild beasts, unless you are able to slaughter them before they expire; and that which is slaughtered on pagan altars. [It is also forbidden for you] to distribute the meat by arrow divination; that is a corrupt practice (*fisq*). Today, the unbelievers have despaired of [overcoming] your religion; do not fear them, fear Me. Today I have perfected your religion for you and completed My blessing/favor upon you; I have chosen islām for your religion. [As for] anyone who is compelled [to eat forbidden meat] by hunger, without any inclination to sin, God is forgiving and merciful. [4] They ask you what is permitted (*uḥilla*) to them. Say: Permitted (*uḥilla*) to you are all pure foods, and that which you have taught birds of prey and dogs to hunt, teaching them as God has taught you; eat what they catch for you, and mention God's name over it. Be aware of God; indeed, God's requital is swift. [5] Today all pure foods have been made permissible (*uḥilla*) to you; the food of the People of the Book is permitted (*ḥill*) to you, and your food is permissible (*ḥill*) to them; [also permitted] are chaste believing women and chaste women from among those who were given the Book before you, if you pay them their due in marriage, not in wantonness, and without taking illicit partners. Whoever denies faith, his works are in vain and he will be among the losers in the next world. [6] O believers! When you arise to pray, wash your faces and your hands up to the elbows; wipe your heads and [wash?] your feet up to the ankles. If you are sexually polluted, purify yourselves. If you are sick or traveling, or one of you has relieved himself [lit: "come from the privy"], or you have touched women, and you do not find water, go to clean sand/dust and wipe your faces and hands with it. God does not desire to burden you, but He wishes to purify you and to complete his favor upon you, that you may be grateful. [7] Remember God's favor to you and His covenant by which He bound you when you said, "We hear and we obey." Fear God; indeed, God is aware of what is within your breasts. [8] O you who believe, be steadfast towards God and stand in witness for equity. Do not let anger against a group of people tempt you not to act justly; act justly, for it is closer to piety, and be aware of God. Indeed, God, is informed of what you do. [9] God has promised those who believe and do good works forgiveness and a great reward. [10] Those who disbelieve and scoff at Our signs, they are the denizens of Hell. [11] O believers, remember God's favor to you when a group of people stretched out their hands against you and He prevented them from harming you. Be aware of God; upon God may the believers rely. [12] God took a covenant from the Children of Israel and sent forth twelve headmen from among them. God said, "I am with you. If you establish prayer, give the prescribed alms, believe in My messengers and support them, and give a goodly loan to God, I will forgive your sins and bring you into gardens beneath which rivers flow. Whoever of you disbelieves after that has strayed from the straight path." [13] Because they violated their covenant, We cursed them and hardened their hearts. They twist words, and have forgotten part of that of which they were reminded. You will always find treachery from them, except for a few of them. [Yet,] pardon them and forgive them; God loves those who do good. [14] From those who call themselves Nazarenes We [also] took a covenant, and they have [also] forgotten part of that of which they were reminded. So We incited enmity and dissension among them until the Day of Resurrection; God will inform them of what they used to do.

At first glance, the opening verses of Sūrat al-Mā'ida seem to present a scattering of loosely linked ritual prescriptions relating to the pilgrimage and dietary restrictions. Careful reading, however, suggests that this passage displays a fairly striking degree of lexical and thematic unity. Far from being a motley set of individual injunctions, it is revealed as a compact and multifaceted exploration of the concepts of the licit and the proscribed, the permitted and the forbidden, giving substance to the initial demand that believers fulfill their obligations.[24] This unity is thrown into relief when we examine the underlying patterns pervading the individual statements in the passage, rather than focusing on the degree of direct logical linkage between each pair of consecutive verses.

The two opening verses, both of which are fairly lengthy, are unified by a repetitive and multifaceted use of the complementary pair "permitted/forbidden" (*ḥ-l-l/ḥ-r-m*) that establishes a pattern extending throughout the opening passage. Although these two roots admittedly relate to a basic theme of the Qur'ān as a whole, the density and—if the word may be permitted—playfulness of their deployment in this passage points to its distinctive qualities. This special character can be defined even on the level of a straightforward word count: Sūrat al-Mā'ida contains five of the Qur'ān's nine uses of the word "*uḥilla*" (including the feminine form, "*uḥillat*") and both of the two incidences of "*ḥill*." Verse one informs the believers that certain livestock (the precise meaning of "*bahīmat al-an'ām*" is disputed by the Arabic exegetes) are permitted to them as food, "*uḥillat lakum*," but warns them that they should not consider it permissible to hunt while on the pilgrimage: *ghayra muḥillī aṣ-ṣayd*, the same (fourth) form of the verb now appearing as an active participle referring to the believers themselves. The reference to the pilgrimage is achieved by specifying that the believers should not hunt when they are "*ḥurum*," interdicted or taboo; technically, the word refers to the exceptional state of ritual purity assumed during the pilgrimage rites, but lexically it is the converse of "*ḥill*," the status of the livestock.

Verse 2 begins by reiterating verse 1's use of the fourth form of *ḥ-l-l* with the believers as subject, with a slight but significant shift in meaning: instead of forbidding the believers to *declare lawful* the game which God has forbidden them to hunt during the pilgrimage, verse 2 forbids them to *violate* God's holy institutions. This carries us one step further from the root meaning of the verb, but it is firmly tied into the web of associations by the pattern already established. The pattern is continued by two uses of the word *ḥarām* (literally, "forbidden") to mean *holy*, in the two phrases "holy month" and "holy house." The verse proceeds to state that hunting is permitted after the pilgrimage rites have been completed and the pilgrim has reentered his ordinary state; you may hunt "*idhā ḥalaltum*," literally, "when you become *ḥill*, permissible," that is, no longer *ḥarām/muḥrim*, taboo. Verse 3, listing forbidden foodstuffs, begins with the verb "*ḥurrimat*"; this passive feminine singular perfect verb directly mirrors the "*uḥillat*" of verse 1. In a punning use of a root aurally similar to "*uḥilla*," one of the interdicted items is described as "*mā uhilla li-ghayr allāh bihi*," that which has been dedicated to someone/thing other than God. This pattern is sustained, although with a lower density and lesser complexity, in verses 4 and 5. Verse 4 once again deals with the permissibility of certain classes of foodstuffs (in this case, game hunted with the aid of dogs), while verse 5 moves from permissible foodstuffs (the foods of the People of the Book) to permissible marriage partners.

An apparent rupture of this thematic continuity occurs in the middle of verse 3, beginning with the word "today" (*al-yawm*). For those who are willing to contemplate the possibility of disruption in the Qur'ānic text, it is possible to hypothesize that the middle of this verse represents an interruption of the original context. If the unusual length and stylistic and thematic unevenness of the verse did not suffice, the close connection between the beginning and end of the verse would be enough to suggest an intrusion. The list of forbidden foods at the beginning of the verse and the closing statement that the believer may consume them under duress clearly belong together; this tight logical nexus contrasts with the apparently loose thematic connection between either statement and the intervening statement about the establishment of the religion of Islam.

However, while its precise placement is perhaps puzzling, the middle of verse 3 is not an extraneous interruption in the context of the passage as a whole; on the contrary, it is thematically very consistent. One element of unity is, of course, the statement that God has "completed My favor (*ni'matī*) to you." The close association between this statement and the following verses is signalled by recurrent references to God's "favor" (*ni'ma*) later in the passage. The use of this term in verse 6 has already been discussed. Similarly, verses 7 and 11 both enjoin the believers to "remember God's favor (*ni'ma*) to you." As has been argued above, this favor is to be interpreted specifically as God's bestowal of His covenant on the community of believers. The injunction to "have no fear of them; fear Me" similarly reflects a recurring element of the complex of motifs associated with the concept of the covenant, as already discussed.

The web of associations surrounding the concept of *ni'ma* is not the only indicator that the opening passage of Sūrat al-Mā'ida should be read in the light of the covenantal motif. In the verses following the description of the *wuḍū'* ablutions (verse 6), the density of covenantal language reaches a peak. The next eight verses contain no less than four uses of the word *mīthāq*, covenant (out of a total of twenty-five in the Qur'ān as a whole, three of which refer to pacts between tribes). Verses 6 through 11 comprise a general exhortation of the believers to fulfill their obligations to God, combining references to God's *ni'ma* (verses 6, 7, 11), His *mīthāq* (verse 7), and, in verse 10, His promise (*wa'd*): "God has promised those who have faith and do good works forgiveness and a rich reward." This sequence is followed by a narrative treatment of the theme, a terse summary of God's successive covenants and their repudiation by their recipients, starting with the Israelites (verses 12–13) and moving through the Christians (verses 14–15).

Another highly significant instance of covenantal language in these verses is the formula "*sami'nā wa aṭa'nā*," "we hear and obey" (verse 7), which specifically evokes the covenant at Sinai. This formula closely approximates the Hebrew words attributed to the Children of Israel in Deuteronomy 5:27 when, sending Moses up to the mountain to relay God's bidding, they aver that "we will hear and do" (*ve-shama'nū ve-asīnū*). The Qur'ān never attributes these precise words to the Children of Israel; however, in a polemical pun clearly evoking the Hebrew wording of the Bible, it twice alludes to the original context of the formula. In verse 2:92–93, God instructs the Prophet to remind the Jews of their ill-treatment of Moses and recounts: "When We made a covenant with you and raised the Mount above you, saying: 'Take what We have given you with willing hearts and hear Our commandments,' you replied: 'We hear but disobey (*sami'nā wa-'aṣaynā*).' " The phonological similarity between the Arabic *'aṣaynā*, "we disobey," and the Hebrew *'asīnū*, "we will do," of the biblical formula allows the Qu'rānic text simultaneously to allude to the original covenental undertaking of the Children of Israel and to evoke their recalcitrance in the very words of their commitment.

Judging from the evidence of the Qurʾān, this formula would seem to have been unusually significant for the early Muslim community as well as for the community which saw its origins in the events at Sinai. On the one hand, as an expression of unquestioning obedience to a commander, it is represented as a practical statement of submission to the authority of the Prophet in his capacity as legal arbiter and military leader. Thus, verse 24:50 notes that "when true believers are called to God and His apostle that he may pass judgement upon them, their only reply is: 'We hear and obey.' " However, the words also seem to have the force of a confession of faith; in the same passage (24:48), this compliant attitude on the part of the believers is contrasted with that of individuals who "declare: 'We believe in God and the Apostle and obey.' But no sooner do they utter these words than some among them turn their backs. Surely these are no believers." The promise of obedience is linked with the statement of faith, which is invalidated by disobedience. The credal context of the formula is best reflected in the final sequence of Sūrat al-Baqara (verses 285–86), which almost certainly represents a fragment of early liturgy. After listing the main articles of faith (believers "all believe in God and His angels, His scriptures, and His apostles: We discriminate against none of His apostles"), it states that the believers

> say: 'We hear and obey. Grant us Your forgiveness, Lord; to You we shall all return. God does not charge a soul with more than it can bear. It shall be requited for whatever good and whatever evil it has done. Lord, do not be angry with us if we forget or lapse into error. Lord, do not lay on us the burden You laid on those before us. Lord, do not charge us with more than we can endure. Pardon us, forgive us our sins, and have mercy upon us. You alone are our Protector. Give us victory over the unbelievers.'

Recognizing the centrality of the motif of the covenant in verses 6 through 15 of Sūrat al-Māʾida reveals a deeper link with the opening verses of the chapter than the stylistic factors mentioned above. It has already been argued that the opening verses are not an arbitrary collection of relatively trivial rules, but a set of variations on the theme of injunction and prohibition, an exploration of the basic categories of *ḥalāl* and *ḥarām*. In essence, they are less about specific rules than about the existence of rules imposed by God and the obligation to adhere to them. This thematic ground makes them unusually appropriate for a covenantal context. It is the acceptance of the covenant that makes divine injunctions binding; conversely, it is the imposition of divinely-bestowed rules that seals the covenant. Thus, in the context of the Hebrew Bible Gerhard van Rad has argued that "there can be no doubt that it is the proclamation of the Decalogue over her which puts Israel's election into effect"; in general, "according to antiquity's understanding, entry into a special relationship with a god was inconceivable without the acceptance and binding recognition of specific ordinances."[25]

The passage at the beginning of Sūrat al-Mā'ida containing the Qur'ānic description of the *wuḍū'* ablutions displays one peculiarity that makes it practically unique among Qur'ānic passages. This is its usage, twice repeated (verses 3, 5), of the word "*al-yawm*" in the adverbial accusative to mean "today." What is unique is not simply the appearance of the word in this meaning, as there are a number of passages in which it occurs, but the fact that in this case it apparently refers to the occasion of the passage's own original promulgation. Unlike most other passages in the Qur'ān, this sequence evokes a specific point of time at which it was made public; whether this is to be taken as the residue of a specific historical present or as a rhetorical device, of course, remains to be determined. The unusual character of the passage comes into relief when we compare it with the other Qur'ānic usages of the word "*al-yawm*" to mean "today." In almost all other cases, the word refers to the Day of Judgment. Here there are two variations in usage: either it occurs within the speech of a participant in the drama of judgment, or it appears within a description of the terrors of that day so intense as to make its events imaginatively present.

As it is implausible that our passage, which deals with an extremely this-worldly catalog of behavioral imperatives, similarly fits into an eschatological scenario, only a few options remain. One argument would suggest that this passage represents the text of a speech. This might be a speech that was actually delivered on a historical occasion by the figure implied (the Prophet Muḥammad, inspired by God), or an example of pseudepigraphy or *Nachdichtung*. The first of these options, of course, may be either extremely orthodox or extremely revisionist in its tendency, depending on whether one wishes to ascribe priority to the text as historical document or to the text as Qur'ān. To suggest that God revealed a text which was then delivered as an address by Muḥammad is to follow a highly traditional paradigm (although, in the case of this passage, without specific traditional warrant);[26] to suggest that it was first delivered as an address and subsequently incorporated into the Qur'ānic canon is quite unorthodox. The notion of *Nachdichtung*, of course, is unavoidably revisionist.

All of these options are interesting and knotty ones, with serious implications for one's attitude towards the text of the Qur'ān as a whole. However, they are not immediately relevant to our main concern, which is to establish the thematic context for the promulgation of the rules governing *wuḍūʾ*. For the traditionalist and the revisionist alike, this thematic context may well be assumed to include an implied link with some juncture in the life of the Prophet Muḥammad. The traditional position holds that the various passages of the Qurʾān were revealed at specific points in a historically known prophetic biography, while the revisionist sees an equally intimate association between Qurʾānic text and prophetic biography arising not from the progress of revelation within the career of the Prophet but from their common origin in a process of community formation and canonization.[27] In either case, we can expect a close linkage between Qurʾān and *Sīra* (the biography of the Prophet Muḥammad).

There are two junctures in the biography of the Prophet which suit the subject matter of our passage. The most obvious of these, and the one which occurred to many of the earliest commentators on the Qurʾān, is the Farewell Pilgrimage of the year ten of the Hijra (632 C.E.).[28] The part of the passage that suggested this context to the exegetes was the center portion of verse 3; its reference to the "perfection" of the religion and the "completion" of God's favor upon the Muslim community inevitably suggested a culminating incident close to the end of the Prophet's life. Although it was the tendency of the exegetes to interpret the Qurʾānic text verse by verse (or even phrase by phrase), this hypothesis might well be extended to the rest of the passage in question. Certainly the opening of the passage fits this context admirably; nothing could be more appropriate to the occasion of the Prophet's final pilgrimage than a discussion of the rites of the *ḥajj*. However, the oldest sources for the biography of the Prophet also preserve the text of the address that the Prophet is supposed to have delivered on the occasion;[29] aside from the repetitive use of the phrase "O people!" which parallels the "O believers!" of our passage and reinforces the idea that it—and other, similar passages of the Qurʾān—might plausibly be regarded as a piece of oratory,[30] it bears no resemblance whatsoever to the opening section of Sūrat al-Māʾida.

Despite the fact that the opening of Sūrat al-Māʾida does not seem to be the text of the "Farewell Sermon," another appropriate setting for the text does suggest itself. This is the incident known as the Truce of Ḥudaybīya. In A.H. 6 (628 C.E.), the Prophet is supposed to have set out with his followers to perform the Lesser Pilgrimage. Although the party's exceptional ritual state and the presence of sacrificial victims were intended to signal their peaceful intentions, the Meccans treated the expedition as a potential raid and turned out in full war regalia. After a tense exchange of emissaries, it seemed that hostilities were inevitable. The apostle took oaths of allegiance from all present, the famous "*bayʿat al-riḍwān.*"[31] In the end, the two sides negotiated a truce requiring that the Muslims withdraw for the present year; in the following year, the Meccans would vacate the holy places so that the Muslims could perform the rites of the pilgrimage. This oath of allegiance to the Prophet by the Muslims was retrospectively regarded as one of several important foundational moments in the history of the community. This setting is appropriate to our passage because it combines its two most obvious preoccupations: the ritual requirements of the pilgrimage and the covenantal relationship between the Muslims and God. The hypothetical association between the opening portion of Sūrat al-Mā'ida and the Truce of Ḥudaybīya is greatly strengthed by the fact that the passage specifically counsels the Muslims to restrain their anger at people who have debarred them from performing the pilgrimage: "Do not allow your anger against a group of people who have blocked you from access to the Sacred Mosque (*al-masjid al-ḥarām*) tempt you to transgress" (5:2). What could be a more appropriate plea in a situation where some believers apparently felt impatient with a prudent truce?

Passages from both Qur'ān and *Sīra* suggest that this incident, in addition to being the occasion for one of the most important historical covenants binding the early Islamic community, was a focus for exploration of the motif of the covenant. The chapter traditionally understood to deal with these events, "al-Fatḥ" (chapter 48),[32] displays some of the same covenantal themes we have seen in the opening passage of Sūrat al-Mā'ida. The first two verses state that "We [that is, God] have given you a glorious victory so that God may forgive you your past and future sins and *perfect His goodness to you* (*yutimma ni'matahu 'alayka*), that He may guide you to a straight path and bestow on you His mighty help" (emphasis mine). Verse 10 asserts that "Those that swear fealty to you [Muḥammad], swear fealty to God Himself. The hand of God is above their hands. He that breaks his oath breaks it at his own peril, but he that keeps his pledge to God shall be richly rewarded by Him" (see also v. 48:18).

The biographical tradition similarly surrounds this incident with covenantal motifs; in this case, however, the traditions evoke the story of Moses and the events at Sinai. The *Sīra* of Ibn Isḥāq relates that when Muḥammad was warned of the approach of the Meccan warriors, he requested a guide who would lead the Muslims towards Mecca by another route where they would not be intercepted by the Meccans:

> [A man of the tribe of Aslam] led them led them by a rough and craggy route between passes. When they emerged from it—it having been very hard on the Muslims—and came into gentle terrain at the valley's end, the Prophet said to the people, "Say, 'We seek forgiveness from God and repent to Him.' " They said that, and he said, "By God, that is the *ḥiṭṭa* that was offered to the Children of Israel, and they did not say it.' "

ncident involving the Prophet's camel,

> ɛ Prophet] said to the people, "Dismount!" Someone replied, "O Prophet of God, there is no water in the valley by which we could stop." [The Prophet] took an arrow from his quiver and gave it to one of his companions, who took it down into one of the [dry] waterholes and planted it within it. Water gushed forth until the people drank their fill from it.[33]

These two motifs, *ḥiṭṭa* and spring, recall the story of Moses and the Children of Israel wandering in the wilderness. The word "*ḥiṭṭa*" appears only twice in the Qurʾān; although it is unclear precisely what the word itself might mean, it is associated with an incident closely associated the miracle of the springs in the story of the Children of Israel.[34] Verses 2:58–60 recount,

> [Remember] when We said, "Enter this town and eat your fill wherever you like. Enter the door bowing down and say '*ḥiṭṭa*'; We will forgive you your sins and give bounteously to the righteous." The wrongdoers distorted what they were told; we sent down upon the wrongdoers a scourge from the sky because of their corruption. [Remember also] when Moses sought water for his people and We said, "Strike the stone with your staff"; twelve springs burst forth from it, and all the people knew their drinking places. Eat and drink of God's bounty, and do not sow corruption in the earth.[35]

It is probably impossible to conclude with certainty whether the Farewell Pilgrimage or the Truce of Ḥudaybīya is the "original" or "true" narrative home of the opening of Sūrat al-Māʾida within the story of the life of the Prophet. Both possibilities have found supporters among Muslim exegetes.[36] In either case, however, we can conclude that the implied setting is a formative moment in the crystallization of the Muslim community and the affirmation of its loyalties. The Qurʾān's fullest elaboration of its purity strictures is associated with an advanced, or even culminating, stage in the definition of the covenantal community.[37]

Patterns within the Qurʾān

Thus far, I have argued that the immediate context of the rules relating to ablutions links them (through the concepts *niʿma* and *mīthāq*) to the motif of the covenantal community; that the same theme dominates the larger passage in which this verse is situated; and that the most probable setting for this passage in the life of the Prophet is an episode which has served as a focus for covenantal imagery and language. Does this pattern hold for the other rules of ritual purity found in the Qur'ān? In addition to verse 5:6, the Qur'ān contains a very small number of other verses that institute practical rules of ritual purity to be observed by the Muslim community.[38]

The second half of verse 5:6 is paralleled by another verse, 4:43:

> O you who believe, do not approach your prayers when you are drunk, but wait until you can grasp the meaning of your words; nor when you are polluted—unless you are travelling the road—until you have washed yourselves; or, if you have relieved yourself or had intercourse with women and you can find no water, take some clean sand and rub your faces and your hands with it. Gracious is God and forgiving.

The general context of this verse is an extended discussion of marriage and familial relations, a theme indicated by the traditional title of the chapter, "al-Nisā'" ("Women"). Its more immediate context, however, echoes the covenantal themes that we have identified in the opening passage of Sūrat al-Mā'ida. The verse is directly followed by a series of references to the infidelity of previous recipients of revelation, particularly the Jews:

> [44] Consider those to whom a portion of the Scriptures was given. They purchase error for themselves and wish to see you go astray. [45] But God best knows your enemies. Sufficient is God as a protector, and sufficient is God as a helper. [46] Some Jews take words out of their context and say: 'We hear and disobey. Hear, [but] as one bereft of hearing. Rā'inā!'[39]—thus distorting the phrase with their tongues and reviling the true faith. But if they said: 'We hear and obey: hear, and look upon us,' it would be better and more proper for them. God has cursed them in their unbelief. They have no faith, except for a few of them.

Although the immediate context of verse 4:43 is not as clearly cohesive as that of verse 5:6, there are discernible commonalities between the two, the most notable being the invocation of the covenantal formula "we hear and obey." Here, as in the opening passage of Sūrat al-Mā'ida, it is adherence to the commands of God and His Prophet that is in question and membership in the rightly-guided covenantal community that is at stake.

One must also consider verse 9:28:

> O believers, the polytheists are unclean; let them not approach the Sacred Mosque after this year. If you fear impoverishment, God will enrich you from His bounty if He so wills; God is all-knowing and wise.

This verse, unlike the previous three, has usually not been interpreted by Sunnī jurisprudence as a legal statement about ritual purity. While nonbelievers were to be barred from the Meccan sanctuary, this was not because they were impure in the technical sense but because they were morally sullied. Only Shī'ite jurists, adhering to what would seem to be the literal meaning of the text, held nonbelievers to be technically impure and drew all of the consequences dictated by the elaboration of the legal concept of *najāsa*. It would be very difficult to determine whether the Qur'ānic text "intends" this statement as a value judgment or as a technical classification, largely because this distinction is itself foreign to the Qur'ān. However, I include this verse in the set of rules relevant to ritual purity for two reasons. The first is that the traditional metaphorical interpretation seems to vitiate the sense of the verse; to state that the infidel is "unclean" in the moral sense is otiose in the context of the Qur'ān, scarcely startling enough to motivate a revolutionary change like the exclusion of a lucrative class of pilgrims from the holy places. The second, and stronger, argument is that there is no internal criterion to distinguish this statement from one like 2:222. In both cases, the text declares something to be unclean (in the case of 2:222, by implication: menstruating women must "become pure," therefore they are unclean), then draws a behavioral consequence: unbelievers must not approach (*lā yaqrabū*) the Sacred Mosque, and men should not have contact with (*i'tazilū*; *lā taqrabū*) menstruating women.

The immediate context of the verse is as follows:

> [25] God has helped you on many battlefields, as on the day of Ḥunayn, when you were elated by your numbers, yet they were of no avail to you. Wide as the land was, it could not hold you; then you turned and fled. [26] Then God sent down His tranquility upon His Prophet and upon the believers, and sent down troops that you did not see and chastized the disbelievers; that is the recompense of disbelievers! [27] Yet, after that, God will forgive whom He will; God is forgiving and merciful. [28] O believers, the polytheists are unclean; let them not approach the Sacred Mosque after this year. If you fear impoverishment, God will enrich you from His bounty if He so wills; God is all-knowing and wise. [29] Combat such of those who were given the Book as do not believe in God and the Last Day and do not

> forbid what God and His Prophet have forbidden, and who do not believe in the true religion, until they pay the poll tax out of hand in utter subjection.

Here we see three of the covenantal motifs we have identified in the first part of Sūrat al-Mā'ida: a reminder of God's support of the Muslims in military conflict against a numerically superior foe; an injunction to fight against those who do not consider illicit (*lā yuḥarrimūna*) what God has forbidden (*ḥarrama*); and a subsequent condemnation of the backsliding of the Jews and Christians. Again, the Muslims' special relationship with God is grounded in their observation of His commands and prohibitions (contrasted with the attitudes of previous covenantal communities) and manifested by divine support in historical crises.

Finally, there is verse 2:222:

> They ask you about menstruation. Say, "It is a harmful thing (*adhan*); keep away from women when they are menstruating, and do not approach them until they become pure again. When they have purified themselves, have intercourse with them as God has commanded you." Indeed, God loves the repentant, and He loves those who purify themselves.

This is the most difficult of the verses under consideration to interpret contextually, due to the staccato and dialogic form of the passage in which it occurs. It is one of a series of answers to questions on a variety of topics (for example, "They ask you about drinking and gambling" [2:219]; "They ask you about orphans" [2:220]). However, in very general terms its broader context echoes many of the same themes we have encountered framing the other purity verses. The entire series of questions and answers constitutes a rudimentary code of religious law, a set of (covenantal) obligations of a kind that we have already encountered. This set of legal injunctions is framed by two passages dealing with the failure of previous communities to fulfill their obligations towards God. The first deals in general terms with the infidelity of previous communities:

> [211] Ask the Children of Israel how many manifest signs We have given them. Whoever alters God's favor after receiving it, God is indeed severe in retribution. [212] This lower life has been made alluring to those who disbelieve. They mock the believers, [but] the God-fearing will be above them on the Day of Resurrection; God gives His bounty to whom He wills without stint. [213] All people were one community. Then God sent the prophets

> as bearers of glad tidings and as warners, and sent down with them the Book bearing truth, that it might judge between the people in their disputes. The only ones who engaged in disputes about it were those who received it after they had received manifest signs, out of mutual envy. God guided the believers to resolve their disputes with truth, by His permission; God guides whom He will to a straight path. [214] Do you imagine that you will enter Paradise without undergoing what was suffered by those who came before you? They experienced trials and tribulations; they were shaken to the point that the prophet and those who believed with him said, "When will God's help come?" Indeed, God's help is near.

Similar themes are echoed by the passage following the presentation of laws relating to women in which the verse on menstruation occurs. After discussing the maintenance of widows, in verse 2:242 the text turns to the issue of fighting in God's cause; the imperative for Muslims to fight is illustrated by the example of the Israelites, who failed to perform this obligation under the leadership of Saul (verses 246–51).

Thus, the dominant theme of the passage as a whole is the Muslim community's accession to the covenantal status forfeited by the Jews and the Christians, and the importance of observing the legal obligations sealing this privileged relationship with God.

It might be argued that the apparent parallels in the immediate contexts of these four verses are simply a function of the relative thematic uniformity of the Qurʾānic chapters in which they occur, rather than of any striking singularity of these particular passages. The failure of successive covenantal communities and their supersession by the Islamic dispensation is, for instance, arguably the theme of Sūrat al-Baqara (chapter 2) as a whole, rather than merely of the verses framing the series of questions in which verse 2:222 finds its place. This may, indeed, be a better way of understanding the text. However, this observation merely broadens the concept of context rather than invalidating it; to argue that the verses imposing purity strictures occur in a thematically cohesive set of *sūra*s is to affirm that they find their place within a distinctive set of Qurʾānic motifs, one which may help us to understand the significance of purity strictures within the symbolic structure of the Qurʾān as a whole.

One obvious opening observation is that all of the verses enjoining purity practices occur within chapters traditionally classified as Medinian. Thus, all are assigned to the second stage in the development of the Muslim community, the stage in which the Muslims had formed a self-governing polity under the leadership of the Prophet. Within the set of Medinian chapters, however, the four verses come from chapters traditionally believed to be widely separated chronologically. While chapter 2 (al-Baqara) is widely believed to have been the first chapter revealed in Medīna, and chapter 4 (al-Nisā') also appears quite early in chronological lists, chapter 5 (al-Mā'ida) and chapter 9 (al-Tawba) are believed to be the last two chapters of the Qur'ān revealed.[40]

While the statements about the chronology of the Qur'ānic text transmitted by medieval authors probably preserve some authentic recollections of the historical revelation of the scripture, in most cases we should probably regard this kind of information as the educated guesses of scholars intimately acquainted with the text itself. As in the case of verse 5:3, where the statement "Today I have perfected your religion for you" was quite logically linked with a culminating moment in the history of Qur'ānic revelation, Muslim scholars often seem to have engaged in a process of textual investigation and inference that we may well continue and—in some cases—very tentatively emend. (With respect to the more detailed narrative settings presented in the *asbāb al-nuzūl* genre, their problematic status makes it advisable to start with the text of the Qur'ān and compare our results with the statements of these traditions.[41]) What, we may thus ask, are the unifying characteristics of the texts of these four chapters—independently of any extrinsic historical data, whatever their accuracy?

The most obvious answer to this question, which I believe can be documented in some detail, is that all four of these chapters fall into a loosely articulated set of chapters which, in various ways and to various extents, display concern with the idea of the Muslim community and the clarification of its boundaries. One index of the relatively high stage of development of the confessional community to which this loose group of "Medinian" chapters is addressed is the relatively complete set of cultic observances and institutions to which they refer. Thus, al-Baqara contains references to *ṣalāt* (prayer), *zakāt* (alms), *ṣiyām* (fasting), *ḥajj* (pilgrimage), and *al-masjid al-ḥarām* (the Holy Mosque at Mecca, the locus of the pilgrimage and the distinctive cultic focus of the religion). al-Mā'ida contains references to *ṣalāt, zakāt, ṣiyām,* and *al-masjid al-ḥarām*; al-Tawba mentions *ṣalāt, zakāt, ḥajj,* and *al-masjid al-ḥarām*, while al-Nisā' mentions *ṣalāt*, *zakāt*, and *ṣiyām.*

The significance of this data is partially chronological; thus, the distribution of these terms in the Qur'ān would suggest that the practices of fasting and pilgrimage were not instituted until the Medinian period. (References to *ṣalāt* and *zakāt* are scattered throughout the Qur'ān, in Meccan and Medianian chapters alike.) The fact that these practices are mentioned in some chapters and not others, however, is not merely a reflection of chronological progression; it also reflects a varying degree of concern with the cultic practices that defined the believing community. References to these defining ritual practices are by no means ubiquitous in the text of the Qur'ān. Thus, *ṣalāt* is mentioned in only 32 of the Qur'ān's 114 chapters; *zakāt* is mentioned in 19; *ṣiyām/ṣawm* is mentioned in 6, and the *ḥajj* is mentioned in only 4. The fact that the chapters under consideration display a high rate of allusion to these practices, then, would indicate a high degree of concern with the practices defining the community.

The same could be said of the remaining constitutive ritual practice of the Muslim community, the first "pillar of Islam." This is the confession of faith, the *shahāda*. While the *shahāda* is not Qur'ānic in its canonical two-part form,[42] the Qur'ān does contain several formulae which may be considered confessions of faith. Significantly, all three of the most likely candidates for a quasi-official confession of faith occur in the chapters under consideration here, two in al-Baqara (verses 2:136 and 285) and one in al-Nisā' (verse 4:136).

Another indicator of concern with community definition and community boundaries can be seen in frequent references to other confessional communities. Thus, three out of the four chapters under consideration here (al-Baqara, al-Mā'ida, and al-Tawba) display an outstanding frequency of reference to Christians and Jews. In fact, these chapters account for a substantial proportion of the references to these confessional groups in the Qur'ān as a whole. *al-Naṣārā* (the Christians) are mentioned fourteen times in the Qur'ān: in al-Baqara (seven times), al-Mā'ida (five times), al-Tawba (once), and al-Ḥajj (once). *al-Ladhīna hādū* ("those who profess Judaism") are mentioned seven times in the Qur'ān: three times in al-Mā'ida, twice in al-Nisā', and once each in al-Baqara, al-Anʿām, al-Naḥl, al-Ḥajj, and al-Jumʿa. *al-Yahūd*, the Jews, are mentioned eight times in the Qur'ān: three times in al-Baqara, four in al-Mā'ida, and once in al-Tawba; al-Baqara also contains three references to *al-hūd*, the Jews.[43]

The most radical assertion of community boundaries is, of course, the waging of war against outsiders. It should not be a surprise, therefore, that the chapters under consideration are also those most concerned with the imperative to combat nonbelievers (more particularly, of course, those who are guilty of aggression against the Muslim community). "Fighting is obligatory for you," admonishes verse 2:216, "much as you dislike it." Several passages in the chapter are devoted to rules of engagement for a relentless yet essentially defensive campaign against the nonbelievers. The theme is addressed by verses 2:190–94 and by the passage beginning with verse 2:244, which follows a summons to battle with a narrative recounting the Israelites' poor record of fighting in God's cause. Sūrat al-Tawba (chapter 9) is equally warlike. Verse 5 commands: "When the sacred months are over, slay the idolaters wherever you find them. Arrest them, besiege them, and lie in ambush everywhere for them." "If you do not go to war," warns verse 9:39,

"[God] will punish you sternly, and replace you by other men." Other verses dealing with warfare include 9:12–16, 9:24–26, 9:29, 9:38–47, and 9:120–23. In Sūrat al-Nisā', verses 76, 84, 89, 91, and 95 deal with the waging of war against nonbelievers. Despite the fact that Sūrat al-Mā'ida seems to describe a situation governed by an uneasy truce, it too emphasizes the general imperative of waging war; thus, verse 5:35 urges: "Believers, have fear of God and seek the right path to Him. Fight valiantly for His cause, so that you may triumph."

Another concept which may be associated with this complex of concerns is, as suggested by our discussion of Sūrat al-Mā'ida, that of the covenant (*mīthāq*). The idea of the covenant is almost exclusively associated with chapters of the Qur'ān considered Medinian; there is only one instance (out of twenty-two uses of the word to refer to a pact between man and God[44]) in which the word appears in a Meccan chapter, al-Aʿrāf (7:169). Fourteen of the twenty-two uses of the word in this sense appear in chapters al-Baqara (chapter 2), al-Nisā' (chapter 4), and al-Mā'ida (chapter 5).

As has already been suggested, the Qur'ānic motif of the *mīthāq* is strongly associated with the covenant at Sinai. Although the Qur'ān is rife with references to Moses and the changing fortunes of the Children of Israel, this unequal concentration of references to the *mīthāq* reflects a real shift in emphasis between the Meccan and the Medinian chapters. The chapters categorized as Meccan—most notably al-Aʿrāf, Yūnus, Ṭāhā, al-Shuʿarā', and al-Qaṣaṣ—include a number of extended sequences dealing with the career of Moses and the events of the Exodus. In these chapters, the focus is almost exclusively on the personal experience of Moses as a prophet, from his confrontation with Pharaoh and his establishment of his prophetic credentials through the contest with Pharaoh's sorcerers to his encounter with the Burning Bush. In the Medinian chapters, in contrast, the focus shifts to the bestowal of the covenant and the infidelity of the Children of Israel. Thus, despite shared narrative material, there is a distinct thematic distinction between the two sets of chapters.

One final feature shared by all four of the chapters containing purity strictures is the reiteration, already noted with respect to Sūrat al-Mā'ida, of the formula *yā ayyuhā'lladhīna āmanū*, "O believers." This formula was already identified by the medieval commentators as an exclusive feature of Medinian chapters.[45] Although the formula appears in a total of sixteen of the twenty-eight chapters classified as Medinian, it is particularly frequent in the chapters al-Baqara (twenty-two uses), al-Mā'ida (sixteen uses), al-Aḥzāb (seven), al-Tawba (six), al-Nisā' (five), al-Anfāl (five), and al-Ḥujurāt (five). The significance of this formula for the idea of the Muslim community is obvious: it assumes the existence of a body of the faithful being addressed, rather than directing its appeal to the individual believer or potential convert.

The association of the reiteration of this formula in the chapters al-Māʾida and al-Tawba with two extremely rare allusions to the chapters' time of promulgation (the "now" of the text) has already been noted, suggesting that these two texts might actually have been delivered to the gathered faithful as an address at a particular point in time. This tantalizing suggestion is supported by the fact, easy confirmed with a copy of the Qurʾān and a concordance, that the formula most often does not occur in isolation; it generally punctuates an extended passage, just as the formula "O people" punctuates the Farewell Sermon (*khuṭbat al-wadāʿ*) as it has been preserved. Thus, we may regard the formula either as a general reflection of the existence of some kind of established community that is addressed in a diffuse way, or as the reflection of a specific situation or situations in which the believers were actually addressed in a body.

Furthermore, the "*yā ayyuhāʾlladhīna āmanū*" passages display a thematic cohesiveness that marks them off as a distinctive group even within the set of chapters considered Medinian. Collation of the verses introduced with this phrase shows that they are overwhelmingly focused on two central themes: the waging of war against infidels and insincere members of the Muslim community (*munāfiqūn*) and the role of the Prophet as the leader and commander of the community. These two themes, of course, do not exhaust this set of verses; subsidiary themes include community unity (the brotherhood of believers and the prohibition of fraternization with nonbelievers), economic ethics (the injunction to give alms, the prohibition of usury, the procedure for making a last will), the main ritual requirements of the religion, and various miscellaneous topics. However, this distribution of topics is highly distinctive when compared with the thematic emphases of the Qurʾān as a whole or of the Medinian chapters as a group. Especially if we examine the passages punctuated by the phrase "O Believers" rather than the individual verses it introduces, we find that the topics of war and the high status of the Prophet are overwhelmingly concentrated in these sections of the text.

The close association between the occurrence of purity rules and the relevant chapters' central concern with issues of community definition can, finally, be confirmed by an examination of the use of purity terms in Sūrat al-Tawba (chapter 9). Here, the link between community boundaries and the motif of purity is pronounced. Sūrat al-Tawba is perhaps more concerned with establishing a well-defined confessional community than any other chapter in the Qurʾān. Its first word, "*barāʾa*" ("a declaration of immunity") proclaims a radical split between the believers and their erstwhile non-Muslim allies, the implications of which are worked out in numerous verses throughout the chapter. The exclusion of nonbelievers from the Holy Mosque in Mecca has already been mentioned; verses 9:17–18 ban nonbelievers from all of "the mosques of God," defining admissible believers as "those who believe in God and the Last Day, attend to their prayers and render the alms levy and fear none but God." Believers, male and female, "are friends to each other" (9:71). Believers should not fraternize with nonbelievers, even if they are close relatives (9:23). It is not even permissible to pray for their redemption, despite an apparent scriptural precedent to the contrary: "Abraham prayed for his father only to fulfill a promise he had made him" (9:113–14). Those who exclude themselves from the community by failing to participate in military campaigns are anathema: "You shall not pray for any of their dead, nor shall you attend their burial. For they denied God and His apostle and remained sinners to the last" (9:84).

This pattern of dissociation from the nonbelievers is linked with a persistent contrast between the purity of the righteous community and the impurity of the unbelievers. Nonbelievers are banned from the Holy Mosque because they are "unclean," *najas*. Hypocrites who excuse themselves from a military campaign on feeble pretexts will try to ingratiate themselves with the Prophet after the campaign, but he should "let them be: they are unclean (*rijs*)." Although they feign belief, they are nonbelievers: "Hell shall be their home, the punishment for their misdeeds" (9:94). The identification of unbelief with impurity is so thorough that in verses 9:124–25 the word *rijs*, "filth," is unambiguously used to mean "unbelief":

> Whenever a chapter of Scripture is revealed, there are those of them that say, "Which of you did this increase in faith?!" As for the believers, it does indeed increase them in faith; they rejoice in it. As for those whose hearts are diseased, it merely redoubles their filth/disbelief (*rijs*); they will die as unbelievers.

The converse identification of belief with purity comes to expression in a somewhat opaque historical reference to a mosque founded with evil intent, which is contrasted with a mosque founded in a spirit of true faith (verses 9:107–8):

> As for those who have established a mosque in spite and disbelief, intending to sow discord among the believers and to await those who have made war on God and His Prophet in the past, they avow, "We had only the best of motives." God bears witness that they are lying. Never stand [to pray] in it! Indeed, a mosque that was founded on piety from the first is more deserving that you stand in it. In it are men who love to purify themselves; God loves those who purify themselves.[46]

Finally, of course, there is the possibility of passing from one realm into the other. While some reluctant elements of the community establish themselves irrevocably as "filthy" by excusing themselves from campaigns, others are not irredeemable: "Others there are who have confessed their sins; their good works had been intermixed with evil. Perchance God will turn to them in mercy. God is forgiving and merciful." The solution, interestingly, is to cleanse them by accepting their financial contributions: "Take alms from them, so that they may thereby be cleansed and purified, and pray for them: for your prayers will give them comfort" (9:102).

The boundary between the pure and the polluted is, thus, the boundary of the community; more precisely, in the militant context of Sūrat al-Tawba, it is that of the *mobilized covenantal community*. This inference is supported by another Qur'ānic passage that makes an oblique yet significant reference to the theme of ritual purity. This is verse 8:11, which occurs in a chapter whose traditional name (al-Anfāl, "The Spoils") accurately reflects its primarily military concerns. The immediate context is a passage recounting the course of a battle—understood to be the Battle of Badr—in an elliptical and theological manner (8:42 provides a few more concrete details):

> [5] Similarly, your Lord sent you forth from your homes in righteousness, yet one faction of the believers was reluctant. [6] They debate with you about the truth after it has become manifest, as if they were being led to death before their own eyes. [7] [And remember] when God promised you that one of the two groups would be yours, you wished that the less mighty would be yours. God wills to confirm the truth with His words and to annihilate the unbelievers—[8] To confirm the truth and cancel falsehood, in spite of the wrongdoers. [9] [Remember] when you sought succor from your Lord and He responded to you, "Indeed, I will reinforce you with a thousand angels in their ranks." [10] God did this only as glad tidings and that your hearts may be tranquil; victory comes only from God. Indeed, God is mighty and wise. [11] [Remember] when you were overcome with drowsiness as security from Him; *[God] sent down rain from heaven upon you, by which to purify you and to cleanse you of Satan's filth*, to make firm your hearts and steady your feet. [12] [Remember] when God revealed to the angels, "I am with you. Steady the believers; I will strike terror in the hearts of the unbelievers. Strike their necks; strike their very fingertips!" (emphases mine)

Here the purification of the Muslim troops is clearly more than merely metaphorical, since it must be carried out by means of water. It would seem that a fortunate rainstorm either washed the troops as they stood or allowed them to perform ablutions, and that this event caused a significant rise in morale, or "strengthened their hearts." This passage thus creates an explicit linkage between purity and military morale, reinforcing the inference that the original context of the motif of purity is the mobilized covenantal community. This implication is even clearer in the exegetical tradition, which remembers or infers the significance of the event in greater detail. "God cast sorrow into the hearts of the believers," recounts one tradition,

> saying: "You claim that there is a prophet among you, and that you are the friends of God; yet you have been barred from the water [by the enemy], and you pray in a state of major and minor impurity (*mujnibīna muḥdithīna*)." God sent down water from heaven, and every river bed flowed; the Muslims drank and purified themselves, and their feet were steadied and Satan's insinuations ceased.[47]

Conclusions

We have established that the Qurʾān's statements about ritual purity—that is, those few passages that enjoin either ablutions or acts of avoidance—occur in a loosely articulated yet quite distinctive set of chapters that display a characteristic set of preoccupations converging on the theme of community boundaries. The theme of ritual purity is associated not only with the unstained devotion of the individual believer, but with the pristine integrity of the believing community, particularly the community mobilized in defense of the religion.

As noted above, Mary Douglas has argued convincingly that a system of ritual purity is "a symbolic system, based on the image of the body"[48] in which "the symbolism of the body's boundaries is used . . . to express danger to community boundaries."[49] In this symbolic system, attention is focused particularly on the places in which the body's boundaries are porous and on substances that cross these boundaries. The intensity and emotional tenor of this attention varies with the status of the community boundaries that they symbolically represent. Concern with the boundaries of the community—both external and internal (that is, between men and women or among the hierarchically arranged elements of the society)—correlates with strict rules of ritual purity; relaxation of this concern, which may be related either to fluid boundaries or with boundaries so well enforced that they require no such symbolic sanction, correlates with mild rules or none at all. With respect to the internal structuring of society, Mikhail Bakhtin has made this point very forcefully from the opposite point of view—that of the willing violation of purity taboos that accompanies temporary dissolution of the normal social boundaries. Discussing the grotesque as it appears in the medieval carnival, Bakhtin remarks that "during carnival there is a temporary suspension of all hierarchic divisions and barriers among men."[50] This exceptional state of social fluidity is expressed by a characteristic attitude towards the human body, one in which

> The stress is laid on those parts of the body that are open to the outside world, that is, the parts through which the world enters the body or emerges from it, or through which the body itself goes out to meet the world. This means that the emphasis is on the apertures or the convexities, or on various ramifications and offshoots: the open mouth, the genital organs, the breasts, the phallus, the potbelly, the nose.[51]

Applying this symbolic correspondence to the laws of ritual purity in the Hebrew Bible, Douglas argues that because "the Israelites were always a hard-pressed minority,"

> in their beliefs all the bodily issues were polluting, blood, pus, excreta, semen, etc. The threatened boundaries of their body politic would be well mirrored in their care for the integrity, unity, and purity of the physical body.[52]

Where does the Qurʾānic law of ritual purity fit in this schema? Firstly, and most importantly, I would argue on the basis of the discussion above that the motif of ritual purity in the Qurʾān is indeed associated with a concern with community boundaries. The passages and, more broadly, the chapters in which the verses dealing with ritual purity are situated are also unusually rich in statements emphasizing the unity and solidarity of the Muslim community and its discontinuity with other confessional communities. The central motif in this affirmation of the distinctive character of the Muslim community is the covenant. Internally, the "O Believers" passages display an unusual concern with the authority structure of the mobilized community, stressing the unique status of the Prophet as commander. Thus, within the Qurʾānic text the expected correlation seems to hold. This is not merely another datum to add to Mary Douglas's roster. Rather, it allows us to retrieve part of the original meaning of the symbolic system constituted by this set of rules. By redrawing the connection between the covenantal community and the institution of the rules of ritual purity, we can regain some of the original resonance of these injunctions and reactivate the meaning of the Qurʾānic command to perform ablutions and "remember God's favor to you and the covenant with which he bound you" (Qurʾān 5:7).[53]

Chapter 2

Interpreting the Qur'ānic Text

The Problem

Having identified the motifs associated with ritual purity in the rhetorical structure of the Qur'ān, we now return to the verses relating to ritual purity to see how they were interpreted by the first generations of Muslims. To treat these two subjects separately is not to imply that Muslims have interpreted the relevant passages incorrectly. The internal thematic patterns that we have tried to bring into relief in chapter 1 are not alternatives to analogous yet different analyses by the early Muslim exegetes. Rather, they fall outside of the purview of Qur'anic exegesis in its traditional forms. Early interpreters of the Qur'an were not primarily concerned with an overall thematic reading of the text of Revelation; rather, as believers with a commitment to the enactment of the text in their daily behavior, they turned their attention to the concrete purport of the individual commands. Their interpretations of these verses were legal, in the sense that they were primarily aimed at the regulation of behavior and only secondarily concerned with the production of meaning.

This chapter pursues two interlocking objectives. One is to trace the substantive content of the debates over the interpretation of the Qur'ānic passages relevant to ritual purity and to examine their implications for the conduct and attitudes of Muslims. The other relates to the ongoing debates within the scholarly community of our own time over the early development of Islamic law.

With respect to the role of the Qur'ān in the early development of Islamic law, traditional and revisionist theories diverge sharply. The received religious view of Islamic law assumes that, in those areas where the Qur'ān makes a relevant statement, the word of the Qur'ān is always historically as well as ideologically primary. Islamic law is presumed to be *generated from* the Qur'ān rather than merely *consistent with* it. Modern Western critical scholarship, on the other hand, has tended to see Islamic legal theory as an ex post facto justification of the substantive provisions of a socially evolving law rather than as an accurate historical account of its development. The sources of Islamic law, in this view, may be logically and ideologically anterior to the rules they "generate"; yet they are historically posterior to them. In accordance with this trend, which he did so much to promote, Joseph Schacht has argued that the the Qur'ān was introduced as a source of substantive rulings in Islamic law only at a secondary stage in its development.[1]

This chapter will address the debate over this issue by concentrating on points of tension in the correspondence between the text of the Qur'ān and the received understanding of the provisions of Islamic law relating to ritual purity. On the basis of opinions attributed to early jurists, the chapter will argue that the relationship between the early development of the law of ritual purity and the text of the Qur'ān is a complex one.[2] One the one hand, I will argue that even when the opinions of early jurists are not transmitted in an explicitly exegetical form, they fall into patterns that clearly reflect the importance of the Qur'ānic text for the understanding of the law. Specifically, early reports demonstrate that all of the major ambiguities in the syntax and semantics of the relevant Qur'ānic passages are reflected in vigorous debates documented by the early sources. Thus, it seems that early jurists attempted to shape their understanding of the law of ritual purity in adherence to the text of revelation; exegetical considerations, overt or implicit, fundamentally shaped the law of ritual purity as a whole. On the other hand, the early reports also clearly indicate that there was a continuous "living tradition" of ritual practice that was transmitted by personal example and was to a certain extent independent of textual sources, including both Qur'ān and *ḥadīth*. Thus, in certain cases early jurists adhered to elements of the living practice that appeared to be at odds with the literal meaning of the relevant Qur'ānic verses and found themselves obliged to justify their understanding of the law.

"When You Rise to Pray"

As stated in chapter 1, the core of the Qur'ānic law of ritual purity is verse 5:6:[3]

> O believers! When you arise to pray, wash your faces and your hands up to the elbows; wipe your heads and [wash?] your feet up to the ankles. If you are sexually polluted, purify yourselves.

> If you are sick or traveling, or one of you has relieved himself [lit: "come from the privy"], or you have touched women, and you do not find water, go to clean sand/dust and wipe your faces and hands with it. God does not desire to burden you, but He wishes to purify you and to complete his blessing upon you, that you may be grateful.

At first glance, this verse may seem painfully explicit in its details. One might with some justification argue that ritual purity is rivalled only by inheritance as the area in which the Qur'anic text enters most fully into the concrete particulars of the law. However, the verse is actually far more elliptical and ambiguous than it may appear at first reading. In fact, on closer inspection it emerges that we need lore external to the Qur'ān to clarify some fairly basic points. What does the Qur'ān mean when it commands the believer to perform ablutions "when you rise to pray"? Is this in contradiction to what is now the universal understanding that one need not perform ablutions before each canonical prayer, but only when one is in a state of impurity? What is the state of *janāba* specified in the second half of the verse ("If you are polluted (*junub*)"), and what exactly is meant by the command to "purify yourselves" (here, one may refer to verse 4:43 for the slightly more specific verb "wash")? How are we to understand the list of conditions at the beginning of the last sentence of the verse? The list literally reads, "But if you are sick or traveling or have relieved yourself or touched women"; all of the elements are linked by the same conjunction, "or" (*aw*). Common sense suggests that the first two items (contact with women and defecation or urination) are causes of ritual impurity while the other two (travel and sickness) are conditions that excuse the worshiper from the normal obligation to perform ablutions with water; however, there is no syntactical signal to indicate a distinction between the two.[4] Similarly, it would be difficult to infer on the basis of this verse alone that there are two different degrees of ritual pollution.

All this is to say that the verse is not completely self-sufficient; it assumes either previous knowledge on the part of the listeners or a source of oral teachings to complement the Qur'ān. The word of the Qur'ān is not in conflict with the received understanding of the causes of impurity and the ablutions that they entail, yet in some cases a certain amount of ingenuity must be deployed to extract the known regulations from a gnomic text.

The most problematic part of the verse from this point of view is its opening phrase: "When you rise to pray, wash . . . " (*idhā qumtum ilā'l-ṣalāt fa'ghsilū . . .*). The most obvious understanding of these words is that the believer is commanded to wash the areas indicated every time he "rises to pray." This is surely how it would have been read in isolation. However, from the earliest period for which we have textual evidence the vast majority of Muslims seem to have been agreed that they were not required to perform *wuḍūʾ* ablutions every time they prayed; ablutions were required only when one was in a state of impurity—that is, when one's purity had been ruptured (or, in legal terminology, "cancelled," *n-q-ḍ*) by one of a limited set of bodily functions. How is the apparent contradiction to be resolved?

One solution is to read these opening words in light of information found elsewhere in the verse. It is true that no specific bodily functions or actions requiring *wuḍūʾ* ablutions are enumerated at the beginning of the verse, where they might be expected. However, such factors are mentioned later in the verse, in connection with the special case of *tayammum* (ablutions performed with dust in the absence of water). Under circumstances that make ablutions with water impossible or perilous to the health, ablutions must be performed with dust after urination or defecation ("coming from the privy") or contact with women. It is a highly natural inference that the causes of impurity mentioned in connection with *tayammum* also apply to the general case of *wuḍūʾ* performed with water. Since the ablutions with dust are a substitute for ablutions with water, they almost certainly occur in the same situations. The inference that the first half of verse 5:6 should be read in light of the additional information in the second half of the verse was indeed advanced by early commentators; the Kūfan exegete al-Suddī, who died in A.H. 127, is supposed to have boldly inserted the missing conditions into the text of the Qurʾān—not, of course, as an emendation, but to fill an assumed ellipsis.[5]

Despite the cogency of this inference, a certain tension between the received understanding of the rules and a narrowly technical reading of the Qurʾān remains. The text of Revelation demands that the believer perform *wuḍūʾ* ablutions when he "rises to pray," and it never *explicitly* limits this injunction to cases of minor impurity. A Qurʾānic literalist might well insist that this command be fulfilled to the letter. If substitute ablutions with dust are to be performed only after certain bodily functions, so be it. God's ways are mysterious, and His ritual demands particularly unfathomable; logical inferences like the one described above need not be taken as binding.

Given this textual dilemma, it is unsurprising that early compilations of traditions preserve numerous reports addressing the question of whether it is necessary to perform *wuḍūʾ* before every prayer or not. Fairly extensive chapters on the subject are found in the *Muṣannaf*s of ʿAbd al-Razzāq[6] and Ibn Abī Shayba[7]; the 3rd/4th century A.H. historian and commentator al-Ṭabarī also presents a large number of relevant opinions from early figures.[8] In the *Muṣannaf* of Ibn Abī Shayba, separate sections comprise the opinions of those who performed *wuḍūʾ* only after polluting bodily functions and of those who performed ablutions before every prayer. The existence of a significant number of early reports addressing the issue might be taken to indicate that it was a contentious one at some early point in time. Examination of the reports, however, reveals that it would be very difficult to adduce any evidence that there was ever a school of thought (as opposed to a constellation of isolated individuals) holding that ablutions were required before every prayer; there is no obvious cluster of people in any specific place or time who are said to have represented this principle. Thus, it is unlikely that the position that ablutions were necessary only after polluting bodily functions was ever under serious attack.

However, it is irrational to suppose that all of the material addressing the issue was generated and preserved gratuitously. The many reports documenting early figures who performed *wuḍūʾ* only after polluting bodily functions must have been recorded in pursuit of some agenda. I would argue that they reflect, not a confrontation between Muslims who held that it was necessary to perform ablutions before every prayer and Muslims who limited ablutions to cases of minor impurity, but a confrontation between a Muslim community that knew full well that it was not necessary to perform ablutions before every prayer and a text that, read in a rigorously literalist fashion, seemed to say that it was.

Most of the reports in question do not make explicit reference to the text of the Qurʾān. However, it is difficult to imagine any factor other than the ambiguous word of Revelation that would have roused an early Muslim to the defense of the apparently well-established belief that ablutions were necessary only in cases of pollution. The underlying exegetical concern is made explicit by a few texts, such as the following report about the Meccan scholar ʿAṭāʾ ibn abī Rabāḥ (d. A.H. 115/733–34 C.E.) and his student Ibn Jurayj (d. A.H. 149-51/ 766–68 C.E.):

> Ibn Jurayj said: I said to ʿAṭāʾ, "Must one perform *wuḍūʾ* for every prayer?" He said, "No." I said, "[God] says, {When you rise to pray . . . }" He said, "The first *wuḍūʾ* suffices you; if I perform *wuḍūʾ* for the dawn prayer, I perform all of the prayers with [those ablutions] as long as I do not have a polluting bodily function (*mā lam uḥdith*)." I said, "Is it desirable (*yustaḥabbu*) for me to perform *wuḍūʾ* for every prayer?" He said, "No."[9]

This report forms part of a corpus which has recently been demonstrated to display many signs of authenticity.[10] While its literal accuracy cannot be regarded as assured, we can take it as a plausible point of departure to suggest a historical setting for the reports relating to this issue. In this report, Ibn Jurayj entertains the possibility that ablutions may be required before every prayer on the basis of the Qurʾānic text. ʿAṭāʾ, somewhat surprisingly, denies this with no other reason but his unshakable commitment to what was presumably the established practice. While ʿAṭāʾ is clearly familiar with the verse, showing no signs of consternation when Ibn Jurayj recites it, he has no detailed interpretation at his disposal that would relate his own position to the letter of the text. It is only his student, a generation younger, who wishes to derive the law rigorously from the letter of revelation. Technical concern with the literal word of the Qurʾān as the supreme source of legislation, this anecdote implies, established itself only in Ibn Jurayj's generation (at least in Mecca, and in the intellectual circles to which these two men belonged, and at least on this particular point). The time frame suggested by the anecdote is the end of the 90s A.H. or the first decade of the second century (roughly 714–28 C.E.).[11]

The chronological inference suggested by the Ibn Jurayj anecdote seems to be supported by the evidence of other reports. That is, explicit and sometimes pointed statements of the principle that *wuḍūʾ* is required only in case of minor impurity are attributed to scholars of the generation of ʿAṭāʾ. (One wonders whether these statements were elicited by the questions of the usually younger students who transmitted them, as was the case with Ibn Jurayj.) A rather defensive statement of the principle that ablutions are necessary only in case of pollution is attributed to ʿĀmir ibn Sharāḥīl al-Shaʿbī, who is supposed to have declared that "I don't care if I pray five prayers with one *wuḍūʾ*, as long as I don't need to defecate or urinate."[12] al-Shaʿbī, a Kūfan, died in the first decade of the second century A.H.[13] The same statement is attributed to Qatāda,[14] a Baṣran who died in 117 or 118.[15] al-Ḥasan [al-Baṣrī], who died in 110, is reported to have stated that "A man can pray all of the prayers with one *wuḍūʾ* as long as he has not had a polluting bodily function; the same applies to *tayammum*."[16] The great Kūfan scholar Ibrāhīm al-Nakhaʿī is supposed to have declared that "I pray the noon, afternoon and the evening prayers with one *wuḍūʾ* as long as I have not had a polluting bodily function (*ḥadath*) or said something reprehensible (*munkar*)."[17] Ibrāhīm died in 95; fairly young at his death, he was of the same generation as the other scholars.[18] A strong statement of principle is attributed to the prominent Ḥijāzī scholar Saʿīd ibn al-Musayyab, an older man who died in the last decade of the first century: "*Wuḍūʾ* without a polluting bodily function is an act of excess (*al-wuḍūʾ min ghayr ḥadath iʿtidāʾ*)."[19]

It is also interesting to observe that scholars of the same generation seem to have shown an interest in adducing the example of prominent members of the previous generation. For instance, in addition to stating his own practice of performing ablutions only when in a state of pollution, Ibrāhīm al-Nakhaʿī is supposed to have reported that "I heard Wahb say, 'I pray the noon prayer with the *wuḍūʾ* of the [previous] night prayer.' "[20] The Wahb in question is probably Wahb ibn Munabbih (the other transmitters of that name being either highly obscure or chronologically too late for Ibrāhīm to have met them). Wahb ibn Munabbih died later than Ibrāhīm al-Nakhaʿī, A.H. 113–16, but he was reportedly born in 34 A.H. and thus more than a decade older than Ibrāhīm, who died in 95 at the age of 49.[21] Interestingly, Wahb's alleged comment is less a direct statement about the occasions of *wuḍū'* than a reflection of a pious practice based on the assumption that one performed *wuḍū'* only for polluting bodily functions. The habit of maintaining one's state of *wuḍū'* from nighttime until the next morning entailed the avoidance not only of elimination and farting but of deep sleep (see below, pp. 70–75); thus, such a statement implied that Wahb held regular vigils. A similar report, from a biographical source, recounts that "for twenty years, he did not perform *wuḍū'* between the night prayer and the dawn prayer (*al-ṣubḥ*)."[22] It is quite likely that this tribute to Wahb's vigils existed before the concern with the legal occasions for *wuḍū'* and was only later found to be relevant to the question (by Ibrāhīm or someone who attributed the report to him).

Similarly, ʿUmāra ibn ʿUmayr, a Kūfan who reportedly died around A.H. 98[23], is cited as reporting the practice of al-Aswad ibn Yazīd, who "used to perform *wuḍū'* with a cup (*qadaḥ*) [of water containing only] enough to satisfy a man's thirst, then pray all of the prayers with that *wuḍū'* as long as he did not have a polluting bodily function."[24] Al-Aswad, a Kūfan and an uncle of Ibrāhīm al-Nakhaʿī, died in A.H. 74–75.[25] The report, with its use of the past tense and its implication that al-Aswad is no longer available for consultation, probably originated sometime between the middle of the 70s A.H. and the end of the 90s (or, of course, was intended retrospectively to depict this period). Again, the report claims that al-Aswad followed the practice of performing *wuḍū'* only after a polluting bodily function, not that he addressed the question as a matter of principle. (Interestingly, the person who seems to have propagated this report is the Kūfan al-Aʿmash, who died in the late 140s A.H.[26]) The Kūfan ʿAṭīya [ibn Saʿd ibn Junāda], who died in A.H. 111, reports that ʿAbd Allāh ibn ʿUmar, who died in the 60s, "used to sit and pray the noon, afternoon, and sunset prayers with one *wuḍū'*."[27] Yazīd [ibn abī ʿUbayd], the client (*mawlā*) of the Companion Salama [ibn ʿAmr ibn al-Akwaʿ], is supposed to have reported that the latter performed all his prayers with a single *wuḍū'*.[28] Salama's death date is extremely uncertain; various reports state that he died in A.H. 64, 74, or after 80;[29] Yazīd ibn abī ʿUbayd died in the 140s.[30]

A particularly interesting case is that of the famous Muḥammad ibn Sīrīn, a Baṣran who died in 110. He is supposed to be the source of one of the few reports documenting supposed instances of people who performed *wuḍū'* for every prayer. Specifically, he attributes the practice to the first three caliphs.[31] However, the same informant who transmits this report from Ibn Sīrīn also states that Ibn Sīrīn himself considered it necessary to perform *wuḍū'* only in case of pollution.[32] The same transmitter relays a third report in which Ibn Sīrīn, apparently in perplexity over the problem, consults with the legendary jurist Shurayḥ. The latter refers him to the popular practice: "Look and see what the people do (*unẓur mādhā yaṣnaʿuʾl-nās*)."[33] These reports, taken together, form a picture consistent with the scholarly opinions discussed so far. A conscious enquiry into the problem of the occasions of *wuḍūʾ* is conducted by Ibn Sīrīn, a member of the generation of ʿAṭāʾ. Ibn Sīrīn, perhaps basing himself on an inference from the Qurʾānic text, believes that *wuḍūʾ* for every prayer is an authentic element of early Islamic practice. However, by reference to the unanimous practice of contemporary Muslims (not *reading* the text of the Qurʾān, but *looking* at what the people do), he is able to convince himself that *wuḍūʾ* is necessary only in cases of pollution, the rule he follows himself.

What is new in the period of the reports examined above, the end of the first century A.H. and the beginning of the second, is a sense of defensiveness about the principle that *wuḍūʾ* is necessary only after a polluting bodily function and the beginnings of a search for evidence to support it. The juristic principle itself seems, if we are to trust the testimony of our sources, to have predated this period. Explicit statements to this effect are attributed to ʿAlqama [ibn Qays], a Kūfan scholar who is supposed to have died in the 60s or 70s;[34] to the Companion Saʿd ibn abī Waqqāṣ, who died in the 50s;[35] and to Abū Mūsā al-Ashʿarī, another Companion of the Prophet, who was governor of Baṣra under ʿUthmān and died sometime between A.H. 42 and 53.[36] However, regardless of one's estimation of the authenticity of these reports about earlier figures, the relatively large number of reports about jurists addressing the question of the occasions of *wuḍūʾ* in the late first and early second centuries A.H. indicates that the question was still lively at that time. The statement that one must perform *wuḍūʾ* only for a *ḥadath* was then noteworthy; a few decades later, it would be banal. Given that the principle itself seems to have been long-established, the only probable cause for a flurry of interest in articulating and defending it is the rise of a new interest in increasingly exacting and technical juristic examination of the Qurʾānic text. The defensive wording of the statements attributed to al-Shaʿbī and to Ibn al-Musayyab suffices to suggest that they were responding to some challenge, and the dialog between ʿAṭāʾ and Ibn Jurayj suggests the nature of that challenge very plausibly.[37]

One interesting report presents a notable exception to the time line we have just suggested. This is an anecdote in which the Companion of the Prophet and pioneering scholar Ibn ʿAbbās, who died in A.H. 68/686–88 C.E.,[38] is confronted with the same textualist challenge later posed by Ibn Jurayj:

> al-Miswar ibn Makhrama said to Ibn ʿAbbās, "Do you have any explanation for ʿUbayd ibn ʿUmayr? When he hears the call to

> prayer he goes out and performs *wuḍū'*." Ibn 'Abbās said, "That is the devil's work. When he comes, tell me." When he came, they informed him. He said, "Whatever prevails upon you to do what you do?" He said, "God says, {When you rise to pray, wash your faces . . . }" and recited the verse. Ibn 'Abbās said, "It is not so; when you perform *wuḍū'*, you are pure as long as you don't have a polluting bodily function (*ḥadath*)."[39]

This report conflicts with the timeline we have suggested in the sense that it represents a Qur'ānic-literalist challenge taking place in the lifetime of Ibn 'Abbās, a teacher of 'Aṭā's who was significantly older than the latter. However, whether or not it actually dates from the time of Ibn 'Abbās, it supports the idea that rigorous Qur'ānic argumentation was introduced into the debate only secondarily, and that a theoretical defense of the established practice was not immediately available. It is interesting that this tradition, which (in giving Ibn 'Abbās, the higher authority, the last word) clearly intends to support the principle that ablutions are necessary only in cases of pollution, gives no justification whatsoever for this position. It is actually rather astonishing that 'Ubayd recites a verse of the Qur'ān and Ibn 'Abbās flatly retorts that "it is not so." Ibn 'Abbās is presumably rejecting 'Ubayd's interpretation rather than the word of God, but he offers no alternate reading. All that is evident from the report is that 'Ubayd's behavior is supposed to be deviant and that Ibn 'Abbās reestablishes the accepted principle.

Overall, these reports—whatever their individual accuracy—suggest two conclusions. Firstly, the established practice of Muslims at least by the final decades of the first century A.H. was to perform *wuḍū'* only after a polluting bodily function. Secondly, sometime around the final decade of the first century A.H. a number of jurists, perhaps under the questioning of their younger students, began to display a palpable defensiveness about this principle and to search for justification in the example of the previous generation and of the first caliphs. This trend seems to have been initiated by increasing interest in rigorous analysis of the text of the Qur'ān.

It is important to stress that the Qur'ān could easily have been the source of the original understanding that *wuḍū'* ablutions were necessary only in cases of minor pollution. This principle is completely compatible with the statements of the Qur'ān, and indeed, as we have already suggested, it is the obvious inference yielded by a commonsense reading of the text. The source of tension was a more rigorous and exacting mode of Qur'ānic interpretation in which general, wholistic understandings of the meaning of the relevant verse were no longer sufficient.

How did legal scholars solve the theoretical dilemma posed by the apparent contradiction between the Qur'ānic text and the established practice?

One might have expected that the continuous practice of the Muslim people would be understood as being modeled on the example of the Prophet, the *sunna*. The Prophetic precedent would then, in this case as in many others, be understood as a clarification of the true intent of the Qurʾānic injunction. Interestingly, however, this is not unqualifiedly the case. On the contrary, some early scholars seem to have suspected that the accepted practice of performing *wuḍūʾ* only after a polluting bodily function was at variance with the personal practice of the Prophet as well with the apparent literal meaning of the Qurʾān. A report recorded by al-Bukhārī recounts:

> Anas said, "The Prophet used to perform *wuḍūʾ* for every prayer." I said, "What did you (pl.) use to do?" He said, "[One] *wuḍūʾ* [used to] suffice us as long as we did not have a polluting bodily function (*ḥadath*)."[40]

Anas ibn Mālik, one of the longest-lived Companions of the Prophet, is supposed to have died between 90 and 95; here, he is probably supposed to be speaking late in life about his increasingly rare firsthand knowledge of the Prophet's lifetime. This scenario suggests an exchange taking place in the 80s or early 90s—a dating that would place it plausibly within the chronological sequence suggested above. Interestingly, one of Anas's greatest claims to fame was his close adherence to the Prophet's example in his prayers.[41] The form of the text is interesting. Upon hearing Anas's report that "the Prophet used to perform *wuḍūʾ* for every prayer," ʿAmr ibn ʿĀmir asks, "What did *you* (pl.) do?" This is not a routine response to a statement about the practice of the Prophet; the ordinary assumption would be that the Prophetic *sunna* was followed by the Companions. The average listener would scarcely be expected to ask a follow-up question suggesting the possibility that the Companions had not followed the example of the Prophet. This exchange thus strongly suggests that ʿAmr ibn ʿĀmir (or the later transmitter who attributed this report to him) had a strong preconception that *wuḍūʾ* was not required before every prayer.[42]

Both the problem of the apparent meaning of the Qurʾānic text and that of the apparently established conviction that the Prophet had performed ablutions before every prayer were resolved by many scholars by an invocation of the principle of abrogation (*naskh*). The idea that an original dispensation requiring *wuḍūʾ* for every prayer was replaced by another requiring it only for polluting bodily functions was based on a widely-circulated *ḥadīth* stating that the Prophet "used to perform *wuḍūʾ* for every prayer, until the day of the Conquest [of Mecca] came and he prayed the noon, afternoon, and evening prayers with one *wuḍūʾ*."[43] This report solved the juristic problem of the occasions of *wuḍūʾ* very neatly. The principle that only the Qurʾān can abrogate the Qur'ān, established by al-Shāfi'ī,[44] need not have been known or accepted by the people who first circulated the report. The earliest practice—presumably based on the Qur'ān—was to perform *wuḍū'* for every prayer, and it was superseded only by a normative action of the Prophet. Very interestingly, chains of transmission for this tradition converge on Sufyān al-Thawrī, a Kūfan who died in 161.[45] Thus, a Qur'ānically-conscious and theoretically rigorous solution to the problem is advanced (although not necessarily created!) by a man of the generation of Ibn Jurayj. The idea that this *ḥadīth* is specifically directed at an exegetical problem is also suggested by its careful specification of a very late date for the shift, placing it after any likely dating of verse 5:6.

A second explanation of the apparent discrepancy between the wording of verse 5:6 and the practice of performing *wuḍū'* only after a polluting bodily function similarly invoked the principle of abrogation:

> Muḥammad ibn Yaḥyā ibn Ḥibbān al-Anṣārī (later known as [*thumma*] al-Māzinī, [i.e.,] Māzin Banī Najjār) said: I said to 'Ubayd Allāh ibn 'Abd Allāh ibn 'Umar, "What do you think was the reason that 'Abd Allāh ibn 'Umar performed *wuḍū'* for every prayer, whether he was in a state of purity or not?" He said that Asmā' bint Zayd ibn al-Khaṭṭāb had reported to him that 'Abd Allāh ibn Ḥanẓala ibn abī 'Āmir ibn al-Ghasīl reported to her that the Prophet had been commanded to perform *wuḍū'* for every prayer, whether he was in a state of purity or not; when this proved onerous to (*shaqqa 'alā*) the Prophet, he was commanded to use a toothpick before every prayer and was excused from performing *wuḍū'* unless he had had a polluting bodily function. ['Ubayd Allāh ibn 'Abd Allāh ibn 'Umar] said, "Since 'Abd Allāh [ibn 'Umar] thought that he was capable (*bihi quwwa*) of doing that [i.e., perform *wuḍū'* before every prayer], he did it until he died."[46]

A very interesting feature of this report is that, although it claims to preserve information about the progressive moderation of God's ritual demands during the lifetime of the Prophet, it suggests that from the point of view of later Muslims it was the purported *practice* of prominent early figures such as 'Abd Allāh ibn 'Umar that was known and that required explanation through retrospective inquiry into the *sunna* of the Prophet. Although there is some dispute over the actual practice of 'Abd Allāh ibn 'Umar[47], there is good evidence that the belief that he had performed *wuḍū'* before every prayer was well enough established to require attention and reinterpretation in light of later consensus. Thus, the sources offer an alternative explanation for the same behavior; in a tradition transmitted by Ibn Māja, ʿAbd Allāh ibn ʿUmar is observed performing ablutions before every prayer and, questioned about his behavior in what are perhaps suspiciously technical terms ("Is *wuḍūʾ* before every prayer a religious obligation [*farīḍa*] or a meritorious Prophetic practice [*sunna*]?"), explains that it is an optional practice that he performs in hope of reward.[48]

Another possible interpretation of the opening words of verse 5:6, "when you rise to pray," is that they refer to arising *from sleep*. One of the exegetical challenges that this interpretation may be understood to have met is that it eliminated the implication that the believer must perform ablutions every time he "rises to pray." From this point of view, the interpretation performs the same function as the abrogation tradition. However, the interpretation that "rising" meant "arising from sleep" also performed another important function: it identified a scriptural warrant for a ritual practice that seems already to have been well-established.[49] Despite some controversy in learned circles, which will be discussed later, there has apparently always been agreement among Muslims that the state of purity required for prayer is cancelled not only by elimination (urination and defecation) and contact with women,[50] but by sleep. This presumed reference to sleep, in combination with the references to elimination and contact with women appearing later in the verse, yields a full set of the major "cancelers of *wuḍūʾ*" (*nawāqiḍ al-wuḍūʾ*). Thus, the received understanding of the rules relating to *wuḍūʾ* can be extracted from the Qurʾānic text with the aid of a small number of semantic and syntactical assumptions, which are presented by an early commentator as follows:

> . . . There is an inversion of order (*taqdīm wa-taʾkhīr*) in the verse, [which should be read] as follows: When you rise from sleep, or you have just relieved yourselves or had contact with women . . . then wash your face [etc.]; if you have no water then perform your ablutions with dust (*tayammamū*)—without mentioning the causes of impurity (*asbāb al-ḥadath*), because the substitute [that is, ablutions with dust] is necessitated by the same conditions that necessitate the original [that is, ablutions with water] (*liʾannaʾl-badal yataʿallaqu bi-mā yataʿallaqu bihiʾl-aṣl*), and no additional elucidation is required. If these assumptions are not made (*matā lam yajʿalū hākadhā*), the verse says nothing about the various things that cause impurity.[51]

The interpretation of the phrase "when you rise to pray" (*idhā qumtum ilāʾl-ṣalāt*) to refer to the performance of ablutions after sleep seems to have been advanced early and with some success; Mālik cites it as the opinion of Zayd ibn Aslam.[52] As Zayd ibn Aslam is supposed to have died in A.H. 136/

753–54 C.E., this report would fit into our general chronological pattern; serious reflection about the textual difficulties of verse 5:6 arises at the beginning of the second century A.H. and leads to a search for technical solutions in the following decades.

Nevertheless, this interpretation of the Qur'ānic phrase "when you rise to pray" is not completely convincing. Although the verb "*qāma*" may sometimes indicate arising after slumber, the phrase "*qāma ilā' l-ṣalāt*" ("to rise to pray") seems to be a generic expression without any necessary reference to sleep. When Qur'ān 4:142 states of the hypocrites that "when they rise to pray (*idhā qāmū ilā' l-ṣalāt*), they stand up sluggishly: they pray for the sake of ostentation," the reference is clearly to the slackness of their devotions in general and not to their somnolence on awaking.[53] Furthermore, interpreting the phrase to mean "when you get up from sleep to pray" creates another exegetical problem; once we have used this part of the verse to indicate the special case of impurity due to sleep, we can no longer use it to specify that the entire set of rules applies to the general situation that one is about to pray. The exegete cited above is really using the same phrase for two different functions simultaneously.

The difficulties inherent in the assumption that the phrase "when you rise to pray" refers to arising from sleep are reflected in the uncertainty about this interpretation expressed by leading legal thinkers. al-Shāfiʿī, who is in fact one of the stronger supporters of this interpretation, presents it in a language of doubt:

> The most obvious interpretation of the verse (*ẓāhir al-āya*) is that anyone who rises to pray must perform *wuḍū'*; [however,] it is possible that it was revealed about some specific [group.] I have heard someone whose knowledge of the Qur'ān I admire claim (*yazʿamu*) that it was revealed about those who arise from sleep. I think (*aḥsabu*) that he was correct in what he said, because there is proof in the *sunna* that anyone who gets up from sleep must perform *wuḍū'*.[54]

Despite al-Shāfiʿī's reference to "proof in the *sunna*," the incentive to discover evidence for the requirement of *wuḍū'* from sleep in the Qur'ān must have been all the greater because it was in fact very difficult to ground this requirement in the *sunna*. It was quite early perceived as a problem that, while most people were firm in the conviction that the rule imposing *wuḍū'* from sleep existed, the available reports about the behavior of the Prophet seemed to document the opposite. The resulting tension is evident in the relevant passage from Muḥammad ibn al-Ḥasan al-Shaybānī's *Kitāb al-Āthār*:

> Chapter on Sleeping Before Prayer and Performing *Wuḍū'* Because of It
>
> Muḥammad [al-Shaybānī] said: Abū Ḥanīfa reported to us from Ḥammād from Ibrāhīm: The Prophet performed *wuḍū'* and went out to the mosque. He found that the *mu'adhdhin* had given the *adhān*. He lay down on his side and slept deeply enough so that it was noticeable—he had a distinctive way of sleeping; he used to snore (*yanfukhu*) when he slept. Then he got up and prayed without performing *wuḍū'*. Ibrāhīm said: The Prophet is not like other people.
>
> Muḥammad said: We adhere to Ibrāhīm's opinion. We have heard (*balaghanā*) that the Prophet said: My eyes sleep, but my heart does not sleep. Thus, the Prophet is not like other people. As for anyone but him, if he lies down on his side and goes to sleep, he must perform *wuḍū'*. This is the opinion of Abū Ḥanīfa.[55]

The formula "My eyes sleep, but my heart does not sleep" seems originally to be part of the material transmitted in the context of the early discussion of the phenomenon of prophecy and the possibility that the dreams of prophets may be true visions. It is cited by the early biographer Ibn Isḥāq (d. A.H. 150/767 C.E.) in the context of the Prophet's Night Journey, whose character as a physical transportation or a visionary experience was hotly contested. Ibn Isḥāq, citing a series of reports suggesting that the journey was a spiritual vision occurring while the Prophet's body was asleep in bed, notes:

> I have heard that the Prophet used to say, "My eyes sleep while my heart is awake." God knows best which of these [states] he was in when he beheld what he beheld of God's doings (*amr Allāh*). Whether he was sleeping or awake, all of it is real and true.[56]

On one level, the application of this maxim to the case of ritual purity was felicitous. The conclusion that the Prophet enjoyed a special dispensation (*rukhṣa*) with respect to this aspect of ritual purity was not an implausible one; other such cases were known, and it seemed not unnatural that a person as exceptional as the Prophet should have certain privileges denied to the common run of mankind. However, in the context of a legal discourse founded on the conviction that the example of the Prophet was normative, it was necessarily a concern to keep such cases to a well-defined minimum. The contention that the Prophet was sufficiently unique to warrant different rules applying to him alone could only weaken his role as a source of binding precedents for the conduct of all believers.[57] The case at hand must have been particularly vexing because the Prophet's alleged behavior was not an exception to a textually well-established rule. The number of his wives was easily identifiable as a special privelege, not merely because his unique status made his multiple marriage alliances vitally important, but because the rule to which they formed an exception was clearly established in the Qur'ān. On what basis did a Muslim of Ibrāhīm al-Nakhaʿī's generation know the rule that the Prophet's immaculate sleep defied? It may have been precisely this dilemma that led thinkers of later generations to seek a warrant for *wuḍū'* from sleep in the text of the Qur'ān.

The difficulty of establishing the requirement for *wuḍū'* after sleep on the basis of *ḥadīth* texts is reflected in the writings of such eminent scholars as al-Shāfiʿī, al-Bukhārī, and Muslim. al-Shāfiʿī (like Mālik before him) documents the requirment for *wuḍū'* from sleep with a report in which the Prophet says, "When one of you awakes from sleep, he should not immerse his hand in the water-vessel before washing it three times; he does not know where his hand was in the night."[58] The main burden of this *ḥadīth* is clearly not the requirement to perform *wuḍū'* after sleep, but the fear that the ablution water will be rendered impure by something (probably semen) that might have gotten onto one's hands in the night. The context may suggest that the awakened sleeper is about to perform *wuḍū'* in preparation for prayer, and thus that *wuḍū'* is mandatory after sleeping, but the *ḥadīth* does not explicitly say so. It could just as well be feared that he would put his hand into the water vessel for a mere morning washing of the hands or the face.

Similarly, al-Bukhārī entitles the relevant chapter in the *Ṣaḥīḥ* "*Wuḍū'* from sleep, and those people who did not consider it necessary to perform *wuḍū'* from brief sleepiness (*al-naʿsa wa'l-naʿsatayni*) or nodding off." However, he offers no *ḥadīth* in support of the positive injunction; both traditions in the chapter support the exception.[59] They are both slightly divergent versions of a tradition in which the Prophet counsels the believer, in case of sleepiness during prayer, to sleep until he is refreshed enough to pray with alertness. Since he does not specify that the nap should be brief or mention *wuḍū'* if it becomes lengthy, this report might be taken to ignore the whole principle that sleep requires *wuḍū'*. Finally, Muslim in his *Ṣaḥīḥ* offers a set of *ḥadīth* under the rubric "Proof that Sleep Does Not Cancel *Wuḍū'* If One Is Sitting Up," but no *ḥadīth* demonstrating the general rule to which this is presumably an exception—that sleep does cancel *wuḍū'* if one is lying down.[60]

There was, however, one *ḥadīth* that did seem to indicate unambiguously the requirement for *wuḍū'* after sleep.[61] Abū Dāwud transmits it from ʿAlī ibn abī Ṭālib: "The Prophet said, 'The eyes are the drawstring of the anus, and when the eyes sleep the drawstring is released, so anyone who sleeps should perform *wuḍū'*.' "[62] Not only does this tradition provide the only direct Prophetic injunction to perform *wuḍū*ʾ from sleep, but it gives a rationale for the rule. Farting, as one more way of expelling something from the anus, is assimilated into defecation under the general rubric of "relieving yourself" (*in jāʾa aḥadukum min al-ghāʾiṭ*). Not only is this a very natural analogical conclusion, but it is mentioned in *ḥadīth* and was clearly familiar to Muslims at a very early date. A person who is sleeping has neither the self-control to prevent himself from farting nor the awareness to note it if he does so. Therefore, anyone awaking from sleep is treated as if he had passed gas and required to perform *wuḍū*ʾ before prayer. However, on inspection it seems that this *ḥadīth* does not constitute documentation that sleep ruptures the state of ritual purity, but a rationale for the established practice of performing *wuḍū*ʾ after sleep that refers it to another (theoretically better established) source of impurity. The tradition does not establish that sleep cancels *wuḍū*ʾ, but conserves the corresponding practice while denying that it does so.

This implication is made explicit, interestingly, in reports about two of the individuals who are supposed to have denied the requirement for *wuḍū*ʾ after sleep. Thus, Abū Mūsā is supposed to have asked his companions after awakening from a nap, "Did you hear me fart?" and prayed without performing *wuḍū*ʾ when they answered in the negative.[63] The statement that "the eyes are the drawstring of the anus" would seem to have been an established formula in ʿIrāq very early indeed; early authorities are quoted as citing it in abbreviated versions that imply its familiarity to their listeners.[64] Whether they were citing a *fiqh* maxim that was later promoted to the status of a Prophetic *ḥadīth* (as the Schachtian theory would dictate), or a familiar Prophetic *ḥadīth* that contemporary practice did not require them formally to identify as such, must remain uncertain. What is certain is that the maxim entailed or reflected an Iraqī reluctance to accept sleep as an independent item cancelling *wuḍū*ʾ, ultimately preserved in the doctrine of the Ḥanafī school.[65]

On examining the Qurʾānic and *ḥadīth* evidence for the requirement of *wuḍū*ʾ after sleep, one is struck by the impression that the sources' conviction that the requirement exists is far stronger than the evidence at hand. As I have already argued, the Qurʾānic text scarcely forces this interpretation on the listener. The evidence of the *sunna*—at least as documented in *ḥadīth* texts—is equally slim. Yet there seems to have been an early and indelible conviction on the part of the majority of legal thinkers that the requirement existed. The only obvious explanation of the discrepancy between the force of the evidence for this rule and the near unanimity of its acceptance is that it was already an established element of popular practice at the time when theoretical discussion of the issue began.

Who, then, rejected the requirement? The sources list a number of prominent individual figures who are supposed to have held that sleep did not require *wuḍū*ʾ at all. There are significant inconsistencies in the lists offered.[66] Among the persons named are the Companions Abū Mūsā al-Ash'arī, who served as governor in Baṣra and Kūfa and died in A.H. 50-54/670–74 C.E.,[67] and 'Abd Allāh ibn 'Umar, who died in A.H. 63–64/682-84 C.E.; the Kūfan 'Abīda al-Salmānī, who died in A.H. 72-74/691–94 C.E. and whose tradition was preserved by the Baṣrans;[68] the Medinian jurist Sa'īd b. al-Musayyab, who died in A.H. 93–100/711–19 C.E.;[69] Abū Mijlaz, a Baṣran who died between A.H. 100 and 110/ 718–29 C.E.;[70] the Syrian jurists Makḥūl, who died between A.H. 112 and 118/730–37 C.E.,[71] and al-Awzā'ī, who died in A.H. 158/774–75 C.E.;[72] and the famous Baṣran traditionist Shu'ba, who died in A.H. 160/776–77 C.E.[73]

One thing that is clear from this list is that the alleged dissenters in the debate over *wuḍū'* from sleep are not clustered in one specific era. Chronologically, they are fairly evenly distributed over the first four generations of Muslims. Thus, it would seem that we are dealing with (if anything) a chronologically dispersed set of individual dissenters rather than a controversy that raged at one specific point in time. Geographically, the dissenters seem to be disproportionately concentrated in Baṣra and Syria. Nevertheless, it does not seem possible to document a Baṣran or Syrian local "school" opinion denying the obligation to perform *wuḍū'* after sleep. In fact, the evidence that even these few scattered figures actually opposed the requirement for *wuḍū'* after sleep is thin and in some cases contradictory.[74] Again, as in the case of *wuḍū'* before every prayer, the tension seems to be, not between two schools of legal thought, but between a virtually unbroken popular and legal consensus on the one hand and a perplexing textual difficulty on the other.

"Wipe Your Heads and Your Feet . . ."

Another point of tension between the apparent meaning of the Qur'ānic text and the received understanding of the law relating to *wuḍū'* relates to the treatment of the feet. The Arabic text of verse 5:6 literally reads, "Believers, when you rise to pray wash your faces and your hands as far as the elbow, and wipe your heads and your feet to the ankle." The text seems to pair the face and hands, which must be washed, and the head and feet, which must merely be wiped. However, as we shall see, the Sunnī tradition unanimously embraced the practice of washing the feet at a very early period. There is a syntactical trick that formally solves the resulting difficulty: instead of reading "and your feet" in apposition to "wipe your heads," it is possible to read "and your feet" in apposition to "wash your faces and your hands." The verse would then be understood to mean, ". . . wash your faces and your hands as far as the elbow, and wipe your heads, and [wash] your feet to the ankle." Due to that fact that the verb "to wipe" requires a preposition, thus placing the noun in the genitive (*wa'msaḥū bi-ru'ūsikum . . . wa-arjulikum*), while the verb "to wash" takes a direct object and thus places it in the accusative (*wa'msaḥū bi-ru'ūsikum . . . wa-['ghsilū] arjulakum*), this alternative parsing of the verse is phonetically distinct from the first. However, despite its technical plausibility, this is a highly artificial solution that scarcely conforms to the standard of perfect eloquence and clarity that believers understand to be exemplified by the Qur'ānic text.

The opinion that the requirement for the cleansing of the feet should follow the most obvious meaning of the Qur'ānic text seems to have been a very widespread one in the early period. This opinion is ascribed to a number of prominent figures of the first and early second centuries A.H. by reports transmitted in the early sources. The opinion that "the feet are wiped" is attributed to al-Ḥasan al-Baṣrī (d. A.H. 110/728 C.E.) and to ʿIkrima (d. A.H. 105/723–24 C.E.).[75] The august ʿAbd Allāh ibn ʿAbbās (d. A.H. 68/686–87 C.E.), regarded as the "father of Qur'ānic exegesis," is supposed to have supported this position with a neat piece of analysis: the *wuḍū'* ablutions consisted of "two wipings and two washings";[76] when God legislated substitute ablutions with dust (*tayammum*), "He substituted two wipings for the two washings and dropped the two [original] wipings."[77] The same logic is attributed to al-Shaʿbī.[78] These men apparently based their opinions directly on the Qur'ānic evidence, probably in the face of popular practice; thus, al-Shaʿbī is supposed to have stated with defiant emphasis that "Gabriel revealed wiping (*nazala jibrā'īl bi'l-masḥ*)."[79] Some early scholars apparently desired to compromise; Anas [ibn Mālik] is said to have "moistened his feet when he wiped them," thus fulfilling both requirements.[80]

A report about the Meccan jurist ʿAṭā' ibn abī Rabāḥ (d. A.H. 115/733–34 C.E.) suggests the tensions among Qur'ānic literalism, Prophetic *sunna*, and popular practice surrounding this minor but practical question:

> Ibn Jurayj said: I said to ʿAṭā', "Why shouldn't I wipe my feet just as I wipe my head, when [God] said [that one should wipe] both of them (*wa-qad qālahumā jamīʿan*)?" He said, "I believe that one should wipe the head and wash the feet (*lā arāhu illā masḥ al-ra's wa-ghusl al-qadamayn*); I heard Abū Hurayra said, 'Woe to the heels from the Fire.' " ʿAṭā' [also] said, "Many people say that [the proper procedure] is wiping; as for me, I wash them."[81]

Here, as in several other instances, ʿAṭā' is challenged by Ibn Jurayj with a discrepancy between his own doctrine and the literal word of the Qur'ān. In many cases, as we have seen, similar anecdotes seem to suggest that ʿAṭā' is not yet concerned with a stringent analysis of the Qur'ānic text on the point in question and is perfectly content with the established practice until questioned by the younger and more theoretically aware Ibn Jurayj. In this text, however,

ʿAṭāʾ is clearly already aware of a difficulty. While his favored approach does not correspond to the most obvious sense of the Qurʾānic text, ʿAṭāʾ seems to be aware of a conflict and is prepared with a piece of counterevidence (a *ḥadīth* of the Prophet) to support his own position. Furthermore, he is aware of "many people" who adhere to the Qurʾānic literalist position.

The chronological development of the doctrine is reflected in the report that "a man said to Maṭar al-Warrāq, 'Who used to say that wiping applies to the feet?' " and received the reply, "Many religious scholars."[82] Maṭar al-Warrāq, who settled in Baṣra, is supposed to have died in A.H. 125 or 129.[83] Although we can know nothing about the anonymous person who is supposed to have asked the question, it is only natural to assume that Maṭar was a fairly old man at the time; the question is a general query about what people "used to say," and thus suggests that the addressee is old enough to offer information about "the old days." The question suggests that the opinion supporting the wiping of the feet is now a fading memory; Maṭar's alleged reply—like the multiplicity of reports attributing this opinion to early figures—suggests that, in contrast, it was once quite possible.

In this case, the historical development in the doctrine would seem to be as follows: by the second half of the first century A.H., Muslims were washing rather than wiping their feet. A number of individual jurists, involved in an increasingly close and technical examination of the text of the Qurʾān and its relationship to the existing practice, advanced the thesis that the feet should in fact be wiped. However, this purist revision of the doctrine ultimately failed; by the end of the lifetime of Maṭar al-Warrāq, it was passing into memory. Why should the doctrine of the wiping of the feet have failed, given that it corresponded to the apparent meaning of the text of the Qurʾān? There are three possible explanations, all of which probably contributed to the final outcome. One is that the evidence of the *sunna* supported the washing of the feet. Another is that the force of established precedent, understood to correspond to the *sunna*, was simply too strong for even a textually compelling revision to prevail. The third is that the issue became charged with political and sectarian overtones. The final outcome of this religio-political polarization was that the wiping of the feet came to be a distinctively Shīʿite practice.

The early sources preserve a number of traditions in which various figures are represented as demonstrating the Prophet's style of performing *wuḍūʾ*. These traditions do not explicitly address the question of the washing or wiping of the feet, but in systematically describing the *wuḍūʾ* ritual they incidentally cover it. Interestingly, almost all assume that the feet are to be washed; one can only conclude that this was the dominant existing practice in the various circles that produced these diverse reports.[84] The striking thing about the various *ḥadīth* preserved on this particular topic is that almost all of them trace the description of the Prophet's practice back to one of the first four caliphs. The most common reference figures are ʿAlī ibn abī Ṭālib (reigned A.H. 35–40/656–61 C.E.) and ʿUthmān ibn ʿAffān (reigned A.H. 23–35/644–56 C.E.), followed by ʿUmar ibn al-Khaṭṭāb (reigned A.H. 13–23/634–44 C.E.).

The form in which these *ḥadīth* texts have been transmitted is also significant. What we may consider to be the paradigmatic form of the *ḥadīth* report consists of a chain of transmission followed either by a statement or action attributed to the Prophet or by an anecdote narrated by the Companion witness who relates the situation in which he saw or heard the Prophet doing or saying the thing in question. These particular *ḥadīth* texts, in contrast, focus not on the situation in which the Prophet is alleged to have performed the action in question, but on the situation in which it was promulgated by the Companion involved. The time frame of the miniature narrative is not the lifetime of the Prophet, but the lifetime of the generation that survived him. Thus, these *ḥadīth* do not make us vicarious witnesses to the practice of the Prophet, but vicarious witnesses to moments at which his precedent was invoked.

The ʿAlī tradition appears in several variations with various chains of transmission. In one of its most elaborate incarnations, it is presented with an Imāmī family *isnād*:

> ʿAbd al-Razzāq - Ibn Jurayj - "someone I trust" - Muḥammad ibn ʿAlī ibn Ḥusayn - his father - his father: ʿAlī called for [water to perform] *wuḍūʾ*. It was brought to him, and he washed his hands three times before putting them into his *wuḍūʾ* water. Then he rinsed his mouth out three times, blew water out of his nose three times, then washed his face three times, then washed his right arm up to the elbow three times, then the left one the same, then [wiped his head once, then washed his right foot up to the ankle bones three times, then the right one the same, then] stood up and said, "Give it to me." I gave him the vessel with the water left from his *wuḍūʾ*, and he drank from the water left from his *wuḍūʾ* while standing up. I was suprised. When he saw that I was surprised, he said, "Don't be surprised; I saw your ancestor (*abāka*) the Prophet do what you have seen me doing"—[the transmitter] said, "[i.e.,] in performing *wuḍūʾ* in this way and drinking his *wuḍūʾ* water while standing."[85]

In another, less lengthy version of the tradition the family *isnād* is absent and the demonstration is made, not individually to his son and successor, but to the public in general. ʿAlī states, "Whoever would like to watch the Prophet's way of performing *wuḍūʾ* should watch this (*man sarrahu an yanẓura ilā wuḍūʾ rasūl allāh faʾl-yanẓur ilā hādhā*)."[86]

Interestingly, there is another *ḥadīth* in which neither ʿAlī nor his descendants of the Imāmī line are cited in the chain of transmission, but the preservation of the Prophet's practice within his broader family is strongly emphasized by the text of the report. In it the Ṭālibid ʿAbd Allāh ibn Muḥammad ibn ʿAqīl ibn abī Ṭālib reports,

> I visited Rubayyiʿ bint ʿAfrāʾ; she said, "Who are you?" He said, [I said:] "I am ʿAbd Allāh ibn Muḥammad ibn ʿAqīl ibn abī Ṭālib." She said, "And who is your mother?" I said, "Rayṭa bint ʿAlī," or "so-and-so bint ʿAlī ibn abī Ṭālib." She said, "Welcome, nephew!" I said, "I have come to ask you about the *wuḍūʾ* of the Prophet." [She said, "The Prophet] used to send us presents and visit us; he used to perform *wuḍūʾ* from this vessel, or one like it—it contains about a *mudd*." She said, "He used to wash his hands, wash out his mouth, and blow water from his nose, then wash his face three times, then wash his hands three times, then wipe his head two times, wipe the inside and the outside of his ears, and wash his feet three times."[87]

Whatever the historicity of this report[88], it seems to represent another point on the spectrum of views on the status of the Prophet's family and their special knowledge of his praxis represented by this set of *ḥadīth*. The first report takes the essentially Shīʿite position that this knowledge is privately transmitted from individual to individual along the line of Imāms. The addition of the mysterious procedure of drinking the water from one's own *wuḍūʾ* gives it a somewhat esoteric cast. The privileged nature of this knowledge is further emphasized by the fact that the listener is represented as being surprised by what he hears. The second report takes the essentially (proto-)Sunnī (although perhaps politically or religiously ʿAlid-loyalist) view that ʿAlī is an authority on the practice of the Prophet, but that ʿAlī's example is available to the community like that of any other Companion. The third takes an intermediate position; while uninterested in the linear succession of the Imāmate, it stresses the special status of the relatives of the Prophet. In the second century, this would have been a perfectly tenable moderate Shīʿite position.

Of course, one must use care when using a word such as "Shīʿite" or "Sunnī" in this context, neither sect having taken definite doctrinal form in the period in which these *ḥadīth* presumably came into existence. Here I am using the terms to denote basic ideological stances that can be discerned in the thinking of various people at various times, whether or not they were individuals belonging to discrete and self-described Sunnī and Shīʿite communities at a time when their doctrines were fully developed. I am terming "Shīʿite" the tenet that religious knowledge is to be sought from the Prophet's family, and more specifically from his direct male descendants of the line who came to be recognized as Imāms. The position that religious knowledge could be reported from the Prophet by any contemporary member of his community I regard as Sunnī. I use these terms, for lack of any better, to designate the schematic gradient of religiopolitical positions along which a given statement can be located.

By this standard, at least two of the above reports show some sign of being Shīʿite. This is despite the fact that no form of the *ḥadīth* attributed to ʿAlī in the Sunnī sources reflects the position that came to be emblematic of Shīʿism. These traditions specify that ʿAlī (emulating the Prophet) *washed* his feet; classical Shīʿite doctrine would dictate that he *wipe* them, in accordance with the most obvious reading of the Qurʾān.[89] Furthermore, the Shīʿite sources hold that ʿAlī performed each action only once or twice.[90]

It is presumably on the basis of such discrepancies that Schacht has argued that "there is no trace of a bias in favour of Shiite legal doctrines in the Iraqian traditions from ʿAlī."[91] However, Schacht's judgement assumes two questionable things: firstly, the *continuity* over time of the Shīʿite position on various issues, and secondly, the *unity* and *unanimity* of the Shīʿite community. It is more likely that the Shīʿite community was diverse and that its positions changed and solidified over time. The fact that the Twelver community that produced the classical Shīʿite compilations of the third to fourth century A.H. and later held a given position thus does not prove that some grouping of ʿAlid loyalists could not have advanced a divergent view in the second century.

It is unlikely to be a coincidence that the other figure most often credited with special knowledge of the Prophet's personal mode of performing *wuḍūʾ* is ʿUthmān, the first caliph of the Umayyad clan and the man whose relative and avenger, Muʿāwiya ibn abī Sufyān, would prove to be ʿAlī's greatest political antagonist after ʿUthmān's assassination. The religious significance attributed to ʿUthmān's knowledge of the Prophet's mode of *wuḍūʾ* is reflected in the more elaborate versions of the text:

> I saw ʿUthmān ibn ʿAffān perform *wuḍūʾ*. He poured water on his hands three times and washed them, then washed out his mouth and blew water out of his nose, then washed his face three times, then washed his right arm to the elbow three times, then washed the left one the same way, then wiped his head, then washed his right foot three times, then the left one three times as well, then said: "I saw the Prophet perform *wuḍūʾ* as I have

> performed *wuḍūʾ*." Then he said, "Whoever performs *wuḍūʾ* the way I just did and then performs a two-*rakʿa* prayer without his mind straying (*lā yuḥaddithu fīhimā nafsahu*) will have his preceding sins forgiven."[92]

This version emphasizes the almost magical efficacy of the Prophet's personal method of performing *wuḍūʾ*.

Another form of the *ḥadīth* concentrates on the caliph's public role in disseminating this information. Although the precise situation is not specified, the scene is clearly a gathering of some sort:

> ʿUthmān said, "Shall I show you (pl.) how the Prophet used to perform *wuḍūʾ*?" They said, "Yes!" He called for water, then washed out his mouth three times, blew water out of his nose three times, washed his face three times and his arms three times, wiped his head and washed his feet. Then he said, "Know that the ears are part of the head." Then he said, "I have sought out (*taḥarraytu aw tawakhkhaytu*) the Prophet's way of performing *wuḍūʾ*."[93]

Whereas the implication of the ʿAlī traditions was presumably that ʿAlī naturally became privy to the Prophet's personal habits as a close member of his family, in this text what is emphasized is ʿUthmān's effort to discover it. As an agent and guardian of the Muslim community, he has sought it out.

Unsurprisingly, the *ḥadīth* attributing this knowledge to ʿAlī are Kūfan, while those tracing it to ʿUthmān are more geographically diverse (Medinian, Baṣran, and Kūfan). It may be significant that most of the Medinian chains of transmission converge on the name of Ibn Shihāb al-Zuhrī. al-Zuhrī seems to have been a particular advocate of this tradition; Muslim follows the body of the report with the comment, "Ibn Shihāb said: Our religious scholars (*ʿulamāʾunā*) used to say, 'This is the most thorough (*asbagh*) *wuḍūʾ* that anyone can perform for prayer.' "[94] To have popularized this *ḥadīth*, which represents the first Umayyad caliph as the custodian of vital and efficacious information about the practice of the Prophet, would of course fit well with what we know of al-Zuhrī's political career as an associate of the later Umayyads.

The inference that this tradition was circulated by al-Zuhrī may, however, be put in question by a report cited by ʿAbd al-Razzāq, in which al-Zuhrī is said to have stated, "If a man were to perform *wuḍūʾ* one time and if he were thorough that one time, it would suffice him (*law tawaḍḍaʾa rajul marratan wāḥida fa-ablagha fī tilkaʾl-marra ajzaʾa ʿanhu*)."[95] I would argue that this statement, which implies that it is somewhat unlikely for a man to perform *wuḍūʾ* only once ("*law*") and merely allows that this procedure is acceptable ("*ajzaʾa ʿanhu*"), not that it is desirable, is perfectly compatible with the belief that full compliance with the Prophet's precedent would dictate three repetitions. However, it should also be noted that this tradition is not included in Mālik's *Muwaṭṭa*ʾ. Given the state of the evidence, it is impossible to come to any firm conclusion about the original popularizer of the *ḥadīth*; it will suffice to note that here al-Zuhrī's name is strongly associated with a tradition with Umayyad overtones.

The traditions attributing special knowledge of the Prophet's *wuḍū*ʾ to ʿAlī and ʿUthmān demonstrate that the question of the proper manner in which to perform *wuḍū*ʾ was very early intertwined with the politically-charged issue of the authority of the *sunna* and the identity of the parties qualified to transmit and represent it. However, despite the polarization of the religio-political stances represented in this set of traditions, they do not represent contrasting positions on the issue of the washing of the feet. Proto-Sunnīs and proto-Shīʿites alike seem to assume that the feet must be washed. How did the specific question of the washing of the feet enter the political arena and become an emblematic sectarian issue? A report in the *Muṣannaf* of ʿAbd al-Razzāq suggests a possible setting in the late Umayyad period. It recounts,

> ʿUthmān ibn abī Suwayd heard that the wiping of the feet was mentioned to [the Umayyad caliph] ʿUmar ibn ʿAbd al-ʿAzīz; he said, "It has been reported to me from three of the Companions of Muḥammad, the least authoritative (*adnā*) of whom is your cousin al-Mughīra ibn Shuʿba, that the Prophet washed his feet."[96]

Here, the unusually pious and well-respected Umayyad caliph ʿUmar ibn ʿAbd al-ʿAzīz (reigned A.H. 99–101/717–20 C.E.) is approached with a query about proper ritual practice: Should one wipe one's feet during *wuḍū*ʾ? The probable background of the question is that ʿUthmān ibn Suwayd, like many scholars of the end of the first century, is increasingly interested in the rigorous analysis and application of the Qurʾānic text, yet is dubious about the possibility of wiping the feet because it conflicts with the established practice. ʿUmar assures him that the *sunna* supports the washing of the feet (and thus, implicitly, that he need not worry about the more obvious reading of the Qurʾānic text).

Such a claim of custodianship of the *sunna* on the part of the Umayyad state might well be expected to have raised opposition. Such opposition is, in fact, reflected in a surviving anecdote attacking a similar authoritative statement allegedly promulgated by the most notorious henchman of the Umayyad regime, the governor al-Ḥajjāj ibn Yūsuf:

> Mūsā ibn Anas said to Anas, "O Abū Ḥamza, al-Ḥajjāj gave the Friday sermon in al-Ahwāz when we were with him and men-

tioned ritual ablutions (*dhakara' l-ṭuhūr*). Instructing us to wash, he mentioned the washing of the feet (*qāla' ghsilū ḥattā dhakara' l-rijlayn wa-ghuslihimā*) and the washing of the heels (*al-'arāqīb wa' l-'arāqib*)." Anas said, "God spoke the truth, and al-Ḥajjāj lied. God Most High said, {Wash your faces and your hands up to the elbows, and wipe your head and your feet}." He [i.e., Mūsā ibn Anas?] said, "When Anas wiped his feet, he would moisten them and say, 'The Qur'ān was revealed with wiping, and the *sunna* brought washing (*nazala' l-qur' ān bi' l-masḥ wa-jā' ati' l-sunna bi' l-ghusl*).' "[97]

In this report two different areas of conflict become manifest. One, addressed by Anas's final comment that "The Qur'ān was revealed with wiping, and the *sunna* brought washing," is purely academic in nature. The basic textual sources of the legal tradition seemed, at least superficially, to be in contradiction. Although the anecdote suggests that he was not able to reach a theoretically satisfactory resolution to the conundrum one way or the other, Anas seems to have been able to resolve the problem in practical terms. Evincing his respect both for the text of revelation and for the precedent of the Prophet, he followed a procedure that combined the two. The other level of conflict reflected by the anecdote was apparently more explosive and less easily resolved. It involved not merely the perplexity occasioned by an apparent conflict between the sources of the law, but the tension generated by different claims to authority in interpreting the law. Anas's son approaches him for his opinion on a statement about the proper practice made by a powerful and oppressive Umayyad governor from an authoritative position afforded him by his rank, the pulpit of the mosque during Friday services. In keeping with the tradition cited above, where an Umayyad caliph advances the claim that the *sunna* of the Prophet dictates the washing of the feet, al-Ḥajjāj implies that the Prophet's example takes precedent over the clear word of the Qur'ān. Whereas Anas's approach to the theoretical conundrum of the apparent conflict of sources was, according to the anecdote, gently respectful of both positions, his reaction to al-Ḥajjāj's alleged pronouncement is harsh and unconditional: "God spoke the truth, and al-Ḥajjāj lied."

It is, of course, impossible to state with certainty whether either al-Ḥajjāj or Anas ever uttered the words attributed to them in this report; it is not even clear whether the report represents one rather complex statement about Anas's attitude toward this thorny legal question or an unstable compound of two anecdotes representing different memories of his views. What is clearly established by stories of this kind, however, is the double nature—theoretical and political—of the issue at hand. Whether or not these specific statements actually originated with al-Ḥajjāj or with Anas, the story suggests that some people in the circles in which this report originated perceived an attempt by caliphs and servants of the caliphal state to promulgate official positions on legal questions relating to ritual purity.

The case of the "wiping of the feet," like the development of the doctrine that *wuḍūʾ* was necessary only after a polluting bodily function, suggests that there was a strong "living tradition" of popular practice that early scholars enquiring into the Qurʾānic text were compelled to treat with respect. This "living tradition" was largely identified with the *sunna*. Thus, it was inferred by many that the existing practice of performing *wuḍūʾ* only after a polluting bodily function must have had its origin in the Prophet's example. Similarly, the practice of washing rather than wiping the feet was seen as part of a living perpetuation of the *sunna* of the Prophet on the part of prominent individuals who modeled it for the community. This "living tradition" of practice (although it came to be enshrined in texts) was originally based on personal example and visual observation rather than on verbal description or textual interpretation. Thus, Shurayḥ instructs Ibn Sīrīn to "*look at* what the people do," and ʿAlī invites people to "*look at* the *wuḍūʾ* of the Prophet." The individuals who are the repositories of this tradition of practice are frequently important religio-political figures. Although, in the present case, both the "ʿAlid" traditions and the "Umayyad" ones support the practice of washing the feet (the position of rejecting this apparently time-honored practice in favor of Qurʾānic literalism apparently not yet having been adopted specifically by Shīʿites), it is clear that the preservation of the correct ritual practice is seen as an important function of the leaders of the community, and that one's views on the identity of the correct leaders of the community thus became intertwined with one's ritual preferences.

This trend of politicization is also evident in the rather elaborate text of one of the most important traditions in the debate over *wuḍūʾ* before every prayer. The anecdote merits close examination:

> Ḥiṭṭān ibn ʿAbd Allāh al-Raqāshī[98] said: We were with Abū Mūsā al-Ashʿarī[99] in an army on the banks of the Tigris when prayer time came; the crier gave the call for the noon prayer. The people got up to perform *wuḍūʾ* and performed *wuḍūʾ*; Abū Mūsā led them in prayer. Then they sat in circles. When the time for the afternoon prayer came, the crier gave the call for the afternoon prayer; the people leapt up to perform *wuḍūʾ* again. [Abū Mūsā] ordered the crier to call out, "No, no one must perform *wuḍūʾ* unless he has had a polluting bodily function (*ḥadath*). Knowledge (*ʿilm*) has almost passed away; ignorance (*jahl*) has prevailed, so that a man strikes his mother with the sword out of ignorance."[100]

I would argue that this report is a narrative polemic rather than (like the brief and sober opinions discussed above) a straightforward account of an early juristic position. Firstly, the report has certain features that make it seem somewhat artificial. The group seems to sit in a circle for several hours merely to make the point that they have already performed *wuḍū'* for the noon prayer and need not do so again for the afternoon prayer. The second, and more striking, distinctive feature of the story is the unexpected passion of Abū Mūsā's condemnation of the practice of performing *wuḍū'* before each prayer. After all, it might seem logical that performing *wuḍū'* before each prayer, if not strictly necessary, would be a nice supererogatory observance. Indeed, as we have seen, the Prophet is often said to have done so himself—an indication that, even if ordinary believers were relieved of such an onerous duty, it was perhaps the ideal practice. Yet Abū Mūsā seems quite enraged. What precisely is at stake in this anecdote?

The intensity of the report's denunciation of the practice of *wuḍū'* before every prayer suggests that it was a polemic against some actual and hated group—yet, as already stated, no such group of jurists supporting *wuḍū'* before every prayer is evident in the sources. However, Abū Mūsā's plaint that "knowledge (*'ilm*) has almost passed away; ignorance (*jahl*) has prevailed, so that a man strikes his mother with the sword out of ignorance" suggests a possible group as the targets of the polemic. Indeed, the identity of this group may be hypothesized.

The reference to "striking one's mother with the sword" evokes the violent practices of the most prominent dissenting group in the early Islamic community, the Khārijites. Furthermore, the practice of performing *wuḍū'* before every prayer undoubtedly (as discussed above) reflects an attitude of Qur'ānic literalism. In this report, conversely, the emphasis is on "knowledge," *'ilm*—in the early Islamic context, primarily the knowledge of the *sunna*. The Khārijites refused to modify Qur'ānic doctrine by reference to the *sunna*; thus, for instance, they rejected the punishment of stoning for adultery.[101] They were also apparently known for adherence to onerous purity practices. Thus, in another early anecdote a woman approaches 'Ā'isha to ask if she must make up all the prayers she misses during her menstrual period; 'Ā'isha retorts, "Are you a Khārijite (*a-ḥarūrīya anti*)?!"[102] The evidence of the chains of transmission suggests that the anecdote was circulated in Baṣra (the *isnād*s seem to converge on Qatāda, who died in A.H. 117). Baṣra being a center of early Khārijism, this would again support a reference to the Khārijites. The inference that Abū Mūsā's fulmination is directed at Khārijite practice would require us to assume that the story is ahistorical; by the time the Khārijites split off from the party of 'Alī, Abū Mūsā was an elderly man who had fled to Mecca in disgrace after the fiasco of his bungled participation in the arbitration between ʿAlī and Muʿāwiya. However, supposing the story is a vehicle for polemical expression rather than a statement of fact, the choice of Abū Mūsā is peculiarly appropriate; as ʿAlī's representative in the arbitration, he would symbolize the event Khārijites resented most.

Whoever was the original target of this story, what it demonstrates clearly is the role of such ritual details as the occasions of *wuḍūʾ* in community formation and in the definition of political loyalty. The people, mobilized in an army, are instructed in ritual practice by a governor and commander clearly intent on unifying their practice.

"If You Have Touched Women . . ."

The last major crux in the text of verse 5:6 (as well as that of verse 4:43) is the interpretation of the phrase "or if you have touched women" (*aw lāmastum al-nisāʾ*). There are essentially two possible understandings of the reference to "touching women," one literal and one figurative. The literal interpretation, of course, is that the phrase refers simply to skin-to-skin contact with a woman, most likely but not necessarily one's wife. The figurative interpretation is that the phrase "if you have touched women" is a metonym or a euphemism referring to sexual intercourse.

Both of these two interpretations have semantic arguments in their favor. In particular, the contention that "touching women" is actually a reference to sexual activity is a quite plausible one in the context of the Qurʾānic text as a whole. The vocabulary of the Qurʾān does not include a word whose primary literal meaning is "to have sexual intercourse." Instead, it employs a more oblique expression very similar to the one we are examining here. Thus, the Virgin Mary marvels at the Annunciation, "How can I bear a child when no man has touched me (*wa-lam yamsasnī bashar*)?" (3:47, 19:20) Men are advised of their duties towards wives whom they divorce before the consummation of the marriage, "before you have touched them" (*mā lam tamassūhunna* (2:236)/*min qabli an tamassūhunna* (2:237)). Thus, the standard Qurʾānic term for sexual intercourse is semantically identical to the one under consideration, but employs a different verb: *massa* instead of *lāmasa*. The strong parallelism with phrases obviously referring to intercourse suggests that we should understand the phrase "if you have touched women" in the same way when it appears in the verses referring to ritual ablutions.

This approach is also suggested by the wording of the phrase that immediately precedes it in these verses, "if you have relieved yourself" (*idhā jāʾa aḥadukum min al-ghāʾiṭ*). The Arabic phrase literally means, "if one of you is coming from the *ghāʾiṭ*"; a *ghāʾiṭ* is a depressed and sheltered spot in open land. The phrase is thus doubly euphemistic, firstly because it refers to "coming from the privy" rather than to the bodily functions one has presumably performed there, and secondly because (like the word "privy" in English) the term used for the place in question is a polite one obliquely implying bodily functions by a reference to the seclusion they demand. The expression as a whole sets a pattern of polite indirection in light of which it is highly natural to interpret the following phrase, "if you have touched women," as a second euphemism.

On the other hand, the Qur'ānic usage of the stem *l-m-s* seems to be distinct from that of the stem *m-s-s*. While the verb *m-s-s* is almost always figurative in its import, referring to sexual contact or to being "touched" by suffering, catastrophe, or madness, this is not true of the usage of *l-m-s*. Of the two other instances of the first form of the verb *l-m-s* in the Qur'ān, one unambiguously refers to reaching out to feel something with the hand. This is verse 6:7, which declares, "If We sent down to you a Book inscribed on real parchment and they touched it (*lamasūhu*) with their own hands, the unbelievers would still assert: 'This is but plain sorcery.' " The second case (72:8), which seems to use form one of the verb as a synonym of form eight (*iltamasa*, "to seek out"),[103] provides no illumination for the case at hand.

The lexicographical tradition, as transmitted by Ibn Manẓūr, also seems to indicate a difference between the usages of the two verbs. Both verbs have the primary denotation of touching with the hand. While both are stated to have the secondary, figurative meaning "to have intercourse," the evidence for this reading seems to be quite thin in the case of "*l-m-s*." In the case of "*m-s-s*" it suffices for Ibn Manẓūr to state that the verb figuratively refers to sexual intercourse and supply appropriate Qur'ānic citations. In the article on "*l-m-s*," where the lack of unanimity about the sense of the relevant Qur'ānic phrase demands that he supply philological evidence, very little seems to be available. His sole documentation is a Bedouin proverb (*qawl al-ʿarab*) about a woman of ill repute: "She does not repel the hand of one who *l-m-s* (*lā taruddu yada lāmis*)." Although the lexicographer Ibn Manẓūr (d. A.H. 711/1311–12 C.E.) seems to imply that this was an established figure of speech, his only textual citation is a *ḥadīth* in which a man approaches the Prophet with this accusation against his wife. The accepted (and obvious) interpretation of the expression is that the woman is liberal in distributing her sexual favors. An alternative interpretation interprets it as an accusation of poor household management: she does not refuse anyone who seeks her husband's wealth. This does not seem to be a very compelling example; even with respect to the sexual interpretation, it makes more sense to understand the saying to mean "She does not repel the hand of anyone who reaches out for her" than to mean "She does not repel the hand of anyone who has intercourse with her" (which anticipates the results of her receptive attitude!).

Thus, on the basis of the Qur'ānic text alone, it would be quite possible to conclude either that any skin-to-skin contact with women rendered one polluted or that one was polluted only by actual intercourse. In fact, both of these exegetical options are reflected in the opinions attributed to authoritative early figures. The position that it is necessary to perform *wuḍū'* after any form of literal "touching" is attributed, through Kūfan chains of transmission, to the Prophet's Companion Ibn Masʿūd.[104] He is supposed to have framed his opinion in an explicitly exegetical form:

> Ibn Masʿūd said, "A man should perform *wuḍū'* from skin-to-skin contact (*al-mubāshara*), from touching with his hand, and from kissing if he kisses his wife"; he used to say about this verse, {*aw lāmastum al-nisā'* }, "It is fondling (*al-ghamz*)."[105]

The statement that it is necessary to renew one's *wuḍū'* after kissing one's wife is also attributed, through Medinian chains of transmission, to the Companion Ibn ʿUmar.[106] The main figurehead for the position that kissing and other forms of skin-to-skin contact with women do not require *wuḍū'* is Ibn ʿAbbās, who is supposed to have denied that such actions were polluting with the typically forceful and humorous statement, "I don't care if I kiss her or smell a sprig of basil (*rayḥān*)."[107] He supported this position with an exegetical argument: " 'Touching' (*al-mulāmasa*) is sexual intercourse."[108]

The controversy over the purity status of kissing and touching is encapsulated in an anecdote narrated by the Baṣran Qatāda (ibn Diʿāma, d. A.H. 117–18[109]):

> ʿUbayd ibn ʿUmayr, Saʿīd ibn Jubayr, and ʿAṭā' ibn abī Rabāḥ argued about "touching" (*al-mulāmasa*, clearly a reference to the language of verse 5:6). Saʿīd and ʿAṭā' said, "It is touching and fondling (*al-lams wa'l-ghamz*), and ʿUbayd ibn ʿUmayr said, "It is sexual intercourse (*al-nikāḥ*)." Ibn ʿAbbās came out to meet them when they were at this point; they asked him [about the controversy] and informed him of their opinions. He said, "The two non-Arabs [lit., "clients": *al-mawlayān*] are in error, and the Arab is correct. It is sexual intercourse, but God preserves decency by using figurative language (*allāh yaʿiffu wa-yaknī*)."[110]

The other major authoritative voice mobilized on behalf of the position that kissing did not require *wuḍū'* is that of the Prophet's wife ʿĀ'isha, who narrates in a *ḥadīth* preserved through geographically diverse chains of transmission that the Prophet used to kiss his wives and then pray without performing *wuḍū'*.[111]

Among the early jurists, the opinion that kissing requires *wuḍūʾ* is attributed to the Kūfans ʿAbd al-Raḥmān ibn abī Laylā (said to have died in A.H. 82),[112] Ibrāhīm (al-Nakhaʿī, d. A.H. 95),[113] al-Shaʿbī (who died in the first decade of the second century A.H.),[114] al-Ḥakam (ibn ʿUtayba al-Kindī, d. A.H. 113-15),[115] and Ḥammād (ibn abī Sulaymān, d. A.H. 119-20).[116] It is also attributed to the Baṣran Qatāda.[117] The Baṣran al-Ḥasan (d. A.H. 110), on the other hand, is supposed to have denied the necessity for *wuḍūʾ* after kissing.[118] His opinion that literally "touching" women did not cause pollution was apparently based on a *ḥadīth* stating that the Prophet had grasped ʿĀʾisha's foot without lust once while he was praying.[119]

Several things can be concluded about the general shape of this debate. The first is that it seems to have been explicitly exegetical in nature. A number of the statements attributed to early figures on both sides of the controversy are overtly framed as interpretations of the verb "lāmasa" ("to touch") used in verse 5:6. Proponents of both positions seem to have been proceeding from the word of the Qurʾān, some of them preferring to understand it literally and others inferring that its true force was figurative. It can be said that, even though in some cases the exegetical nature of the reports is not explicit, both major positions were "Qurʾānically aware." Thus, unlike in the case of several of the other controversies discussed in this chapter, there are no reports in which a scholar adhering to an opinion based on popular practice or on the Prophetic *sunna* is embarrassed by the citation of an apparently conflicting locution from the Qurʾān. Furthermore, there is no discernible evidence of an established popular practice that rendered jurists loath to explore one or the other of the exegetical alternatives. This is probably because, on the level of practice, this was a rather technical question.

The other major pattern that emerges is that, like the other controversies discussed in this chapter, the debate over the true meaning of verse 5:6's reference to "touching" is a theoretical one in which scholars in any given locality developed individual positions based on their own evaluation of the evidence available. Neither of the two interpretations that competed in this debate can be inferred originally to have been the *local* opinion in one of the metropolises of the early Islamic world; both of them were apparently *personal* opinions based on theoretical considerations.

This conclusion contradicts the analysis of the debate offered in one of the earliest literary sources, Muḥammad ibn al-Ḥasan al-Shaybānī's *Kitāb al-Ḥujja ʿalā ahl al-madīna*. Al-Shaybānī attributes the opinion that kissing cancels *wuḍūʾ* to the Medinians and contrasts it with the Kūfan position (exemplified by Abū Ḥanīfa) that no *wuḍūʾ* is required: "Abū Ḥanīfa said of the man who kisses his wife after having performed *wuḍūʾ* that it does not cancel *wuḍūʾ*. The people of Madīna said, 'That requires *wuḍūʾ*'."[120] However, the same author's compilation of the opinions of his teacher Abū Ḥanīfa represents the distribution of opinions in a more complex way. In this book, which does not structure its presentation around the dichotomy between ʿIrāq and Medina, both opinions are attributed to Kūfan scholars:

> Muḥammad said: Abū Ḥanīfa reported to us from Ḥammād from Ibrāhīm about the man who comes back from a journey and is kissed by his paternal or maternal aunt or [another] woman from his immediate family [lit., "whom he cannot marry"]: he said, "He does not have to perform *wuḍūʾ* if he kisses a woman who is closely related to him [lit., "whom he cannot marry"]; but if he kisses someone he is permitted to marry he must perform *wuḍūʾ*, and it is equivalent to a polluting bodily function (*ḥadath*)." Muḥammad said, "This is Ibrāhīm's opinion (*qawl*); we do not follow it. We do not consider it necessary to perform *wuḍūʾ* from kissing under any circumstances, unless [the man] has a discharge. This is the opinon of Abū Ḥanīfa."[121]

Indeed, examination of the early sources suggests that until the beginning of the second century A.H. this debate proceeded primarily within ʿIrāq. Thus the origins of the disagreement would seem to lie not in discrepancies between two local traditions of popular practice that confronted each other and sparked theoretical debate in an age of synthesis, but in the generation of divergent opinions by scholars within one locality (Kūfa). The conflict between "the Medinians" and "the ʿIrāqīs" documented in *Kitāb al-Ḥujja* emerges less as an encounter between two originally isolated indigenous traditions than as a debate between followers of Mālik and followers of Abū Ḥanīfa, neither of whom necessarily represented the single or the original position of the people of his city of origin. The roots of the controversy probably lay in divergent interpretational strategies adopted by scholars increasingly involved in close and rigorous examination of the Qurʾānic text.

The question of *wuḍūʾ* after skin-to-skin contact with women was, of course, one with a practical and symbolic significance of its own.[122] However, the interpretation of the Qurʾānic reference to "touching women" was rendered even more important by the fact that one's exegetical choice with respect to this phrase dictated the implicit structuring of verse 5:6 as a whole. Due to the loose syntactic structure of this lengthy and important Qurʾānic verse, reinterpretation of the phrase "if you have touched women" entailed an implicit realignment of the entire sentence. Because of the complex nature of the questions raised by the interpretation of this phrase, I will begin by discussing the syntax of the verse in detail.

If we read the phrase as an allusion to mere skin-to-skin contact with women, it is natural to regard it as a source of minor impurity parallel to defecation and urination. The phrase "if you have touched women" is thus placed parallel with the preceding phrase, "if you have relieved yourselves." Those who promote this reading are thus implicitly parsing the verse as follows:

a.) relieved yourself
1. When you rise to pray, having <], then [perform *wuḍū'*].
b.) touched women

2. If you are in a state of major impurity, cleanse yourselves [i.e., bathe (*ghusl*)].

ill
3. If you are < and you can find no water,
travelling

a.) relieved yourself
and you have< [i.e., are in a state of minor impurity],
b.) touched women

then [perform ablutions with dust].

In this reading, the pair "if you have relieved yourselves or touched women" describes the two conditions of minor impurity. These are implied to be the conditions under which one must perform the *wuḍū'* ablutions and explicitly stated to be the conditions under which one may perform ablutions with dust (*tayammum*) if no water is available. Between the clause relating to *wuḍū'* ablutions and the clause relating to ablutions with dust, there is a clause relating to major impurity. If one is in a state of major impurity, which the tradition unanimously interprets to mean impurity resulting from sexual activity, then one must cleanse oneself—according to the tradition, a full bath known as *ghusl*. According to this reading, it should be noted, the verse says nothing about what you should do if you are in a state of major impurity and you are ill or do not have access to water.

While mere touching best fits into the schema of ritual purity in the capacity of a source of minor impurity (requiring *wuḍū'* ablutions), sexual intercourse has always been recognized to be a source of major impurity (requiring full bathing, *ghusl*). In this case, the phrase "or [if] you have touched women" is not paired with the phrase "if you have relieved yourself" as a source of minor impurity, but contrasted with it as a reference to sexual pollution. The implicit structuring of the verse would thus be:

1. When you rise to pray <
   a. [and you are in a state of minor impurity], wash your hands, etc. (i.e., perform *wuḍū*ʾ)
   b. if you are in a state of major impurity, cleanse yourselves (i.e., perform *ghusl*)

2. If you are < ill / travelling and you can find no water,

   and you have <
   a. relieved yourself (i.e., are in a state of minor impurity)
   b. had sexual intercourse (i.e., are in a state of major impurity),

   then [perform ablutions with dust].

Here the verse is structured into two basic cases, each with two subcases related to the availability of water. The first half of the verse, relating to ablutions with water, clearly implies the case that water is at hand. In this case, one must either perform *wuḍū*ʾ ablutions (understood but not stated to apply to unspecified cases of minor impurity) or, if one is in a state of major impurity, cleanse oneself completely. The second half of the verse deals with cases in which no water is at one's disposal. In this case, whether you are in a state of minor impurity after relieving yourself or in a state of major impurity after having intercourse with ("touching") a woman, you may perform ablutions with dust. This structuring of the verse has the appeal of symmetry and also enjoys the substantive advantage of covering the case that one is in a state of major impurity without access to water. Here, the specification of the causes of minor impurity would have to be based on the assumed parallelism between the two halves of the verse. The first half deals with minor impurity of unspecified source and with major (sexual) impurity; the second deals with urination and defecation ("coming from the privy") and with sexual impurity ("touching women"). The symmetry of the two halves would then imply that, just as the major (sexual) impurity of the first half of the verse is mirrored by the "touching women" of the second, the unspecified minor impurity of the first half of the verse corresponds to the "coming from the privy" of the second.

The structural ambiguity of verse 5:6, arising from the uncertain denotation of the reference to "touching women," thus leaves it in doubt whether one can perform *tayammum* in case of sexual pollution. The second half of the verse states that, in case of illness or in the absence of water, one can perform *tayammum* after urinating or defecating ("coming from the privy") or after "touching women." If "touching women" is interpreted as a literal reference to skin-to-skin contact (understood to be a source of minor impurity), then the instructions relating to *tayammum* say nothing about sexual pollution. If, on the other hand, "touching women" is interpreted as a euphemism for sexual intercourse, the verse clearly indicates that *tayammum* is permissible in case of sexual pollution.

If early jurists constructed their opinions with reference to the text of the Qurʾān, one would expect this ambiguity to have generated a difference of opinion on the issue of *tayammum* for sexual pollution. This is, in fact, the case. The opinion that one may not perform *tayammum* in case of major (sexual) pollution is most widely attributed to Ibn Masʿūd, who is supposed to have stated, "If I were to become sexually impure and didn't find water for a month, I would not pray."[123] The same opinion was also attributed to ʿUmar[124] and to ʿAbd Allāh [Ibn ʿUmar] (perhaps suggesting an original ambiguous reference to "ʿAbd Allāh"[125]). It is probably not a coincidence that Ibn Masʿūd and Ibn ʿUmar are the two authorities most often associated with the doctrine that it is not permissible to perform *tayammum* in case of sexual pollution. As mentioned above, they are also the two authorities associated with the interpretation that "touching women" literally refers to skin-to-skin contact, including kissing—which, as indicated above, is the very interpretation of verse 5:6 that leaves the possibility of *tayammum* from major impurity in suspension. The interconnection between these two legal conundrums (the interpretation of verse 5:6's reference to "touching women" and the question of *tayammum* from sexual pollution) is indicated by an anecdote recorded by ʿAbd al-Razzāq:

> Ibn Jurayj said: I said to ʿAṭāʾ, "Do you think (*a-raʾayta*) that [God's] statement {or you have touched women} refers to sexual intercourse (*al-muwāqaʿa*)?" He said, "Yes." I said to him, "If someone in a state of sexual impurity is traveling and does not find water, how does he purify himself?" He said, "It is the same as the purification for the person who needs to perform *wuḍūʾ* and cannot find water: both of them wipe their faces and their hands [with dust]."[126]

As suggested by ʿAṭāʾs rejoinder, the idea that sexual impurity could render prayer impossible in a situation where sufficient water for full ablutions was unavailable (one that, for camel nomads, could potentially last for a very long time) was unacceptable to most jurists of the late first and early second centuries A.H. Thus, the opinion that *tayammum* was not permitted in this situation seems to have been rejected even by some jurists who transmitted it from such authorities as Ibn Masʿūd. ʿAbd al-Razzāq follows Ibn Masʿūd's supposed dictum with a comment by its transmitter: "Sufyān said, 'This opinion is not followed (*lā yuʾkhadhu bihi*).' "[127] Other jurists argued that Ibn Masʿūd had recanted (*nazala ʿan, rajaʿa ʿan*) his opinion that someone in a state of sexual impurity should not pray until he performed full ablutions.[128]

Given the fact that many jurists followed the interpretation that the reference to "touching women" in verse 5:6 literally denoted skin-to-skin contact, and thus that verse 5:6 had nothing to say about *tayammum* in case of sexual pollution, how did they derive this dispensation from the Qurʾānic text? It seems that they resorted to the other major passage on ritual purity in the Qurʾān, verse 4:43:

> O believers, do not approach prayer when you are intoxicated, until you know what you are saying; or when you are sexually polluted, unless passing on the way (*illā ʿābirī sabīl*), until you wash yourselves. If you are sick or traveling, or one of you has relieved himself [lit., "come from the privy"] or you have touched women, and you cannot find water, go to clean sand/dust (*tayammamū ṣaʿīdan ṭayyiban*) and wipe your faces and hands with it. Indeed, God is forgiving and clement.

Verse 4:43's statement that one may "approach prayer" in a state of major impurity if one was "passing on the way" was interpreted by some scholars to mean that one could not enter *places* of prayer (that is, mosques) in a state of pollution except in passing.[129] However, this ambiguous locution was also subject to an interpretation relevant to the issue of *tayammum* from sexual pollution:

> al-Ḥasan ibn Muslim[130] said [about the Qurʾānic phrase,] {when you are in a state of major impurity—unless in passing on the way}: "That is, unless you are traveling; then perform *tayammum*."[131]

Similar interpretations are attributed to ʿAlī ibn abī Ṭālib,[132] Ibn ʿAbbās,[133] and the Damascene jurist Sulaymān ibn Mūsā (d. A.H. 115–19/733–38 C.E.).[134]

The vexing question of *tayammum* from major pollution, generated by the literal interpretation of the reference to "touching women" in verse 5:6, was also resolved by various appeals to the *sunna* of the Prophet.[135] The texts of some of the relevant *ḥadīth* indicate that the question was a controversial one, probably as a result of the ambiguity of the Qurʾānic text.

> A man of the desert came to ʿUmar ibn al-Khaṭṭāb and said, "O Commander of the Faithful! We sometimes spend a month or two

> without finding water [with which to perform full ablutions]. ʿUmar said, "As for me, I would not pray until I found water." ʿAmmār ibn Yāsir said, "Don't you remember that you and I were out pasturing our camels, and don't you remember that I became sexually impure?" [ʿUmar] said, "Yes." [ʿAmmār said,] "I rolled around [*tamaʿʿaktu*] in the dust; [later] I mentioned that to the Prophet, and he laughed and said, 'I would have sufficed you to do this with the dust'—and he struck the ground with his hands, blew on them, and wiped his face and his hands up to close to the middle of the arm with them." ʿUmar said, "Fear God, O ʿAmmār!" ʿAmmār said, "For all that I owe to you, I am willing not to mention it for the rest of my life, O Commander of the Faithful." ʿUmar said, "No, by God; I will let you take responsibility for your own actions (*uwallīka min amrika mā tawallayta*)."[136]

Al-Bukhārī transmits an early juristic dialogue about this tradition, perhaps somewhat unlikely on a literal level but reflecting the complexity of the debate as perceived by early jurists:

> Shaqīq ibn Salama said: I was with ʿAbd Allāh [ibn Masʿūd] and Abū Mūsā. Abū Mūsā said [to Ibn Masʿūd], "What do you think (*a-raʾayta*) someone should do if he becomes sexually polluted and does not find water?" ʿAbd Allāh said, "He should not pray until he finds water." Abū Mūsā said, "What do you do with ʿAmmār's report where the Prophet said to him, 'It would have sufficed you [to perform *tayammum*]'?" [ʿAbd Allāh] said, "Don't you see that ʿUmar wasn't convinced by it?" Abū Mūsā said, "Let's forget ʿAmmār's report; what do you do with this verse (*hādhihiʾl-āya*)?" ʿAbd Allāh did not know what to say, and replied, "If we gave them a dispensation (*rakhkhaṣnā*) to do this [i.e., to perform *tayammum* from sexual pollution], pretty soon anyone who found his water cold would leave it and perform *tayammum*." I [al-Aʿmash] said to Shaqīq, "This was ʿAbd Allāh's only reason for disliking it?" He said, "Yes."[137]

It is not completely clear to which verse of the Qur'ān Abū Mūsā is referring in this version of the story; in another, there is an explicit citation of verse 5:6.[138] If this is, in fact, the verse that was originally intended, the transmitter of this story clearly understood "touching women" to refer to sexual intercourse—an interpretation that, according to other reports, ʿAbd Allāh ibn Masʿūd is not supposed to have shared. This dialogue is clearly intended to discredit Ibn Masʿūd's supposed refusal to accept the possibility of *tayammum* from sexual pollution, and thus does not arm him with the obvious rejoinder that the verse refers to literal "touching" and has nothing to do with sexual pollution. Whatever the true opinion of Ibn Masʿūd, it is clear that this was a vexing exegetical issue. The deep and contentious uncertainty surrounding the possibility of *tayammum* from sexual pollution, arising as it does from the related exegetical issue of "touching women," reinforces the conclusion that juristic thinking in this area was informed by critical reading of the Qurʾānic text at a very early and fundamental stage in its development.

Conclusion: Revealed Text and Personal Example in the Law of Purity

Close examination of the relationship between the word of scripture and the accepted understanding of the law reveals that neither of the two dominant paradigms for the role of the Qurʾān in the genesis of the law is adequate to the evidence. Those who would see the text of revelation as the ultimate source of Islamic conceptions in this area (as in all others) have no explanation for the discrepancies between the accepted practice and the apparent meaning of the Qurʾānic text. In cases of apparent contradiction, it is the received practice that prevails, even when there is no significant support for the popular practice in the *ḥadīth* of the Prophet. Thus, the command to perform *wuḍūʾ* "when you rise to pray" did not produce any significant school of thought advocating ablutions before each prayer. Similarly, the popular predilection for washing of the feet was imposed on an unaccommodating text by an ingenious yet problematic syntactical maneuver. Both cases provide ammunition for those who would claim that explicit reference to the Qurʾānic text intruded onto the natural development of popular practice at a secondary stage. It should be emphasized that this need imply no true conflict between the text of revelation and the ongoing practice of the community; but these cases suggest that we can claim only that the practice is compatible with the Qurʾān, not that it is generated from it.

However, our study of the textual ambiguities of the verses of the Qurʾān dealing with ritual ablutions suggests that the text of the Qurʾān, far from being irrelevant to the early development of the law of ritual purity, itself generated controversies of a very fundamental nature. For instance, a very subtle structural ambiguity in the text of verse 5:6 raised the question of whether *tayammum* was permissible in case of major impurity.

How are these results to be interpreted? One obvious conclusion is that self-conscious and systematic juristic discussion of the rules relating to pollution and ablution was preceded by the emergence of a quite coherent and unified tradition of popular practice whose authority was such that it generally prevailed in the face of theoretical challenge. This "living tradition" was perhaps more closely identified with the crystallizing concept of Prophetic *sunna* than with the rigorous exegesis of the Qur'ānic text, but it was fundamentally independent of either. This is not to say that this popular practice may not have been ultimately rooted in implicit understandings of the Qur'ānic text, with which it was generally compatible, or in authentic living memories of the practice of the Prophet's example; however, it was apparently generated neither from *ḥadīth* in the textual sense or from conscious engagement with the word of the Qur'ān.

However, while the text of the Qur'ān did not generate all thought and behavior on this subject in the systematic and supreme way that might have been expected by later generations, it did play a decisive role in the definition of the law at a very early stage in its development. Almost every major ambiguity in the vocabulary and syntax of the verses relating to ablutions produced a genuine difference of legal opinion that can be traced at least to the first decades of the second century A.H.[139] Furthermore, the content of the debates demonstrates that the text (at least of the relevant verses) was extant and known in its present form by the earliest jurists to whose thought we have access. It existed, with the structural anomalies and ambiguities we see today, to puzzle and provoke the earliest Muslim thinkers whose recorded opinions survive.

While a reconstruction of the interaction between Qur'ānic exegesis and popular practice in the case of *wuḍū'* ablutions is obviously of some relevance to our understanding of the general development of Islamic law, it should be remembered that ritual law is to a certain extent a special case. Ritual purity and prayer were such fundamental elements of the spiritual life as understood by Muslims that they were reluctant to associate their introduction with any specific point in the progressive revelation of the Qur'ān, certainly not any point as late as that understood by the majority of scholars to be the occasion of revelation of verse 5:6. This is a military expedition, dated in the year 6 A.H., on which the Prophet's young wife ʿĀ'isha is supposed to have lost her necklace and thus detained the party in a place without water while they carried out a search. The revelation of the "verse of *tayammum*" (either 5:6 or, according to some scholars, 4:43) was then revealed.[140] One solution to this problem was to infer that what was revealed on this occasion was neither verse 5:6 nor verse 4:43, but the rule relating to *tayammum* that is included in them both; the muḥaddith Ibn Ḥajar al-ʿAsqalānī (d. A.H. 852/ 1449 C.E.) writes:

> [This *ḥadīth*] has been used as proof . . . that *wuḍū'* was incumbent upon them before the revelation of the verse of *wuḍū'*; for this reason, they considered it a terrible thing to sojourn in a

> place where there was no water, and Abū Bakr did what he did to ʿĀʾisha. Ibn ʿAbd al-Barr said, "All the experts on the Prophet's biography (*ahl al-maghāzī*) know that the Prophet never prayed after prayer was made obligatory for him without *wuḍūʾ*; only someone who was ignorant or stubborn would deny it." He said, "The fact that in this *ḥadīth* he says 'the verse of *tayammum*' indicates that the new information that was given to them at that time was the rule relating to *tayammum* (*ḥukm al-tayammum*), and not the rule relating to *wuḍūʾ*." He said, "The wisdom in the revelation of the verse of *wuḍūʾ* [on this occasion], despite the fact that people were already performing [*wuḍūʾ*], is that the obligation to perform it would be recited in the Revelation."[141]

However, even without associating the revelation of verse 5:6 with this particular incident, it was impossible for most scholars to link the initial introduction of the rules relating to *wuḍūʾ* with the revelation of verse in which they are described, which (as we have discussed) is found in a Medinian chapter of the Qurʾān. Instead they traced the practice of *wuḍūʾ*, like the prayer ritual itself, back to the Prophet's Night Journey (an event that occurred at an indeterminate point in the Meccan period) or, preferably, to the very inception of Muḥammad's prophetic mission. Ibn Isḥāq writes:

> A scholar informed me that when prayer was made obligatory upon the Prophet, Gabriel came to him when he was on the heights of Mecca. He jabbed the side of the valley with his heel, and a spring burst forth. Gabriel performed the *wuḍūʾ* ablutions as the Prophet watched, in order to show him how to purify himself for prayer. Then the Prophet performed *wuḍūʾ* as he had seen Gabriel perform *wuḍūʾ*. Then Gabriel led him in prayer; the Prophet followed him in prayer. Then Gabriel went away. The Prophet came to Khadīja and performed *wuḍūʾ* for her to show her how to purify herself for prayer. The Prophet led her in prayer as Gabriel had led him in prayer, and she followed him in prayer.[142]

What is rather remarkable about his account, from the earliest fully preserved biography of the Prophet, is that it makes the introduction of the *wuḍūʾ* ablutions completely independent of the verbal revelation of the Qurʾānic passage relating to *wuḍūʾ*. Gabriel is not represented as instructing the Prophet in words at all. Instead, the process is one of personal example by the teacher (Gabriel) and physical emulation by the disciple (Muhammad). The process is repeated when the Prophet descends from the mountain and instructs Khadīja by example. The verbal form of God's communication with mankind is completely eclipsed by personal example in the transmission of the ritual.

With this paradigm in mind, it becomes clear why the supporters of various candidates to the legitimate religio-political leadership of the community so fervently attempted to appropriate for them the role of modeling *wuḍū'*. A person who taught the proper form of the ritual of *wuḍū'* to the community took his place in an unbroken line of personal and intimate acts of guidance stretching back to the angel Gabriel himself.

Chapter 3

"Cancelers of *Wuḍū*ʾ" and the Boundaries of the Body

Early scholars proposed and debated several sources of pollution in addition to those enumerated by the Qurʾān. While there was no doubt that major pollution (*janāba*) was caused by sexual acts and emissions, however defined, the set of actions and bodily functions that might cause minor impurity (entailing *wuḍū*ʾ ablutions of the extremities, rather than *ghusl* ablutions of the entire body) was more eclectic and less clearly delimited. The exact number and nature of the "cancelers of *wuḍū*ʾ" were significant because, taken as a group, these sources of pollution suggested to scholars the basic shape and meaning of the idea of ritual defilement. A single "canceler of *wuḍū*ʾ" more or less could suggest a significantly different underlying rationale for the entire group. From this point of view, the content of these controversies is a reflection of the community's continuing effort to define the nature of ritual impurity and its relationship to Islamic conceptions of the body, sexuality, and morality. As will emerge from the following examination of several of the debates that engaged the interest of early religious scholars, in many cases they represent not only substantive disagreements over matters of detail but different overall conceptualizations of the law of ritual impurity as a whole.

*Wuḍū*ʾ from Cooked Food

Michael Cook has proposed that it is precisely those legal controversies that are defunct that will provide us with the most illuminating and undistorted glimpses of the early development of Islamic law.[1] Pursuing this line of thought, we will begin by examining a case that seems to have lost its relevance before the establishment of the classical schools of law (in the late second to third centuries A.H.). This state of affairs may avert the danger of viewing the issue through the eyes of those later ages whose views are so much better preserved than those of the earliest believers. It may be hoped that a postmortem examination of this controversy, so long passed away, will recover for us some aspects of the idea of ritual purity as it was lived and puzzled over by vanished generations of Muslims.

The legal controversy in question involves *wuḍūʾ* from cooked food, or "that which has been touched by fire" (*al-wuḍūʾ mimmā massat al-nār*). The issue of cooked food addresses a question that might well be raised by reflection on the rules of *wuḍūʾ* as they were known from the Qurʾān. It was well-established that *wuḍūʾ* was canceled by the elimination of wastes from the body. If purity was violated by substances exiting the body at the end of the digestive cycle, what of substances entering the body at the beginning? Might not all transgressions of the surface of the body entail ruptures in purity?

To conceive of eating as a transgression of the surface of the body is, as it happens, an approach that was to be seriously explored over the years by legal thinkers reflecting on the nature of fasting. Some theorists focused on the more obvious aspect of fasting as a form of self-denial, arguing that only the ingestion of such substances as would relieve hunger or thirst invalidated a fast (liquids, foods, and those non-food substances, such as oil used for grooming, that happened to have nutritive value). Others, however, pursued the ramifications of fasting conceived as a sealing of the boundaries of the body from intrusions of any kind. This approach was to receive its fullest expression in the rules relating to fasting established by the Shāfiʿī school. According to these rules, fasting is invalidated not merely by eating or drinking but by introduction of anything at all into the interior (*jawf*) of the body, through any orifice—not only the mouth but the nose, the ear, the anus, and so forth. Thus, a fast can be broken simply by sticking a reed into one's ear.[2] Defined in this way, breaking a fast (transgressing the boundaries of the body by introducing something into its interior) presents an obvious converse and complement to canceling *wuḍūʾ* by elimination.[3] That this analogy was perceived—and ultimately rejected—by participants in the controversy over *wuḍūʾ* from cooked food is demonstrated by arguments such as the comment, attributed to the Companion of the Prophet ʿAbd Allāh ibn Masʿūd, that "*Wuḍūʾ* is from what comes out, and fasting is from what goes in and not from what comes out."[4] Nevertheless, this principle had to assert itself through controversy and debate.

Why precisely cooked food should have been singled out as canceling *wuḍūʾ* is not completely clear. One possible explanation lies in the wording that is almost invariably used to characterize such food: "*mā massat al-nār*," literally, "that which has been touched by fire." I have translated the phrase as "cooked food" because this is the interpretation suggested by the texts of the various traditions involved in the controversy; the category seems to include not only things that have literally been touched by fire (like grilled meats), but things that are baked or boiled (bread, cheese). This inference is supported by a few reports that speak of "that which has been changed by fire" or "that which has been cooked by fire" (*mā ghayyarathu al-nār, mā anḍajathu al-nār*).

The somewhat stilted phrase "*mā massat al-nār*" draws attention to the role of fire in the cooking process; and fire, *al-nār*, was and is far from being a neutral term in Islamic religious discourse. In a religious context, it could hardly escape its association with hellfire. In the symbolic structure of the Qurʾān, heat and fire are just as ineluctably associated with divine punishment as coolness and water with faith's heavenly reward.[5] To be "touched by fire" is to burn in Hell.[6] This association did not escape Muslims reflecting on the significance of *wuḍūʾ*, who linked the process of bathing the body with cool water with their hopes to escape the Fire. "It is said," reports one early author, "that whoever washes between his fingers and toes with water, God will spare them from the Fire; whoever does not take care in washing his heels when performing *wuḍūʾ*, they will be touched by the Fire (*massathā al-nār*)."[7]

No surviving school of law holds that the consumption of cooked food cancels *wuḍūʾ*, and the legal compendia of the late Middle Ages dispatch the issue summarily if they do not (as is more frequently the case) pass it over in complete silence. The great Ḥanbalī jurist Ibn Qudāma, whose practice it is to survey all strands of opinion on a given issue, states that "we know of no controversy over it today [that is, in the seventh century A.H./fourteenth century C.E.]."[8] The fifth-century A.H. Mālikī scholar al-Bājī suggests that dispute had died out long before his own time: "the debate (*khilāf*) about it was only in the time of the Companions [of the Prophet] and the following generation," he writes; "then a consensus emerged abandoning [*wuḍūʾ* from cooked food]."[9] Nevertheless, it would appear that at a certain point in the past the question of cooked food was the focus of lively contention. Despite his confidence that the legal scholars of his own day are unanimous in denying that cooked food cancels *wuḍūʾ*, Ibn Qudāma is able to present impressive lists of witnesses among the Companions of the Prophet and the following generation on both sides of the issue, as well as a Prophetic *ḥadīth* in *favor* of the practice. Such early compilations as the *Muwaṭṭaʾ* of Mālik and the *Āthār* of Muḥammad ibn al-Ḥasan al-Shaybānī (both dating from the second century A.H./eighth century C.E.) devote comparatively substantial space to the documentation of the question.

The *locus classicus* of the controversy over cooked food is a *ḥadīth* of the Prophet enjoining, "Perform *wuḍūʾ* from that which has been touched by fire" (*tawaḍḍaʾū mimmā massat al-nār*)." It is transmitted in different narrative settings from several different Companions of the Prophet:

> Abū Sufyān ibn al-Mughīra ibn al-Akhnas visited Umm Ḥabība. She gave him some *sawīq* to drink, then he got up to pray; she said to him, "Perform *wuḍūʾ*, Nephew! I heard the Messenger of God say, "Perform *wuḍūʾ* from cooked food (*mā massat al-nār*)."[10]

> Abū Hurayra said: Do you know why I am performing *wuḍūʾ*? I am performing *wuḍūʾ* from chunks of cheese (*athwār aqiṭ*[11]) that I ate. I heard the Messenger of God say, "Perform *wuḍūʾ* from cooked food."[12]

The *ḥadīth* is also reported from Zayd ibn Thābit,[13] from the Prophet's wife ʿĀʾisha,[14] and from several other figures.[15] It is, by the standards of criticism that were to develop among specialist scholars, very well authenticated. It is both *marfūʿ* and *muttaṣil* (that is, attributed to the Prophet himself through an unbroken chain of transmitters); it is transmitted from more than one Companion; and it was transmitted by figures generally considered reliable. With these qualifications in its favor it is unsurprising that it came to be enshrined in the *Ṣaḥīḥ* of Muslim, thus finding a permanent place among the Prophetic *ḥadīth* most implicitly trusted by the Sunnī faithful.

Indeed, despite the universal abandonment of the stricture it enjoins, the report itself was forsaken by neither traditionists nor legal scholars. Instead, they had recourse to the doctrine of *naskh* (abrogation): This statement of the Prophet, while held to be authentic, was deemed to have been overruled by his later actions. These actions were documented by a number of reports attributed to Companions stating that they witnessed him eating cooked food and then praying without renewing his ablutions. Unlike the report in favor of *wuḍūʾ* from cooked food, which is uniform in its formulaic wording, these reports display many variations in form and content.

> The Prophet ate a shoulder of meat, then wiped his hand with a coarse cloth that was under him, then got up to pray.[16]

> The Messenger of God performed *wuḍūʾ*, then cut off a piece from a shoulder of meat and ate, then went to pray without performing *wuḍūʾ*.[17]

> The Messenger of God ate from a bone or gnawed at a rib, then prayed without performing *wuḍūʾ*.[18]

Thus, Muslim follows his section on "*Wuḍūʾ* from cooked food (*mā ghayyarat al-nār*)," which contains three versions of the *ḥadīth* requiring *wuḍūʾ* for cooked food, with another entitled "The abrogation of *wuḍūʾ* from cooked food (*mā massat al-nār*)," containing ten traditions to the opposite effect. The view that *wuḍūʾ* from cooked food had been enjoined by the Prophet but superseded by his later actions was embodied in a report from one of the Prophet's Companions; Bukhārī's commentator al-ʿAynī notes, with respect to the *ḥadīth* texts requiring *wuḍūʾ*, that they are "abrogated by what was transmitted by Jābir [ibn ʿAbd Allāh al-Anṣārī, d. A.H. 73–78 /692–98 C.E.[19]]: 'The later of the two dispensations (*ākhir al-amrayn*) from the Messenger of God is the abandonment of *wuḍūʾ* from cooked food.' " This report was itself to experience no small success, achieving a place in more than one of the canonical "Six Books" and several other respected compilations.[20] The case of "cooked food" was to become one of the classic examples of abrogation of the *sunna* by the *sunna*; in his classic study of the discipline of *ḥadīth*, Ibn al-Falāḥ (d. A.H. 643/1245–46 C.E.) cites it as one of his two examples of *naskh* known through the statement of a Companion.[21]

It is clear why such a bald statement of chronology was necessary for the successful application of the theory of *naskh* in favor of the anti-*wuḍūʾ* school of thought. The more common procedure, in the numerous cases where the application of the chronological principle is not conveniently attributed to a Companion witness, is to infer the sequential order of conflicting reports from the dates of the respective Companions' association with the Prophet. Abū Hurayra, the source of one of the main forms of the report in favor of *wuḍūʾ* from cooked food, did not convert to Islām (and thus become a Companion well situated to observe the Prophet and competent to transmit *ḥadīth*) until the year of Khaybar, in A.H. 7. Thus, he associated with the Prophet only for the last three years of the latter's life. Ordinarily, this circumstance would create a strong presumption that he was reporting the Prophet's later, and thus final, position on the issue. The presumption would have been strengthened by the fact that the reports of the Prophet's eating cooked food and not performing *wuḍūʾ* are primarily attributed to figures who associated with him from a far earlier date: Jābir ibn ʿAbd Allāh himself, who may have fought at Badr (and certainly participated in many of the Prophet's subsequent campaigns);[22] Suwayd ibn al-Nuʿmān, who gave the oath of allegiance under the tree and fought at Uḥud;[23] and even Ibn ʿAbbās who, despite his youth at the death of the Prophet, was his kinsman and probably observed him from an early age. The awkwardness of the situation is intensified by the fact that the Suwayd tradition is dated: it speaks of the year of the expedition of Khaybar—the very cutoff point that would mark it as earlier than any observation by Abū Hurayra![24]

It may be a reflection of dissatisfaction with the argument of abrogation that other solutions were put forward. al-ʿAynī reports that some people, who apparently accepted the word of the various reports enjoining *wuḍūʾ* from cooked food while rejecting their most obvious interpretation, argued that "*al-wuḍūʾ*" in the formula "*al-wuḍūʾ mimmā massat al-nār*" (ablutions from cooked food) did not refer to the mandatory canonical ablutions ("*wuḍūʾ al-ṣalāt*") but to the washing of the hands.[25] A similar line of reasoning is probably represented by a report recounted in the *Āthār* of al-Shaybānī:

> We were sitting in the mosque with Ibn Masʿūd when they brought a large bowl and a pitcher of water towards us from Bāb al-Fīl. Ibn Masʿūd said, "I believe this is for me." One of the people said, "Yes, Abū ʿAbd al-Raḥmān; there was a banquet in the quarter." It was set down; he ate from it and drank some of the water, then poured [water] on his hands and washed them and wiped his face and his arms with the moisture from his hands. Then he said, "This is the *wuḍūʾ* for someone who has not ruptured his ritual purity."[26]

Despite the report's position in the section on *wuḍūʾ* from cooked food, al-Shaybānī does not comment on its relevance to this particular issue, preferring to conclude from it that it is permissible to perform *wuḍūʾ* in the mosque "if it is not from something dirty (*idhā kāna min ghayr qadhar*)."[27] Nevertheless, it would seem to be a response to the dilemma posed by a successful *ḥadīth* in favor of *wuḍūʾ* from cooked food for those who rejected its legal implications. It is good to "perform *wuḍūʾ*" in some sense after consuming what we presume to have been cooked food (Ibn Masʿūd's portion from the banquet); nevertheless, it is not *wuḍūʾ* in the technical sense (*wuḍūʾ al-ṣalāt*, in the terminology used by al-ʿAynī), and eating cooked food does not cancel the state of ritual purity.

Why were legal scholars of all schools so determined to discover a way to dismiss the legal implications of this highly respectable *ḥadīth*? One obvious reason is that the requirement to perform *wuḍūʾ* from cooked food defied one of the fundamental regularities that could be observed among the basic rules regarding minor impurity (that is, impurity requiring *wuḍūʾ* rather than full-body ablutions). The universally agreed-upon causes of minor impurity were urination and defecation—in other words, as some legal thinkers came to formulate it, the expulsion of impure substances from the body. Eating cooked food shared with these functions neither the element of elimination nor that of impurity. The many analogical arguments disputing the requirement of *wuḍūʾ* from cooked food, most of them ascribed to the distinguished scholar and Companion of the Prophet Ibn ʿAbbās, revolved around these two issues: food is pure and good, all the more so when it is cooked; and it enters the body rather than issuing forth from it.

> ʿAṭāʾ informed me that he heard Ibn ʿAbbās say: "Fire is a blessing of God; it does not make anything permissible or forbidden. There is no *wuḍū*ʾ from what has been touched by fire. . . ."
>
> [Ibn Jurayj (?) comments:] As for his saying that it does not make anything permissible, it addresses their statement that if *ṭalā*ʾ (boiled wine) is touched by fire it is permissible; his saying that it does not make it forbidden addresses their statement that it is necessary to perform *wuḍū*ʾ from what is touched by fire.
>
> ʿAṭāʾ said: I heard Ibn ʿAbbās say to someone who asked him about this: If you perform *wuḍū*ʾ from what has been touched by fire, [what about the fact that] people perform *ghusl*[28] with heated water (he did not see any harm in performing *ghusl* with heated water and [also] performed *wuḍū*ʾ with it); oils have [also] been touched by fire, and people do not perform *wuḍū*ʾ from them.[29]
>
> Ibn ʿAbbās was asked about performing *wuḍū*ʾ from what had been touched by fire; he said, "The fire only made it more pure (*lam yazidhu illā ṭīban*)."[30]
>
> I saw Ibn ʿAbbās and Abū Hurayra waiting for a goat (*jady*) of theirs that was in the oven; Ibn ʿAbbās said, "Take it out for us, so that it doesn't make us miss prayers." They took it out, and they ate some of it; then Abū Hurayra performed *wuḍū*ʾ, and Ibn ʿAbbās said: "Did we eat something unclean (*rijs*)?" Abū Hurayra said, "You are better and more knowledgeable than I"; then they prayed.[31]
>
> Ibn ʿAbbās said, "It is necessary to perform *wuḍū*ʾ from what comes out [of the body], not from what goes in (*al-wuḍū*ʾ *mimmā kharaja wa-laysa mimmā dakhala*)."[32]

The traditionist response to such arguments may be seen in a dialogue, contrived yet telling, transmitted by Ibn Māja:

> Abū Hurayra said, "The Prophet said, 'Perform *wuḍū*ʾ from cooked food.' " Ibn ʿAbbās said, "Should I perform *wuḍū*ʾ from hot water?!" [Abū Hurayra] said to him, "Nephew! When you hear a *ḥadīth* from the Prophet, don't coin similitudes about it (*lā taḍrab lahu*ʾ*l-amthāl*)!"[33]

Up to this point, we have traced the basic contours of the debate over cooked food without regard to time or place. We have seen that, despite the apparently impeccable documentation of this practice, it met with universal disfavor in all of the classical Sunnī schools of law. Part of the resistance to the requirement for *wuḍūʾ* from cooked food may, as we have seen, have resulted from systematic considerations. However, there is no compelling reason why these considerations should have overcome the testimony of a strong *ḥadīth*. In addition to abstract, theoretical concerns, might the course of the debate be elucidated by the historical context in which the issue was discussed?

In terms of the chronological and geographical placement of the dispute, several remarks are in order. One is that the positive statement in favor of *wuḍūʾ* from cooked food is logically, and thus presumably chronologically, prior to the statements to the contrary. Without the claim that it was necessary to perform *wuḍūʾ* from cooked food, the reports stating that early individuals were observed eating and then praying without performing *wuḍūʾ* would be completely unmotivated. This order of precedence is clear on the face of the analogical arguments, which are explicit rejoinders to a preexisting opinion. Nevertheless, to say that the existing *reports* denying the requirement must be younger than those advocating it is not to say that the earliest *practice* of the Islamic community involved performing *wuḍūʾ* from cooked food. In fact, there is every reason to assume the contrary. As has been noted, *wuḍūʾ* from cooked food was fated to utter extinction in the legal tradition despite the existence of a respectable *ḥadīth* supporting it. It is scarcely likely that a widespread early practice would have perished without a trace with such a plausible credential in its favor. Whether or not the Prophet actually ever enjoined the Muslims to observe such a stricture, the *ḥadīth* to this effect must have fallen on inhospitable soil. Here, as in other cases, it seems likely that Prophetic Tradition has diverged sharply from practice ("tradition" in the generic rather than the technical sense), and practice has won.

In fact, the texts of the two main forms of the *ḥadīth* themselves support this assumption. Neither presents the alleged word of the Prophet unadorned; each presents a brief narrative frame in which the rule is imparted to later Muslims who have apparently never heard of it. Abū Sufyān [ibn Saʿīd] ibn al-Mughīra ibn al-Akhnas is apparently unfamiliar with the practice;[34] he owes the information to his access to his aunt, Umm Ḥabība. Similarly, Abū Hurayra assumes that the reason for his ablutions will be news to his listeners. Both texts embody what might be called the activist model of the *sunna*. Far from being the verbal embodiment of a continuous community practice, on the model assumed by Mālik,[35] the transmission of a *ḥadīth* text is here an instrument for the reform of community practice.

In terms of the geographical distribution of the chains of transmission, these various reports create a distinctive pattern. While the ʿIrāqī chains of transmission of the reports supporting *wuḍū*ʾ from cooked food are disproportionately Baṣran, those of the reports rejecting the practice are strongly Kūfan. The coherence of the pattern is increased by the fact that the Prophetic *ḥadīth* supporting the practice are strongly identified with Madīna, while the favorable reports from Baṣra tend to be traced to Companions or the following generation. Very schematically, then, we have a distribution of opinions conforming to the most traditional conceptions of the legal values of the various metropolitan centers: while Madīna appears as the home of the Prophetic *sunna*, Kūfa teems with analogical arguments riding on their own logical cogency.

However, despite the fact that the geographical distribution of opinions suggests this basic pattern, it cannot be so easily reduced to a geographical schema. The doctrine of *wuḍū*ʾ from cooked food cannot be clearly associated with any specific local school. While almost all reports advocating the practice are Medinian and Baṣran, not all Medinian and Baṣran reports are in favor of the rule. Our sources do not allow us to hypothesize a stage at which it was the local consensus in either place. The *Muwaṭṭa*ʾ of Mālik, which may be taken to represent the Medinian opinion of his day, cites a set of reports on the subject that are unanimous in their rejection of *wuḍū*ʾ from cooked food. On the Baṣran side, not only do the reports directed against the practice in Sunnī sources include a few of apparent Baṣran provenance, but the Khārijī tradition (which can be taken as another witness of Baṣran sentiments) similarly rejects it.[36]

In sum, the opinions on this issue display a pattern that is clearly related to geography but is not purely a function of geography. While Kūfans seem to have been unanimous in rejecting the practice and Baṣrans seem to have been largely in favor of it, opinion in Madīna was sharply split. Both in Madīna and (to a lesser extent) in Baṣra, the practice seems to have been promoted in some circles and rejected in others. The key to the identity of these circles must thus lie in some factor other than geography. Since the reports in support of the practice are far fewer than those opposing it, it is easier to begin by attempting to identify those who were active in promoting it than by surveying its myriad opponents. The task is simplified by the obvious common elements in the chains of transmission.

The most salient common denominator in the chains of transmission supporting most of the reports advocating *wuḍū*ʾ from cooked food is the name of Muḥammad ibn Muslim ibn Shihāb al-Zuhrī. al-Zuhrī's prominent role in the dissemination of the practice is immediately suggested by his name's ubiquity in ʿAbd al-Razzāq's section on the subject; of ten reports, six are transmitted through al-Zuhrī.[37] Two of them contain additional, corroborative comments in the voice of al-Zuhrī;[38] one report that is not transmitted by al-Zuhrī nevertheless concludes with a comment on his personal practice in this regard.[39] A similar pattern emerges upon examination of the various chains of transmission for the reports tracing the practice back to the Prophet. The requirement to perform *wuḍū'* from cooked food is attributed to the Prophet in two different reports, one in the voice of Umm Ḥabība and one with Abū Hurayra. The Umm Ḥabība report is supported by two basic chains of transmission. One, which appears in the *Muṣannaf*s of both ʿAbd al-Razzāq and Ibn Abī Shayba (twice in each compilation), is unform up to al-Zuhrī and then diverges into many different strands. According to chains of transmission found in various compilations, at least eight different people are supposed to have transmitted the report from al-Zuhrī.[40] There is another chain of transmission without al-Zuhrī that appears in the classical *ḥadīth* compilations, but not in the *Muṣannaf*s; it seems to be less widely disseminated than the first.[41] The same is true of the *ḥadīth* of Abū Hurayra; most of the chains of transmission converge on the name of al-Zuhrī, with a few isolated strands that do not.[42]

In addition to being the main authority of his generation explicitly to attribute this saying to the Prophet, al-Zuhrī is supposed to be the source of almost all of the statements attributing the formula or the practice to other early figures. According to various reports he is supposed to have attributed it to ʿAbd Allāh ibn ʿUmar, ʿUmar ibn ʿAbd al-ʿAzīz, ʿĀ'isha, Abū Salama, and Zayd ibn Thābit.[43]

Joseph Schacht has pointed out that the various chains of tradition for a given *ḥadīth* frequently prove to converge on a single figure, whom he designates "N.N.," despite the existence of multiple lines of transmission to and from this individual. "The existence of a significant common link (N.N.) in all or most isnāds of a given tradition," Schacht writes, "would be a strong indication in favor of its having originated in the time of N.N."[44] A crude application of Schacht's "common link" theory, which in its simplest form attributes the origination (that is, forgery) of a *ḥadīth* to the individual in question or to people using his name no earlier than the date of his death, would suggest that al-Zuhrī might very well have been the originator of the dictum in its form as a Prophetic *ḥadīth*.

While I would hesitate to make gratuitous assumptions of outright forgery as lightly and mechanically as Schacht was wont to do, the centrality of al-Zuhrī's apparent role does suggest that we might approach the *ḥadīth* with a certain measure of additional caution. It also suggests that, whatever the ultimate provenance or authenticity of the report, we can hypothesize that the formula was circulated as a report from the Prophet either by al-Zuhrī or by circles who held his name in high esteem.

In Baṣra, where the saying is generally not explicitly attributed to the Prophet, it is associated overwhelmingly with the names of two main figures:

al-Ḥasan al-Baṣrī and Abū Qilāba.[45] al-Ḥasan is quoted as stating that he followed the practice himself;[46] he is also the alleged source of reports stating that Abū Mūsā al-Ashʿarī observed it.[47] One particularly interesting report states that Maṭar al-Warrāq, a resident of Baṣra said to have died in A.H. 129/746–47 C.E.,[48] "was asked . . . 'From whom did al-Ḥasan get [the practice] of performing *wuḍū'* from cooked food?' He said, 'He got it from Anas and from Abū Ṭalḥa, who got it from the Prophet.' "[49] This is a particularly intriguing story for two reasons. One is that, like the anecdotes in which the formula "*tawaḍḍa'ū mimmā massat al-nār*" ("perform *wuḍū'* from that which has been touched by fire") is presented as a Prophetic *ḥadīth* to Muslims who have apparently never heard of it, it suggests that the practice probably was not current among the broader public in the earliest days. The questioner clearly considers it to be a distinctive practice of al-Ḥasan's, and wants to know where he got the idea. The second is that, although the evidence certainly is not conclusive, it strongly suggests the phenomenon of the "growth of *isnāds*"—the process by which, according to the theories of Schacht and other revisionist scholars, a given statement or ruling acquired links to progressively earlier and more authoritative figures with the passage of time. Here the association between this particular practice and the name of al-Ḥasan seems to be well-established; a questioner of a later generation is not satisfied with this authority, however, and elicits a pedigree linking the practice to the Companions and ultimately to the Prophet. The controversial status of the reports about *wuḍū'* for cooked food is also suggested by a report cited by Ibn Saʿd, where al-Ḥasan first states that he heard the formula from Abū Hurayra and then defiantly declares, "And I will never abandon it (*lā adaʿuhu abadan*)."[50]

Somewhat similar questions are raised by a report attributed to the other great Baṣran authority for this practice, Abū Qilāba al-Jarmī. He recounts,

> I saw Anas ibn Mālik leave al-Ḥajjāj talking to himself. I said, 'What's wrong with you, Abū Ḥamza?' He said, 'I left this man; he called for food for the people, and he ate and they ate, then they got up to pray without performing *wuḍū'*' (or he [may have] said, 'without touching water').

In the version of the report cited by Ibn Abī Shayba, Abū Qilāba asks Anas, "Didn't you (pl.) use to do that?"; Anas denies it.[51] (The ʿAbd al-Razzāq version, on the other hand, ends with the remark that "Anas used to perform *wuḍū'* after eating cooked food.") Here again, an entire group of Muslims seems to be oblivious to the requirement for *wuḍū'* from cooked food. In the Ibn Abī Shayba version of the report, Abū Qilāba even seems to believe that Anas and his associates themselves used to pray without performing *wuḍū'* from cooked food. If Abū Qilāba ever entertained doubts about the practice, however, he seems to have overcome them. He is supposed to have transmitted the requirement from an anonymous Companion of the tribe of Hudhayl and to have actively promoted its observance.[52]

What do these three key transmitters of reports promoting *wuḍū'* from cooked food have in common? One obvious common denominator is the age in which they lived. Abū Qilāba died between 104 and 107; al-Ḥasan al-Baṣrī died in 110; and al-Zuhrī died between 123 and 125. The seventeen- to twenty-one-year spread in their dates of death is insignificant in light of the length of their lives; although Abū Qilāba's birthdate is unknown, al-Ḥasan is supposed to have been eighty-eight at the time of his death,[53] while al-Zuhrī is said to have lived to be seventy-two.[54] Thus, despite some difference in age, all three were contemporaries who were active adults at the turn of the second century A.H. However, they are united by more than contemporaneity. They are also bound together by their cordial relationships with another important promoter of the practice of *wuḍū'* from cooked food, the Umayyad caliph ʿUmar ibn ʿAbd al-ʿAzīz (ruled A.H. 99–101/717–20 C.E.).

ʿUmar is al-Zuhrī's source for the Abū Hurayra version of the Prophetic *ḥadīth* enjoining the practice; he is also one of the authorities whom al-Zuhrī cites as having followed the practice themselves. For al-Zuhrī, a good relationship with ʿUmar ibn ʿAbd al-ʿAzīz would have been merely an extension of a close relationship with the Marwānid house dating from the earliest days of its rise to power. According to one report, he is supposed to have traveled to make contact with Marwān ibn al-Ḥakam (ruled A.H. 64–65/684–685 C.E.) as a young man.[55] Other stories have him traveling from Madīna to the court of ʿAbd al-Malik and using a display of his learning to extract financial favors from that caliph.[56] The relationship thus initiated led to patronage by a series of Marwānid rulers. More than one anecdote retailed by the classical sources suggests that several Marwānid caliphs regarded al-Zuhrī as a valuable source of learned endorsement for various controversial policies, to the point that his scholarly integrity was severely challenged. A famous anecdote cited by al-Yaʿqūbī has ʿAbd al-Malik (ruled A.H. 65–86/685–705 C.E.) promoting Jerusalem as a site of pilgrimage with the help of a Prophetic *ḥadīth* transmitted by al-Zuhrī.[57] Another attempt to use al-Zuhrī as a propagandist for the Umayyads is supposed to have met with resistance on the part of the scholar; requested to state that ʿĀ'isha's anonymous accuser in verse 24:11 of the Qur'ān was ʿAlī, al-Zuhrī firmly maintained that it was ʿAbd Allāh ibn Ubayy.[58] Whatever the truth of the individual anecdotes, these stories indicate a perception of strong ties to the palace.

al-Zuhrī is also supposed to have been appointed judge by Yazīd II (ruled A.H. 101–105/720–724 C.E.) and tutor to the royal sons by Hishām (ruled A.H. 105–125/724–743 C.E.).[59] The latter apparently also cultivated an interest in al-Zuhrī's traditions; al-Zuhrī's student Shuʿayb ibn abī Ḥamza, who served as a secretary under Hishām, is said to have taken dictation from him on behalf of the caliph ("*kataba ʿan al-Zuhrī imlāʾan liʾl-sulṭān*").[60] The Umayyad archives are supposed to have contained many works that he wrote for Hishām.[61]

While information is thin, it would seem that al-Zuhrī's connection with ʿUmar ibn ʿAbd al-ʿAzīz was typical of his close patronage relationship with the Marwānid house in general. ʿUmar seems to have admired him greatly; he is supposed to have told his companions of al-Zuhrī that "there remains none more knowledgeable about the established *sunna* (*sunna māḍiya*) than he."[62] Another report speaks of an audience in which al-Zuhrī presents *ḥadīth* to ʿUmar.[63]

While al-Zuhrī's reputation for collaboration with the Umayyads is well established, al-Ḥasan al-Baṣrī seems at first glance a much less likely figure to associate with the authorities. He is known through the epistles attributed to him as an austere character who was unafraid to rebuke the powers that be when rebuke was in order.[64] However, his political record was one that could ultimately only gratify the Marwānids. During the revolt of Ibn al-Ashʿath against ʿAbd al-Malik's notorious governor al-Ḥajjāj ibn Yūsuf, al-Ḥasan was steadfast in his opposition to the rebels. While evincing no enthusiasm for the ruling house, let alone for al-Ḥajjāj (whom he execrated), al-Ḥasan counseled peaceful endurance of unjust rule, which he allegedly regarded as a punishment from God.[65]

What is more, al-Ḥasan seems to have exchanged his attitude of pained toleration towards the authorities for one of cautious cordiality in the reign of the pious ʿUmar ibn ʿAbd al-ʿAzīz. He is supposed to have briefly served as a judge during his reign, before submitting a successful request to be relieved of the job.[66] He is also said to have accepted the accumulated stipend payments that had been withheld from him in earlier reigns, which ʿUmar ibn ʿAbd al-ʿAzīz offered to him and to Muḥammad ibn Sīrīn upon ʿUmar's accession to the throne. Here al-Ḥasan appears as the more accommodating party; Ibn Sīrīn is supposed to have refused the payment on the grounds that there was not enough money in the treasury to repay all the people of Baṣra.[67] It has been argued that al-Ḥasan was, in fact, the main architect of ʿUmar's ideology as caliph.[68] Upon hearing the news of ʿUmar ibn ʿAbd al-ʿAzīz's death, al-Ḥasan is supposed to have said, "The best of people has died."[69] Indeed, the two men had much in common temperamentally. A certain Mazyad ibn Ḥawshab is said to have declared, "I have never seen anyone more fearful (*akhwaf*) than al-Ḥasan and ʿUmar ibn ʿAbd al-ʿAzīz; it was as if hellfire (*al-nār*) had been created only for the two of them."[70]

As for Abū Qilāba, the second main authority for reports on this subject in Baṣra, he was also apparently an associate of ʿUmar ibn ʿAbd al-ʿAzīz. ʿUmar is supposed to have been a great admirer of his; he is cited as saying, "O people of Syria (*Shām*), it will be well with you as long as you have this one among you."[71] Unlike al-Zuhrī, he is supposed to have been very sparing in his transmission of *ḥadīth*, although he cherished the *sunna*.[72] However, ʿUmar ibn ʿAbd al-ʿAzīz is supposed to have sought him out as an authority. Abū Qilāba himself is said to have narrated a story in which ʿUmar visited him and asked him to recite *ḥadīth*.[73] He apparently took an unusually hard line against the heterodox (*aṣḥāb al-ahwāʾ*); like al-Ḥasan, he was particularly energetic in his condemnation of their resort to insurrection ("the sword," *al-sayf*).[74] This position was, of course, a boon to the authorities; according to one anecdote (existing in more than one version), it was particularly valued by ʿUmar ibn ʿAbd al-ʿAzīz. He is supposed to have visited Abū Qilāba when he became seriously ill, exhorting him to "muster your strength (*tashaddad/tajallad*), so that the Hypocrites do not gloat over us."[75]

Abū Qilāba's main source for his opinion on *wuḍūʾ* from cooked food, Anas ibn Mālik, is also said to have admired ʿUmar. Although he had a history of opposition to the Umayyad dynasty, having fought with ʿAlī against Muʿāwiya and with Ibn al-Ashʿath against al-Ḥajjāj,[76] he seems to have been an admirer of this particular member of the Marwānid house. While he died before ʿUmar acceded to the caliphate, he apparently encountered him as a young man in Madīna, when ʿUmar was governor there. He is supposed to have declared, "I never saw anyone pray as much like the Messenger of God as this youth."[77]

Certainly, not all of the scholars linked to ʿUmar ibn ʿAbd al-ʿAzīz are supposed to have supported the practice of *wuḍūʾ* from cooked food. The Kūfan faqīh al-Shaʿbī (d. 104–10), who served as a judge during ʿUmar's caliphate,[78] is supposed to have rejected the practice on the basis of his own legal discretion (*raʾy*), remarking that "It is a poor kind of food for which you have to perform *wuḍūʾ*."[79] There is also one chain of transmission in which Sulaymān ibn Yasār (d. 103–7) appears transmitting a pointed rejection of the practice from Ibn ʿAbbās.[80] Sulaymān ibn Yasār administered the markets of Madīna when ʿUmar ibn ʿAbd al-ʿAzīz was governor;[81] he is also mentioned in one report among the ten Medinian legal scholars whom ʿUmar is supposed to have recruited as advisors.[82] The practice of performing *wuḍūʾ* from cooked food was apparently not promoted by all of ʿUmar's learned associates, but by a small and zealous group.

In contrast with the reports advocating the practice of *wuḍūʾ* from cooked food, which revolve around a small number of individuals joined by personal ties, those opposing it seem to reflect a broad-based consensus. Far from converging on any particular figures, the reports bear chains of transmission from all major intellectual centers of the contemporary Islamic world and are diffusely distributed over a large set of transmitters. However, a few generalizations may be ventured. One is that the links contemporary to the main disseminators of the *ḥadīth* discussed above (al-Zuhrī, al-Ḥasan, and

Abū Qilāba) tend to be figures at least somewhat less closely associated with the Marwānids in general and with ʿUmar ibn ʿAbd al-ʿAzīz in particular. Thus, in Baṣra we can contrast al-Ḥasan with his contemporary Muḥammad ibn Sīrīn (who died in the same year, 110, reportedly at the age of seventy-seven), who reportedly opposed *wuḍū*ʾ from cooked food. In a tradition preserved in two different versions, he is supposed to have related:

> I asked ʿAbīda about cooked food [lit., what has been touched by fire].[83] He ordered that a sheep be slaughtered; then he was called away—I think the governor called him. He called for milk, butter and bread, and he ate and we ate with him. Then he got up to pray and prayed without performing *wuḍū*ʾ. Ibn Sīrīn said: I suspected *(ẓanantu)* that he only wanted to show me that.[84]

Both the summons from the governor (*amīr*) and the fact that ʿAbīda answers Ibn Sīrīn only obliquely may subtly suggest that this was a sensitive issue that was felt to be debated under the eyes of the regime. In any case, the contrast between al-Ḥasan's and Ibn Sīrīn's positions on this point of law is paralleled by the contrast between their attitudes to ʿUmar ibn ʿAbd al-ʿAzīz. The tradition that al-Ḥasan received his government stipend from ʿUmar, while Ibn Sīrīn declined, has already been mentioned. The symbolic distinction between the two men's stances was significant; posterity would remember that, as stated in a pithy report cited by Ibn Saʿd, "ʿUmar ibn ʿAbd al-ʿAzīz sent to (*baʿatha ilā*) al-Ḥasan, and he accepted; he sent to Ibn Sīrīn, and he did not accept."[85]

In Madīna, the opposition to the practice of *wuḍū*ʾ from cooked food similarly seems to have been drawn from circles not distinguished by their zeal for the Umayyads. Muḥammad ibn al-Munkadir, the figure on whom several of the Medinian traditions rejecting the practice converge,[86] was an ascetic who was apparently not remembered by posterity for any political activities or associations at all.[87] ʿAṭāʾ ibn Yasār, whose name also appears repeatedly,[88] apparently was similarly apolitical.[89] A tradition opposing the practice is attributed to the formidable Saʿīd ibn al-Musayyab (d. A.H. 93 or 94),[90] who is supposed to have observed ʿUthmān eating cooked food and then praying without performing *wuḍū*ʾ.'[91] Ibn al-Musayyab has been noted by posterity for his attitude of unrelieved contempt towards the Marwānid dynasty and all of its representatives, which reportedly led to at least one episode of imprisonment and persecution.[92] While he himself did not live to see the reign of ʿUmar ibn ʿAbd al-ʿAzīz, he is thus an appropriate authority for an implicitly oppositional tradition.

Interestingly, the opposition to *wuḍū*ʾ from cooked food also seems to have included Shīʿite elements. Independently of the Shīʿite compilations (which date from a later period and probably reflect the ultimate pansectarian rejection of *wuḍūʾ* from cooked food), the *Muṣannaf*s of ʿAbd al-Razzāq and Ibn Abī Shayba suggest that figures revered by the Shīʿite movement were consistently linked with the opposition to this practice. *Ḥadīth* confuting the injunction to perform *wuḍūʾ* from cooked food are found with several different Imāmī chains of transmission. Muḥammad ibn ʿAlī ibn Ḥusayn—that is, the fifth Imām, al-Bāqir (d. A.H. 114–18/734–37 C.E.)—is supposed to have transmitted from his father that the Prophet ate meat and then prayed without performing *wuḍūʾ*;[93] he is also credited with a Prophetic *ḥadīth* to the same effect transmitted from Ibn ʿAbbās.[94] Jaʿfar ibn Muḥammad (the sixth Imām, al-Ṣādiq, d. 148) is supposed to have declared that "ʿAlī did not perform *wuḍūʾ* from cooked food."[95] There is also a report stating that the Kaysānī Shīʿite figurehead Muḥammad ibn al-Ḥanafīya—the nominal leader of what was probably the strongest Shīʿite faction of the period leading up to the ʿAbbāsid revolution—"used to eat *tharīd* (a meat dish) and drink *nabīdh* (boiled wine) and pray without performing *wuḍūʾ*."[96] Since this report is traced to a figure who is supposed to have drawn his traditions about Muḥammad ibn al-Ḥanafīya from a document *(ṣaḥīfa)* of unknown origin,[97] it is more likely to represent the opinion of the community that revered him than of Ibn al-Ḥanafīya himself. While the *Muṣannaf*s of ʿAbd al-Razzāq and Ibn Abī Shayba, as traditionist works largely uninterested in communicating a coherent legal message, preserve extensive traces of a completely defunct Sunnī movement in support of *wuḍūʾ* from cooked food, they thus seem to document a Shīʿite consensus against the practice from the outset.

Overall, there seems to be ample evidence to associate the reports enjoining *wuḍūʾ* from cooked food and the controversy they provoked within the circle around ʿUmar ibn ʿAbd al-ʿAzīz. As we have seen, traditions in its favor were circulated almost exclusively by ʿUmar's warmest supporters, while the opposition to the practice included several elements of the opposition to the dynasty. Furthermore, the overall chronological and political setting of the controversy is corroborated by the texts of more than one of the more elaborate reports. One of these is the anecdote, already cited, in which Anas ibn Mālik is supposed to have left an audience with al-Ḥajjāj enraged by the governor's neglect of this principle of purity. Perhaps playing on ʿUmar's well-known defiance of al-Ḥajjāj while governor of Madīna, when he offered a haven for refugees from al-Ḥajjāj's repression in ʿIrāq, the report neatly associates observance of the injunction of *wuḍūʾ* from cooked food with opposition to al-Ḥajjāj. Whatever its literal accuracy, the scenario points directly at the political context we have been suggesting for this controversy.

An intriguing report in the *Musnad* of Aḥmad ibn Ḥanbal corroborates both the Marwānid setting of the dissemination of this practice and the prominent role of al-Zuhrī in its promotion.

> Qatāda said: Sulaymān ibn Hishām said: "This fellow"—meaning al-Zuhrī—"will not let us eat a thing without ordering us to perform *wuḍūʾ* from it"—meaning cooked food (*mā massat al-nār*). [Qatāda] said: I said, "I asked Saʿīd ibn al-Musayyab about it, and he said, 'When you eat [food] it is pure (*ṭayyib*) and you are not obligated to perform *wuḍūʾ* from it; when it comes out it is impure (*khabīth*) and you are obligated to perform *wuḍūʾ* from it.' " [Sulaymān] said: "Is there anyone in town [who can confirm this]?" [Qatāda] said: I said, "Yes; the man with the oldest learning in the Arabian Peninsula (*aqdam rajul fī jazīrat al-ʿarab ʿilman*)." [Sulaymān] said, "Who?" I said, "ʿAṭāʾ ibn abī Rabāḥ.". . . So [Sulaymān] sent someone to ask him (*baʿatha ilayhi*) and he said, "Jābir informed me that they ate bread and meat with Abū Bakr al-Ṣiddīq, and [Abū Bakr] prayed without performing *wuḍūʾ*."[98]

The Sulaymān ibn Hishām who is irritated by al-Zuhrī's zeal for ablution is almost certainly Sulaymān ibn Hishām ibn ʿAbd al-Malik, son of the Umayyad caliph Hishām who ruled from A.H. 105 to 125 (724–43 C.E.); he is the only well-known figure of this name.[99] al-Zuhrī, as mentioned earlier, is supposed to have acted as tutor to Hishām's sons, and this situation may be the most appropriate setting for the anecdote; the implication that al-Zuhrī exercises some kind of supervision over Sulaymān's personal habits is otherwise somewhat perplexing, and the first-person plural ("won't let *us*") could then refer to Sulaymān and his brothers. The likely historical setting for the incident would be sometime between A.H. 105 and 115, when Hishām was already caliph but ʿAṭāʾ was still alive and venerated as an increasingly rare link to the first generation of Muslim scholars. More specifically, it is plausible to imagine that this scene is set in A.H. 113, when Sulaymān was deputed to lead the ḥajj in the company of al-Zuhrī;[100] this scenario would explain why the Meccan ʿAṭāʾ is represented as being available "in town."

A report on the opposite side of the controversy points just as clearly at a Marwānid and politically charged setting for the debate. This is the anecdote attributed to one ʿAbd Allāh ibn Shaddād ibn al-Hād:

> Abū Hurayra said, "One must perform *wuḍūʾ* from cooked food." Marwān said: "How can anyone [else] be asked about this when the wives of our Prophet and our mothers are among us?" [ʿAbd

> Allāh] said, "So he sent me to [the Prophet's wife] Umm Salama and I asked her . . ."[101]

Here Marwān ibn al-Ḥakam, the founder of the Marwānid dynasty, responds to Abū Hurayra's presentation of a *ḥadīth* by rhetorically asking how any self-selected transmitter can report statements from the Prophet when the people most intimately familiar with his habits are still available for consultation. When he sends ʿAbd Allāh ibn Shaddād to question Umm Salama on this point, she reports that she served the Prophet meat and that he prayed without performing *wuḍūʾ* after eating it. Perhaps, as is not uncommon in polemical exchanges, this riposte to the Abū Hurayra *ḥadīth* tries to beat its disseminators at their own game; associates of a later Marwānid caliph are confounded by the invocation of the founder of their line. Alternatively, the report could have served to enhance the reputation of Marwān, who is here represented as a guardian of the prophetic *sunna* who ensures that the most authoritative sources are consulted about the authentic practices of Muḥammad. In any case, the report would seem to have a political point to make, one related to Marwān's identity as the founder of the eponymous caliphal line.

If the evidence points to the Marwānid dynasty in general and to ʿUmar ibn ʿAbd al-ʿAzīz in particular, what motives and understandings might have informed the ultimately futile effort to popularize *wuḍūʾ* from cooked food? Why would ʿUmar ibn ʿAbd al-ʿAzīz have encouraged the circulation of reports advocating *wuḍūʾ* from cooked food? In fact, such an effort would fit what we know of the ideological foundations of his reign on several different levels. Firstly, it seems to be in harmony with what we know of ʿUmar's attitude towards the *sunna* (the "way" or "practice" established by the precedent of the Prophet and the early Islamic community). ʿUmar seems to have based his appeal to a large extent on the idea that he was *restoring* an Islamic practice that had fallen into neglect. A number of reports cite him as emphasizing the revival or resuscitation (*iḥyāʾ*, *inʿāsh*) of the *sunna*. In the words attributed to him in one report recorded by Ibn Saʿd, "If it were not that I could revive a *sunna* (*unʿisha sunnatan*) or establish what is right, I would not want to live for an instant."[102] To view our set of *ḥadīth* reports in the context of this position would explain an otherwise anomalous feature of the complex. As has already been noted, several of the reports would lead us to believe that the practice of performing *wuḍūʾ* after eating cooked food was unfamiliar to most Muslims at the time when the various forms of the *ḥadīth* advocating it were first widely circulated. What is unusual is that the novelty of the practice is implied by several texts *in its favor*—they represent it as a practice that is authentic yet at the same time unknown. To admit that the practice one is advocating is alien to the continuous practice of the community would usually be a liability; in the context of a commitment to revival of the *sunna*, it here becomes an advantage.

Secondly, 'Umar's involvement with the issue of *wuḍū'* from cooked food—his own reported adherence to the practice, his personal dissemination of one of the major *ḥadīth* in its support, and the patronage of its other circulators that we are suggesting here—fits into what seems to have been a wider concern with ritual purity. The sources supply us with a number of small reports about his purity practices that, trivial as they may appear individually, cumulatively constitute a remarkably complete description of the ritual purity practices of an individual of his time. Given the minor role that ritual purity seems to have played in the public images of most pious figures, these statements together indicate an unusual degree of interest in the subject. 'Umar ibn 'Abd al-'Azīz is said to have been so scrupulous about *wuḍū'* from cooked food that he performed ablutions after eating sugar.[103] However, he did perform *wuḍū'* with water that had been heated.[104] He performed *wuḍū'* if he touched his genitals.[105] He performed *wuḍū'* with water from a brass vessel; he also used a towel to wipe off his face after his ablutions.[106] He reportedly took positions on both of the extraordinarily vexed questions relating to the treatment of the feet in the *wuḍū'* ablutions: the question of wiping versus washing[107] and the question of "the wiping of the shoes" (*masḥ al-khuffayn*), which has been a major intersectarian issue over the centuries.[108] He apparently followed the school of thought that favored maintaining a continuous state of ritual purity (as opposed to limiting it to its role as a preparation for prayer); as a result of his sexual abstinence, he reportedly did not perform the major ablution (*ghusl*) for an emission of semen from his accession to the caliphate until his death—that is, for almost two years.[109] He was also known for his opinions on several issues located on the boundaries between ritual purity and the closely related spheres of personal hygiene and physical modesty. Thus, he forbade Muslims to wash themselves in public baths without covering their private parts, and himself performed the major ablution (*ghusl*) at home wearing a loincloth (*izār*).[110]

It cannot be emphasized enough that these practices, nugatory as they may seem to people culturally at a great remove from the ritual life of the Muslim community of the late first century A.H., address questions that were hotly debated in their time. Issues such as the use of brass ablution vessels and the permissibility of drying oneself off after performing *wuḍū'* were important enough in their day to leave appreciable traces in the early sources. Positions such as 'Umar's support of *wuḍū'* from cooked food and from touching the genitals also raised important theoretical issues that were vital to the understanding of ritual purity as it was apparently developing in his day. While it would not be wise to place too much credence in the content of any individual report about 'Umar's purity practices—which are rarely supported by enough chains of transmission even to permit speculation about their origins—it seems undeniable that ʿUmar's image as a ruler unusually concerned with issues of this type is well established. While specific details are questionable, the underlying trend is probably reliable.

Indeed, it would seem that we can discern a distinctive basic appreciation of the nature of ritual purity underlying a number of ʿUmar's various personal choices in this area. Many of his contemporaries, particularly those associated with the teachings of Ibn ʿAbbās, seem to have been involved in elaborating ritual purity as a strictly circumscribed and rigorously systematic set of rules applied to a limited set of bodily functions and impure substances. ʿUmar's opinions are a counterpoint (possibly archaic, or at least archaicizing) to this emerging consensus, insisting that the ingestion of pure foods and contact with certain parts of one's own body could cancel *wuḍūʾ*. How could licit food or contact with the penis, neither of them in itself impure, cancel one's state of ritual purity? Why would the permissibility of heating one's *wuḍūʾ* water even be in question? The answer seems to be that many of the views imputed to ʿUmar imply a vision of ritual purity not as a field that was self-contained and governed by conceptions about the inherent impurity of certain substances, but as one that was continuous with and largely defined by issues of ethics and morality as embodied in Qurʾānic terminology.

Central to this view of the nature of ritual purity is ʿUmar's understanding of the word "*ṭayyib*" (licit, pure). In the Qurʾān, it designates (among other things) those foods that are permissible to the believer; along with *ṭahūr* it is, in fact, the major Qurʾānic term that may be taken to designate pure substances. Thus, although it largely lost out to derivatives of the root "*ṭ-h-r*" in the classical terminology of ritual purity, it was frequently used as a technical term in the early period. This is clearly how it is being used in the analogical arguments against *wuḍūʾ* from cooked food, where it is protested that it is impossible for food that is "*ṭayyib*" to cancel a state of ritual impurity. ʿUmar, at least in the memory preserved by the sources, did not follow this usage. For him, the primary thrust of the word "*ṭayyib*" always seems to be "licit" in the sense of "rightfully acquired," not "licit" in the sense of "substantively pure." It is not impure substances such as urine and menstrual blood that represent the primary antithesis of the "*ṭayyib*," but ill-gotten gains. This view is made explicit in an anecdote about ʿUmar's eating habits:

> ʿUmar ibn ʿAbd al-ʿAzīz had associates (*aṣḥāb*) who attended him and aided him with their opinions and from whom he heard [*ḥadīth*]. One day they came to him and he took a long time to appear in the morning. They said to each other, "Do you fear that he has changed [in his attitude towards us]?" Muzāḥim heard

> this; he went in and ordered someone to wake him, and reported to him what he had heard from his associates. He gave them permission to enter, and when they came in to him he said, "Last night I ate chickpeas and lentils, and they gave me gas." One of them said, "O Commander of the Faithful, God says in His book, 'Eat of the good/licit things (*ṭayyibāt*) We have provided for you.' " ʿUmar said, "No indeed, you have interpreted it wrong (*dhahabta bihi ilā ghayr madhhabihi*); He meant legal earnings (*ṭayyib al-kasb*), not good/licit foods (*ṭayyib al-ṭaʿām*)."[111]

This understanding of the key term "*ṭayyib*" did not simply entail the disjunction of the term from the realm of ritual purity and its transfer to the field of economic ethics. Rather, it entailed a melding of the two spheres. This becomes clear in the anecdotes about his attitude towards heated water. Although he is said to have used heated water for purposes of ablution, other statements report scruples relating to water that was heated in a public oven.[112] It emerges from these reports that his concern was not with any possible effect of the heating process on the cleanliness of the water, but with the costs involved in feeding the fire and his own legitimate entitlement to the fuel. Thus, in one anecdote he solves the problem by paying for the fuel:

> Water for ʿUmar ibn ʿAbd al-ʿAzīz's ablutions was heated in the public kitchen (*maṭbakh al-ʿāmma*) without his knowledge. When he found out about it he said, "For how long have you been warming it?" They said, "About a month." He contributed that amount of wood to the public kitchen.[113]

Here ʿUmar's extreme economic scrupulosity and his concern for purity of the kind that is achieved by ablutions are inextricably conjoined.

This view seems to arise naturally from a Qurʾānic world-view where the two semantic fields, economic ethics and ritual purity, intersect in the key term *tazakkā*/*zakāt*.[114] In the understanding embodied in the reports about ʿUmar, as well as in the text of the Qurʾān, there is no absolute disjunction between the purification of wealth and the purification of the body. Indeed, according to one report ʿUmar is supposed to have made *zakāt* a precondition for the validity of prayer precisely parallel to ablution: "He who has [paid] no *zakāt* has no prayers (*innahu lā ṣalāta li-man lā zakāta lahu*)."[115] This is an exact, and likely intentional, parallel to a Prophetic *ḥadīth* stating that "He who has no *wuḍū*ʾ has no prayers (*lā ṣalāta li-man lā wuḍūʾa lahu*)."[116]

Aside from any concern for financial probity, why was ʿUmar's general willingness to perform his *wuḍū*ʾ ablutions with warm water worthy of note? Scruples relating to hot water may be understood in the Qurʾānic context.

Some reports speak not of "heated water" (*al-mā᾿ al-musakhkhan*) but of "hot water" (*al-ḥamīm*).[117] This is precisely the word that is repeatedly used in the Qur᾿ān to refer to the scalding liquid with which God torments the damned in Hell.[118] As is specified in a Qur᾿ānic reference to the prophet Ayyūb (Job), who is supposed to have been healed by his ablutions, the righteous cleanse themselves with cool water (*mughtasal bārid*).[119] Hellfire was, of course, one of ʿUmar's most characteristic pious preoccupations. His extreme rectitude is supposed to have been sustained by a constant awareness of the peril of Hell, and the sayings attributed to him are peppered with references to the Fire. This was no preoccupation with an abstract divine displeasure; in one anecdote, ʿUmar explains his unwillingness to extend financial favors to his relations by throwing a *dīnār* into the fire until it glows red, then casting it out so his companion can hear it sizzle.[120]

It does not require an enormous intuitive leap to imagine that the scruples about heated water may also have applied to cooked food. Both the financial and the Qur᾿ānic rationales would apply.[121] As has already been mentioned, the wording of the stricture, requiring *wuḍū᾿* from "that which has been touched by fire," strongly suggests Qur᾿ānic language relating to Hell. The stricture also, of course, dovetails with ʿUmar's extreme caution in the enjoyment of food. While complete abstinence from food (unlike complete sexual abstinence, with which he is credited) was not an option, he seems to have practiced a kind of continence with respect to eating. Among the many reports describing the meager and humble nature of his meals, one states that he never ate to the point of satiety.[122]

In the case of *wuḍū᾿* from cooked food I would tentatively argue that ʿUmar ibn ʿAbd al-ʿAzīz adopted a somewhat obscure purity practice that was probably already current in ascetic circles in Baṣra and patronized its circulation in the form of a dictum of the Prophet.[123] The Iraqī origin of the practice—or at least the ʿIrāqī odium attaching to it in some circles—is reflected in a tradition in which Anas ibn Mālik, one of the alleged Companion witnesses for the practice, is supposed to have been chided for his adherence to it by an assembly of other Companions:

> Anas ibn Mālik said: I went to Madīna and had supper with Abū Ṭalḥa before the *maghrib* (sunset) prayer; a number of the companions of the Messenger of God, including Ubayy ibn Kaʿb, were at his house. The prayer time arrived and I got up to perform *wuḍū᾿*. They said: What is this ʿIrāqī innovation you have introduced (*mā hādhihi᾿ l-ʿirāqīyatu᾿ l-latī aḥdathtahā*)? Are you performing *wuḍū᾿* from good food (*al-ṭayyibāt*)? They all performed the *maghrib* prayers without performing *wuḍū᾿*.[124]

ʿUmar's attempt to popularize this practice was most likely inspired by his commitment to the revivification of neglected practices of the Prophet and dramatized his ambitions for a radical (and possibly messianic) purification of the Islamic community. However, his efforts met with acceptance only among a small number of scholars who were loyal to the Umayyads or placed pious hopes in the reforms of his reign; due to widespread theoretical skepticism and the staunch resistance of elements in the political and religious resistance, the initiative was doomed to failure.

*Wuḍū*ʾ from Touching the Genitals

As will be remembered, performing *wuḍū*ʾ from touching the genitals was another purity practice noted to have been followed by ʿUmar ibn ʿAbd al-ʿAzīz. Like *wuḍū*ʾ from cooked food, this practice was apparently sufficiently distinctive to be associated with him by posterity. Unlike *wuḍū*ʾ from cooked food, however, it was a successful position that ultimately asserted itself in three out of the four classical schools of law. Only the Ḥanafīs, faithful to the Kūfan tradition, persisted in rejecting the practice. From the point of view of the substance of the debate, this case presents a strong parallel to the previous one of *wuḍū*ʾ from cooked food. The support for the practice of *wuḍū*ʾ from touching the genitals is purely tradition-based; that is, whether the authority be the Prophet, a Companion, or an early legal figure, the stricture is enjoined without any supporting legal reasoning. What matters is simply the appeal to an authoritative early precedent. The opposition, once again centered in Kūfa, rebuts it in on the basis of systematic legal reasoning. Although they are often placed in the mouths of authoritative early figures, the refutations of the requirement draw a significant element of their power to convince from the cogency of their content.

Despite the lack of explicit rationales attributed to early figures, it is not difficult to divine the general tendencies underlying the idea that touching the genitals cancels *wuḍū*ʾ. It is one of the possible logical extensions emerging from the close interrelationship of sexuality and ritual purity. One of the possible theoretical bases on which this interrelationship could be approached by jurists is indicated by al-Shāfiʿī, who writes in *Kitāb al-Umm* that a person's *wuḍū*ʾ is canceled if he touches his own genitals or anus or those of another human being, alive or dead, but that

> if he touches any of the parts in question on an animal he does not have to perform *wuḍū*ʾ, on the basis that human beings have physical inviolability (*ḥurma*) and acts of worship (*taʿabbud*) are incumbent upon them, while no such [rule applies] for animals or towards animals.[125]

Here, *wuḍū*ʾ is canceled by touching the most intimate parts of the human body, which are seen to have a sanctity extending beyond death. The underlying principle is *ḥurma*, "physical inviolability," a broad legal concept which has been variously applied to unwarranted medical intervention in the body, intrusion into the intimate areas of the anatomy, and violation of the sanctity of corpses. It is difficult to judge whether Shāfiʿī's appeal to the *ḥurma* of the human body reflects the approach of the earliest jurists who debated the question of *wuḍū*ʾ from touching the genitals; there is some reason to think that not all of his predecessors shared his reasoning.[126] However, the concept of *ḥurma* is an extraordinarily relevant and useful one for the study of ritual purity. There is a striking homology between the strictures relating to ritual purity and those derived from the concept of *ḥurma*. Like the rules of ritual purity, which shadow forth the ideal of the self-contained and nonporous body, the concept of *ḥurma* demands that the intactness of the human body be preserved unless urgent need requires its violation. Like the rules of purity, which invite the preservation or restoration of a body unriven by the intrusions and extrusions of sexuality, the concept of *ḥurma* hedges around human sexuality with protective prohibitions. Both reflect similar concerns relating to the body that must have been shared by many Muslims; it is no coincidence that in this particular case the two sets of principles are seen to be substantively in harmony.

However congenial to the general climate of opinion relating to the body the rule may have been found in some circles, however, it was theoretically problematic. The crux of almost all of the responses, like those to the traditions about *wuḍū*ʾ from cooked food, is the absence of any clearly impure substance involved in the action alleged to cancel *wuḍū*ʾ. The genitals are not impure, opponents to the practice object. Touching your genitals is not (technically speaking) any different from touching the tip of your nose, your elbow, or any other part of your anatomy.[127] If you really think that a part of your body is impure, you should cut it off.[128] In the final analysis, "[the penis] is merely a part of you."[129]

Furthermore, it was impossible to adopt the position that the genitals *were* impure in any rigorously systematic way. This problem is reflected in a dialogue between the Meccan scholar ʿAṭāʾ ibn abī Rabāḥ (d. A.H. 115) and his student Ibn Jurayj, a younger man who was clearly more affected than his teacher by the rising trend towards systematization:

> Ibn Jurayj said: I said to ʿAṭāʾ, "[What if] I touched my penis through my clothes?" He said, "*Wuḍū*ʾ is only necessary for direct contact and touching." I said, "[What about if I touch it] with the thigh or the calf?" He said, "*Wuḍū*ʾ is only necessary for [touching] with the hand." I said, "What's the distinction between

> those [two cases?]" He said, "It is simply part of the man; how can it not touch the man[ʿs body]? The hand is not the same as the leg in that respect."[130]

Ibn Jurayj apparently accepted his mentor's teaching despite his logical reservations. However, he was himself unable to defend it in the face of more sophisticated ʿIrāqī systematic thinking. In this case the anecdote is narrated (unsurprisingly) by the victor in the debate, the Kūfan scholar Sufyān al-Thawrī (d. A.H. 161):

> A certain governor (*baʿḍu umarāʾihim*) called me and Ibn Jurayj and asked about touching the penis. Ibn Jurayj said, "[A man who touches his penis] performs *wuḍūʾ*"; I said, "No *wuḍūʾ* is necessary for him." When we had differed [thus,] I said to Ibn Jurayj: "What do you think about the situation [*a-raʾayta*] if a man puts his hand on semen?" He said, "He washes his hand." I said, "Which of the two is more impure, the semen or the penis?" He said, "No, it's the semen." I said, "Then how can that be [i.e., how can you claim that he must perform *wuḍūʾ* from touching his penis but merely wash his hand if he touches semen]?" He said: "It is surely a devil who inspired you with this (*mā alqāhā ʿalā lisānika illā shayṭān*)."[131]

As this example suggests, the debate tended to follow a clear geographical pattern, with Ḥijāzīs supporting the practice and (mostly Kūfan) ʿIrāqīs opposing it. In the case of *wuḍūʾ* from cooked food, we saw an intriguing instance in which an ostensibly Medinian *ḥadīth* seems to represent, not the continuous and accepted practice of the Medinians, but a Prophetically-sanctioned reworking of an ʿIrāqī (Baṣran) legal position. The situation is different with respect to *wuḍūʾ* from touching the genitals. Here, to judge from the available information about Companion traditions and the opinions of early legal scholars, there apparently were well-entrenched regional traditions underlying the debate—despite some difference of opinion in ʿIrāq. At the Companion level, the Medinian authority Ibn ʿUmar is the figure most frequently cited as having performed *wuḍūʾ* if he touched his genitals. The chains of transmission are Ḥijāzī and ʿIrāqī (i.e., mainly Baṣran).[132] On the level of the early legal scholars, the Meccans ʿAṭāʾ ibn abī Rabāḥ,[133] Mujāhid [ibn Jabr],[134] Ṭāwus [ibn Kaysān],[135] and Ibn Jurayj[136] are supposed to have supported the practice, as is the Syrian authority Makḥūl.[137] On the other hand, the position of the Medinian authority Saʿīd ibn al-Musayyab is disputed, or perhaps errors in transmission have produced contradictory statements.[138]

In Kūfa, statements denying the necessity of *wuḍū'* in this situation were attributed to such figures as Ibn Mas'ūd,[139] 'Alī,[140] Ḥudhayfa ibn al-Yamān,[141] and 'Ammār ibn Yāsir.[142] The Kūfan authority Sa'īd ibn Jubayr, who appears as a transmitter for the Ibn Mas'ūd traditions, also appears as a final authority through a couple of non-Kūfan *isnāds*.[143] Largely Kūfan traditions from both sides of the dispute contested the precedent of Sa'd ibn abī Waqqāṣ, who was variously stated to have enjoined the practice or to have ridiculed it.[144] Among the Kūfan legal scholars, Ibrāhīm al-Nakha'ī is adduced in the chains of transmission of traditions deprecating the requirement;[145] he is also supposed to have stated that it was all right if a man touched his penis during prayer.[146] Such somewhat later Kūfan figures as Abū Ḥanīfa[147] and Sufyān al-Thawrī (d. 161)[148] are similarly supposed to have opposed it. The situation in Baṣra was more confused; reports on both sides of the conflict seem to have enjoyed circulation there. In terms of local material, Baṣran traditions cite 'Imrān ibn Ḥuṣayn as a Companion witness against the practice,[149] and such authorities as al-Ḥasan[150] and Qatāda[151] are supposed to have opposed it. Based on the slight evidence available, al-Ḥasan seems to have been a (or the) main circulator of the reports about 'Imrān ibn Ḥuṣayn.[152]

From the point of view of classical law, this multiplicity of Companion testimonies and statements from early local authorities was reduced to relative insignificance by the presence of a Prophetic *ḥadīth* requiring *wuḍū'* from touching the genitals. The text of the *ḥadīth* (referred to henceforth as the "Busra *ḥadīth*"), which appears with slight variations in different sources, is as follows:

> 'Urwa ibn al-Zubayr and Marwān debated the question of touching the genitals. Marwān said: "Busra bint Ṣafwān reported to me that she heard the Messenger of God command *wuḍū'* from touching the genitals." It seemed that 'Urwa was not convinced by what he said, so Marwān sent an officer (*shurṭīyan*) to her; he returned and informed them that she heard the Messenger of God command *wuḍū'* from touching the genitals.[153]

The first distinctive element of the text of the tradition is the identity of the main character in the anecdote, Marwān. As is explicitly stated in some versions of the chain of transmission, this is none other than the caliph Marwān ibn al-Ḥakam (reigned A.H. 64–65/684–85 C.E.), the progenitor of the Marwānid line. It should be emphasized that Marwān is not the obvious choice for this particular role. It is not completely implausible in light of the biographical sources; he is said to have consulted with the Companions during his tenure as governor of Madīna,[154] and 'Urwa is said to have had a personal regard for him as a transmitter.[155] However, the sources also amply document that Marwān was best known neither as a legal thinker nor as a transmitter of *ḥadīth*. The political implications of his presence in the *isnād* would, one suspects, have completely overshadowed any scholarly reputation attaching to his name. The Umayyad overtones of the *isnād* are intensified by the presence of Busra bint Ṣafwān as the Companion link. Busra is supposed to have been an early emigrant to Madīna and to have given the oath of allegiance to the Prophet. She reportedly lived into the caliphate of Mu'āwiya, which would be consistent with the assumption that she was available for consultation when Marwān was governor of Madīna (the most likely setting for his consultation with 'Urwa). Her precise identity, however, is obscure. Her lineage is disputed, beginning with the father of Ṣafwān; she is variously claimed to have been from Banū Asad or Banū Kināna. What is unmistakable is her association with the Marwānids. According to her Asadī genealogy she was a relation by marriage, the great-grandmother (on the maternal side) of Marwān's son and heir, 'Abd al-Malik ibn Marwān. According to her alternate, Kinānī, genealogy, she was Marwān's maternal aunt.[156] In a possible harmonization of the two lines of thought, al-Mizzī makes her Marwān's mother-in-law and aunt and 'Abd al-Malik's grandmother.[157]

The second unusual feature of the *ḥadīth* is its form. The anecdote that introduces the alleged statement of the Prophet is not a description of the circumstances of that statement by the Companion witness to the event. We are not told anything about the circumstances of the Prophet's pronouncement. In fact, the legal statement itself is presented as merely the final element in the byplay between the second transmitter, Marwān, and the third, 'Urwa. Even if the text and its chain of transmission were to be regarded as sober statements of historical fact, it remains to be asked why the report is framed in this particular form—with Marwān as the protagonist of a pointed little anecdote, rather than merely a link in the *isnād* between Busra and 'Urwa. A tradition that depicts Marwān setting straight a scholar and traditionist of the stature of 'Urwa ibn al-Zubayr almost certainly does so with an agenda in mind. One such agenda might simply be to enhance the religious stature of the Marwānid family by emphasizing its access to Prophetic lore through a female relation of Busra's early Islamic credentials. This hypothesis is supported by an alternate version of the *ḥadīth* in which the dictum is reported not from Busra by Marwān, but from Umm Ḥabība by Mu'āwiya's brother 'Anbasa ibn abī Sufyān.[158] The ostensible provenance of the *ḥadīth* has changed, but its Umayyad pedigree is conserved. A second agenda, which seems to be hinted by the text of the anecdote itself, relates to one of the themes discussed above: the revivification of the Prophetic *sunna*. Like the traditions we have discussed relating to *wuḍū'* from cooked food, this report makes a point of noting that—far from reflecting a universally-known and continuous practice of the Muslim community—the Prophet's alleged statement *surprises* an eminent and knowledgeable Muslim.

It is also striking how closely the form of this *ḥadīth* echoes that of one we have already encountered, the report in which Marwān sends ʿAbd Allāh ibn Shaddād to question Umm Salama about *wuḍūʾ* from cooked food (see above, pp. 117–118). One might well wonder whether the motif underlying both stories, in which the caliph Marwān uses his connections with aged female associates of the Prophet to investigate points at issue about the Prophet's purity practices, is a topos with no necessary historical basis.

Suspicions about the provenance of this *ḥadīth* may also be raised simply by its obvious effectiveness within the context of interschool debates about the occasions of *wuḍūʾ*. Despite the cogency of systematic objections to the practice, mere analogical reason ultimately could not hold its own in the face of a Prophetic *ḥadīth* in its favor; Ḥanafī refusal to enjoin this practice (although it could be voluntarily followed as an act of piety) would find its justification in a counter-*ḥadīth* attributed to the Prophet. In the eyes of many revisionist scholars, these facts would in themselves suggest that the *ḥadīth* in question was forged and put into circulation at some period after the debate had already run its course on the level of local legal authorities or Companion traditions. As the advent of a Prophetic *ḥadīth* would inevitably render these categories of evidence obsolete, the surviving non-Prophetic reports must be relics of a stage before its assumed fabrication. In the words of Norman Calder, speaking of the various types of report on the very topic under discussion here, "The Prophetic hadith must have been one of the last to emerge. Once in existence and allied to a theory advocating the sufficiency of Prophetic hadith as legal authority, it would prevent the continued accumulation of Companion and other exempla."[159] Unlike in the case of *wuḍūʾ* from cooked food, where the Prophetic *ḥadīth* is identified with an archaic stage of the legal debate by the early and unanimous rejection of its substantive content, it would be natural to assume that this *ḥadīth* is very late indeed.[160]

In this particular case, in fact, there are more than a priori reasons to conclude that the *ḥadīth* in question was not in wide circulation in the first century. Whether it is authentic, in the sense that the Prophet actually made this statement and it was transmitted under the circumstances stated, is another question. It can best be approached by believers using the criteria provided by the various legal schools. What a given individual living more than a millennium ago may or may not have actually remembered his aunt to have said is not a question that can be resolved by historical methods. The issue that we *can* approach, at least by educated conjecture, is whether this contention was widely known. On this level, there is a fair amount of evidence that the tradition was not a major factor in debates over this issue before the end of the first century. It does seem reasonable to conclude, as a general distillation of the many specific reports surviving, that the practice of performing *wuḍū*ʾ from touching the genitals was practiced by some people quite early on. However, on those rare occasions when we have explicit statements about the rationales behind various early figures' support for the practice, it is not a *ḥadīth* of the Prophet that they adduce.

The most famous early attempt to ground this rule in an authoritative source is attributed to ʿAbīda al-Salmānī, a Kūfan who died in the early to middle 70s.[161] He is supposed to have discovered the requirement for *wuḍū*ʾ from touching the genitals in Qurʾān 4:43, in the words ordinarily read as "*aw lāmastum al-nisā*ʾ" ("or if you have touched women").[162] To derive this ruling from the wording of this verse would require that he read "*al-nasā*" instead of "*al-nisā*ʾ," "*al-nasā*" being a vein running down the inner thigh (and thus a discrete reference to the groin).[163] Given the fact, reflected in the orthography of the Qurʾān as it came to be established, that the dialect of Quraysh apparently did not pronounce the *hamza*, this would be a perfectly acceptable reading of the word. It would be possible to attribute the entire idea of performing *wuḍū*ʾ from touching the genitals to this reading of the Qurʾān, assuming it to have been widespread earlier on (or even, one might venture, original—whatever that might mean). However, the somewhat strained semantics of the reading, as well as the fact that it is attributed to ʿAbīda and to no one else, suggests that this was a display of exegetical ingenuity on the part of an individual. Believing that it was necessary to perform *wuḍū*ʾ after touching the genitals, ʿAbīda (or someone using his name) found a peg for the rule in the text of Revelation.

This apparently remained the best available explanation of the doctrine (or the only one known to some scholars) for some time. In one report Ibn Sīrīn (d. A.H. 110/728–29 C.E.), cites this Qurʾānic reading from ʿAbīda and continues, "I was informed that Ibn ʿUmar used to perform *wuḍū*ʾ if he touched his genitals, and I inferred that Ibn ʿUmar and ʿAbīda were of the same opinion."[164] Apparently this interpretive maneuver was the only basis that Ibn Sīrīn knew to ascribe to Ibn ʿUmar.[165]

A report from the Meccan jurist ʿAṭāʾ (d. A.H. 115/733–34 C.E.), drawn from the Ibn Jurayj tradition in the *Muṣannaf* of ʿAbd al-Razzāq, allows a similar inference. As Harald Motzki has demonstrated, in the corpus of reports attributed to Ibn Jurayj in this compilation, ʿAṭāʾ is almost always cited for his own *ra*ʾ*y*.[166] In some cases, it seems natural to infer that his statements were actually based on Prophetic traditions known to him; Motzki adduces some examples where ʿAṭāʾ explicitly cites the relevant traditions in response to questions from his younger and more *ḥadīth*-oriented students. Here, however, ʿAṭāʾ supports his statement with an explicit attribution, and it is not to the Prophet but to Ibn ʿUmar:

> ʿAṭāʾ said: Anyone who touches his penis should perform *wuḍūʾ*; this is related from Ibn ʿUmar (*innamā uthira dhālika ʿan Ibn ʿUmar*).[167]

This is all fairly conjectural, as it must be given the state of the evidence. However, there is evidence that the practice of performing *wuḍūʾ* from touching the genitals gained ground slowly and met with a certain amount of resistance in wider circles. This resistance is reflected in parenthetical remarks attached to a report about a related issue, the question of touching the armpit (*ibṭ*). The report, stating that anyone who touches his armpit should perform *wuḍūʾ*, is supposed to have been transmitted through the chain ʿUmar ibn al-Khaṭṭāb - "a man" - ʿUbayd Allāh ibn ʿAbd Allāh ibn ʿUtba - al-Zuhrī - Ibrāhīm - ʿAbd al-Razzāq. One of the transmitters, who unfortunately remains unidentified, expresses his unease about circulating the report:

> He said, "I have not heard this *ḥadīth* from anyone but him." He said, "We transmit to people that they should perform *wuḍūʾ* from touching the genitals, and they don't believe us. What [do you think it will be like] if we transmit to them [the same] about the armpit? (*innā nuḥaddith al-nās biʾl-wuḍūʾ min mass al-farj fa-mā yuṣaddiqūnanā fa-kayfa idhā ḥaddathnā bi-mass al-ibṭ*)."[168]

It is not clear whether the transmitter in question is talking about a *ḥadīth* of the Prophet or a report about ʿAbd Allāh ibn ʿUmar. In any case, the statement implies that traditions supporting the practice were introduced secondarily into a somewhat inhospitable environment.

Does this all mean that the *ḥadīth* in question is a forgery of very late date indeed? This has, in fact, been argued by Norman Calder. Despite the fact that the tradition appears in the earliest compilations available, he argues, it does not belong to the historical period its presence would imply. Rather, it was inserted into them in the course of a long period of development. Specifically, he argues that its presence in al-Shaybānī's *Kitāb al-ḥujja ʿalā ahl al-Madīna* is due to secondary revision and does not reflect the actual age of the *ḥadīth* text, which is better indicated by its absence from al-Shaybānī's recension of the *Muwaṭṭaʾ*. Because of the importance of Calder's arguments, I will examine them in detail.

Calder's dissection of the passage on this issue in the *Ḥujja* is based on two different indices: the occasional ruptures in coherence of the text as it stands, and the correspondence of a large section of the text (paragraphs 9–25 in Calder's division, which I will follow here) to that of the same section in *Muwaṭṭaʾ Shaybānī,* which does not contain the Busra tradition (the tradition, cited above, in which the Prophet enjoins *wuḍūʾ* from touching the genitals). The second fact is indisputable, and Calder's argument that the natural and original home of the excerpt is in the *Muwaṭṭa'* rather than in the *Kitāb al-Ḥujja* is convincing.

The chronological conclusion that Calder hopes to base on these observations is, however, not equally compelling. The *Ḥujja* "knows the text of the *Muwaṭṭa' Shaybānī*," Calder writes; "The *Ḥujja*, then, is undoubtedly later than the *Muwaṭṭa' Shaybānī*."[169] In light of Calder's own thesis of organic development, we must take this to mean not that the *Ḥujja* as a whole is later than the *Muwaṭṭa' Shaybānī* as a whole, but that the recension of the *Ḥujja* that has reached us achieved its *present form* later than the recension of the *Muwaṭṭa' Shaybānī* we have received.[170] In fact, Calder himself ends up by arguing that in its original strata the *Ḥujja* is very probably "older than the *Muwaṭṭa' Shaybānī*."[171] Obviously, the thesis that the *Ḥujja* was "closed" later than the *Muwaṭṭa'* does not mean that any given material in the *Ḥujja* is later than the material in the *Muwaṭṭa'*. What Calder has masterfully demonstrated is that it is very difficult to draw chronological conclusions from the supposed sequential ordering of books at all. It remains true that the Busra tradition appears in one collection and not in another supposedly originating with the same individual. This should make us worry. However, the conclusion that the *Muwaṭṭa' Shaybānī* lacks the *ḥadīth because* it is the older compilation and the *ḥadīth* did not exist at the time of its composition is a broad inferential leap. The *Ḥujja* has the tradition; the *Muwaṭṭa'* has the tradition outside of the recension of al-Shaybānī; to assume that the instances where it occurs are always late and the one instance where it does not occur is early may possibly be correct, but it does not arise from any independent knowledge we have about the chronology of these texts. Rather, it is an argument *from* certain assumptions about the development of the Islamic legal tradition *to* the chronology of the composition of the texts.

Thus, Calder's chronological argument really rides on his contention that the Busra tradition represents a late interpolation in the *Ḥujja*. His arguments about the logical divisions in this problematic text, however, are questionable. In order to make the somewhat involved argumentation that follows intelligible, I reproduce Calder's division and numeration of the relevant text of the *Ḥujja*:

> [1] Abū Ḥanīfa said: If someone who has performed *wuḍū'* touches his genitals (*farj*), his *wuḍū'* is not cancelled.
>
> [2] The Medinians (*ahl al-Madīna*) say: If someone who has performed *wuḍū'* touches his genitals, he must perform *wuḍū'* again. The touching must be with the inner side of the hand; if it is with the back of the hand, this does not necessitate *wuḍū'*.

[3] Earlier (*qabla dhālika*), the Madīnans used to say: If he touches his genitals with any of the parts of the body that are washed in *wuḍūʾ* (*mawāḍiʿ al-wuḍūʾ*), it necessitates *wuḍūʾ*. Then they abandoned this opinion and said: He must perform *wuḍūʾ* only if he touches it with the inner side of the hand.

[4] Muḥammad and al-Ḥasan said: What is the difference between the inner side of the hand and the back? If *wuḍūʾ* is cancelled by touching it [with the inner side of the hand], isn't it cancelled by touching it with the back?

[5a] Do you hold (*a-raʾaytum*) that if he touches the anus . . . does this cancel *wuḍūʾ*? They said: Yes; that and the genitals (*farj*) are the same,

[5b] because we have heard a *ḥadīth* of the Prophet that was mentioned by Busra bint Ṣafwān, [stating] that she heard the Prophet say, "If one of you touches his penis, he should perform *wuḍūʾ*."

[6] The response to this is: We have heard it reported from the Prophet that he was asked about that and said, "Is it anything but a piece of your body?" and did not consider it necessary to perform *wuḍūʾ*.

[7] What none of us dispute (*waʾl-ladhī lā ikhtilāfa fīhi ʿindanā*) is that ʿAlī ibn abī Ṭālib, ʿAbd Allāh ibn Masʿūd, ʿAmmār ibn Yāsir, Ḥudhayfa ibn al-Yamān, and ʿImrān ibn Ḥuṣayn did not consider it necessary to perform *wuḍūʾ* for touching the penis—and who is Busra ibnat Ṣafwān in comparison to them?

[8] And have you transmitted [this *ḥadīth*] from anyone but her? They say: Ibn ʿUmar used to say that. The response to that is [*qīla lahum*]: Ibn ʿUmar was a man who was extremely scrupulous about *wuḍūʾ* and *ghusl*; you have transmitted from him that he used to splash water into his eyes when he was sexually polluted, and you don't follow that opinion of his. This is clearly an example of Ibn ʿUmar's personal scrupulosity (*mimmā yushaddidu bihi Ibn ʿUmar ʿanhu ʿalā nafsihi*).

[26] How can we abandon all of these people's reports and their agreement on this matter for the *ḥadīth* of Busra bint Ṣafwān, a woman [whose testimony is] without [the corroboration of] a man, given women's tendency to be untrustworthy in transmission? Fāṭima bint Qays informed ʿUmar ibn al-Khaṭṭāb that her husband divorced her three times and the Prophet did not award her residence or support, and ʿUmar refused to accept her statement.[172]

The difficulties in this passage are sufficiently obvious. The most obvious problem is that the *ḥadīth* of Busra bint Ṣafwān does not have any clear relevance to the function that its position in the argument clearly requires it to play: refutation of the Medinian contention that the anus is legally analogous to the penis. Calder concludes that the original text of the *Ḥujja* consisted of paragraphs 1, 2, 4, and 7.[173] Paragraphs 5 and 6 are later insertions, added to reflect a later and more refined (that is, more *ḥadīth*-oriented) stage of the debate. The reference to the *ḥadīth* of Busra would thus not represent an element of the earliest layer of the text at all, a point which is central to Calder's vision of the development of Islamic legal argumentation.

However, there is more than one serious problem with this line of argument. One is that paragraph 7 explicitly refers back to paragraph 5's citation of the Busra *ḥadīth*. Calder rather weakly suggests the idea of paragraph 7 "possibly [!] excluding at first the rhetorical question."[174] However, in fact we need to make rather extensive adjustments to disentangle the issue of the Busra *ḥadīth* from the remainder of the passage, including Calder's further assumption that paragraph 8—which, like paragraph 26 (which follows it, excluding the *Muwaṭṭa'* citation), deals with Busra—represents yet another interpolation.[175] Unlike the issue of the anus, the Busra *ḥadīth* is not a discrete and incongruous stranger in a text that otherwise knows nothing about it. If it is a late insertion, we must assume that the entire passage (after paragraphs 1 and 2, which could be original) was restructured to revolve around it.

A far simpler explanation of the most glaring discontinuities in the text, however, would be merely to assume that the analogical argument involving the anus is an interpolation, or that some bridging material that would return the discussion to the main issue of touching the genitals has dropped out. This would eliminate the most obvious fault line, the logical non sequitur in which we expect Busra's *ḥadīth* somehow to comment on the issue of the anus. The following exchange would then make a great deal of sense, following the structure:

1. *You* allege that a statement is preserved from the Prophet supporting your position.

2. *We*, on the contrary, transmit a statement from the Prophet supporting our position.

3. What is *undisputed* is that a number of Companions held our position.

4. While you also have a Companion witness to your position, he is widely agreed to have had eccentric personal sensitivities on this particular issue.

The third step (paragraph 7 in the text) makes sense only in light of the preceding conflict, that is, the citation of the two contradictory *ḥadīth*. The sense of it is: We disagree on the position of the Prophet, but what we *do* agree on is . . . (*waʾlladhī lā ikhtilāfa fīhi*). The two sides have reached parity in the Prophetic arms race; tacitly declaring a draw on this level, the author moves to the level of Companion testimony, where his side is able to win handily.

The remainder of the argument addresses a weakness in the Ḥanafī side that the author is apparently loath to bring up explicitly: the Ḥanafī tradition is anonymous ("it *has reached us* [*fa-qad balaghanā*] from the Prophet"), while the Medinian tradition has a respectable Companion transmitter. Therefore, it is necessary to impugn the qualifications of Busra bint Ṣafwān as far as possible. Calder finds this illogical: "Busra, after all, does not act as an authority in her own right, but as a transmitter of the Prophet's ruling."[176] The slight incongruity of the argument derives, I would argue, not from discontinuity in the text but from the fact that the Ḥanafī author quite naturally wishes his side to come out on top.[177]

Furthermore, Calder is not correct in arguing that we can divide the text into chronologically graded strata on the basis of Companion citations per se. If true, of course, this would have given us an independent criterion with which to prise paragraph 7 free of the Busra tradition. However, it is simply not the case that "the technique of listing authorities but not citing exempla in detail" is "an older type of argument which was phased out as the principle of (near exclusive) appeal to Prophetic hadith began to predominate."[178] If this were the case, we would not have to puzzle over the provenance of Prophetic *ḥadīth*; we could simply assume that they were always later than any existing Companion traditions, since the latter would never have been cited when a Prophetic *ḥadīth* was available. However, this is actually far from true. Lists of the Companions (and, for that matter, *tābiʿūn*[179] and prominent legal scholars of later generations) who allegedly held a given position continued to be perfectly acceptable ancillary arguments throughout the classical period and, indeed, up until our own day.

Thus, while Calder's argument about the composite nature of the text is powerful, his specific proposals about the different elements of the text and their chronological distribution are—though plausible—not compelling. His argument that the Busra tradition is a late element whose very presence proves the final recension of the *Ḥujja* to be later than *Muwaṭṭaʾ Shaybānī* reflects, rather than dictates, his conception of the development of Islamic legal argumentation.

Especially in light of Calder's thesis of the organic development of the legal texts, which renders argumentation from the date of individual books difficult, it may be more rewarding to attempt to base hypotheses about the origins of this *ḥadīth* on internal evidence. This specific *ḥadīth,* as we have seen, seems particularly rich in internal clues to its own provenance and agenda.

As already noted, there are grounds to argue that the invocation of the figure of Marwān is a trope. Certainly the Busra *ḥadīth*, like the ʿAbd Allāh ibn Shaddād text on *wuḍū'* from cooked food, makes a point about the role of the caliph in the determination and dissemination of the *sunna.* Marwān is implied to be a figure whose court serves as a clearinghouse for religious knowledge, whose state resources (such as the officer, *shurṭī*, dispatched to question Umm Salama) are mobilized in the service of pious inquiry, and whose family connections provide authentic information about the Prophet. Unlike in the case of ʿUmar ibn ʿAbd al-ʿAzīz and his associates, there seems to be very little corroborative context that might strengthen the plausibility of these anecdotes. Yet, I would argue, precisely because of the repetitive and pointed nature of the appearance of members and henchmen of the Marwānid house in the reports surrounding these two debates, we must assume that they originated at a time when the Marwānid dynasty was still the political frame of reference, that is, sometime before the ʿAbbāsid revolution of A.H. 132.

The case of *wuḍū'* from touching the genitals seems to present a strong parallel to the first case in this chapter, that of *wuḍū'* from cooked food. Again a rigorous purity stricture, perhaps contradicting popular practice, is promoted in Madīna and meets resistance (largely in ʿIrāq) on systematic grounds. Again, the circulation of a Prophetic *ḥadīth* supporting the practice would seem to have taken place in the Marwānid period and to have been promoted by Umayyad government circles or circles loyal to the government. The only key difference is that in this case the more rigorous practice demanded by the *ḥadīth* was able to assert itself in some circles.

Blood and Other Bodily Issues

In addition to the circulation and promotion of authority statements traced to the Prophet and/or his Companions, systematic inference (going under the rubric of *ra'y* or, later and more restrictively, of *qiyās*) was a generative factor in the formation of the law of purity. The conclusion that "*wuḍū'* is required for what comes out, not for what goes in" (*al-wuḍū' mimmā kharaja wa-laysa mimmā dakhala*) raised the possibility that the category so defined included more that the universally accepted "cancelers of *wuḍū'*" (urination, defecation, farting). What of other bodily issues? Early debates considered the purity implications of a wide range of bodily issues, including blood, vomit, and pus.[180] Interestingly, the content of reports about the opinions attributed to early figures, as well as the texts of the earliest literary works available, suggest that these discussions revolved not primarily around the contestation of authoritative precedents, but almost completely around the effort to generate a coherent set of categories into which the various bodily issues could be fit. al-Shaybānī writes in his *Ḥujja ʿalā ahl al-Madīna*,

> Abū Ḥanīfa said: Anyone who has a nosebleed, vomits or coughs up (*qalasa*) a mouthful or more, or who has blood or bloody or clear pus flowing or dripping from a wound must perform *wuḍūʾ*. The Medinians say, "*Wuḍūʾ* is obligatory only for a pollution (*ḥadath*) coming out of the penis or anus or for recumbent sleeping; if someone coughs up food or vomits he need not perform *wuḍūʾ*, but should rinse it out of his mouth and wash his mouth."[181]

Interestingly, al-Shaybānī has reports about two early figures and one *ḥadīth* of the Prophet which report behavior that is perplexing for classical understanding of purity law: They are said to have had nosebleeds during prayer and to have gone to perform *wuḍūʾ*, returned, and resumed their prayers from where they left off.[182] Either because these reports were late or not widely accepted, or because they did not seem to resolve the theoretical question satisfactorily, the text's most vigorous argumentation is purely conceptual. The Medinians are made to say, "We consider the blood and vomit that emerge to be equivalent to sweat, mucus, spit and tears; if we required *wuḍūʾ* for [blood and vomit] we would also require it for [sweat, mucus, spit, and tears]." The followers of Abū Ḥanīfa then retort that this is a false parallel, as blood, pus, and vomit are substantively impure (*najis*), while emissions such as spit, tears, and sweat are not. They compel their Medinian opponents to admit that they would require someone who had blood, pus, or vomit on his clothing to wash it off before prayer, while they would not require him to wash off any of the other substances mentioned.[183]

A generation later, a *ḥadīth* enthusiast of the stature of al-Shāfiʿī argues the point purely as a critique of the underlying analogy (*qiyās*). The *sunna* indicates, he points out, that *wuḍūʾ* is necessary for a range of things coming out of the genitals or the anus, whether excrement, urine, or a fart. Everyone agrees that *wuḍūʾ* is not required for a range of things coming out of the mouth or the nose, including spit, breath, and mucus. This proves, Shāfiʿī argues, that *wuḍūʾ* is not required for nosebleeds, cupping, or anything else that does not involve something coming from the genitals or the anus. The key factor cannot be the impurity of the substance issuing forth; isn't it true that one must perform *wuḍūʾ* for a fart, even though a fart is not a substance that can make anything impure?[184]

The most detailed consideration of the emission of a substance across the boundary of the body was focused on the issue of bleeding. Interestingly, reports about the opinions of early jurists suggest the early emergence of a geographically widespread consensus on the subject. The basic rule accepted by almost all of the early scholars whose opinions are preserved is that the shedding of blood does rupture a person's state of purity (and thus require *wuḍū*ʾ), but only if the blood is actively flowing. No *wuḍū*ʾ is required if the blood is merely visible within a wound or if it is passively transferred out of the body, for instance on one's finger. Unlike the injunction to "perform *wuḍū*ʾ from that which has been touched by fire," which was a set formula gaining its force from the authoritative names with which it was associated, the principle that active bleeding required *wuḍū*ʾ seems to have been hammered out by legal thinkers who phrased it in various ways and had to work out its implications by trying out different scenarios such as nosebleeds, scrapes, and running sores.

In Kūfa, the rule was attributed to Ibrāhīm al-Nakhaʿī, in several differently worded but mutually corroborative versions.[185] Through a Syrian chain of transmission, the thought is also attributed to the Kūfans al-Shaʿbī and al-Ḥakam.[186] In Baṣra, the rule is reported from the prominent figures Qatāda,[187] al-Ḥasan al-Baṣrī,[188] and Abū Qilāba.[189] The same basic position is attributed to the towering Syrian figure Makḥūl.[190] The greatest amount of information is available on the Meccan ʿAṭāʾ ibn abī Rabāḥ. The *Muṣannaf*s of ʿAbd al-Razzāq and Ibn Abī Shayba give his opinion on a number of different specific scenarios, all converging on the principle that *wuḍū*ʾ is necessary only for blood that actively flows.[191] He is also supposed to have stipulated that this rule applies only to blood, not to pus, tears, or mucus.[192] Another Meccan figure cited on this issue is the Qurʾānic commentator Mujāhid. Here the evidence is somewhat contradictory; while one report (with a completely Meccan *isnād*) reports that he required *wuḍū*ʾ whenever blood was visible,[193] another (with a Kūfan *isnād*) claims that he held some form of the dominant opinion, making a concession for blood that did not flow out of the wound.[194] He is also supposed to have transmitted a somewhat ambiguous latitudinarian position from Abū Hurayra ("he saw no harm in a couple of drops of blood during prayer")[195] and the opinion already cited from Abū Qilāba.[196]

One notable thing about this, in general, drably uniform set of opinions is that they are attributed to a set of legal thinkers who were almost precisely contemporaneous to each other. (Here I am limiting my comments to explicit expressions of the principle involved, rather than claims that various early figures were observed behaving in specific ways.[197]) The opinion that *wuḍū*ʾ is required for dripping or flowing blood is supposed to have been explicitly enunciated, in one form or another, by eight different early legal scholars: Ibrāhīm al-Nakhaʿī (d. "four months after the death of al-Ḥajjāj [which was in 95]"), al-Shaʿbī (d. A.H. 103–10/721–29 C.E.), al-Ḥakam [ibn ʿUtayba] (d. A.H. 113–15/731–34 C.E.), al-Ḥasan al-Baṣrī (d. A.H. 110/728–29 C.E.), Qatāda [ibn Di'āma] (d. A.H. 117–18/735–37 C.E.), Abū Qilāba al-Jarmī (d. A.H. 104–7/722–26 C.E.), 'Aṭā' ibn abī Rabāḥ (d. A.H. 115/733–34 C.E.), and Makḥūl (d. A.H. 112–18/730–37 C.E.). The one early dissenting opinion is from Ṭāwus ibn Kaysān (d. A.H. 100–6/718–25 C.E.). Thus, all of the people involved died within a single period of less than twenty-five years. Despite the range of birth dates and life spans that may lie behind these dates of death, these data clearly imply that all of the individuals involved were alive at the same time. Thus, for instance, the lifetime of the last to die (Qatāda) overlapped that of the first to die (Ibrāhīm al-Nakha'ī) by thirty-two to thirty-four years.[198] Despite the discrepancy between their death dates, Qatāda can thus be considered a contemporary of Ibrāhīm, who was alive well into his adulthood. Furthermore, there were multiple strands of personal contact between the members of the group. To use Qatāda as an example once again, he is supposed to have transmitted traditions from al-Ḥasan al-Baṣrī, 'Aṭā' ibn abī Rabāḥ, Abū Qilāba al-Jarmī, and al-Sha'bī—four of the other seven members of the group.[199]

The one major counter-argument to the dominant position that flowing blood required renewal of one's ablutions seems to have originated in the Arabian Peninsula. In a report in the *Muṣannaf* 'Abd al-Razzāq, the early Medinian authority 'Urwa ibn al-Zubayr is questioned on the subject by his son:[200]

> Hishām ibn 'Urwa said: I had boils. I asked my father about them and he said, "If they stop bleeding, wash them and perform *wuḍū'*; if they do not stop bleeding, perform *wuḍū'* and pray. Do not worry if something comes out; 'Umar prayed while his wound was spouting blood."[201]

Here 'Urwa apparently combines the *fiqh* doctrine that *wuḍū'* is necessary for flowing blood, which is implied by his instructions to "wash them and perform *wuḍū'*," with a concession to necessity. His concession that it is permissible to pray while bleeding if the flow of blood is chronic may very well be based on an analogy with the case of the *mustaḥāḍa*, the "woman with an issue of blood," who may pray even while bleeding if she performs *wuḍū'*. On this level, he is not necessarily diverging from the consensus described above. However, this report introduces a vital new element into the discussion: the citation of an authoritative precedent, in this case from the second caliph, 'Umar ibn al-Khaṭṭāb. The reference, oblique but comprehensible to any well-informed Muslim, is to the final hours of 'Umar's life; 'Umar was assassinated by stabbing.

The reference to 'Umar formed the basis for the Mālikī argument that, in fact, bleeding did not cancel *wuḍū'* at all. The *Muwaṭṭa'* cites a fuller, more vivid version of the same story:

> [al-Miswar ibn Makhrama] visited ʿUmar ibn al-Khaṭṭāb after praying the dawn prayer on the night when he was stabbed. ʿUmar was awakened and they said to him, "Come, pray the dawn prayer (*al-ṣalāt al-ṣalāt li-ṣalāt al-ṣubḥ*)!" ʿUmar prayed while his wound spouted blood.[202]

Another pious anecdote sometimes used to make the same argument is found in Ibn Isḥāq's biography of the Prophet and reproduced in Ṭabarī's *Taʾrīkh al-Rusul waʾl-Mulūk.* It recounts the story of two Muslims who held watch at night during a raid in the lifetime of the Prophet. The enraged husband of a woman who has been killed by a Muslim during the raid approaches the camp during the night and spots one of the watchmen, who is performing his prayers. The attacker hits him with one arrow after another, but he merely plucks out the arrows and continues with his devotions. Only after completing his prayers does he wake his companion and inform him that he has been wounded; asked why he did not seek help earlier, he says that he was determined to finish the Qurʾānic chapter he was reciting.[203]

Both of these anecdotes are historical narratives that clearly began their career in circles other than those concerned with the technical elaboration of purity law. They have far greater power and coherence as narratives about the undaunted courage of early Muslims than as legal precedents. Even if it was accepted that the stories established that the shedding blood did not cancel *wuḍūʾ*, for instance, legal-minded Muslims were left to wonder how it was possible for the Muslim guard to pray with blood on his body and his clothes.

To summarize: the majority of the preserved reports about the opinions of early jurists on the subject of *wuḍūʾ* from bleeding suggest that their opinions were essentially examples of *raʾy* (prudential opinion). It seems most plausible to assume that the many statements requiring for *wuḍūʾ* from bleeding recorded from authorities of the late first and early second centuries A.H. were inspired primarily by overall systematic considerations. The frequent co-occurance of statements and arguments about such other bodily emissions as sweat, saliva, mucus, and tears suggests that early jurists were involved in general reflection about the underlying patterns in the law of purity.

The line of thought that coalesced in the Ḥanafī tradition explored the possibility that the underlying rationale for cancellation of *wuḍūʾ* was the emission of substances across the boundaries of the body. This logic, however, was limited by the popular recognition that some such emissions (like the shedding of tears and the exudation of sweat) did not require *wuḍūʾ*. Here, as in other cases, we presumably encounter the influence of existing practice. Jurists did not work with a clean conceptual slate; their argumentation had to introduce theoretical refinement into the framework of established assumptions. To distinguish between polluting and nonpolluting emissions they had recourse to the concept of *najāsa* (substantive impurity). However, it seems probable that this was not a completely technical concept, but a set of understood perceptions of the "dirtiness" of various kinds of bodily flux. al-Shaybānī, for instance, proves the distinction between blood or pus and sweat or tears by pointing out that his opponents would immediately instruct someone with a bloody garment to wash or change it before prayer, but not someone with a garment sullied with sweat or dampened by tears. This is less a technical argument about the purity status of the substances involved than an appeal to established practice based on shared sensibilities.

In contrast, the line of thought that coalesced in the Mālikī position rejects the transgression of the boundaries of the body as a focus of theoretical concern. By invoking images of heroically embattled early Muslims praying as their very lifeblood ebbed, they challenged the implicit ideal of the ritually pure body as integral and sealed. The image of ʿUmar at prayer with a wound spouting blood is perhaps the most dramatic affirmation imaginable that one's bodily boundaries may be dangerously porous without causing ritual impurity. As blood is also substantively impure, both technically and (presumably) in popular sensibility, attention is also diverted away from the purity status of the substances emitted. Instead, the focus of concern is on the two bodily orifices from which the known cancellers of *wuḍūʾ* (urine, feces, farts) issue forth. It is very consistent with this logic that Mālikīs also early concluded that *wuḍūʾ* was cancelled by touching either of these orifices, despite objections from their Kūfan debating partners.

Because of such deeply-rooted and theoretically significant differences in the construal of the law of purity, it may be futile to attempt theoretical readings of Islamic purity law as a whole. Like modern secular scholars, early Muslims formed and elaborated hypotheses about the overall shape and significance of the category of polluting bodily functions. Multiple construals were possible, and multiple understandings of the underlying nature of purity and pollution are expressed in the *sharīʿa*.

Conclusions

One general conclusion that we might draw from these three samples of the early Muslim debates about purity is that the late first and early second centuries A.H. seem to have been a decisive time for the development of legal doctrine. In the first two case studies, there was reason to believe that the Prophetic *ḥadīth* in question came into wide circulation sometime around the end of the first or the beginning of the second century. While the traditions in question may conceivably be authentic, in the sense that they reflect the Prophet's actual words or actions, they do not seem to have assumed a paramount role in the legal debate before this period. In the third case examined, an explicit legal consensus seems to have emerged by the end of the first century. A time frame this early would be rejected out of hand by some revisionist scholars, such as Joseph Schacht, who identifies "the beginning of the second century A.H. as the time in which [Islamic] jurisprudence started."[204] However, I believe that bringing together large numbers of reports about the ostensible opinions of early legal scholars has, in the cases I advance here, rendered a picture of early Islamic juristic development that is plausible in its general outlines and whose very coherence recommends it to our serious consideration. In the words of G.H.A. Juynboll, I would argue that "a judicious and cautiously formulated overall view of what all those early reports . . . collectively point to, may in all likelihood be taken to be not very from from the truth . . ."[205]

In the first two cases (of *wuḍū'* from cooked food and from touching the genitals), in addition to the general time frame, the relevant reports seem to suggest extensive involvement of Umayyad court circles, particularly those around the caliph ʿUmar ibn ʿAbd al-ʿAzīz. The role of members of the Umayyad dynasty in the early development of Islamic law is a vexed issue in Western scholarship. It is among Joseph Schacht's theses that many elements of the *sharīʿa* are actually rooted in Umayyad administrative practice.[206] This does not mean, however, that he accepts the authenticity of individual reports attributing rulings or (particularly) the transmission of *ḥadīth* to individual Umayyad caliphs. With respect to ʿUmar ibn ʿAbd al-ʿAzīz in particular, Schacht repeatedly makes summary judgments against the authenticity of reports about his statements.[207] Such attributions are particularly questionable, in Schacht's eyes, because of the regard ʿUmar enjoyed among later generations; he argues that "the 'pious' Umaiyad ʿUmar b. ʿAbdalʿazīz . . . became a favorite authority of Auzāʿī and the Medinese for the fictitious 'good old' practice."[208] The image of ʿUmar ibn ʿAbd al-ʿAzīz as a transmitter of *ḥadīth* is also placed in doubt by the work of Patricia Crone and Martin Hinds. In the context of a study of Umayyad caliphal ideology, they have pointed out that sources such as panegyric poetry indicate that the Umayyad caliphs understood themselves as independent sources of sacred guidance for the Muslim community whose religious stature in no way depended upon a perceived role as guardians of a specifically prophetic *sunna*.[209]

The material examined here is thus suspect for two reasons, in addition to the generally controversial nature of reports alleging to record the judicial positions of Umayyad caliphs. One is that the primary Umayyad figure involved is ʿUmar ibn ʿAbd al-ʿAzīz, the only caliph of his dynasty who would retain an aura of religious authority in the eyes of the classical tradition. Thus, at least on the basis of the identity of the authority involved, later back-projection cannot be ruled out. The second, and more important, issue is that the reports examined here conform at least roughly to the classical conception of the caliph as a guardian of the *sunna*, rather than as a source of authoritative rulings in his own right. Crone and Hinds would presumably regard this as a secondary revision of the Umayyad caliphs' role as independent religious authorities in the light of the later supremacy of the prophetic *sunna*.

Such suspicions would be particularly apposite with respect to the two reports (see pp. 117–8, 126) in which Marwān himself (the founder of the Marwānid line of the Umayyad dynasty) is represented as a royal facilitator of the Muslim community's quest for authentic reports of the Prophet's normative practice. The report in which Sulaymān ibn Hishām questions Qatāda about al-Zuhrī's enthusiasm for *wuḍū'* from cooked food (see p. 117), however, presents a more complex and perhaps more plausible picture of the state of legal development. While only the beginning of the report is relevant to the issue of *wuḍū'* from cooked food and has been quoted above, its continuation gives a broader picture of the participants' ideas about the sources of religious authority. As may be remembered, the narrative begins with Sulaymān complaining to Qatāda of al-Zuhrī's tiresome requirement that he perform ablutions after eating cooked food. Qatāda responds that he himself consulted a prominent (and now deceased) authority on the subject, and was told that performing *wuḍū'* for cooked food does not cancel a person's ablutions. Sulaymān is thus presented with two conflicting statements by authoritative legal scholars; he decides to resolve the matter by consulting a third authority and is referred to ʿAṭā'. ʿAṭā's answer is that one of his own authorities saw an early caliph (Abū Bakr) eat cooked food and pray without performing ablutions.

In the continuation of the narrative, Sulaymān asks Qatāda, "What is our opinion (*mā taqūlu*) about grants for life (*al-ʿumrā*)? Qatāda responds with a *ḥadīth* of the Prophet supported by a full chain of transmission. al-Zuhrī then interjects a conflicting opinion, apparently on his own authority. Sulaymān—again faced with two conflicting scholarly opinions—asks ʿAṭā' for his view; ʿAṭā' replies with another report from his previous authority (Jābir) confirming Qatāda's statement about the Prophet's ruling on this subject. At this point, al-Zuhrī objects, "The caliphs/commanders do not make this ruling (*inna'l-umarā'/al-khulafā' lā yaqḍūna bi-dhālika*)!" ʿAṭā' responds, "ʿAbd al-Malik made this ruling in the case of such-and-such (*kadhā wa-kadhā*)!"[210]

In light of classical legal theory, it would be nonsense for al-Zuhrī (who is apparently unable to ground his position in a statement traceable to the Prophet) to respond to a *ḥadīth* complete with chain of transmission by objecting that caliphs do not make the ruling in question. In the context of this narrative, however, ʿAṭā' finds the objection completely apposite, and responds with evidence in the same spirit: the precedent of the Marwānid caliph ʿAbd al-Malik. The importance of caliphal example is also implied by ʿAṭā's first transmitted text, which involves the practice of the caliph Abū Bakr. The implied theoretical background of this debate is an eclectic or transitional position in which scholarly transmission of oral texts from the Prophet and reference to the authoritative actions of the ruling dynasty are alternative and coexisting frames of reference. In its very messiness, I would argue, this picture is quite plausible. It may reflect a point in transition from one theory of religious authority to another, the interaction of varying views of religious authority arising from different circles, or both. In general, both the density of references to ʿUmar and his contemporaries and the wealth of historically plausible detail contained in the reports suggests that this material is at least largely based in fact. This conclusion aligns with that of G.H.A. Juynboll, who argues that ʿUmar's reign marks the beginning of historically discernible caliphal involvement in the dissemination of prophetic *sunna*, the theory and practice of which had been merely embryonic before that time.[211]

Insofar as the Umayyad references are considered credible, the material examined here confirms one of the inferences drawn by Crone and Hinds: that, given that Umayyad ideology gave the caliph far more than merely an administrative role, we should expect to see caliphal interventions in areas apparently unrelated to the practical concerns of statecraft. Interestingly, however, Crone herself suggests that there is an "almost total absence of Umayyad caliphs from early Ḥadīth on ritual law."[212] This absence is to be attributed to secondary revision; it "is thus likely to mean that it was in this field that their legal competence was first rejected."[213] Further examination of archaic debates in ritual law may be expected to turn up more material of this kind; on the basis of the present material alone, it may be hypothesized that caliphal involvement in the development of ritual law was considerable, but that this involvement was—at least by the Marwānid period—far more complex than the unilateral imposition of explicitly caliphal directives.

Through the anecdotes about early debates such as those surrounding cooked food, touching the genitals, and bleeding, we can dimly discern an archaic stage at which even the basic lineaments of the idea of purity were still largely undefined. Consider the statement of Saʿīd ibn al-Musayyab elicited by the Umayyad prince Sulaymān ibn Hishām: "When you eat it it is pure (*ṭayyib*) and you are not obligated to perform *wuḍūʾ* from it; when it comes out it is impure (*khabīth*) and you are obligated to perform *wuḍūʾ* from it." Like the similar statement attributed to Ibn Masʿūd, this is a very elementary generalization that represents a necessary first stage in theoretical consideration of the causes of impurity in Islamic law: it is related to the expulsion of substances from the body. This basic conceptualization would very naturally lead to other questions that are in fact recorded to have been discussed by the generation of scholars that flourished at the turn of the first to second century A.H., such as the issue of *wuḍūʾ* from bleeding.

We can also discern in such reports an archaic terminology of purity. Instead of using the technical terminology that later predominates in discussions of ritual purity (*ṭāhir* and *najis*), for instance, the formula attributed to Saʿīd ibn al-Musayyib uses two Qurʾānic terms (*ṭayyib* and *khabīth*) that are far broader and more multivalent. This is the same terminology we encounter in the anecdotes about the purity practices of ʿUmar ibn ʿAbd al-ʿAzīz. As we have seen in the case of ʿUmar, this Qurʾānic terminology fits into a broader ethical and cosmological schema than that invoked by the classical law of ritual purity. A phrase such as *mā massat al-nār* similarly draws on a Qurʾānic terminology that is inextricably linked to eschatological narratives. The religious ideas evoked by the debate over cooked food, which map the opposition of pure and polluted directly onto the ethical and eschatological dichotomies of permitted and forbidden, heaven and hell, can occasionally also be glimpsed in reports about other archaic purity debates. One early source, reporting on the debate surrounding the permissibility of using sea water for ablutions, states:

> It is reported from ʿAbd Allāh ibn ʿUmar that he used to say, "This is a sea; below it are seven (other) seas, and below them are the Fires [of Hell]." He used to forbid people to perform *wuḍūʾ* with sea water.[214]

To say that such terminology and such understandings of the law of purity are archaic is not necessarily to imply that they are "original." As we have seen, some of the arguments that display these features may have been innovative in their time. However, they are archaic in the sense that they must have preceded the full elaboration and entrenchment of a separate and technical juristic vocabulary for the analysis of issues of purity. After the basic terminology and structure of the juristic understanding of purity law were established, fundamentally variant understandings were excluded. Later Muslims, such as Ṣūfīs, who wished to reintegrate purity law into larger ethical and eschatological discourses did so as a secondary symbolic elaboration of an established framework.

Chapter 4

Substantive Impurity and the Boundaries of Society

The Fluidity of the Law

Debates over "cancelers of *wuḍūʾ*" focused on the frontiers of the individual Muslim body, examining how various bodily functions or fluxes might affect its purity status. The inevitable and quotidian nature of many of these "cancelers" meant that each believer must pass through the cycle of pollution and purification on a daily basis, if not more often. The transient nature of such pollutions and the routine ease of their ritual reversal made the alternation of purity states into a background rhythm of ritual life, one that could be slowed by devotional exercises such as fasting and vigils but never definitively halted. The Islamic law of ritual purity, however, recognizes not only such secondary and cyclical purity states but fundamental and stable purity statuses. While a believer alternates daily or hourly between the purity required for prayer and the pollution that precludes it, some substances and living beings are permanently categorized as impure and defiling. In classical legal terminology, this status is known as *najāsa*. To draw distinctions between that which is *najis*—substantively and inherently impure—and that which is fundamentally pure (although perhaps experiencing temporary states of pollution) is to draw abiding classificatory barriers between different groups of substances, animals, and (potentially) people.

In the Sunnī tradition, such questions are far less extensively and comprehensively treated in traditional legal compilations than those relating to polluting bodily functions. The major motivating thrust of Islamic legal discourse has always been toward the definition and documentation of forms of right action, rather than toward the theoretical elaboration of abstract systems. Accordingly, early classical legal works with sections on ritual purity (for example, the *Muwaṭṭa*ʾ of Mālik, the *Umm* of al-Shāfiʿī) subdivide their treatment of the topic into sections corresponding to the various types of ablution: a section on *wuḍū*ʾ and the bodily functions that occasion it, one on *ghusl* and the bodily functions that occasion it, and one on *tayammum* (ablutions performed with dust in the absence of water). While there may be a subsection devoted to the qualifications of water used for ablution (*al-miyāh*) or to the removal of substantive impurities (*najāsa*) from the body or the clothing, in general early compilations never systematically address the question of the nature of substantive impurity or enumerate the substances regarded as impure. Attitudes towards substantive impurity do emerge from the content of specific arguments within this format, although the question is rarely addressed frontally.

Perhaps because questions of substantive purity are frequently interstitial, with systematic principles emerging only obliquely from comments on concrete issues of purity practice, significant issues in this subject area in some cases remained unresolved through the classical period and into the present. It is often assumed that with the crystallization of the four classical schools of law the Islamic system of ritual purity (like other areas of the law) achieved a state of synthesis and stability marred only by insignificant points of disagreement among the four schools. Islamic law of the classical period and beyond has traditionally been regarded as stable, if not static; while more recent research has demonstrated that there was a significant degree of dynamism and change up to the modern period in certain areas of the law, such as land tenure and taxation,[1] ritual law has generally been excluded from this new picture of a fluid and protean Sharīʿa. It has generally been assumed, at least tacitly, that ritual law is immune from the practical pressures to which other areas of the law are subject, and thus that Muslim ritual practices can be described equally well by texts from any period subsequent to the emergence of the canonical schools. Similarly, differences in ritual practice among the four schools have been assumed to be matters of detail, significant only in their role as marks of school identity.

In this chapter, on the contrary, I will argue that the law of ritual purity was neither unified nor frozen in the classical period. There were, as this chapter will demonstrate, various areas in which the earliest comprehensive works of Islamic law reflected (or established) more or less universal consensus regarding the basic shape and meaning of the law of ritual purity—consensus that, in many cases, is surprising in light of the sources on which the law is based. Nevertheless, significant points of disagreement remained. Furthermore, some issues (such as the purity status of human corpses) were never definitively resolved even within individual schools. These interschool debates and chronological developments were not, as has frequently been implied, trivialities that served only to fuel the hairsplitting debates of effete jurists. Instead, they addressed some of the most fundamental questions relating to the shape and significance of the law of purity. Like the early controversies described in previous chapters, these evolving opinions probed and transformed the semantics of the law.

The emergence of a juristic understanding of the concept of *najāsa* (substantive impurity) involved the examination of two major questions. One of these questions involved the relationship between this form of impurity and the passing states of pollution experienced by believers as a result of their bodily functions. As will be clear from the discussion of the Qurʾānic provisions pertaining to ritual purity in chapters 1 and 2, the Qurʾānic material on the subject focuses overwhelmingly on states of personal pollution, the bodily functions that occasion them, and the ritual processes by which they can be reversed. The sole Qurʾānic use of the root that became the technical legal term for substantive impurity, *n-j-s*, refers not to an inanimate substance but to nonbelieving humans, and (as will be discussed below, pp. 157–64) was almost universally understood by early jurists to be metaphorical. The Qurʾān did refer to several physical substances (shed blood, pork, and wine) in terms understood to refer to ritual impurity,[2] but provided no indication of the ritual consequences of contact with these substances. If one came in contact with shed blood that had not issued from one's own body, was one obliged to perform ablutions? Merely to remove the blood? The Qurʾānic references did not address these questions, nor did the available *ḥadīth* texts clarify the issue completely. Conversely, it remained to be determined to what extent the states of personal pollution occasioning the ablutions described in the Qurʾān should be understood to imply the presence of substantive impurity analogous to that attributed to pigs or blood. Most obviously, many wondered whether water used for ablutions was assumed to have removed some form of substantive impurity and thus itself should be considered impure.

The second issue examined by jurists striving to define the concept of *najāsa* related to the basic category distinctions that structure the system of ritual purity as a whole. Like the rules governing most areas of human activity, from kinship to food preparation, the strictures of ritual purity may be regarded as constituting (among other things) a system of classification. This system of classification is based on a limited number of distinctions or oppositions, to which it draws attention and which must be observed in order to deploy the rules correctly. On this level, the system of ritual purity may be compared to the grammar of a language. In order to conjugate a verb in English, one must place it on the axes of person, number, and tense. In many other languages, one must also place it with regard to gender. In yet other languages, one must observe further distinctions which are completely unknown to the grammar of Indo-European languages; a verb's conjugation may, for instance, vary according to the shape or size of the subject of the action. Furthermore, a given category distinction may be given greater or lesser prominence in a system where it is observed. English has masculine and feminine pronouns referring to sexual beings; French has grammatical gender for inanimate objects; while, on the other extreme, Persian (like Turkish) has no grammatical gender at all. "He," "she," and "it," are all expressed by the same pronoun ("*u*"); gender can only be expressed through semantics (" '*u*' is my mother"), never through grammar.

In linguistics, of course, it is not (or is no longer) accepted that the category distinctions imposed by the morphology of a language determine the perceptions or cognition of its speakers. Iranian society is no less rigorously gendered for Persian's lack of masculine and feminine pronouns. A system such as Islamic law, however, differs from a language in that it is explicitly value-laden and prescriptive. In the terminology of Clifford Geertz, it is a model for, as well as a model of, social practice. The imposition of social categories is one of the main idioms in which Islamic law speaks to Muslims. Independently of the content of its requirements, the law speaks volumes by its divisions of the society which acknowledges it and of the cosmos within which it functions.

Terse as the Qurʾānic treatment of the subject of ritual purity is, it does seem to reflect several category distinctions that might well have emerged as basic structural principles of the Islamic law of ritual purity. One of these is gender; both verse 2:222, which requires men to "avoid women" when they are menstruating, and verses 4:43 and 5:6, which require them to perform ablutions after they have "touched women," suggest that the female sex is a major focus of concerns about pollution. Although no other category distinction is invoked as prominently as gender, the handful of Qurʾānic verses dealing with ritual purity suggest two other category distinctions that might have been taken as fundamental to the system: faith versus unbelief, and life versus death. The importance of the category distinction between believers and nonbelievers is, of course, suggested by verse 9:28's statement that "the unbelievers are unclean (*najas*)." While the Qurʾān's short list of food prohibitions consists primarily of individual items (such as pigs) that establish no clear categorical principles, the prohibition on "dead things" (*mayta*, technically defined as things that have expired without the benefit of ritual slaughtering; see verses 2:173, 5:3, 6:145, 16:115) suggests a general principle that—in the absence of special ritual interventions—death is a cause of pollution.

The selection and comparative emphasis of category distinctions within the system of purity was inextricably intertwined with the evolving definition of the concept of substantive impurity. Each of the category distinctions discussed above arguably involved the concept of substantive impurity, and each at least potentially pertained to human beings. If "touching women" canceled one's ablutions, it might well be inferred that women were substantively impure—at least with respect to men. Nonbelieving humans are Qurʾānically described with the very term (*najas*) that came to be the technical designation for substantive impurity. While the Qurʾānic references to carrion appear in the context of food prohibitions, and thus presumably relate to animals that would be appropriate for eating if properly slaughtered, the rule that dead bodies are impure could obviously be understood to include human corpses—all the more so since human beings are never ritually slaughtered and thus always technically "carrion."

The development that I wish to trace in this chapter is the process by which the concept of substantive impurity was separated from that of personal pollution, leading to a consistent denial by mainstream Sunnīs that human beings were ever substantively impure. The female, the infidel, and the dead were all cleared of the stigma of substantive impurity at the outset of the classical period. The idea of the inherent substantive purity of the human person was further elaborated in subsequent centuries, resulting in a postclassical synthesis of the law that was both humanistic and universalistic to a remarkable degree. Nevertheless, individual legal schools retained distinctive positions on subordinate matters that continued to generate meaningful differences in the semantics of the law.

Women, Nonbelievers, and the Dead

There is evidence in the early sources that some of the legally-concerned elements within the first generations of Muslims actively considered the idea that women were in some sense ritually polluting. Although not explicitly framed in an exegetical form, the debate on this subject was probably inspired at least in part by the Qurʾānic requirement that the (implicitly male) believer perform *wuḍūʾ* after "touching women." Many early legal opinions and reports about the practice of prominent early figures address the question whether direct physical contact with women required one to renew one's ablutions. As discussed in detail in chapter 2, opinions were divided; while some early jurists (primarily of the school of Ibn ʿAbbās) chose to construe the wording of verses 4:43 and 5:6 as a euphemistic reference to sexual intercourse, others embraced the literal interpretation that literally "touching" a woman rendered one ritually polluted.

This line of thought led to further questions. Early jurists wondered whether, if physical contact with women indeed required a man to renew his ablutions, women could transmit pollution to other substances such as water. Traces of this early debate are reflected in chapters in such early compilations as the *Muṣannaf*s of ʿAbd al-Razzāq[3] and Ibn Abī Shayba[4] addressing such questions as whether one can drink or perform ablutions with water from which a woman has drunk or with which she has made her own ablutions (*suʾr al-marʾa, faḍl al-marʾa*). The context as well as the content of these selections of reports indicate the line of thought being pursued, which ranged women among a set of animals that were deemed impure or whose purity status was doubtful; in the *Muṣannaf* of ʿAbd al-Razzāq, the chapter on "water from which a woman has drunk" follows chapters on "dogs lapping from vessels," "water from which a cat has drunk," and "water from which riding animals (*dawābb*) have drunk." The very existence of these chapters indicates that at least some early Muslims contemplated the possibility that women per se were contagiously impure;[5] substantive conclusions on the permissibility of ablutions with water already used by a woman varied.[6] Again, the position vindicating the purity of women is most outspokenly represented by the school of Ibn ʿAbbās. Just as Ibn ʿAbbās is represented as identifying "touching women" as intercourse, thus excluding mere physical contact with women as a source of pollution, he is reported to have denied that there is anything wrong with water previously used by a woman: "She has cleaner clothes [than a man], and smells better (*hiya anẓaf thiyāban wa-aṭyab rīḥan*)."[7]

In the absence of systematic expositions of the system of ritual purity from the earliest period, it is probably impossible to reconstruct the precise understanding of the ritual purity status of women that underlay the opinion that "touching women" rendered a man impure in the minds of early jurists. The questions asked by some of these early scholars clearly reflect understandings of the nature of impurity that are different from, and more fluid than, the ones that came to prevail by the classical period. As we will discuss in greater detail below, in the classical understanding of the law of ritual purity there came to be a sharp distinction between states of pollution experienced by human beings, which are counteracted by appropriate ablutions, and the status of substantive impurity, which is irreversible.[8] As the fundamental lineaments of the system of ritual purity came into focus, the idea that women might be in some sense substantively impure became incoherent; such an assumption would have made nonsense of the fact that female believers purified themselves for prayer.

However, in the earlier period such distinctions were not as clear. In the earliest period of the development of the Islamic law of ritual purity there seems to have been a certain ambiguity and interchangeability in the use of the concepts of *janāba* (the state of sexual pollution experience by human beings) and *najāsa* (the status of substantive impurity). Thus, for instance, Qatāda is supposed to have glossed the word "*najas*" in the Qurʾān, verse 9:28, as "*janāba*" or "*ajnāb*."[9] It was similarly initially unclear whether sexual pollution affected only the person who had originally incurred it or in some sense rendered him or her an "impure substance" with respect to other believers; some early Muslims seem to have worried that persons suffering from major pollution might be contageously impure. This concern was addressed, and largely dispelled, by a formula establishing that the two categories of pollution were distinct: "A believer is never substantively impure (*"laysa yanjasu' l-mu' min"* or *"inna' l-mu' min lā yanjasu"*).[10] While al-Shāfiʿī neither identifies this formula as a *ḥadīth* nor supplies it with an *isnād*,[11] al-Bukhārī presents it as a *ḥadīth* in which the Prophet reassures a man who hesitates to shake hands with him due to his state of sexual pollution.[12] Similarly, ʿAbd al-Razzāq trasmits a report in which Ibn ʿAbbās states, "A garment does not become sexually impure; the ground does not become sexually impure; a man who is touched by a[nother] man who is sexually impure does not become sexually impure; water does not become sexually impure . . . (*laysa ʿalā' l-thawb janāba wa-lā ʿalā' l-arḍ janāba wa-lā ʿalā' l-rajul yamassuhu' l-junub janāba wa-laysa ʿalā' l-mā' janāba*)."[13] In another tradition recorded in the *Musnad* of Aḥmad ibn Ḥanbal, ʿĀʾisha reports that she and the Prophet used to perform *ghusl* from the same vessel of water and notes, "We were both sexually impure, but water does not become sexually impure (*innā la-junubān wa-lakinna' l-mā' lā yajnabu*)."[14] The idea that personal pollution, including *janāba*, was a phenomenon distinct from substantive impurity (*najāsa*) was thus not intuitively obvious to everyone, but had to be explicitly established. Early speculation that appears to reflect concern about the substantive purity status of women thus probably belongs to a time before the disjunction between personal and substantive impurity was definitively established.

[margin note: Distinction of sexual & inherent impure]

Perhaps the most important question that the recorded early opinions leave in suspension is whether the rules in this area were considered to be reciprocal—that is, whether touching a man was considered by these same jurists to render a woman impure. This is, in fact, a question that is left unanswered by the Qurʾānic text itself. The earliest jurists on record as supporting the position that "touching women" canceled one's state of ritual purity were concerned specifically with the problem of men touching women; the problem of the purity status of the woman as it affected her own readiness to engage in prayer does not seem to have been addressed. Either they considered the rule to be a nonreciprocal one applying only to women, or they assumed that their listeners shared a tacit understanding that rules stated in androcentric terms in fact applied to both sexes. Ibn Abī Shayba records a rare report representing an early jurist as explicitly addressing the question of reciprocity. The following opinion is ascribed to Ḥammād (probably Ḥammād ibn abī Sulaymān, d. A.H. 119–20/737–38 C.E.[15]):

If a man kisses his wife without her volition (*wa-hiya lā turīdu dhālika*), only he is obliged to perform *wuḍūʾ*; she is not obliged

> to perform *wuḍūʾ*. If she kisses him, only she is obliged to perform *wuḍūʾ* and not he. If he feels pleasure (*shahwa*), he is obliged to perform *wuḍūʾ*. If he kisses her without her volition and she feels pleasure, she is [similarly] obliged to perform *wuḍūʾ*.[16]

The question of reciprocity relates not only to the symmetry of the rule regarding "touching women," but to its underlying rationale. A construal of the rule limiting its application to men who touch women lends itself to an interpretation based on a concept of substantive impurity applying specifically to women. As we have seen, this is in fact a line of reasoning that was pursued by some early jurists who wondered whether impurity was transmitted to other substances, such as water, coming into contact with the bodies of women. A reciprocal understanding of the rule, in contrast, is not conducive to this approach. Although many early jurists may tacitly have assumed that women should perform ablutions after touching men, there is no evidence that anyone ever explored the assumption that men were substantively impure. Instead, a reciprocal understanding of the rule suggested that the source of pollution was not the body of either of the individuals concerned, but the act of touching itself. This inference established a parallel between the act of "touching women" and the other acts requiring the renewal of one's *wuḍūʾ* ablutions, all of which are bodily functions one has oneself performed rather than instances of contagion by another person or substance. What is envisioned is not a quality of substantive impurity inherent in bodies of either sex, but a quality of pollution ascribed to heterosexual contact. In Ḥammād's construal of the rule, cited above, there are two causal factors involved: initiative or intent (here, *irāda*) and sexual pleasure or desire (*shahwa*). They seem to operate independently: one is polluted by heterosexual contact if one initiates it—even, apparently, if it turns out not to be pleasurable—and if it is pleasurable, even if one did not initiate it.

Although the precise causal factor involved in the rule continued to be debated, the reciprocal understanding of the rule was apparently well established by the beginning of the classical period. al-Shāfiʿī makes the point in detail:

> If a man touches a part of the body of a woman directly with his hand or part of his body, without any barrier between them, with or without (sexual) desire, he is required to perform *wuḍūʾ* and so is she. The same applies if she touches him; both of them must perform *wuḍūʾ*. In all of this, it is immaterial which of their bodies directly touches the other's, whether he directly touches her skin or she directly touches his with part of her skin. If he directly touches her hair with his hand without touching her skin he is not required to perform *wuḍūʾ*, regardless of whether he did

> it with or without (sexual) desire—just as, if he desires her without touching her, he is not required to perform *wuḍū'*. Desire has no effect, because it is in the heart and the effect depends on the action; hair is different from skin. (He said): If he were to perform *wuḍū'* when he touched her hair as a pious precaution (*law iḥtāṭa*), it would be preferable to me.[17]

On certain fundamental points of the law relating to the rationale behind *wuḍū'* from "touching women," almost universal agreement prevailed by the outset of the classical period. All jurists were agreed in rejecting the possibility that women were in any sense substantively impure. The majority agreed that the necessity to renew one's *wuḍū'* ablutions after "touching women" arose from the act of (hetero)sexual touching and applied symmetrically to members of either sex.[18] Nevertheless, the law continued to be elaborated in symbolically potent ways within the various schools of law. Not only did differences of interpretation persist between the individual schools of law, but these variant understandings of the law reflected and in turn imposed different understandings of the individual's social environment and the ways in which it was charged with sexual desire. Let us summarize the majority opinions of the classical schools.[19]

According to the Shāfiʿīs, *wuḍū'* is canceled by skin-to-skin contact between a man and a woman who are not sufficiently closely related to preclude marriage. Any barrier between the two, be it only a thick layer of dust, prevents the cancelation of *wuḍū'*. This rule applies regardless of whether either party acted out of desire or experienced pleasure, and even if the touching occurred completely inadvertently. The person touched must be in principle desirable (*yushtahā*), but this category is defined in the broadest possible terms: a man's *wuḍū'* is canceled even if he touches a "hideous crone (*ʿajūz shawhā'*)." (In support of this ruling, it is argued that although a man does not usually experience pleasure when touching an aged and repulsive woman, in principle it is conceivable to take pleasure in her as long as she is alive.) In contrast, a man cannot cancel his *wuḍū'* by touching another man, even if the individual involved is a "handsome prepubescent youth" (*amrad jamīl*), although it is *sunna* (a commendable practice in the spirit of the Prophet's example) to renew one's ablutions in such a case. Similarly, women cannot cancel their *wuḍū'* by touching other women; a hermaphrodite cannot cancel his or her *wuḍū'* by touching anyone at all. All Shāfiʿites agree that the *wuḍū'* of the person performing the act of touching is canceled; there is a difference of opinion about someone who passively is touched, with some members of the school holding that his or her *wuḍū'* is canceled and others denying it.

The Mālikīs hold that touching cancels *wuḍū'* if the person touched is one who would normally give (sexual) pleasure (*yultadhdhu bihi ʿādatan*), but only on the condition that the person performing the act of touching either intends to experience pleasure or in fact experiences it. *Wuḍūʾ* is canceled if the person performing the touch seeks pleasure, even if he or she does not experience it, and if he or she experiences it, even if no such intention existed. Under these conditions, *wuḍūʾ* is canceled even if there is a barrier, such as a garment, between the two. The category of people who would "normally" be desired is defined somewhat more narrowly than among the Shāfiʿīs; thus, touching a woman does not cancel *wuḍūʾ* if she is old enough to be repellent to the ordinary person. On the other hand, the touching need not be between persons of opposite sexes; under the stated conditions, *wuḍūʾ* is canceled by a man touching another man or by a woman touching another woman. Contact between parts of the body that have no sensation, like the hair or fingernails, does not cancel *wuḍūʾ*. Kissing on the mouth always cancels *wuḍūʾ*, even if no pleasure is intended or received. Kisses of compassion or farewell (presumably on other parts of the face or body) cancel *wuḍūʾ* only if sexual pleasure is involved.

Finally,[20] the Ḥanafī position is that touching does not cancel *wuḍūʾ*, even if it is between the full bodies of a naked man and women, unless their genitals touch or the man experiences a pre-ejaculatory emission. The holding that *wuḍūʾ* is canceled by genital contact even if the man experiences no emission is considered an example of *istiḥsān*—that is, a prudential exception to a general principle.

As we see from this exposition of the dominant opinions within the various schools of law, each of them has selected different key factors in determining the purity implications of skin-to-skin touching (*mulāmasa*, *lams*). One difference lies in the different degrees of emphasis placed, on the one hand, upon pollution construed as an automatic consequence of an external act and, on the other hand, upon pollution construed essentially as an intrapsychic phenomenon generated by subjective factors of experience and desire. The Shāfiʿī view, essentially shared by the Ḥanafīs and Ḥanbalīs, tends to emphasize the external and objective (the gender of the individuals involved) over the internal and subjective (the presence or absence of sexual enjoyment). This emphasis does not necessarily imply that the pollution incurred is itself external and objective. As we shall see below, Shāfiʿī himself argues that rituals of cleansing as well as the states of personal pollution that required them are essentially the arbitrary decrees of an inscrutable God. Ritual impurity of the human person (in contrast, for instance, to the impurity of excrement or blood), in his view, is not "real" in the sense of having a correlate in the physical world. Nevertheless, in the Shāfiʿī, Ḥanafī, and Ḥanbalī interpretation of the rules relating to "touching," God's decrees in this area are taken to refer primarily to concrete external actions.

In contrast, the Mālikī approach to the rule focuses attention on the subjective erotic charge of the act. Although Mālikīs, like Shāfiʿīs and Ḥanbalīs, require that some external action be involved ("touching" excludes pure fantasy or visual fondling), the polluting or neutral quality of a touch is determined by the active and passive participants' sexual enjoyment. Indeed, it would seem that to some extent the pursuit of sexual pleasure is the essential "act" involved; by anticipating pleasure from the touch, the passive partner is considered to become active: "As for the person being touched, if he . . . intends to experience pleasure, he is considered to be [actively] performing the act of touching (*ṣāra lāmisan*)," presumably even if he is physically immobile. By excluding some acts that fit the physical requirements of polluting "touch" yet are nonerotic in intent and experienced as such (for instance, kisses of compassion and farewell), the Mālikī interpretation of the rules relating to "touching" focuses attention on the examination and disciplining of one's subjective erotic urges.

With respect to their categorization of the possible objects of the act of touching, the various schools of law construct different divisions of the sociosexual world of the individual (male) Muslim. The Shāfiʿī interpretation of the rules divides the believer's social environment starkly into two categories, men and women. Physical contact between members of the two categories are symbolically sexualized, regardless of the age or attractiveness of the individuals involved. The only cross-gender touching that is not eroticized is that occurring between close blood relatives (or women who are permanently prohibited as marriage partners through milk-sisterhood or affinage). Conversely, physical contact between members of the same gender category is desexualized—despite the sexual pleasure that may be experienced or desired from contact with a person of the same sex. The Mālikī view, in keeping with its greater emphasis on subjective erotic experience, makes a more nuanced division. It desexualizes contact with aged women (and, one assumes, also men), simultaneously acknowledging that physical contact between members of the two sexes is not in all circumstances erotic and establishing certain expectations or assumptions about the sexuality of the old. It also blurs the stark heterosexual categorization advanced by the Shāfiʿīs, regarding some men as the potential objects of male sexual desire.[21]

Another category of human bodies that suffered the suspicion of impurity in the preclassical period comprised the bodies of the dead. Here again, the understanding that human corpses were substantively impure in the technical sense would create a logical rupture in the system of ritual purity as it came to be understood.[22] Just as the hypothesis that women were substantively impure threatened to make nonsense of the ablutions of female Muslims, the idea that Muslim corpses were impure stood in obvious tension with the universally recognized requirement that they be washed before interment. Here again, however, it must be remembered that the basic outlines of the system of impurity were far more fluid in the early period. The practice of washing corpses apparently did not prevent early Muslims, like members of many other religious communities, from viewing contact with corpses as a source of pollution. Thus, it seems that many early Muslims both understood it to be necessary to wash corpses before burial and assumed that it was necessary for the person who had washed a corpse in turn to perform full ablutions *(ghusl).*

The practice of performing *ghusl* after washing a corpse is supported by a number of reports from figures of the first two generations; in some cases, the requirement is traced back to the Prophet himself.[23] However, the rule was also widely questioned. It may be that the practice of performing the major ablution after touching a corpse in the course of its preparation of burial was a preexisting custom that persisted in the Islamic period; whatever its origin, it seems to have been quite well entrenched in the early Muslim community. A number of traditions both reflect the existence of the practice and attempt to deny its necessity, like this story recorded in the *Muwaṭṭa'* of Mālik:

> Asmā' bint ʿUmays, the wife of Abū Bakr al-Ṣiddīq, reported that she washed Abū Bakr when he died. She said to the Emigrants who were with her, "I am fasting, and this is an extremely cold day. Am I obliged to perform *ghusl* (*hal ʿalayya min ghusl*)?" They said, "No."[24]

While Mālik's tradition explicitly states only that ablutions may be omitted under duress, it gently implies that they are in any case not obligatory. Many reports attack the requirement for *ghusl* after washing the dead much more vigorously and more directly. This opposition to the practice was grounded in an important consideration of principle. An obligation to perform *ghusl* after touching a corpse entailed more than the possibility of inconvenient exposure to water in circumstances of bodily weakness or insalubrious weather. For many people, the practice's implicit suggestion that the corpse was substantively impure was insulting to the deceased companions and relatives they were laying to rest. A number of reports, attributed to several different early jurists and to the Prophet himself, thus ground their denial of the necessity of the practice explicitly in a protest against the implication that the bodies of the believers' dead are impure.[25] Opposition to the requirement for *ghusl* after washing a corpse finds expression in a series of anecdotes in which early legal authorities such as Ibn ʿAbbās, Ibn Masʿūd, Ibn ʿUmar, Ibrāhīm [al-Nakhaʿī], and Abū'l-Shaʿthā',[26] questioned about the practice, deny its necessity simply by pointing out that it implies that the dead are impure. Their replies range from cool understatement ("If your friend [*ṣāḥib*] is impure, then wash"[27]) to impassioned ridicule ("Do you not fear God? You wash from [touching] your dead; are they impure (*a-anjās hum*)??!"[28]).

Another expression of opposition to the practice of *ghusl* after washing the dead is the formula, cited above, used to deny the substantive impurity of persons suffering from sexual pollution: "A believer (or: a Muslim) is never substantively impure (*lā yanjasu*)." In the context of the controversy over ablutions after washing a corpse, the formula is sometimes extended to address the problem more explicitly: "A believer is never substantively impure, alive or dead."[29] Finally, the Prophet was credited with the simple injunction, "Do not deem your dead impure (*lā tunajjisū mawtākum*)." Significantly, neither al-Bukhārī nor al-Shāfiʿī sees fit to supply an *isnād* for one of these dicta. Al-Bukhārī attributes the first formula, without *isnād*s, both to the Prophet and to Ibn ʿAbbās.[30] Al-Shāfiʿī not only declines to offer an *isnād* for the second formula, but seems reluctant to accept its content:

> I prefer that [someone who washes a corpse] perform *ghusl*; I do not consider it obligatory—God knows best. *Ḥadīth* denying that it is necessary to perform *ghusl* have been transmitted, including [the statement] "Do not treat your dead as impure (*lā tunajjisū mawtākum*)."[31]

The welter of statements by early jurists and the paucity of *ḥadīth* involved in this particular controversy suggest that the question of the ritual purity status of corpses was addressed rather late and remained open at the start of the classical period. The idea that corpses were ritually impure was probably an old and well-established idea that surprised no one until reflection on the unique status of believing human beings in Islamic theology led some Muslims to question it. My tentative reconstruction of the development of doctrine on this point is that the practice of performing full ablutions after washing a corpse prevailed unchallenged until, at some relatively late point, systematic reflection on the system of ritual purity focused attention on the implicit assumption that deceased believers were polluting and deemed it an affront to the dignity of the dead.

The final category of human beings placed under the suspicion of substantive impurity by the Qurʾānic text was, of course, nonbelievers. In the light of the emergence of the root *n-j-s* as a technical term for substantive impurity, verse 9:28 of the Qurʾān raised the question of the substantive purity status of nonbelievers too urgently to be ignored.[32] The very formula that served to free the bodies of believers from the imputation of substantive impurity, dead or alive, simultaneously reflected or promoted the idea that nonbelievers might indeed be substantively impure. It is almost certainly no coincidence that the formula used to create the definitive disjuncture between passing states of personal pollution and the permanent status of substantive impurity is "a *believer* is never substantively impure (*innaʾl-muʾmin lā yanjasu*)." There is a clear and pointed symmetry between this categorical statement and the converse Qurʾānic statement that "polytheists are unclean/ impure (*innamāʾl-mushrikūna najas*)."[33] One cause of the incredulous sarcasm with which early jurists greeted the implication that the bodies of deceased believers were impure was very likely that they understood substantive impurity to be supremely the attribute and the shame of nonbelievers. The argument that dead believers were not impure did not necessarily imply the same of other human corpses, as indicated in this report:

> Saʿīd ibn Jubayr said: I asked Ibn ʿUmar, "Should I perform *ghusl* from [touching] a dead person?" He said, "Was he a believer (*a-muʾmin huwa*)?" I said, "I hope so!" He said, "Wipe yourself off (*tamassaḥ*) from [touching] a [dead] believer; do not perform *ghusl* from [touching] him."[34]

The idea that nonbelievers were ritually impure was one that apparently enjoyed acceptance from some early Muslims in the community at large, and not merely among legal scholars. The *Sīra* of Ibn Isḥāq, the original recension of which dates from the first half of the second century A.H., includes a number of anecdotes reflecting this assumption and the avoidance behaviors to which it apparently gave rise. A Muslim named ʿĀṣim is said to have "taken God to witness that he would never let a polytheist touch him or touch a polytheist, out of fear of pollution (*tanajjusan*)."[35] The same avoidance is indicated in an anecdote about a visit by the arch-polytheist Abū Sufyān to a daughter of his who is married to the Prophet Muḥammad:

> Abū Sufyān . . . went in to visit his daughter Umm Ḥabība bint Abī Sufyān. He was about to sit on the Prophet's mat; she rolled it up so he would not sit on it. He said, "My girl, I don't know whether you think the mat is too good for me, or that I am too good for it!" She said, "It is the Prophet's mat, and you are an impure polytheist (*mushrik najis*); I did not want you to sit on the Prophet's mat." He said, "By God, you have fallen on evil days since you left me."[36]

Other anecdotes in the *Sīra*, however, suggest that the impurity imputed to polytheists was not an irreducible attribute of their physical beings but a secondary effect of their bad habits. In an anecdote about the pre-Islamic period, the tribe of Hudhayl craftily encourages the king of Yemen to plunder the treasure at the sanctuary at Mecca, hoping that he will violate the sanctity of the temple and incur divine destruction. The king consults two rabbis on the subject, and they explain that the plan to seize the Meccan sanctuary will inevitably lead him to perdition. Instead of sacking it, they advise him to "circumambulate it, glorify and honor it, shave your head by it and humble yourself before it until you leave it." The king asks, "What prevents you from doing so yourselves?" and the rabbis reply, "By God, it is indeed the house of our father Abraham and it is as we have told you; but the people there have driven us from it with the idols they have set up around it and the blood they shed there; they are unclean polytheists"—or something to that effect.[37]

This anecdote, while invoking the idea that "polytheists are unclean," refers less to the purity status of the nonbelievers' bodies than to their habit of trafficking in filth. Another anecdote in the *Sīra* similarly suggests that, although polytheists were considered to be impure, this was not a substantive impurity dispelled only by the transformative act of conversion to Islam, but a simple function of nonbelievers' failure to perform the necessary ablutions to render themselves pure. When the fiery and as yet unconverted ʿUmar discovers his sister Fāṭima reading a page from the Qurʾān, he asks her to let him read it. She replies,

> "My brother, you are unclean in your polytheism and only the clean may touch it."[38] So ʿUmar got up and washed himself and she gave him the page, which contained [the Qurʾānic chapter] Ṭā Hā. He read it, and when he had read the opening portion he said, "How fine and noble is this speech."[39]

Only after reading the Qurʾānic passage does ʿUmar declare his intention to go to the Prophet and render his Islām. His ablutions have rendered him pure and capable of touching the Qurʾān, even though he remains a nonbeliever.[40]

The idea that nonbelievers are in some sense impure is also reflected in the practice, required by some jurists[41] and also mentioned at several points in the *Sīra*,[42] of performing the major ablution (*ghusl*) upon conversion to Islam. At some stage, this practice may possibly have implied a transition from an abiding state of impurity as a nonbeliever to the purity of belief. This inference is supported by the occasional mention of other rites of purification (ones which fall outside of the purview of the classical law of *ṭahāra*, but nevertheless are associated with the concept of purity) in connection with conversion. In one report, transmitted by ʿAbd al-Razzāq, a new convert proclaims his Islam and the Prophet tells him, "Cast from you the hair of unbelief"; shaving the head, a rite also performed in the context of the *ḥajj*, is clearly associated with purification.[43] The same is true of circumcision, another operation mentioned as having been performed on new converts.[44]

According to Ibn Manẓūr, " 'So-and-so purified (*ṭahhara*) his son' means that he performed the *sunna* of circumcising him."[45] Despite the graver implications of these more extreme rites of purification, however, the practise of performing full ablutions at conversion could be taken simply to mean that the new convert was assumed to be in a state of ritual pollution due to his previous ignorance or rejection of the law of purity. This is the interpretation that many later jurists gave to the practice.[46]

In fact, there is reason to believe that the doctrine of the ritual impurity of nonbelievers was not an archaic Muslim belief but a controversial doctrine that was actively promoted at a specific point in history. The fact that several of the anecdotes cited above about the impurity of nonbelievers adopt the precise vocabulary of the Qurʾān suggests that the stories are not merely matter-of-fact accounts of forms of thought and behavior that were taken for granted by contemporary Muslims, but narrative commentaries on the wording of the Qurʾān. The wording of Umm Ḥabība's objection that "you are an unclean polytheist" (*anta rajul mushrik najis*), as well as that tentatively attributed to the two rabbis, echoes that of Qurʾān 9:28 too closely for the parallel to be merely accidental. In the case of the speech attributed to ʿUmar's sister Fāṭima, the Qurʾānic reference is double: both to 9:28 and to 56:77–79, "This is a glorious Qurʾān, safeguarded in a book which none may touch except the purified." The pointed, although implicit, evocation of Qurʾānic proof texts suggests that the anecdotes are not merely reflecting an existing doctrine but arguing in favor of a novel one. This suspicion is particularly powerful with respect to the story about ʿUmar's sister, which seems to present an implicit argument about the contested meaning of not one but two controversial Qurʾānic passages.

One reason for the rather high incidence of explicit (and faintly polemical) invocations of the idea that nonbelievers are in some sense ritually impure in the *Sīra* of Ibn Isḥāq, a text originally dating from the first half of the second century A.H., may be that this idea was at the time a relatively new and controversial one whose implications were gradually being worked out. Early opinions relevant to the interpretation of verse 9:28 transmitted in the classical sources suggest both that the verse was not originally understood in the context of the law of ritual purity and that it was injected into the debate over ritual purity sometime around the turn of the second century A.H. Firstly, a number of the transmitted opinions of early figures suggest that their originators were completely oblivious to the issue of ritual purity. Most importantly, a variety of early opinions (some of which appear in the form of *ḥadīth*) suggest that verse 9:28 was not understood to exclude nonbelievers from the Meccan sanctuary categorically. Instead, many people understood it to require that nonbelievers be admitted only in roles of subordination to Muslims:

> The Prophet said, "No polytheist shall enter the Sacred Mosque forever after this year, except those who have a treaty with the Muslims (*ahl al-'ahd*) and their servants."
>
> The Prophet said about the verse [9:28], "except slaves or Protected People (*ahl al-dhimma*)."
>
> Qatāda said: ". . . No polytheist could approach the Sacred Mosque after that year except someone who pays the *jizya* or the slave of a Muslim."[47]

These traditions are clearly incompatible with the doctrine that nonbelievers are ritually impure. While satisfying the political intent of the Qur'ānic passage, which is to establish Muslim supremacy and independence in the holy precincts, the exception allowing access to nonbelievers allied or subordinated to believers does nothing to still fears of defilement through ritual pollution. Significantly, these opinions are not polemics against the doctrine that nonbelievers are ritually impure; they ignore the issue of ritual purity altogether. They thus may very well reflect a stage when verse 9:28 had not yet been drawn into the dialogue about ritual purity.

Classical sources also reflect the process by which another authoritative text, this time the accepted account of an event in the life of the Prophet, was in some cases recounted without reference to ritual purity and in others made explicitly to address the purity debate. I would argue (tentatively and speculatively) that in their innocence of the technical purity issue involved, the former are likely to be earlier in date.[48] The incident in question involves the delegation sent to the Prophet by the tribe of Thaqīf in Ramaḍān of the year A.H. 9/630–31 C.E., when the tribe realized that it was unable to resist the new Muslim coalition but wished to negotiate favorable terms of conversion. The received version of the story, recounted in *Sīra* of Ibn Isḥāq and adduced in various reports from early figures, included a potentially disturbing detail: the delegation, consisting of men who remained officially idol-worshipers until the conclusion of the negotiations over the terms of the tribe's conversion, sojourned within the confines of the Prophet's mosque. Unlike the anecdote about Umm Ḥabība, this story does not appear to be originally a polemic addressing the issue of the ritual purity of nonbelievers. In the version recorded by Ibn Isḥāq, the anecdote makes no reference to this issue at all; it is merely one of a set of details illustrating the Prophet's warm yet firm treatment of an initially proud and obdurate group of men. The fact that the Prophet accommodates the delegation in the mosque, like the fact that he feeds the men food from his own household, indicates a generosity of spirit standing in sharp contrast with the small-minded suspicions of the nonbelieving visitors—who will not eat the Prophet's food until it has been tasted by a mediator.[49] The "original" setting of the anecdote, if one may speak of such a thing, has to do with moral character and not with ritual purity.[50]

A series of reports recorded in the *Muṣannaf*s of ʿAbd al-Razzāq and Ibn Abī Shayba demonstrates that the story of the delegation of Thaqīf was at some point drawn into the debate over the substantive purity status of nonbelievers.[51] The form of the anecdotes suggests that an already established narrative was being interrogated for its implications in a newly significant debate. One use of the anecdote was a straight retelling (shorn of its original context), now strategically deployed in the context of a debate over ritual purity to suggest that nonbelievers need not, in fact, be excluded from Muslim places of worship for fear of pollution. Another set of reports retools the anecdote more significantly, this time in support of the idea that nonbelievers are indeed substantively impure. In several versions of the anecdote attributed to al-Ḥasan [al-Baṣrī], the anecdote is revised to address the very objection that was probably foremost in the minds of later believers who heard about the delegation of Thaqīf:

> Al-Ḥasan said: When the delegation of Thaqīf came to the Prophet, they stayed in a pavilion (*qubba*) that was in the back of the mosque. When it was time for prayers, a man from among the people said, "O Prophet it is time for prayers; those are non-believing people (*qawm kuffār*), and they are in the mosque." The Prophet said, "The ground is not subject to pollution (*innaʾl-arḍ lā tanjasu*)," or something to that effect (*aw naḥwa hādhā*).[52]

The addition of this exchange neatly reverses the initial implications of the story. Where the Prophet's accommodation of nonbelievers within a mosque superficially suggests that they are not substantively impure, the statement that "nothing pollutes the ground" suggests the opposite: nonbelievers are indeed impure, and it is only the inability of earth to contract or transmit pollution that averts their threat to the sanctity of the mosque.[53]

The fact that the story in its most unadorned form is completely oblivious to any issue of ritual purity, as well as the somewhat contrived nature of the reports endeavoring to bring it into harmony with the doctrine of the substantive impurity of nonbelievers, suggests that this doctrine was probably unknown to the anecdote's first transmitters. The belief that nonbelievers were substantively impure was most likely a secondary development in the law of ritual purity, one either inspired or (at least) supported by a new understanding of verse 9:28 in the context of emergent ideas about substantive impurity.

How and when did the question of the substantive purity status of nonbelievers, and thus the permissibility of their admission to places of Muslim worship, become an issue? Although the evidence is very slim, some sources suggest that the issue may have been raised by the Caliph ʿUmar ibn ʿAbd al-ʿAzīz, who is reported to have promulgated an edict barring non-Muslims from mosques and appended a supporting reference to verse 9:28 of the Qurʾān.[54] Like the positions discussed in chapter 3, this directive emerges from the sources as a novel initiative, one that was legitimated by reference to the fundamental sources of the faith (in this case, the text of the Qurʾān) but that apparently ran counter to the prevailing practice. The reports supporting the two sides of the debate over the ritual purity status of nonbelievers, like those in the controversy over *wuḍūʾ* from cooked food, cluster in the lifetime of ʿUmar and seem to correlate to some extent with contemporary political alignments.[55]

The two major legal figures associated with the doctrine that nonbelievers were substantively impure are al-Ḥasan al-Baṣrī (d. A.H. 110/728–29 C.E.) and Ibn ʿAbbās. Both are is supposed to have said, with reference to verse 9:28, that Muslims should not shake hands with polytheists; if they did so, they should perform *wuḍūʾ*.[56] Regardless of the authenticity of the tradition about Ibn ʿAbbās (which does not seem to appear in the earliest sources), the sources suggest that al-Ḥasan was the key figure in the dissemination of the doctrine of the ritual impurity of nonbelievers. Not only did he advance the opinion that one should perform ablutions after shaking hands with a nonbeliever; he is also, as mentioned above, the person credited with recounting a version of the story of the delegation of Thaqīf pointedly recast to suggest that they posed a potential threat of pollution. Here we see a repetition of a pattern established in chapter 3; although generally censorious and aloof from those in power, al-Ḥasan appears to have been a supporter of ʿUmar ibn ʿAbd al-ʿAzīz and an enthusiastic propagator of his distinctive doctrines regarding ritual purity.

The controversy over the ritual purity of nonbelievers seems to have drawn other contemporary figures into the fray. Thus, Ibn Abī Shayba transmits a report that an Ibn Abī Muḥayriz was seen shaking hands with a Christian man in the mosque of Damascus.[57] Ibn Abī Muḥayriz was a member of the generation following the Companions of the Prophet (according to a weak report he was a Companion); he is supposed to have died either in the reign of al-Walīd ibn ʿAbd al-Malik (A.H. 86–96/705–15 C.E.) or in that of ʿUmar ibn ʿAbd al-ʿAzīz (A.H. 99–101/717–20 C.E.). Significantly, he was known for his critical stance towards the Umayyad regime. According to two reports from Ibn Abī Khaythama recorded by Ibn Ḥajar, he was one of the few Syrians who condemned al-Ḥajjāj openly.[58] This report meshes very neatly with the hypothesis that the interpretation of Qurʾān 9:28 classifying nonbelievers as substantively impure and banning them from mosques was first disseminated by ʿUmar ibn ʿAbd al-ʿAzīz. Assuming that he did in fact live until the reign of ʿUmar, we might infer that Ibn Abī Muḥayriz publicly defied the state-sponsored interpretation of the verse in the most provocative possible venue: the Friday mosque of the capital of the Umayyad empire. Apparently always politically outspoken, Ibn Abī Muḥayriz would presumably have been protected by his advanced age. It then becomes comprehensible why this anecdote is at pains to record such an apparently trivial detail as the location of the alleged handshake; without its political context, this touch is at best a weak effort at verisimilitude. It is also probably not a coincidence that it is specifically a handshake that is involved; the gesture can be seen as a direct riposte to the legal opinion advanced by al-Ḥasan. Even if Ibn Abī Muḥayriz had, in fact, died during the previous reign, it would be very natural for pious people offended by a legal interpretation promoted by the authorities to refer to the example of a recently deceased model of piety—particularly if the latter had been known for his fearless public criticism of the Umayyad administration.

Similarly, Ibn Abī Shayba transmits a report that Mujāhid "saw no harm in the People of the Book sitting in the mosque." Mujāhid ibn Jabr al-Makkī, Abū'l-Ḥajjāj al-Makhzūmī, best known for his knowledge of Qurʾānic interpretation, died in A.H. 100–4 /717–22 C.E.;[59] he was thus a contemporary of ʿUmar ibn ʿAbd al-ʿAzīz and al-Ḥasan al-Baṣrī. Perhaps not insignificantly, he was accused of getting his exegetical material from the People of the Book (i.e., Jews and Christians); he was thus to some extent himself the victim of increasingly negative and exclusive attitudes towards nonbelievers.[60]

If the doctrine that non-Muslims were substantively impure was indeed promoted in the lifetimes of al-Ḥasan and ʿUmar ibn ʿAbd al-ʿAzīz, the initiative was doomed to failure. A Sunnī consensus that nonbelievers were substantively pure (at least while alive) eventually emerged in contrast, and perhaps even in reaction, to the Imāmī Shīʿite holding that they were impure and defiling.

Children of Adam

By the outset of the classical period, Sunnī scholars had largely rejected or marginalized the doctrines that women, human corpses, or nonbelievers were substantively impure. For classical and postclassical scholars, the significance and structure of the system of ritual purity thus clearly were not generated by the category distinctions (male versus female, believer versus unbeliever, and life versus death) suggested at first glance by the Qurʾānic text. How, then, did they conceive of the shape and meaning of the system of ritual purity as a whole? It will not, by this point, come as a surprise that classical and postclassical conceptualizations of the system of ritual purity were changeable and diverse. However, some major themes and tendencies are discernible in the classical and postclassical texts. We may begin by examining the treatment of ritual purity in what is arguably the first unitary and comprehensive rendition of substantive Islamic law, al-Shāfiʿī's *Kitāb al-Umm*.[61]

Al-Shāfiʿī rejects the idea that human beings might be categorized as substantively impure (*najis*) according to gender or confessional identity so completely and unquestioningly that he never feels moved to argue the point explicitly. His lack of concern with the possibility that nonbelievers might be substantively impure is reflected in his discussion of water obtained from Christians, where he declares:

> There is no harm (*lā baʾs*) in performing *wuḍūʾ* with water owned by a polytheist (*mushrik*) or with which he has performed *wuḍūʾ* [*sic*], as long as one does not know that there is an impure substance in it; water has a quality of purity (*ʿindaʾl-māʾ ṭahāra*), no matter who possesses it or where it may be.[62]

Although this passage evinces concern with the possibility that water owned by a nonbeliever may be polluted, in fact it is founded on the assumption that the bodies of nonbelievers are not themselves substantively impure. Were nonbelievers substantively impure, water with which they had performed ablutions would inevitably be polluted. Although they are not explicit in this regard, al-Shāfiʿī's remarks seem to address the suspicion that water owned by a nonbeliever may be sullied with forbidden substances (wine, pork, dog saliva) unbeknownst to its Muslim recipient. Tacitly basing himself on the principle that the state of ritual purity is not ruptured by doubt (and thus remains valid unless canceled by a known pollutant), al-Shāfiʿī establishes that the purificatory value of the water is not removed by such suspicions in the absence of actual knowledge of such a pollutant.

The passage in which *Kitāb al-Umm* most directly addresses the question of the purity status of different categories of human beings occurs in a section entitled "persons in a state of sexual impurity and polytheists passing over ground and walking on it" (*mamarr al-junub waʾl-mushrik ʿalāʾl-arḍ wa-mashyuhumā ʿalayhā*):

> Al-Shāfiʿī said, "Do not approach prayer when you are drunk, but wait till you can grasp the meaning of your words; nor when you are polluted—unless you are travelling the road (or: "passing along your way")—until you have washed yourselves . . ." [Qurʾān 4:43] Al-Shāfiʿī said: A person learned in the Qurʾān has interpreted God's statement "nor when you are polluted—unless you

> are travelling the road" to mean, "Do not approach the places of prayer"; what he said is very convincing, since there is no "passing through" prayer—there is only "passing through" its place, which is the mosque. Thus, there is no harm in someone in a state of sexual pollution (*al-junub*) passing through the mosque; he may not abide there, because God said, "unless you are passing on your way." Al-Shāfiʿī said, Ibrāhīm ibn Muḥammad reported to us from ʿUthmān ibn abī Sulaymān that when the polytheists of Quraysh came to Medina to ransom their prisoners they used to spend the night in the mosque, including Jubayr ibn Muṭʿim. Jubayr said, "I used to hear the Prophet reciting [the Qurʾān]." Al-Shāfiʿī said, "There is no harm in a polytheist spending the night in any mosque but the Sacred Mosque [in Mecca], because God said, "Believers, know that the idolators are unclean. Let them not approach the Sacred Mosque after this year is ended." [Qurʾān 9:28] Thus, no polytheist should enter the Sacred Mosque under any circumstances. He said: If a polytheist can spend the night in a mosque other than the Sacred Mosque, a Muslim may also do so. Ibn ʿUmar relates that he used to spend the night in the mosque in the time of the Prophet when he was single, and the "ascetics of the porch" (*masākīn al-ṣuffa*) [also did so]. He said: The ground is not polluted (*lā tanjasu*) by the passing of a menstruating woman, a person in a state of sexual impurity (*al-junub*), a polytheist or the corpse of a polytheist, because no living human being is ever substantively impure. I consider it undesirable for a menstruating woman to pass through the mosque, but if she does so she does not pollute it.[63]

The title and general contents of the section imply that al-Shāfiʿī is equating polytheists (*mushrikūn*) with Muslims in a state of major ritual pollution, either menstrual or sexual; this in itself suggests that al-Shāfiʿī may merely be categorizing nonbelievers as persons who are in a state of impurity due to their failure to follow Islamic purity practices, rather than contemplating the possibility that they are substantively impure in the manner of pigs. He implies a figurative understanding of verse 9:28, "the idolators are unclean," when he restricts its application to the Holy Mosque of Mecca; any understanding of the verse that applied it to nonbelievers' actual purity status would, of course, have implications for their admittance to any place of worship. Al-Shāfiʿī's chief objective in the section is not to determine the purity status of nonbelievers but to assert that living human beings as such never enter the category of substantive impurity at all. The principle finds explicit expression in the culminating words of the passage: "no living human being is ever substantively impure (*laysa fī l-aḥyā' min al-ādamīyīn najāsa*)."[64]

The striking thing about the general logic of this paragraph and about its concluding statement is that it introduces a category that is not established either by the Qur'ānic materials relating to ritual purity or by the relevant *ḥadīth* texts. This is the category of *al-ādamī*, "the human being," literally, "the descendant of Adam." By categorizing the passing states of pollution applying to the human person—including nonbelievers—as fundamentally different from the substantive impurity adhering to inanimate objects, this logic sharply emphasizes the unique status of human beings. The prevailing denial that nonbelievers were substantively impure had already implicitly suggested that all human beings, and not exclusively members of the Muslim community, fell into one category with respect to the rules of ritual purity. However, in the preclassical period the idea of "humanity" as a relevant category for the analysis of the laws of ritual purity had been merely a tacit and negative implication of this denial. In the thought of al-Shāfiʿī and his successors, the category of "humanity" became an overtly articulated and centrally important element in the understanding of the law of ritual purity.

An emphasis on the unique status of the human person informs al-Shāfiʿī's understanding of the underlying structure of the law of ritual purity as a whole. As we have seen, a disjunction between the purity status of nonhuman substances and the states of purity and pollution experienced by believers had already been established on a basic level by the juristic formula that "a believer is never substantively impure." al-Shāfiʿī both explicitly extends this logic to include all human beings and further elaborates the logical implications of this disjunction. For al-Shāfiʿī, there is a sharp distinction between two domains of ritual purity: that of substantive impurity (*najāsa*), where pollution and cleansing are both treated as instrumental processes focusing on the manipulation of physical pollutants existing in the external world, and that of personal states of purity and pollution, which are purely subjective states conceived of by the believer in adherence to God's command and have no discernible correlates in the physical world.

One place where this sharp dichotomy between substantive impurity and purely notional states of personal pollution comes to expression is in al-Shāfiʿī's severing the connection between bodily functions entailing personal pollution and the purity status of the bodily secretions being expelled. According to al-Shāfiʿī, personal pollution can be incurred through the expulsion of substances that are themselves pure, most notably semen. The element of impurity arises, not from the purity status of any of the substances involved, but from the unfathomable decree of God. Consequently, ablutions restoring the human person to a state of purity are not instrumental processes removing physical pollutants (even of a subtle and invisible nature), but pure acts of submission to the commands of the creator: in al-Shāfiʿī's terminology, *taʿabbud*.[65] "Don't you see," al-Shāfiʿī argues, "that semen is not substantively impure, but [emission of] it requires *ghusl*? *Wuḍūʾ* and *ghusl* are *taʿabbud*."[66] The word *taʿabbud* has no direct English equivalent; it is a verbal noun meaning "to act as an *ʿabd*." In a sociological context, the noun *ʿabd* means "slave"; in a theological context, it means "worshiper, creature." Every human being is thus an *ʿabd* of God. The Qurʾānic text repeatedly uses the word *ʿabd* to mean "human being," and this is the primary meaning of the word recorded by such lexicographical works as Ibn Manẓūr's *Lisān al-ʿArab*.

Al-Shāfiʿī's argument that the rules relating to states of personal purity and pollution are *taʿabbud* thus has two basic dimensions. Firstly, it implies that, as the states involved are completely dissociated from the physical pollutants observable in the external world, the rules cannot be subjected to logical scrutiny or to analogical reasoning; they are grounded exclusively in the sovereign will of the Creator. Secondly, it defines the purificatory force of the ritual ablutions as a function of human faith that is sharply differentiated from the processes of physical cleansing applied to inanimate objects. This disjunction is clearly illustrated by al-Shāfiʿī's contention that water already used for *wuḍūʾ* ablutions cannot be reused for another person's ablutions, yet is not substantively impure (*najis*).

> If someone were to ask, "Why can't someone perform *wuḍūʾ* with [water that has already been used for *wuḍūʾ*], if it is not substantively impure (*najis*)?" the answer is: "Because people have an obligation to obey the decrees of God with respect to purifying themselves even if their bodies have not come into contact with impure substances (*innaʿalāʾl-nās taʿabbudan fī anfusihim biʾl-ṭahāra min ghayr najāsa tumāss abdānahum*); garments and earth have no obligation to obey the decrees of God or to wash with water without [having come into contact with] impure substances."[67]

Thus, in al-Shāfiʿī's view, ritual ablutions remedying states of personal pollution find their significance not in a realm of states of purity and impurity shared with the physical world, but in the uniquely human experience of conscious creaturehood and obedience towards God. The essential element is not the removal of pollutants but the realization of one's status as an *ʿabd*.

Consistently with this underlying logic, al-Shāfiʿī holds that the central element in the ritual ablutions is the worshiper's conscious intention (*niyya*). Although jurists had long agreed that *niyya* was a necessary element in the *wuḍūʾ* ablutions, al-Shāfiʿī emphasizes the centrality of *niyya* to an extreme extent. According to al-Shāfiʿī, the proper intention renders *wuḍūʾ* ablutions valid even in the absence of any of the individual acts of washing prescribed in the Qurʾān; someone who immerses himself in pure water or stands under a rainspout while intending to perform *wuḍūʾ* has discharged his ritual obligation. The important element in the process is not the set of physical actions prescribed in the Qurʾān, but the subjective intent of the believer. Conversely, even after the initial framing of one's ritual intent it is possible to invalidate one's ablutions by conceiving an incompatible intention, such as physical cleansing (*tanaẓẓuf*) or cooling oneself with the water.[68] The correctness of one's subjective attitude with respect to one's ablutions consistently takes precedence over the correctness of one's physical actions. Thus, al-Shāfiʿī argues that if a person is in doubt as to whether he legally qualifies as a traveler and nevertheless wipes his boots in the minor ablutions for a period of more than twenty-four hours (a special dispensation for travelers), he must repeat all of the prayers performed after the first twenty-four-hour period—*even if* he later proves to have qualified as a traveler. This is because, despite the fact that as a traveler he was technically entitled to wipe the boots for three days, he did it *in the belief* that he might not be entitled to do so.[69]

Thus, it can be argued that for Shāfiʿī the central motif of the system of ritual purity is human life, understood as a state of creaturehood defined by obedience to God. Unlike the rules of purity relating to inanimate or nonhuman beings, those relating to humans focus almost exclusively on subjective factors. The key term in this conception is *al-ādamī*, "the human being." As we have remarked, this term seems to have entered the juristic terminology of ritual purity only in the classical period; it is represented neither in the Qurʾān nor in the *ḥadīth* on the subject, nor is it commonly used in the legal opinions transmitted from the preclassical period.

Al-Shāfiʿī's conception of the unique purity status of human beings is exemplified by his distinctive position regarding the purity status of semen, which most jurists considered to be impure:

> God began the creation of Adam from water and earth (*ṭīn*) and He made both of them purificants, and he began the creation of [Adam's] children from gushing liquid (*māʾ dāfiq*); His beginning the creation of Adam with the two purificants that are the source of all purity (*al-ṭahāratayniʾ llatayni humāʾ l-ṭahāra*) is an indication that He begins the creation of others as well only from a pure substance and not from an impure one. The *sunna* of the Prophet indicates the same thing. Al-Shāfiʿī said: ʿAmr ibn abī Salama reported to us from al-Awzāʿī from Yaḥyā ibn Saʿīd from al-Qāsim ibn Muḥammad from ʿĀʾisha that she said, "I used to scratch the semen from the Prophet's garment (*thawb*)." Al-Shāfiʿī

> said: Semen is not substantively impure. If someone were to say, "Then why is it scratched or wiped off?" the answer is that [it is scratched off] as mucus, spit, mud, or food that has gotten stuck to a garment are scratched off, for the sake of cleanliness and not because they are substantively impure; if one were to pray before it was scratched or wiped off, there would be no harm in it. None of these things can communicate impurity to water or anything else. al-Rabīʿ ibn Sulaymān said: al-Shāfiʿī dictated to us (*qāla al-Shāfiʿī imlāʾan*), "Anything wet that comes out of the penis, urine, pre-ejaculatory fluid (*midhy*), the fluid that emerges after urination (*wady*), anything that can or cannot be identified, it is all substantively impure except semen. Semen is the viscous fluid from which children are made and which has an odor like pollen; nothing else that comes out of the penis has a pleasant odor."[70]

It should be emphasized that this is a distinctive and striking departure in the understanding of the law of ritual purity. While al-Shāfiʿī's arguments about the creation of Adam and the analogous conclusion about the purity status of semen are certainly not inconsistent with the basic textual sources he had at his disposal, neither are they obvious or mechanical conclusions from these basic materials. Most obviously, his insistence that Adam was created from pure substances is not an obvious inference from the Qurʾān's several different statements about the materials from which God created humankind. In fact, the more obvious implication of the relevant Qurʾānic passages is exactly the opposite: that God's original creation of human beings is all the more astonishing because He chose to produce the pinnacle of His creation precisely from those substances that were most lowly, offensive, and impure. The creation of human beings is associated Qurʾānically with semen, with blood or bloodclots, and with earth (dust, clay, or mud). The first two have obvious associations with ritual pollution, semen because of its close link with sexual pollution, and blood because it is a central Qurʾānic food taboo. Earth is an ambiguous substance in the context of the Qurʾānic law of ritual purity. On the one hand, as al-Shāfiʿī emphasizes, when clean and dry it can be used in substitute ritual ablutions (*tayammum*) in the absence of water. In contrast, however, many of the references to the earth that was used to form Adam emphasize that he was created from wet soil or mud.[71] In three places the Qurʾān refers to this soil as *ḥamaʾ masnūn*,[72] which the majority of early interpreters took to mean mud that had fermented or spoiled (literally, "changed": *taghayyara*) and become foul (*muntin*).[73]

Not only are semen, blood, and mud substances that might be seen as inherently impure in the context of the Qurʾānic text as a whole, but the passages dealing with the creation of humankind explicitly emphasize their lowly and distasteful qualities. The Qur'ān recounts that when God created Adam, He commanded the angels to prostrate themselves before him. The only one who balked at this commandment was Iblīs (Satan), who protested: "I am nobler than he; you created me from fire, and You created him of clay."[74] The unfathomability of God's sovereign will is exemplified in His decision to fashion His supreme creation from unprepossessing materials; lowly or impure substances are ennobled and purified by human beings' role as worshipers of their creator. As several other passages emphasize, the lowliness of humankind's constituent ingredients also suggests the absolute qualitative transformations a person undergoes in the journey from inchoate matter to earthly human life, from the dissolution of death to renewed life in the resurrected body. A human being's state before the infusion of the spirit is just as unpromising of future life as his state after death; the unformed fetus is no better than the decomposed corpse. A God who can bring life to a droplet of semen or a clot of blood can bring life to scattered remains.[75] In emphasizing the purity of human life from the very beginning of its formation, al-Shāfiʿī departs from a Qur'ānic emphasis on the discontinuity of human development. In the Qur'ānic schema, the physical existence of human beings is a dramatic cycle of transitions from death to life and from impurity to purity. For al-Shāfiʿī, the substantive purity of the human person is a constant from the inception of the creation of the first man.

Later thinkers adopted and expanded on the idea that the dignity of the human person was the central motif of the system of ritual purity. Although no final consensus ever emerged on the purity status of dead bodies, a strong school of thought came to affirm that believers at least were pure even beyond death.[76] The link between this perduring substantive purity and the inherent dignity of human beings was supported with a Qur'ānic proof text, 17:80: "We have favored (or "ennobled": *karramnā*) the children of Adam and guided them by land and sea. We have provided them with good things (or "pure foods": *al-ṭayyibāt*) and exalted them above many of Our creatures." Ritual purity does not seem to be one of the issues that were related to this verse in the early period. Traditional interpretations included general reference to the status of humans as rational beings as well as variations on the subject of food and transportation (including the domestication of beasts of burden), suggested by the second half of the verse. Al-Qurṭubī reports:

> Included in this dignity (*karāma*) is creating them in this tall-statured and comely form and giving them transportation by land and sea—whereas no animal but the children of Adam is transported by its own will, desire, and planning—and honoring them with special food, drink, and clothing, in which no animal has the same scope as the children of Adam, for they alone of all animals

> earn money, wear clothes, and eat complex foods. The best any [other] animal can achieve is to eat raw meat or simple food. Al-Ṭabarī transmits from a number [of interpreters] that the favor is that [human beings] eat with their hands, which the rest of the animals eat with their mouths. . . . Al-Ḍaḥḥāk says, "He honored them with speech and discernment." ʿAṭāʾ says, "He honored them with erectness of bearing and height of stature." Yamānin: "With comeliness of form." Muḥammad ibn Kalb: "By making Muḥammad one of them." It has also been said that he honored men with beards and women with locks (of hair: *al-dhawāʾib*)." Muḥammad ibn Jarīr al-Ṭabarī says, "[God honored them] by giving them mastery over other created beings (*al-khalq*) and making other created beings obedient to them." It has also been said [that God honored them] with speech and writing.[77]

It is difficult to know precisely when verse 17:70 was drawn into a discourse of ritual purity increasingly focused on the dignity and uniqueness of human beings. By the time of the Ḥanafī jurist al-Kāsānī (d. A.H. 587/1191 C.E.), the association between the verse and the law of ritual purity seems to have been well enough established among jurists to require nothing but an oblique reference. He writes, "Muḥammad ibn Shujāʿ al-Balkhī mentions that human beings (*al-ādamī*) are not rendered substantively impure by death and the [consequent] absorption of shed blood (*al-dam al-masfūḥ*) by their members, *as a sign of their dignity* (*karāmatan lahu*)." Kāsānī himself follows the classical Ḥanafī position that a human corpse is defiled and defiling (for instance, if it falls into a well) until washed; he argues that the deceased must have had a polluting bodily function while expiring, given the "loosening of the limbs" and the waning of consciousness experienced by the dying. In this case, he says, the special dignity (*karāma*) accorded to human beings lies in the possibility of purifying a human corpse (unlike any other carrion).[78] Regardless of the specific position chosen, al-Kāsānī reflects a received understanding that the purity status of human corpses must somehow manifest the special dignity accorded to human beings in verse 17:80; the key word *karāma* indicates the connection to anyone familiar with the juristic application of this Qurʾānic passage. In a similarly formulaic reference assuming widespread knowledge and acceptance of this Qurʾānic interpretation, Ibn Ḥajar al-Haytamī (d. A.H. 974/1567 C.E.) writes:

> [Carrion] is any [animal] whose life has passed away without ritual slaughter or its equivalent (*al-dhakāt al-sharʿīya*); . . . human beings are excepted because their dignity is established scripturally (*ustuthniya minhā al-ādamīyu li-takrīmihi biʾl-naṣṣ*).[79]

Given that verse 17:80 speaks of the "children of Adam," application of this verse to the juristic problem of the purity status of human corpses tended to de-emphasize possible distinctions between believers and nonbelievers. The privileged status indicated by the verse is usually understood to be shared by all humankind. al-Haytamī continues,

> This applies to the non-believer from the point of view of his essence; this is not in contradiction to the fact that his blood is rendered licit by an accidental characteristic inhering in him. [The purity of the human corpse] is also established by the well-authenticated (*ṣaḥīḥ*) report [that the Prophet said,] "Do not declare your dead to be impure (*lā tunajjisū mawtākum*); a Muslim is not impure, alive or dead." He mentioned "a Muslim" because it was the most common case (*liʾl-ghālib*). The meaning of the "impurity" of the polytheists (*najāsat al-mushrikīn*) in the Qurʾānic verse is that their beliefs are impure, or that one should avoid them as one avoids impure things. There is disagreement over [the purity of the corpses of human beings] other than the prophets and the martyrs.[80]

Although it seems to have started among jurists rather than exegetes, the idea that verse 17:70 implied the purity of human corpses seems gradually to have joined the classic list of interpretations of the verse noted by commentators on the Qurʾān. The nineteenth-century commentator al-Qinūjī glosses the verse,

> That is, "we favored all of them; this favor includes creating them in this comely and symmetrical form, [granting them] purity after death, and distinguishing them with special kinds of food, drink, and clothing of which other kinds of animals have nothing comparable."[81]

The continuation of verse 17:70, stating that God has "exalted [the children of Adam] over many of our creatures," had long been the focus of controversy over the cosmic rank of humankind, either above or below that of angels and *jinn*.[82] The purity of human dead having been taken as a manifestation of God's special favor to the human race, mentioned at the beginning of the verse, it was natural to ask whether this particular advantage was shared with mankind's cosmic competitors. al-Ḥaytamī's commentator al-Shirwānī writes, elaborating on the statement that human corpses are pure,

> Similarly, angels and genies (*jinn*); their dead bodies (*mayta*) are pure. . . . It is supported . . . by [the Prophet's] statement, "The

> believer is not substantively impure, alive or dead," since he did not qualify it by [saying] "human." It is not a problem that this implies that unbelievers (*al-kāfir*) are impure, because the qualification "believer" here and in similar contexts (*fī hādhā wa-naẓā'irihi*) is not for the purpose of excluding non-believers, but of praising faith and making people desire it.[83]

The concept of the unique status of human beings was not applied only to the issue of the purity status of dead human bodies. It could also be seen as the decisive factor in the understanding of the concept of substantive purity in general. For al-Haytamī, the role of human beings as the pinnacle of creation is the determining factor in the purity status of all things in existence, which are pure but for a small number of exceptions:

> The general case (*al-aṣl*) is that substances (*al-a'yān*) are pure, because they were created for the benefit of human beings (*al-'ibād*) and they can only perform this function—or can best perform it—if they are pure.[84]

Why, then, were there impure substances at all? The increasingly detailed and explicit discussions of the categories of substantive purity and impurity came to emphasize the fact that most things in the world were pure and to define with increasing precision the small number of things that were not. al-Shirwānī explains:

> Know that substances are either non-animal or animal (*jamād wa-ḥayawān*). All non-animal substances are pure, unless the [divine] Lawgiver has specified that they are impure. . . . Similarly, all animals are pure unless the [divine] Lawgiver has named them as exceptions. . . . An "animal" is anything that has a living spirit (*rūḥ*), and a "non-animal substance" (*jamād*) is anything that is not an animal, the source (*aṣl*) of an animal, a [severed] piece of an animal, or expelled from (*munfaṣil 'an*) [the body of] an animal. The source of any animal—which is sperm, a bloodclot, or a clump of flesh (lit., "morsel": *muḍgha*)—is pure if the animal is pure and impure if it is impure. A [severed] piece of an animal is like its carrion. Substances expelled from [the bodies of] impure animals are always impure. [Substances expelled] from [the bodies of] pure animals are pure if they are secretions (*rashḥ*) such as sweat, saliva, and the like; if they have undergone a change in the interior of the body (*lahu istaḥāla fī'l-bāṭin*), like urine, they are impure. Things that change for the better, like the

> milk of pure animals and human beings and like eggs, are pure. In short, everything in the universe is either a non-animal substance, an animal, or the waste product of an animal; you [now] know how they are classified.[85]

The purity or impurity of a given living being or substance is thus, according to al-Shirwānī, determined by two different forms of categorization. One is a systematic categorization of all items encountered in the physical world into animals, the waste products of animals, and substances that are not derived from animals. Animals and nonanimal substances are (generally speaking) pure; animal wastes are impure. The other is an internal division of two of these three categories (animals and nonanimal substances) into two groups, those that are pure and those that are impure. Rather than being based on some meaningful category distinction, this second set of impure items is merely a list of exceptions defined only by divine decrees whose motivations are unknown. Thus, the only kind of impurity constituting a known and meaningful category comprises the bodily wastes of living beings.

The key element that in turn defines the category of animal wastes is their quality of having undergone a process of transformation within the body, a transformation that renders them useless and offensive. The prime location of this transformation, the classic example of which is the transformation of pure and nourishing food into worthless and evil-smelling feces, is the stomach. The paradigm of change (*taghayyur*) and passage through the stomach was extended to cover other substances expelled from the body. Thus, al-Ḥaytamī remarks:

> [Impure substances include] {pus} because it is blood that has spoiled (*dam mustaḥīl*), and *ṣadīd*, which is a thin liquid mixed with blood [that runs out of wounds]; similarly, the liquid that runs out of sores or blisters [is impure] if it has turned (*in taghayyara*). {And vomit}, even if it has not changed or remained for a long time in the stomach (*wa-in lam yataghayyar wa-illā'staqarra fī'l-ma'ida*), because it is a waste product (*faḍla*); and the phlegm (*balgham*) that comes from the stomach [is impure], unlike that which comes from the head or the chest, like what flows from the mouth of a sleeping person, unless he knows that it comes from the stomach.[86]

In the same vein, the Ḥanafī jurist al-Zayla'ī cites Abū Yūsuf's opinion that phlegm "that rises from the stomach (*al-jawf*) cancels [*wuḍū'*], unlike that which descends from the head, because it is a kind of vomit and thus becomes like the other kinds of vomit, and also because it becomes impure (*yatanajjasu*) in the stomach, unlike that which descends from the head, *because the head is not a source of impurity and the stomach is a source of impurity* (*al-ra᾿s laysa bi-maḥall al-najāsa wa᾿l-ma῾ida maḥall al-najāsa*)."[87]

The result of the developments under discussion is a universalistic and humanistic understanding of the law of purity, focusing on the unique status of the "children of Adam" and perceiving the stomach cavity and the transformations that occur there as the primary sources of substantive impurity. The connection between these two key elements, the human predicament and the process of digestion, and the broader thematic context in which they find their place can best be understood through examination of the narratives which Muslims recount about their common origin. It is significant that, as we shall see below, the basic themes underlying the law of ritual purity are most fully developed in the narratives relating to Adam (and, to a lesser extent, to Eve). Adam is, of course, symbolic of the things that all human beings have in common; we all are, in the words of the classical legal texts, *ādamīyūn* (Adamites) or *abnā᾿ ādam* (children of Adam). To a large extent, these narratives probably preexisted many of the universalizing developments in the law of ritual purity described above. From this point of view, technical legal argumentation may merely have been catching up with a strong strain of universalism already expressed in the narrative heritage transmitted from the earliest Muslims.

The traditional narrative of the creation of Adam establishes from the outset that his fundamental imperfection is his "hollowness," in other words, his possession of a digestive tract. It is this imperfection that belies his initial promise as a being more imposing than the angels. Al-Tha῾labī reports,

> ῾Abd Allāh ibn Sallām asked the Messenger of God, "How did God create Adam?" He said, "He created Adam's head and forehead from the dust of the Ka῾ba, his chest and his back from Jerusalem, his thighs from the soil of the Yemen, his shanks from the soil of Egypt, his feet from the soil of the Ḥijāz, his right hand from the soil of the East, his left hand from the soil of the West; then he cast him at the gate of heaven, and every time a band of angels passed by him they were astonished by his beautiful appearance and his tall stature; they had never seen a form that resembled him. Then Iblīs passed by and saw him; he said, "For what were you created?" Then he struck him with his hand, and lo and behold he was hollow (*jawf*). He entered his mouth and went out from his anus, and said to his companions from among the angels who were with him, "This is a hollow creature (*khalq ajwaf*) that will not stand firm or remain in control of himself (*lā yathbitu wa-lā yatamāsaku*)."[88]

It is here, and not in the strictly juristic development of the concept of ritual pollution, that we encounter a distinct enunciation of the concept of "lack of control" from within the Islamic tradition. The concepts of hollowness, lack of control, and the transformation of substances all appear intertwined in the following comments on the incident, presented by Ibn Manẓūr:[89]

> In the *ḥadīth* about the creation of Adam it says, "When he saw that he was hollow, he knew that he was a creature that would not be master of himself (*lā yatamālaku*)." [. . .] Ibn al-Athīr said, "What is meant by ʿ*al-jawf*ʾ here is anything that has a transformative power (*quwwa muḥīla*), like the stomach and the brain." . . . "*al-ajwafāni*" are the stomach and the genitals because of their large inner cavities (*li-ittisāʿ ajwāfihimā*). Abū ʿUbayd says in his statement in the *ḥadīth*, "Do not forget the *jawf* and what it holds," that is, the food and drink that enter it. There are two opinions about [this statement]. One is that it means both the stomach and the genitals, as when he said, "What makes me most fearful for you is the two hollow things (*al-ajwafāni*)." It is also said that he meant by "*al-jawf*" the head and what it holds and retains of the knowledge of God.

The quality of hollowness appears as the defining attribute of Adam at the time of his creation in other contexts as well. One of the words used to describe the clay from which he was formed is thus interpreted by some early commentators to indicate hollowness. Thus "*kaʾl-fakhkhār*" (Qurʾān 55:14), according to one early interpretation, means "like something that has an opening and not solid (*muṣmat*)."[90] Adam's quality of hollowness was seen in direct opposition to the attributes of God; thus, al-Ṭabarī presents sixteen reports stating that "*al-ṣamad*," a mysterious attribute of God mentioned in verse 112:2, means "solid" (*muṣmat*), "without an inner cavity" (*lā jawfa lahu*), or "not eating or drinking."[91] This opposition was made explicit in some versions of the narrative of Adam.

One, recorded by al-Ṭabarī, relates that after God creates Adam from the dust, he casts down the as-yet lifeless body and leaves it for forty years. The story continues,

> Iblīs would come and strike it with his foot, and it would clang (*yuṣalṣilu*) and ring; this is what God refers to when he says "*min ṣalṣāl kaʾl-fakhkhār*" (55:14), meaning "like something that has an opening and not solid (*muṣmat*)." Then he would enter into his mouth and pass out of his anus, and enter into his anus and pass

> out of his mouth, and then say, "You are nothing because of [your] hollowness (*ṣalṣala*); what were you created for? If I am given dominion over you I will bring you to destruction; and if you are given dominion over me I will disobey you."[92]

In another version of the story, Iblīs says to the angels, "Do not be in awe of this one; your Lord is solid (*ṣamad*) and this one is hollow (*ajwaf*), and if I am given dominion over him I will bring him to destruction."[93]

Why was the possession of an inner cavity such a damning quality? The answer seems to lie in the neediness of that empty interior space, the inevitability of hunger and the voraciousness and greed it draws in its wake. This has already been suggested by the pairing of the stomach and the genitals as "*al-ajwafānī*," a term which may not adequately describe the shape of the organs involved (at least so far as males are concerned) but vividly suggests the neediness and hunger of these two "empty" body parts. The same interpretation is suggested by the narrative recounting the gradual, top-down vivification of Adam's body by the breath of God:

> The scholars say, "When God wanted to breathe the spirit into Adam, he ordered it to enter his mouth. It said, "Its bottom is deep and its entrance is dark." He said it to the spirit again, and it answered the same. The same thing happened the third time. Finally, the fourth time He said, "Enter against your will, and go out against your will." When God ordered it in this way, it entered his mouth. When He first breathed the spirit into him, it entered his brain and revolved there for a hundred years; then it descended to his eyes. The wisdom in that is that God wanted Adam to see the beginning of his [own] creation and his origin, so that when he experienced successive miracles he would not become haughty or conceited. Then [the spirit] descended into his nostrils, and he sneezed. When he was done sneezing, the spirit descended into his mouth and his tongue. God taught him to say, "Praise to God, Lord of the universe." That was the first thing that he uttered. God replied, "May your Lord have mercy on you, Adam; it was for mercy that I created you." God said, "My mercy preceded my anger." Then the spirit descended into [Adam's] chest and his ribcage. He began to try to get up, but he was not able. That is why God said, "Truly, man is ever impatient (*wa-kānaʾl-insānu ʿajūlan* [Qurʾān 17:11])" and "Impatience is the very stuff man is made of" (*khuliqaʾl-insānu min ʿajal* [Qurʾān 21:37]). When the spirit reached his stomach (*jawf*), he hungered for food (*ishtahā al-ṭaʿām*). That was the first covetousness (*ḥirṣ*)

> that entered Adam's insides (*jawf*)[94] . . . Then the spirit spread throughout his entire body, and he became flesh, blood, bones, veins, and tendons.[95]

The second episode in the life of Adam that is of interest from the point of view of the themes underlying the system of ritual purity is the expulsion from Paradise. Interestingly, the theme of the interior cavity or *jawf* is one that is echoed and repeated throughout the narrative of the Fall. Thus, a narrative attributed to Wahb ibn Munabbih recounts:

> When Iblīs wanted to cause [Adam and Eve] to slip, he entered into the stomach (*jawf*) of the serpent; the serpent [then] had four legs and was like a Bactrian [camel] (*bukhtīya*), one of the most beautiful creatures that God had created. When the serpent entered the garden, Iblīs came out of its stomach (*jawf*); he took [a fruit] from the tree that God had forbidden to Adam and Eve and brought it to Eve.

After Iblīs successfully tempts Eve to eat the fruit and she in turn tempts Adam, the latter hides in his shame:

> The two of them saw their private parts (*saw'āt*); Adam went inside of the tree (*fī jawf al-shajara*). His Lord called him saying, "O Adam, where are you?" He said, "Here I am, O Lord." [God] said, "Won't you come out?" [Adam] said, "I am ashamed before you, O Lord."[96]

Here, the narrative adds to the appetitive qualities of the interior cavity its potential for concealment and deception.

From the moment of his creation, Adam's hollowness stands in contrast to the self-sufficient "solidity" of God. In contrast, the permeability of his body—associated with the expulsion of wastes and the processes of digestion and change that produce them—is a result of the Fall that stands in contrast to the condition of Adam's body in the Garden. The need to expel wastes is a result of the expulsion from the Garden; according to one tradition, it was even its cause: "The [forbidden] tree made anyone who ate from it defecate (or fart: *aḥdatha*); it was not fitting for there to be any *ḥadath* in paradise."[97] It was this understanding of the nature of the transgression that led some to identify the Forbidden Fruit as the fig, a food known for its laxative properties.[98] Thus, as the story proceeds to the expulsion from the Garden, we see that Adam's body becomes subject to a veritable flood of boundary violations:

> Wahb ibn Munabbih said, "When God made Adam descend to earth and he settled down in a seated position on the earth, he sneezed and his nose ran with blood. When he saw the blood flowing from his nose, not having seen blood before, he was terrified by what he saw. The earth did not soak up (lit., "drink": *tashrab*) the blood; it blackened on the earth like cinders. Adam was very alarmed by this; he remembered heaven and the peace he had had there, and he fell down in a faint and cried for forty days. God sent an angel to him; he rubbed (*masaḥa*) his back and his stomach and put his hand on his heart, and the sadness and faintness passed from him and he was relieved of the grief that had afflicted him."[99]

Interestingly, Adam is supposed to have had a harder and more impermeable outer boundary during his sojourn in Paradise; of this original integument, only his fingernails remained after the Fall.[100]

As the story proceeds, the bodily functions associated with ritual pollution are systematically linked with the new conditions surrounding Adam's existence after the Fall. Adam first feels his unaccustomed need for clothes and is taught how to make them.

> Then, after covering his nakedness, Adam complained [again]. Jibrīl said to him, "What's the matter?" He said, "I feel an unease and agitation within myself that will not allow me to pray; I feel a creeping like the creeping of ants between my flesh and my skin." Jibrīl said to him, "That is called hunger." He said, "How does one get rid of it?" He said, "I will lead you to it." He disappeared, then [returned] bringing two red bulls, an anvil, bellows, a hammer, and some tongs. Then he brought him sparks from hell. They fell on Adam's hand, and a spark flew from it and fell into the sea. Jibrīl went into the sea and brought it to Adam; it flew from him again, until he had done this seven times. This is why the Prophet (PBUH) said, "Your fire is one-seventieth of the fire of heaven, after it has been washed with water five times." When he brought it for the eighth time, the fire spoke, saying, "O Adam, I will not obey you; I will take revenge on those of your children who are disobedient on the Day of Resurrection." Jibrīl said, "O Adam, it will not obey you; but I will imprison it for you and your children so that you and your children will benefit from it." He imprisoned it in stone and iron; this is why God said, "Observe the fire which you light . . . [Qur'ān 56:71]." It is related that when Adam took hold of the fire and it

> burned his hand and he let go of it, he said to Jibrīl, "Why does it burn my hand and not yours?" He said, "Because you disobeyed God and I did not disobey Him." Then Jibrīl ordered him to make agricultural implements; he was the first one who worked iron. Then he brought him a bag of wheat and said, "O Adam, two grains are yours and one grain is Eve's." This is why a man gets twice a woman's share [in inheritance]. The weight of a grain was 180,000 dirhams. Adam said, "What should I do with all this?" He said, "O Adam, take it; it is the means of stilling your hunger. It was by means of it that you were expelled from paradise, by means of it you will live in this world, and by means of it you and your children will meet temptation (*al-fitna*) until the Hour comes." Then he ordered him to tie the two bulls, break some wood, and place it upon the two of them. He did that and began to till the earth upon them; he was the first one to till the earth. The two bulls wept for the peace of paradise that they had lost; their tears dripped onto the earth, and millet sprouted. They urinated, and chickpeas sprouted. They defecated, and lentils sprouted. Then Jibrīl split those grains so that they became numerous, then sowed them; they sprouted immediately.

After being taught all the many laborious steps in the cultivation of wheat, the preparation of flour, and the baking of bread, Adam finally produces an edible loaf.

> When he ate it, tears ran from Adam's eyes. He said, "What is this weariness and fatigue?" He said to him, "This is what God warned you of"—That is God's statement, "This is an enemy to you and your spouse; do not let him expel you from paradise so that you are wretched." "As for now, you may eat of the labour of your hand and the sweat of your brow, you and your children." When Adam finished the food, he felt a pain in his stomach and did not know what it was. He complained of it to Jibrīl, who said, "That is thirst." He said, "How can I quiet it?" He went away, then returned with a pickaxe and said to him, "Dig a hole in the ground." He kept on digging until the pit came to his knees, and water as cool as ice and sweeter than honey sprang up from beneath his feet. He said, "O Adam, take a drink from it." He drank from it, and felt better. Then, after that, he felt a pain worse than the first and the second. He said to Jibrīl, "What is this that I'm feeling?" He said, "I don't know." God sent an angel to him, and [the angel] pierced his front and his anus (*qubulahu*

> *wa-duburahu*); before that there was no place for the food to exit. When something offensive came out of him and he smelled it, he cried about it for seventy years.[101]

The intimate link between the consumption of food and the cycle of finitude and decay that defines mortal life is vividly illustrated by the process in which the oxen produce various staple food crops from their bodily wastes. The enjoyment of nourishment from the fields is merely a link in the progression from dung-enriched soil to human excrement, from waste to waste. The sweet scents of Paradise give way to the evil exhalations of decay. The cycle of consumption and elimination and the bodily permeability which it requires stand in stark contrast, not only to the paradisiac conditions that prevailed before the expulsion from the Garden, but to the condition that awaits the blessed after their return to the eternal Garden. Of course, the Qurʾānic description of the gardens of Paradise includes both food and drink. However, in the Garden one eats and drinks purely for pleasure; there is neither hunger nor thirst.[102] Freed from biological drives, one is also freed of their inevitable consequences; food and drink consumed in Paradise do not lead to the expulsion of unpleasant wastes. Instead, according to a number of early reports, they will evaporate through the skin as a sweet-smelling vapor of musk.[103] Interestingly, some commentators indicate that this phenomenon will lead to a diminution of mankind's "hollow" qualities:

> Ibn ʿAbd al-Aʿlā - Ibn Thawr - Maʿmar - Abān - Abū Qilāba: When the people of heaven have eaten and drunk as much as they wish, they call for the pure drink and drink it. It purifies their stomachs (*buṭūnahum*); what they have eaten and drunk becomes a vapor and the scent of musk, and for this reason their stomachs shrivel up (*taḍmuru buṭūnuhum*).[104]

The absence of digestion and elimination is paralleled by an absence of other processes of putrefaction and decay. Thus, commentators note that the fruits of the world and those of paradise are the same, "except that the former go bad (lit., "change": *tataghayyaru*) and the latter do not go bad (*lā tataghayyaru*)."[105] The same idea is reflected in interpretations of Qurʾān 76:19's reference to "young men of everlasting youth" (*wildān mukhalladūn*):

> The interpreters have differed regarding the meaning of "*mukhalladūn*." Some of them have said that it means that they do not die. . . . Others have said that it means wearing bracelets (*musawwarūn*) . . . Others have said that, rather, it means that they are wearing earrings (*muqarraṭūn*). It has also been said that it means

> that they are eternally youthful and do not change from that age (*lā yataghayyarūna ʿan tilkaʾl-sinn*). It is reported from the [Bedouin] Arabs that they say of a man if he becomes old and his hair remains black that he is "*mukhallad*." Similarly, if he becomes old and his molars and teeth remain in place it is said that he is "*mukhallad*," because he remains in one condition (*huwa thābit al-ḥāl*). This is an emendation to Qatāda's statement that [the verse's] meaning is that they do not die, because if they remain in one condition and do not change by becoming old or white-haired or by dying, then they are *mukhalladūn*.[106]

Thus, a paradisiac state of static perfection is contrasted with an earthly state of flux and change.[107] The motif of change and putrefaction is not, however, the only symbolic resonance of the theme of food and digestion as it relates to ritual purity. The cycle of appetite, consumption, transformation, and expulsion centering on the digestive tract (and secondarily—but only secondarily—the cycle of desire, procreation, and death centering on the other "hollow one," the genitals) has a double significance. In addition to exemplifying our nature as needy, limited, and ultimately mortal beings, it exemplifies the acquisitiveness and greed that lead to injustice and domination among human beings. The hunger for food, and thus for grain and ultimately for land, entailed by the hollowness of the human interior is poignantly evoked in a passage which only narrowly missed inclusion in the Qurʾānic canon. Classical sources record that the following verse was once recited as part of the Revelation:

> If a human being (lit., "son of Adam," *ibn ādam*) had one valley [of land], he would wish for a second; if he had the second, he would wish for a third. Nothing will fill the stomach (*jawf*) of a human being but dust.[108]

The desire for food is not only a reflection of mortal neediness, but a basic source of inequality and injustice in the world. In a world where humans need grain, there will always be those who have more grain than their fellow men; and there is no end to human cupidity but death, the result of the Fall.

It is this second aspect of the complex that explains the deep and organic association between ritual purity and economic ethics in the Islamic tradition. As has already been noted, the second primary thematic association of purity vocabulary in the Qurʾān (after bodily functions) is financial, as exemplified by the duty to "purify" one's wealth by paying *zakāt*. The continuing vitality of this connection between ritual purity and economic rectitude is manifested in many aspects of the Islamic tradition. The double significance of the word "ṭayyib" as used by early Muslims, including ʿUmar ibn ʿAbd al-ʿAzīz, has been discussed in chapter 3. The understanding of financial probity as a prerequisite for food purity is one that persisted among pious Muslims, particularly among Sufis, who frequently refused to eat food suspected of having been bought with ill-gotten gains or money that had not been purified by *zakāt*. Like food, wealth must be *ḥalāl*; if it is not, it robs the food itself of its purity. An account of the pre-Islamic reconstruction of the Kaʿba by the Quraysh in the *Sīra* of Ibn Isḥāq reflects, as always, Islamic values when one of the builders is made to say: "O people of Quraysh, do not bring into the building of this [sanctuary] ill-gotten gains, nor the wages of a harlot, nor money taken in usury, nor anything unjustly taken from its owner."[109] Like objects or humans who are ritually impure, illicitly-gained wealth can pollute a sanctuary.

The story of Adam clarifies this connection by dramatizing the double role of food in an agrarian society. It is not merely humble and benign nourishment, but the primary object of human desire—a desire that transcends the biological need of fallen and mortal beings and shades into acquisitiveness and greed. It is wheat for which we were expelled from Paradise.[110] It is significant that the narrative represents Adam as initiating the practice of inheritance when he is instructed to divide his grains of wheat between himself and Eve—two for himself, one for her. In the world in which these narratives originated, food (that is, agricultural produce) *was* wealth. It is no coincidence that the *ḥadīth* forbidding usury deal with foodstuffs, including grains, as well as gold and silver.[111] The idea of transacting a usurious exchange in wheat may seem odd to us now, but in the world of this *ḥadīth* grain is money; the medium of economic exploitation is not only precious metal but food. It is probably not accidental that it is wheat, and not apples or any other perishable and luxurious fruit, that most Muslim commentators accepted to be the Forbidden Fruit; grain, not only a staple food but a semi durable commodity, was far more symbolic of economic power than any sweet treat.[112] The intimate connection between the lust for food/wealth that led to the Fall and the opportunity to regain Paradise by sharing one's food/wealth is exemplified by the interpretation of the story of Adam presented by a modern-day Iranian villager:

> In paradise Hazrat-i Adam was given paradisic fruits to eat. These fruits became sweat and evaporated without defecation. But then the devil seduced him, saying, "Eat from this wheat! It's a good fruit, better than all others." And Adam ate the wheat. He didn't know that the wheat has the effect of bowel movement. No one who has eaten it is allowed to stay in paradise any longer. So Adam was expelled from paradise . . .

> About this, Hajji Hafiz said: "My father sold the garden of paradise for two grains of wheat. I wouldn't be a worthy son of my father if I wouldn't buy it back with one grain of barley." That means, Hazrat-i Adam was deceived into selling paradise for two grains of wheat, but his offspring can buy paradise back even *with barley, that is, with worldly possessions*—by giving help to the poor and destitute and miserable, by giving bread, by giving a shirt to one who is naked.[113]

The contrast between the timelessness of Paradise and the finitude and dependence of earthly humanity, dramatized in the story of Adam and Eve, also encompasses the final source of personal pollution recognized by Islamic law: sleep. The close interconnection between the two most unavoidable bodily drives, for food and for slumber, is manifest in the following passage describing Adam's first hours:

> God caused a bunch of grapes to draw near to Adam, and he ate it; and that was the first food of Paradise Adam had eaten. When he had finished, he said, "Praise be to God." God said, "For this have I created you, O Adam. It is to be a custom for you and your children to observe until the end of the ages." Slumber then overcame Adam and he slept, for there is no rest for the body except in sleeping. The angels, alarmed, said, "Sleep is the brother of death: this one will surely die!" When Iblis heard that Adam had eaten food, he rejoiced and said, "I shall lead him astray!" Wahb ibn Munabbih said that one of the signs of death is sleep and one of the signs of resurrection is wakefulness.

Like the hollowness of the human anatomy, the human need for slumber is opposed to the perfection and power of God:

> The Children of Israel asked Moses, "Does our Lord sleep?" And God said unto Moses, "O Moses, were I to sleep, the heavens would tumble to earth and the universe and all its contents would pass away altogether." Ibn Abbas said, "The Jews asked our Prophet Muhammad about this, and God revealed to him: *God! there is no God but he; the living, the self-subsisting: neither slumber nor sleep seizeth him* (2:255).

As in the case of excretion and sexuality, human beings will attain some semblance of the attributes of God in their paradisiac state:

> Then they said, "O Muḥammad, do the people of Paradise sleep?" He said, "They do not sleep, because sleep is the brother of death; neither do they die."[114]

The idea that (with the exception of sleep[115]) the bodily functions requiring ablution originated with the disobedience of Adam and Eve and their expulsion from Paradise explains one of the most puzzling aspects of the lore surrounding the *wuḍū'* ablutions: the strong association between *wuḍū'* and the cleansing of sins. This connection is manifested in complexes of traditions stating that ablutions expiate offences and depicting the process of *wuḍū'* as a quasi-physical cleansing of the individual limbs from sin; it is also apparent in the texts of prayers traditionally recommended for use in conjunction with the *wuḍū'* ablutions, which speak of repentance and forgiveness. One popular *ḥadīth* states,

> The Prophet said: When someone stands to perform *wuḍū'* and washes his hands, the sins come out of his hands; when he washes out his mouth, the sins come out of his mouth; when he blows water out of his nose, the sins come out of his nose, and so on until he washes his feet.[116]

On a very general level, this association between ablution and expiation is unsurprising; just as filth is an almost universal metaphor for sin, cleansing is an almost universal metaphor for contrition and absolution. However, this symbolic nexus becomes more perplexing when one considers the specific situations in which the *wuḍū'* ablutions are performed. Although, as we have discussed, various minority opinions recommended ablutions following morally repugnant actions such as evil speech, the overwhelming consensus held that *wuḍū'* was to be performed only after a limited set of bodily functions. These bodily functions, as has been frequently noted, are in no way sinful or even avoidable. Rather, they are an inevitable part of the regular functioning of the healthy human body. Why, one might one ask, should one be moved to reflections on sin and forgiveness while cleansing oneself from urination? The answer may be that urination, like the other bodily functions requiring *wuḍū'*, is emblematic of the condition of the *fallen* body. It is a commonplace that Islam has no concept of original sin; Adam and Eve are alone responsible for their crime, and none of their descendants are born with an inherited guilt requiring the intervention of a savior. However, the children of Adam and Eve live out their earthly lives outside of the Garden; they do not share their foreparents' sin, but they share their expulsion from Paradise. The human condition is fallen; the perfection of Paradise can be restored only after resurrection.

Thus, al-Shirwānī argues that the choice of limbs for purification in *wuḍūʾ* is not at all arbitrary:

> Prayer is a private conversation (*munājāt*) with the Lord, so he requested that we cleanse ourselves for it. . . . The four limbs [that are cleansed in the *wuḍūʾ* ablutions] are selected for this because they are the means by which sins are performed; or, because Adam headed for the [Forbidden] Tree with his face, walked to it with his feet, and picked [a fruit] from it with his hands, and the leaves brushed his head.[117]

Purity and Gender

The analysis in this chapter thus far has suggested that the category of gender, like that of confessional identity, was essentially eclipsed by more universalistic concerns in the classical and postclassical understanding of the law of ritual purity. Not only did the practical provisions of the law come to be understood in a way that minimized the distinction between the sexes, but there was an increasingly important thematic linkage between the phenomenon of ritual pollution and the mortal condition of the fallen Adam—a *human* predicament exemplified primarily by a *male* prototypical figure. Ritual pollution, according to this paradigm, is ungendered; in an androcentric vision of the world, Adam is symbolic not of males but of all humankind. The story of the Fall emphasizes, not sexuality, but voracious hunger and the mortal coil into which it leads. This understanding of the Islamic system of ritual purity as it is symbolically embedded in the story of the Fall is aptly described by Peter Brown, writing of the importance of fasting in the religious life of the Christian Desert Fathers:

> It was widely believed, in Egypt as elsewhere, that the first sin of Adam and Eve had been not a sexual act, but rather one of ravenous greed. It was their lust for physical food that had led them to disobey God's command not to eat the fruit of the Tree of Knowledge. By so doing, they had destroyed the perfect physical equilibrium with which they had been first created. No longer content to contemplate the majesty of God largely (if not wholly) unconscious of the needs of their body Adam and Eve had reached out to devour the forbidden fruit. *In this view of the Fall, greed and, in a famine-ridden world, greed's blatant social overtones—avarice and dominance—quite overshadowed sexuality.*[118]

This is not, of course, the received understanding of the Islamic system of ritual purity among Western scholars of the phenomenon. Instead, the system has been perceived to emphasize gender or, indeed, to function fundamentally as a mechanism for the disempowerment of women or the stigmatization of female sexuality.[119] This argument, as we shall see, arises quite naturally from a basic homology between the prevailing Western understanding of the Islamic system of ritual purity and that of Islamic conceptions of gender. As we have discussed repeatedly in the course of this study, the prevailing view of the Islamic law of ritual purity is that it is fundamentally shaped and motivated by a concern with bodily and psychological control. Any rupture in an individual's mastery over his body, as well as in his emotional composure, results in a rupture in his state of ritual purity, which must be restored through appropriate ablutions. Similarly, it is widely argued that female sexuality is regarded in the Islamic tradition as a chaotic antithesis to a fundamentally male holy order.

It should be noted that a similar conceptualization of gender has been proposed as a cross-cultural constant. In her classic (although now widely and convincingly criticized) article "Is Female to Male As Nature to Culture?" Sherry Ortner proposed in 1972 that the universality of female subordination could be explained "by postulating that women are being identified or symbolically associated with nature, as opposed to men, who are identified with culture."[120] This opposition swiftly reduces to a concern with "control" similar to that articulated by students of ritual purity, as Ortner defines culture as "the notion of human consciousness, or . . . the products of human consciousness (that is, systems of thought and technology), by means of which humanity attempts to assert control over nature."[121] Significantly, although she does not explicitly refer to Mary Douglas or any other theorist of ritual purity, Ortner presents rites of purification as a prime example of this "purposive manipulation of given forms toward regulating and sustaining order," arguing that they are "in large part (though not, of course, entirely) . . . concerned with the relationship between culture and nature." This interpretation, she reasons, clarifies one of the most obvious conundrums arising from the interpretation of systems of ritual purity: if pollution is, cross-culturally, regarded as powerfully and chaotically contagious, how is it that rites of purification are able to contain it? Defining pollution as "the unregulated operation of natural energies," she reasons that

> The answer . . . is that purification is effected in a ritual context; purification ritual, as a purposive activity that pits self-conscious (symbolic) action against natural energies, is more powerful than those energies.[122]

According to this logic, which identifies both women and pollution with the chaotic forces of the natural world and both men and purification with the structuring and controlling efficacy of conscious symbolic action, one would expect systems of ritual purity cross-culturally to regard women as prime sources of pollution. Ortner's hypothesis that the symbolic association of women with nature and men with culture is the constant underlying the subordination of women in all societies has not withstood critical scrutiny in the years following the publication of her article. The universality both of the binary opposition between nature and culture and of the association of each of these realms with one gender has been challenged by anthropologists working in societies where other conceptualizations of the relationship between the social and the natural worlds prevail.[123] However, I believe that it can be argued that the basic logic underlying Ortner's arguments is somewhat more plausible in the specific context of Islamic culture than it has proved to be cross-culturally.

It is frequently held that female gender is associated both in the classical Islamic literary tradition and in many contemporary Islamic societies with the forces of entropy and disorder. Female sexuality, it is argued, is regarded as uncontrolled and uncontrollable, a formidable challenge to the structures and boundaries of a patriarchal culture. This deeply ingrained association between women and disorder is crystallized in the multiple significations of the Arabic root "*f-t-n*," a key term in Islamic religious ethics and political science as well as in the vocabulary of gender. "*Fitna*" is a multivalent term denoting sexual or moral temptation, dissension, conflict, or chaos. It is associated with the social breakdown caused by civil strife, and thus came to be the most common Arabic term used to designate the interludes of internecine warfare that repeatedly rent apart the early Islamic community. It is also strongly associated with the female gender. The Prophet is supposed to have warned his community that women were the direst *fitna* that would face them after his passing; the word is also associated with female allure in a positive sense, and Fātin is a fairly common female name. The two semantic clusters, political and sexual, intersect in the traditions about the Prophet's widow ʿĀʾisha, who was a prominent participant in the Muslim community's first civil war (*fitna*).[124]

If, as these two widely accepted approaches to the topics of ritual purity and gender suggest, both discourses are defined by an underlying preoccupation with order and control, it seems only natural to hypothesize that they must be intimately interrelated. If, as many studies of Islamic attitudes towards women have suggested, women are confined in their homes and their hair confined under the *ḥijāb* in order to prevent the boundary transgressions constantly threatened by their supposedly voracious sexuality, cannot women be regarded as potential "matter out of place" in the sense suggested by Mary Douglas?

A survey of the anthropological literature on Muslim women quickly reveals that this conclusion, although generally not explicitly articulated, has been made by several prominent recent students of Islamic culture who have touched on the subject of ritual purity. Examining the purity practices of a Bedouin group in the Western Desert of Egypt, Lila Abu-Lughod asks why childbirth and menstruation should be regarded as occasions of pollution when reproduction is such a positive social value. Why should the "association with reproduction" resulting from these biological functions, she asks, "contribute to the moral inferiority of women"? An important element of the solution to this conundrum, she argues, is that

> sexuality and reproduction, like menstruation, are negatively valued as "natural" events over which females have little control, thereby providing the avenue through which others come to control them. As such they diminish women's capacities to attain the cultural ideal of self-mastery.[125]

In a study on women in contemporary Turkey, Julie Marcus has made an even more comprehensive argument about the links between the law of purity and the desire to bind and control the transgressive power of women. Marcus argues that purity practices, not the strictures of Islamic family law, are the fundamental mechanism by which normative Islam achieves the subordination of women. Laws of purity, she contends, tend to be applied broadly and unthinkingly and thus play a pervasive and insidious role in the structuring of Turkish society.[126]

Despite the formal gender neutrality of the rules of ritual purity in Islamic law, Marcus argues, they create a deep and fundamental gender asymmetry through their differential impact on the two sexes. The irreduceable difference between the male and female experiences of the Islamic law of ritual purity is related to menstruation, the only polluting bodily function that is not subject to conscious control:

> The law books accord female and male sexuality and bodily secretions absolute equivalence, so that, like men, women are also constructed as sexual. However, unlike male sexuality, women's sexuality is located within a body beyond the control of the mind. The need to control that body in order to achieve purity operates in a way that it does not for its male counterpart.[127]

This hypothesis, in Marcus's view, reveals Islamic purity practices and the strictures relating to female modesty as but two manifestations of the same preoccupation with control. Thus, she can offer a distinctly Douglasian interpretation of the requirement that women conceal their hair:

> Against the background of pollution law, women's hair can be seen as a rather difficult substance, perhaps ambiguous in its nature. Although it flows across the body boundary and it is uncontrolled, it is not of itself polluting, for it is constantly present and in movement; presumably such a process would be difficult to eliminate. . . . Hair is, however, quite clearly defined as a substance in need of control and it is closely linked to the order of the moral community. Women also defined as uncontrolled, are further identified as such through wearing the head hair long. . . . However, head hair seems to be used to state a lack of control which has already been established elsewhere; like so much of cultural practice, it reinforces pollution categories but does not appear to determine them.[128]

Of the two studies, Abu-Lughod's is by far the more successful in embedding her hypotheses about ritual purity in an explication of her subjects' *own* cultural categories. She is able to relate the theme of control, which she perceives to underlie the categorization of women's reproductive functions as polluting, to a broader set of concerns relating to emotion and self-expression. However, her conclusions are of limited relevance to us here because of the scrupulous specificity of her discussion. She avoids essentializing the beliefs she studies as "Islamic," and skirts the subject of Islamic law as a system and the degree to which it generates, or even corresponds to, the practices she observes. Marcus's conclusions are of far greater potential significance for this study, as she explicitly argues that her subjects' practices reflect conscious adherence to the strictures of Islamic law; her arguments purport to apply not merely to the concrete practices of a specific local group of believers, but to Islamic law as a system. Unfortunately, her arguments fail to explain adequately either the significance of the system of ritual purity as experienced concretely by Turkish women (or men) who follow it or the precise nature of the relationship between this concrete experience and the high-cultural discourse that supposedly determines it.

Marcus's thesis is based on the idea that purity strictures underlie the physical circumscription of Turkish Muslim women's lives, limiting them to the domestic sphere and excluding them from the symbolic public constitution of the community of the faithful on Fridays and festivals. In framing this argument, Marcus intermittently conflates several levels of analysis which must be carefully separated for the purpose of our discussion here. The first of these is the level of explicit gender ideology, which itself functions on several different planes: in the high-cultural discourse of the classical legal texts and their modern successors, and in the colloquial discourse of the women and men who adhere to some or all of the practices the texts enjoin. The second is the functional level, on which purity practices may have pragmatic effects on the power relations and mutual perceptions of the sexes without these effects necessarily being acknowledged either by legal scholars or by ordinary believers. Marcus generally seems to assume a close correspondence between the prescriptions of the legal texts and the practices of believers. Thus, her arguments are supported far more often by citations from normative texts than by examples of the statements or behavior of her informants. However, this focus on the analysis of normative texts is to some extent undermined by her further assumption, never set forth in detail, that the actual significance of the purity practices in question lies in pragmatic effects that are mystified and erased by the surface egalitarianism of the legal texts: despite the fact that "the law books accord female and male sexuality and bodily secretions absolute equivalence," when applied to women the law of purity "*operates* in a way that it does not for its male counterpart."[129]

On the level of the explicit content of Islamic legal texts, Marcus's argument is extremely problematic. While a menstruating woman should not tarry in the mosque, and ultimately has very little motive to do so because she is precluded from prayer, there is no basis in the law of ritual purity for the blanket exclusion of women as such from communal prayer. Outside of the mosque setting, there is no basis in ritual purity for the exclusion even of menstruating women from any activity whatsoever. The rationale for the limitation of women to the domestic sphere and their exclusion from communal prayer relates to modesty, and not to purity. As we have seen, Marcus regards the two as effectively synonymous, equating flowing hair and flowing blood alike with boundary transgression and violation of control. Because she never cites statements by the Turkish women whose lives she studied, it is unclear whether this interpretation reflects these women's own conceptualization of the system of ritual purity or merely Marcus's devotion to a Douglasian explanation of ritual purity systems in general. It is, of course, quite possible that the women conceptualized the system in this way. This concept is demonstrated by a study far more sensitive to its subjects' own categories and terminology, Carol Delaney's work on women in a contemporary Turkish village:

> The uncontrolled mixing of the sexes, like the mixture of sexual fluids during intercourse, is felt to be *bulaşık*. *Bulaşık* means

> soiled, tainted, contagious, and is the word used to describe both dirty dishes and contagious diseases. The city (as well as Europe and America), in which this kind of mixing takes place, is considered *bulaşık*, unlike the village, which is *temiz* (clean). The village, where the sexes are relatively segregated, is clean because it is *kapalı*,[130] as are its women.[131]

However, to the extent that the women studied by Marcus actually identified modesty with ritual purity, they were enacting an understanding of ritual purity that is *distinct* from that represented in Islamic legal texts. While the system of ritual purity as understood by legal scholars may have symbolic potentialities that promote the conflation of modesty strictures with the rules of ritual purity, the fact remains that the two domains are completely distinct on the level of explicit legal discourse. A scantily dressed woman, or one who ventures obtrusively into the public domain, may be blameworthy according to the standards of normative Islam; but this has no effect whatsoever on her ritual purity status. Any interpretation of Islamic legal discourse as such must be able to explain the fact that an improperly exposed woman may have to do a range of things to restore her lost propriety, but she will never have to perform ablutions. Urinating in private renders a woman (or a man) ritually polluted; uncovering her hair in public does not.

Despite the analytical weaknesses of Marcus's argument, which represents a valiant initial attempt to address a set of problems too complex to be adequately addressed in a single study, it does make an enormously valuable contribution in suggesting the many levels on which this problem deserves to be addressed in the future. Marcus is, of course, completely correct in observing that the most significant impact of the rules of ritual purity may lie in practical effects never acknowledged (and perhaps never even envisioned) on the level of explicit legal discussion. It is undeniably true that, just as economic policies that are officially blind to socioeconomic status may for this very reason be unusually prejudicial to the poor, legal systems that are formally gender-neutral may by their very denial of the significance of gender be unusually prejudicial to women. Furthermore, explicit legal discourse may itself be produced and interpreted on many different levels. Legal discourse exists not only in classical and modern scholarly texts, but in the minds of ordinary Muslims who interpret, select, and enact the provisions of the law and relate them to other symbolic structures. These popular understandings of the law may not be uniform among different sectors of the population; men and women, for instance, may or may not understand the law and its implications in the same way.

The practical impact of purity strictures on the lives of Muslim women is a complex problem which can be studied only in the context of specific cultural environments and specific periods in history. The factor most relevant to the specifically female experience of the Muslim rules of ritual purity, menstruation, is not a stable or unchanging part of women's biological functioning. Depending on the nutritional and reproductive conditions of a given woman's life, she may menstruate monthly for forty years or a mere handful of times in her entire reproductive life. Anecdotal evidence suggests that many Muslim societies have encouraged reproductive practices (including frequent pregnancy and extended nursing) that have tended to minimize the frequency of menstruation. Geraldine Brooks reports an extreme case from contemporary Saudi Arabia:

> One British doctor, on an eighteen-month posting to a Jeddah hospital, thought his interpreter had failed him during an ante-natal checkup on a twenty-eight-year-old Bedouin. "I asked her when she'd had her last period, and she said, 'What's a period?' It turned out she'd never had one. She'd been married at twelve, before her menarche, and had been pregnant or lactating ever since."[132]

While this has surely never been the norm in any society, Muslim or otherwise, the close spacing of pregnancies in some traditional societies does seem to have minimized the impact of menstruation on ritual purity for some Muslim women in traditional societies. While pregnant and nursing women are permitted to break the Ramadan fast in the interests of their health (in contrast to menstruating women, who cannot hold a valid fast due to their impurity), for many women pregnancy provides a welcome opportunity to fast the entire month without the interruption occasioned by menstruation. Marjo Buitelaar recounts the statements of a group of women in contemporary Morocco:

> That women would prefer to fast all days of Ramadan is expressed in the proud statement of some women that they had fasted throughout Ramadan during their pregnancies. In fact, none of my informants could produce the name of a woman who had not done so. With a broad smile on her face, one women told me about the early years of her marriage, when, for five successive years, she had managed to fast the whole of Ramadan because of being pregnant.[133]

The impact of menstruation is also affected by more modern developments in women's reproductive experience. Buitelaar notes that "these days, many women use birth-control pills, which makes it possible to postpone menstruation until Ramadan has passed."[134]

The fact remains that menstruation inevitably has some impact on women's ritual lives, and that this fact is recognized (and accentuated) in popular concepts of the relationship between gender and religiosity—particularly by men. Buitelaar notes that among the Moroccans she studied "the depreciation of women's fasting activities appears to be shared generally," and that this devaluation is directly related to the necessity that women break their fast during their menstrual periods. While it was distinctly more pronounced among men, who suggested that women failed to make up the fasting days they missed, women also regarded their fasting as defective.[135]

In this study, our concern is specifically with the high-cultural discourse of Islamic law. Thus, the relevant questions for us here are to what extent the idea of women's menstrual impurity is emphasized in the classical textual tradition, and to what extent the idea of ritual purity is symbolically linked with an image of chaotic and uncontrolled female sexuality. As the following examples will demonstrate, it is, in fact, perfectly possible to locate narratives from the classical textual tradition in which the concepts of female sexuality, ritual impurity, and lack of control appear in association. A misogynistic understanding of the concept of ritual pollution is thus not a purely "popular" phenomenon that can be cleanly distinguished from a more universalistic "scholarly" tradition. However, investigation of classical texts also suggests that the thematic cluster female sexuality/disorder/pollution is not characteristic of strictly *legal* discourse.

One of the narratives suggesting the thematic cluster female sexuality/disorder/pollution is a minority opinion (although a fairly well-represented one) about the interpretation of a Qur'ānic verse, 12:31, describing a scene in the story of Joseph. The wife of Joseph's master, having tried in vain to seduce him, becomes the subject of malicious gossip among the women of the town. Hoping to vindicate herself by demonstrating that the youth is in fact irresistible, she invites the women to a repast where she supplies them with fruit and fruit knives before ushering Joseph into the room. When they behold him, according to the text, "*akbarnahu*"—a verb usually intrepreted to mean "they exalted him"—and cut their hands with their fruit knives in their arousal. Other interpretations of the verb "*akbarna*," however, link it with bodily functions causing pollution:

> Abū'l-Shaykh transmitted from (*min ṭarīq*) ʿAbd al-ʿAzīz ibn al-Wazīr ibn Kumayt ibn Zayd ibn al-Kumayt the poet that he said: my father told me from my grandfather: I heard my grandfather say regarding [God's] statement "when they saw him *akbarnahu*," "[it means,] 'they ejaculated (*amnayna*).' And he recited . . ."

There follows a line of Arabic poetry supporting this understanding of the verb *k-b-r*.

> Ibn Jarīr, Ibn al-Mundhir, and Ibn abī Ḥātim transmitted through the chain of transmission ʿAbd al-Ṣamad ibn ʿAlī ibn ʿAbd Allāh ibn ʿAbbās from his father from his grandfather Ibn ʿAbbās that he said regarding [God's] statement {*fa-lammā raʾaynahu akbarnahu*}, [it means,] "When Yūsuf came out to them they menstruated from joy."

He cites a line of Arabic poetry in support of this understanding of the verb *k-b-r*, as well.[136]

The story, according to these interpretations, links female sexual desire both with bodily emissions and with a lack of control that leads the women to inflict bodily harm on themselves. Even in the majority interpretation of the verse, in which the women merely admire Joseph before accidentally cutting their hands, the bodily uncoordination resulting from their lust leads to the shedding of a polluting bodily fluid. The connection among the three elements of sexuality, lack of control, and pollution is clear.

A similar linkage among women, lack of control, and ritual impurity is established in another place in the classical textual tradition, in what may be the most notoriously misogynistic *ḥadīth* in the established corpus:

> The Messenger of God said, "O women! Give alms, and ask forgiveness frequently; I have seen that you are the majority of the inhabitants of Hell." An intelligent woman among them said, "What is wrong with us, that we are the majority of the inhabitants of Hell?" He said, "You curse [people] frequently and are ungrateful to your companions; I have never seen people deficient in intellect and religion who can overcome a man of intelligence as you [women] can." She said, "O Prophet! What is [our] deficiency in intellect and religion?" He said, "As for the deficiency in [your] intellect, the testimony of two women is equivalent to the testimony of one man. That is the deficiency in [your] intellect. [A woman] passes nights without praying and breaks her fast in Ramaḍān; that is the deficiency in [your] religion."[137]

Although the *ḥadīth* makes no explicit reference to the theme of ritual pollution, it was universally understood to refer to women's exclusion from ritual worship during their menstrual periods. Similarly, the theme of loss of control is implicit yet integral to the text. Given the etymology of the word, the *ḥadīth*'s attack on women's intellect (*ʿaql*) naturally lent itself to interpretations focusing on the idea of control. The word *ʿaql* is placed by scholars commenting on the *ḥadīth* in the context of a series of images relating to the concept of binding and restraint:

> Ibn Durayd said, "It is derived from the hobble (*ʿiqāl*) of the she-camel (*nāqa*), because it restrains (*yaʿqilu*) its owner from intemperacy (*jahl*); that is, it holds him back (*yaḥbisuhu*). For this reason, it is said that "the medicine bound (*ʿaqala*) his stomach," meaning that it kept him from defecating (lit., "detained him": *amsakahu*). . . . In al-Azharī's *Tahdhīb* it says, "The person of intellect (*al-ʿāqil*) is the one who holds himself back and restrains himself from [following] his passions, based on the expression, 'He held (*iʿtaqala*) his tongue,' meaning that he restrained it and prevented it from speaking."[138]

The version of the tradition presented by al-Bukhārī contrasts the woman's lack of *ʿaql* with the *ḥazm* (resoluteness) of the men she threatens to entrance. Here again, the image is one of control; the basic meaning of the root *ḥ-z-m* is "to bind, to tie."

Perhaps the place where the interlinkage among the motifs of female sexuality and desire, lack of control, and ritual purity is most pronounced is in the etiological narratives presented by the classical texts to explain the origins of menstruation. It is also in the presentation and interpretation of the alternative scenarios representing this event, however, that the deep ambivalence of legal thinkers towards the nature and meaning of menstruating comes most clearly to expression.

One of the competing narratives is, of course, the story that menstruation was inflicted on Eve as a punishment for her initiative in plucking the Forbidden Fruit. God is made to declare, "As for you, Eve, just as you have made this tree bleed you will bleed every month."[139] Here the themes of female desire, loss of control (exemplified in defiance of the divine decree), and the resulting stigma of monthly pollution are unmistakably intertwined. Another story traces the origins of menstruation not to Eve but to the Israelite nation:

> This is the opinion of ʿAbd Allāh ibn Masʿūd and ʿĀʾisha which is cited by ʿAbd al-Razzāq. The precise wording is: "The men and women of the Children of Israel used to pray together, and women would look at the men (*kānat al-marʾa tatasharraf li-lʾrijāl*). So God visited menstruation upon them and banned them from the places of worship (*manaʿahunnaʾl-masājid*)."[140]

This tradition presents the precise thematic construct suggested by Marcus: female desire, manifesting itself in uncontrolled ogling of men in a setting intended for prayer, leads directly to ritual pollution and to permanent exclusion from the sites of public religious expression. In this case, the complex is enriched by another motif, the association with the Israelites. Lack of control and the resultant pollution are linked not only with a subordinated gender but with a subordinated religious community.

Significantly, however, these narratives of sexuality and sin are challenged and (in the classical legal tradition) largely displaced by an alternative narrative, one which takes a pointedly universalistic approach. This is the statement, attributed to the Prophet Muḥammad, that menstruation "is something that God has decreed for the daughters of Adam." It is framed in a story which clearly demonstrates an intent to remove the stigma from menstruation:

> ʿĀʾisha [recounted] that the Prophet came to see her and found her weeping, having started to menstruate in Sarif before entering Mecca [on the Ḥajj]. He said, "What's the matter; have you gotten your period (*a-nafisti*)?" She said, "Yes." He said, "This is something that God has decreed for the daughters of Adam. Perform all the rites of the Ḥajj (*iqḍī mā yaqḍīʾl-ḥājj*), except that you may not circumambulate the House."[141]

Spare as it is, this statement gently but unmistakably implies that menstruation is not an extrinsic product of female desire imposed as a result of some transgression, but an integral part of God's plan. It is not *imposed* on the daughters of *Eve* (presumably, as a result of her sin) but *decreed* for the daughters of *Adam*—that is, for the females of all humankind. Menstruation is simply a biological fact. It is this tradition about the origins of menstruation that is favored by al-Bukhārī, in preference to the opinion that it was first visited upon the Israelite women.[142]

Thus, the association among the motifs of female sexuality, disorder, and pollution is present (although contested) in Islamic classical discourse. However, as we have seen in the first half of the present chapter, gender does not seem to be a primary organizing category within the specifically *legal* discourse on ritual purity. In fact, specifically legal analysis tended to challenge misogynistic assumptions even within the dialogues surrounding the very texts that have just been advanced as manifesting the association among female sexuality, disorder, and pollution. Thus, legal scholars found it quite difficult to define the precise grounds on which women could be categorized as "deficient in religion" on the basis of the ritual limitations imposed by menstrual pollution. On narrowly legal grounds, it was very difficult to determine precisely where women's shortcomings lay. True, they periodically abandoned their devotions under specified conditions; however, this applied to men who were sick or traveling as well, and no one argued that *they* were deficient in religion. This kind of argument prompted heated rejoinders:

> One should not object that travelers [are a counterexample because] they shorten [their prayers] and are not considered to be deficient in religion, because [a menstruating woman's] refraining from prayer is due to God's holding himself too exalted to allow himself to be worshiped by [women] when they are in a state that is considered dirty (*tanzīh lillāh ta'ālā an ya'budnahu mustaqdhirāt*), in contrast to the traveler. Also, the deficiency is not inevitable (*lāzim*) for the traveler, because he has the option of not traveling, while women do not have the option of not menstruating. It may not be necessary [to resort to this argument], because the traveler merely changes the number [of prayers], while [menstruating women] refrain from prayer altogether.

These arguments themselves were insufficient to convince later commentators on the text; one author commented,

> His first distinction breaks down because [menstruating women] are allowed to engage in meditation (lit., "recollection of God": *dhikr*) and Qur'ānic recitation (*al-tilāwa*)—which is equivalent to prayer (*wa-huwa fī ma'nā' l-ṣalāt*)—and perform all the rites of the Pilgrimage except circumambulation [of the Ka'ba]; a woman engaging in a pious retreat (*al-mu'takifa*) [who begins to menstruate] can do everything that she was doing before except pray and remain in the mosque, according to one of the two opinions current in our school (*'alā aḥad al-qawlayn 'indanā*).[143]

A subsequent commentator, al-Washtānī, went on to argue that

> The Imām's second distinction [actually] results in the opposite [conclusion], since the objection referred to a traveler who shortened [his prayers]; if he shortened [his prayers] and had the option of not traveling, it is more appropriate that he be [regarded as] deficient [i.e., than the woman, who has no such option].[144]

Indeed, legal authors were perplexed by the question of whether menstruating women were in fact credited by God for the prayers they were compelled to omit—a special favor that was considered to apply to sick persons and travelers who were accustomed to performing supererogatory prayers.[145] In general, it was very difficult to explain with reference to legal conceptions of obligation how a menstruating woman could possibly be penalized for omitting a religious observance that she was forbidden to perform.

Thus, it would seem that the classical Islamic discourse on gender is not homogeneous; in this case, the legal discourse seems to be far more egalitarian than the *ḥadīth*. Indeed, as we have seen above, the Islamic law of ritual purity as a whole does not seem to be founded on the concept of control per se. The theme of control, to the extent that it is invoked at all, finds itself specifically within the context of the "hollowness" of Adam. Instead of finding its place in a dichotomy between "male" culture and "female" nature, it is placed in the context of a contrast between the dependency and mutability of life in this world and the self-sufficiency and eternity of God. The gender-neutrality of the rules themselves is reinforced by their grounding in a myth of origins that associates the advent of pollution with the actions of a specifically male (and symbolically universal) figure, Adam. "Male" cultural activities, like farming, are closely associated with the cycle of hunger, consumption, digestion, and excretion which forms the focal point of the system of ritual purity. By abandoning a single-minded focus on the theme of "control," it would seem that we have escaped the paradigm in which pollution must be identified structurally with women.

This conclusion would seem to be challenged by the findings of Carol Delaney. Basing herself on the results of her fieldwork among Turkish village women, Delaney depicts the concept of ritual purity among these contemporary Turkish villagers in much the same way that I have above, basing myself on the classical sources: it is based on a contrast between the change and decay experienced in the physical world (exemplified by polluting bodily functions) and the unchanging eternity of the world to come. However, Delaney finds this understanding of the system of ritual purity to be a highly gendered one. In her Turkish village setting, the pollution experienced in this world is exemplified primarily by menstruation rather than defecation:

> In Muslim Turkish village society, I suggest, menstruation is a fecund symbol for both condensing and expressing a complex set of notions about women, life, and the world. As an index of fertility, it heralds the possibility of life in "this world" (*bu dünya*), as seen in Islam. But earthly life, as the earth itself, is characterized by its mutability and susceptibility to corruption, decay, and death. Existence in this world is juxtaposed to that in the "other world" (*öbür dünya*), considered to be one's original home and the one to which all true Muslims will return.

> The other world is a potent reality to villagers, heightening the contrast to life in this world. In the other world there is said to be food and drink of an ambrosial sort. However, metabolic processes do not occur: the "body" is incorruptible and self-contained. As we shall see, that is the ideal image of the self, and it is associated with and can be approximated in this world only by men. Women, on the other hand, are associated with the physical and perishable aspects of life—that is, with corporeality.[146]

In keeping with this opposition between life on earth and existence in Paradise, Delaney records that the women she studied associated menstruation specifically with Eve's sin and her expulsion from the Garden.[147]

Returning to the classical sources, it is difficult to discern an association between gender and pollution analogous to that discovered by Delaney in modern Turkey. In fact, there is remarkably little linkage between the mortality/eternity dichotomy and any specifically female form of pollution. As discussed, the idea that menstruation originated specifically with the sin of Eve is contested in the classical sources. Similarly, the contrast between the eternal existence of heaven and the flux of mortal existence is articulated by the classical sources in largely gender-neutral terms. This gender neutrality is reflected, for instance, in the medieval exegetes' interpretation of the Qur'ān's reference (verse 2:25) to the "purified companions" who will accompany the blessed in Heaven. As is to be expected, the "purity" of these heavenly creatures is understood to consist in freedom from boundary-violating bodily discharges. As these "companions" are understood to be female, one might have expected that the focus would be on specifically female bodily functions. However, this is not the case; the many interpretations cited by al-Ṭabarī speak of urination and defecation, spitting, and ejaculation as well as menstruation and childbirth. Specifically female functions are mentioned, but they do not dominate the field; the concern is with the polluting functions of the human, not specifically the female, body.[148]

Is the Islamic law of ritual purity, then, gender-neutral? I would like to propose that the evidence under discussion here manifests a principle developed by Victor Turner: that the category distinctions evoked in a specific ritual are highly situational, and that we should not expect the relevant category distinctions to be active in all ritual activities within one religious system. Turner writes:

> There is no single hierarchy of classifications that may be regarded as pervading all types of situations. Rather, there are different planes of classification which transect one another, and of which the constituent binary pairs (or triadic rubrics) are only temporarily

connected: e.g., in one situation the distinction red/white may be homologous with male/female, in another with female/male, and in yet another with meat/flour without sexual connotation.[149]

Thus, we may understand Sunnī legal discourse to have declined (increasingly over time) the distinctions of gender, confessional identity, and even biological life as organizing principles of the law of ritual purity; this does not imply that the same is true for Islamic legal discourse as a whole. A particularly clear example of this phenomenon is presented by the strictures relating to physical modesty. Islamic law has developed an intricate set of specifications dictating which parts of the body must be covered both during worship, which is invalidated by immodest exposure, and in the presence of other people. The degree of coverage required varies according to the social categorization both of the person whose body is revealed or concealed and of the others to whose gaze he or she is exposed. Most obvious, or perhaps most notorious, is the distinction between men and women; thus, women may expose only their faces and hands during prayer, while men must be covered only from the navel to the knees. The other significant distinction relating to the person whose body is revealed divides slaves from the free; a slave woman may expose as much of her body as a man. The remaining distinctions relate to the identity of the beholder; the required degree of coverage depends on whether one is exposed to the gaze of someone of the same or of the opposite sex, a member of one's immediate family or a stranger, and a Muslim or a nonbeliever. The criteria of gender, freedom, kinship, and Islam may or may not correspond directly to attributions of positive or negative value. The ways in which the license to expose extensive flesh may simultaneously dignify men and devalue female slaves are subtle and ambiguous. Yet it is indisputable that the selection of these particular criteria for attention is distinctive and significant to the underlying values of the law. This set of rules would have expressed different values if, for instance, it had prescribed differing degrees of coverage based on generational differences as well as differences in gender. Furthermore, as we have seen, the same category distinctions need not be taken as the organizing principles of other areas of Islamic law.

The classical and postclassical jurists' gender-neutral structuring of the law of ritual purity must, thus, be understood as a specific case reflecting these jurists' understanding of the true nature and symbolic resonance of one limited area of the law. Specifically, it can be understood to find its place in the context of the Islamic affirmation of the equal spiritual dignity of all believers that is most vividly expressed in Muslims' ritual lives. Although gender distinctions are introduced into various aspects of Islamic ritual (primarily dress and the physical placement of male and female worshipers) by considerations of modesty and propriety, ritual law—unlike family and economic law—is overwhelmingly dominated by the universalistic theological principles of the faith.

Conclusions

The fact that the narrative of the creation and fall of Adam and Eve is saturated with the themes of bodily integrity and its rupture, control, and loss demonstrates that the Islamic law of ritual purity can usefully be understood against the background of the Islamic creation myth. That this should be the case is unsurprising in the light of general patterns in the history of religions. Mircea Eliade has hypothesized that all rituals are grounded in myths of origins; they "acquire the meaning attributed to them, and materialize that meaning," he writes, "only because they deliberately repeat such and such acts posited *ab origine* by gods, heroes, or ancestors."[150] In this particular instance, I would argue, ritual actions gain their resonance not from the recapitulation of ontology but in the anticipation of its reversal. In relating how humans came to be embodied, porous, and fatefully dependent on food and sleep, the story of Adam evokes the human predicament and demands a ritual response.

In its revelation of Adam and his progeny as beings that "are hollow and cannot control themselves," the story of Adam provides evidence that, in some sense, the eternally frustrated human desire for control lies at the heart of the law of ritual purity. However, the narrative demands an altered and limited understanding of the concept of control. Agriculture is, after all, a fundamental manifestation of culture as a force binding and controlling nature; yet the cultivation of the earth—like weaving, toolmaking, and cooking—appears within the story as deeply implicated in the cycle of pollution and death. The control underlying the system is neither emotional composure nor cultural mastery, but control over the voraciousness that underlies life after the Fall.

Similarly, a common-sense application of the concept of control would dictate that vomiting is unambiguously polluting: it represents a violation of the boundaries of the body that is unpredictable and involuntary, shattering the strongest composure. To understand the competing opinions that were actually advanced by Muslim jurists, one must have some explanation for the two criteria they applied to the question: the substantive purity status of the matter expelled from the body and the orifice through which the matter is expelled. The idea that the stomach is "the locus of impurity," the idea that food cast up from the stomach is impure if it has "changed," and the idea that the genitals and the anus are the "two exits" causing pollution are all conceptions outside of the purview of the concept of "control." The law of purity's focus upon the stomach and the process of digestion can be understood only in the context of a more culturally specific set of concepts revolving around the opposition between eternity and stasis on the one side, and mortality and "change" on the other.

Interestingly, the theme of mortality and decay has recently been proposed as a key to the understanding of purity practices cross-culturally. While the Islamic belief in eternal life (and in a paradisiac realm that presents a purified and incorruptible mirror image of this world) informs the concrete content of the Islamic discourse of purity, the connection between pollution and decay appears to have some cross-cultural relevance. Anna Meigs has argued that the opposition between life and death underlies the concept of pollution among the Papuans she studied, and proposes that the same structure underlies modern Americans' sensibilities. The life-death opposition, she argues, permits an understanding of the concept of pollution that structuralist concepts of "ambiguity" do not:

> We experience sexual fluids, faeces, urine, sweat, blood as substances well on the road to decay if not already decaying, as things which are dying, separated from that which can make them alive. . . . Body emissions are polluting because they begin to decay as soon as they leave the body. The fear and revulsion which humans feel at decaying substances, at polluting, undoubtedly reflects our fear of the decay which often precedes death and which, of course, always follows it.[151]

Nevertheless, the opposition between paradisiac perfection and earthly neediness and decay is not *the* underlying logic of the Islamic law of purity; rather, it is one symbolic context among several. The degree of disagreement and change manifested in juristic discussions of ritual purity from the preclassical to the postclassical period demonstrates that the provisions of the law cannot be mechanically derived from any single generating principle. The individual cases examined in the various chapters of this study suggest that differences of opinion were not merely technical matters of detail; rather, they manifest deep and ongoing reflection on the underlying shape and significance of the law of purity. The law of purity did not merely undergo a trajectory of change in a single direction. A number of different tendencies and meanings always persisted within Muslim understandings of the law.

Thus, the universalism generated by the integration of the law of purity with the story of the Fall stands in tension with the covenantal exclusivity of the Qur'ānic law of purity. Of course, the covenant binding Muslims could be (and was, in some cases) understood in a universalistic fashion; Muslims understood all the children of Adam to be covenantally bound to their Creator.[152] However, the community-defining role of the law of ritual purity always remains the opposite pole to its universalistic meanings. The function of the law of purity in defining the boundaries of the community may be most prominent in minority and sectarian communities (for instance, among the Muslims of China[153] and among Shīʿites), but it is always available; it is always *one of* the meanings of the law.

The debate over the purity status of dead human bodies reflects another deep and productive tension within the law of purity. It arises from the tension between a symbolic logic in which pollution is fundamentally an expression of the tragedy of mortal life (and thus centrally associated with death) and a theology that affirms eternal life.

The Muslim uncertainty regarding the purity of human corpses is particularly striking in light of the attitudes of neighboring religious communities. Death is the central source of human pollution as understood by Zoroastrians; all substances issuing from the body, from breath and saliva to blood and urine, are regarded as "dead matter of the living" and "are open to grave pollution from the Corpse Demoness."[154] It is also frequently and, I believe, accurately argued that the pollution of death is the supreme organizing principle of the entire Jewish system of purity. The primacy of the opposition between life and death is clearly indicated by the biblical language used to describe many aspects of the law of purity, as well as by the structure of the system elaborated by the rabbis. A person suffering from a defiling skin disease (*tzaraʿat*, traditionally, although inaccurately, translated as "leprosy"), one of the major sources of impurity in Jewish law, is referred to in the Hebrew Bible as being "like one who is dead."[155] The consumption of blood is biblically forbidden because "the life of the flesh is in the blood."[156] A woman polluted by menstruation must be purified with "living water."[157] Most importantly, in the rabbinic system the "father of the fathers of impurity"—the only source of pollution that causes three degrees of contagion—is the corpse.[158]

In light of this pattern, the development of a strong current of Muslim opinion denying the impurity of human corpses is striking. The subtraction of the corpse from the set of defiling substances represents not merely the elimination of one item from a rather extensive list, but a revolutionary rethinking of the whole system. Interestingly, this Islamic development recapitulates a similar development within Christianity. Philippe Ariès writes,

> Despite their familiarity with death, the ancients feared the proximity of the dead and kept them out of the way. . . . Whether they were buried or cremated, the dead were impure; if they were too near, there was danger of their contaminating the living. In order to avoid all contact, the abode of the dead had to be separated

> from the domain of the living, except on the days of propitiatory sacrifices; this was an unbreakable rule. . . . But this aversion to the proximity of the dead soon gave way among the early Christians, first in Africa and later in Rome. The change is remarkable, for it reflects a profound difference between the old pagan attitude and the new Christian attitude toward the dead.[159]

In a similar vein, Peter Brown notes that

> the Christian cult of saints rapidly came to involve the digging up, the moving, the dismemberment—quite apart from much avid touching and kissing—of the bones of the dead, and, frequently, the placing of these in areas from which the dead had once been excluded.[160]

Unlike the Christian innovations described by Ariès and Brown, the Islamic development described here is primarily a change in classificatory thought rather than in the physical treatment of the dead. Fondling human remains never became a common element of Islamic piety. However, Ariès's explanation for the Christians' swift rejection of the "old repugnance" for the dead could just as well describe the Muslim case: it occurred "through faith in the resurrection of the body."[161]

Conclusion

While it is impossible to demonstrate the literal accuracy or exact date of any individual report dealt with in this study, I believe that the cumulative picture is surprisingly credible. The reports as a group yield, not a blatantly idealized projection into the past of the consensus of later generations, but a plausible picture of gradual and contested progress towards a coherent understanding of the law. With respect to the Qur'ān, for instance, they suggest that an overall correspondence with the text of the Qur'ān is noticeable from the outset, more rigorous textual analysis raises questions by the early second century A.H., and technical solutions are discernible by the middle of the second century. (The chronology of the development of Qur'ānic argumentation in this area of the law, of course, may or may not be the same as that for other subject areas.) The generation that flourished in the late first and early second centuries A.H. also appears to be engaged in a search for authoritative precedents, frequently resorting to the example of the previous generation but sometimes also invoking the Prophet himself. The opinions attributed to jurists of this generation imply a lively formative stage in which a number of important questions are still open, or at least still worth debating. In the cases of *wuḍū'* from cooked food and of touching the genitals, as discussed in chapter 3, politicized elements in the texts of a number of reports suggest the historical setting of the Marwānid period, and specifically the closing first and opening second centuries A.H., for the dissemination of relevant *ḥadīth*. While the origins and literal accuracy of such *ḥadīth* texts have not been examined here and are perhaps ultimately undeterminable by purely historical means, this period of time seems to have been crucial for their promotion and incorporation in the juristic circles that developed the law of purity.

The examples we have discussed here show the lively interaction between a set of authoritative texts (including Qur'ān, *ḥadīth*, and the statements of prominent early Muslims) and a vital community whose living practice also seems to have exercised considerable authority. In contradiction to the arguments of revisionists such as Schacht, the material reviewed in chapter 2 suggests that the complexities and ambiguities of the Qur'ānic text entered into the formation of Sunnī purity law at the earliest and most formative stage; almost every nicety of syntax in the relevant wording of the Qur'ān has given rise to a significant corresponding debate in the earliest strata of of juristic discussion to which we have access. However, the interpretive activities of early jurists were also clearly constrained by the force of existing practice. Like the conviction that it was necessary to perform *wuḍū'* after arising from sleep in the morning, some aspects of purity practice seem to have been so firmly established that quibbling over possible textual rationales played a strictly secondary role. The double nature of the community's transmission of purity law, which was passed on both through texts and through personal example, is reflected even in the purely textual material examined here. Unlike some other aspects of the *sharī'a*, a rite such as *wuḍū'* was disseminated both as an abstract set of rules and as a bodily praxis. The authority to *say* what *wuḍū'* entailed (and what entailed *wuḍū'*) was thus paralleled by the authority to *show* it. Interestingly, a number of the examples covered here suggest that both types of authority were actively claimed and contested not only by early scholars, but by the Umayyad caliphs and members of the ruling family. Purity law thus emerged from the social and political interplay among rulers, scholars, and ordinary Muslims as well as from the theoretical interplay between authoritative text and unifying theory.

Perhaps the most striking element of the developments I have tried to trace in these pages is the flexibility of the patterns and meanings that have been imposed on the basic rules of ritual purity. Chapter 1, examining the Qur'ānic context of the purity verses on a number of different levels, argued that their most consistent thematic association was with the motif of the covenantal community. The verses enjoining ablutions are both accompanied by covenantal language and located in passages and verses emphasizing the themes of community unity and integrity and separation from nonbelievers. The purity practices attributed to 'Umar ibn 'Abd al-'Azīz, which integrate purity and pollution into the ethical and eschatological frameworks of the Qur'ān (chapter 3) while emphasizing separation from nonbelievers (chapter 4), seem to be very much in harmony with this reading of the Qur'ān. However, the possible meanings of the purity practices involved were not exhausted by such an understanding. As argued in chapter 4, the classical Sunnī schools of law did not embrace an interpretation in which separation and hierarchy were the underlying rationales; rather, perhaps in harmony with a theological view in which all humankind were latent members of the covenant, they elided more exclusivist readings of the law to yield a highly universalist and egalitarian understanding of purity.

Furthermore, understandings of purity law were never unified or frozen. Although legal texts do not focus on the meaning of the rules they set forth, relatively insignificant differences in substantive law can yield far-reaching variations in implied meaning. Whether or not touching one's genitals cancels one's state of purity is not, on the face of it, a question of enormous practical import. However, when one contrasts such a belief with the statements attributed to early scholars that the genitals are "just a part of your body" and that touching them is no different from touching one's nose, it is difficult to deny that there is a genuine symbolic and psychological difference between the two. One view hierarchizes parts of the body and stigmatizes some of them as unclean; the other affirms that the human person is pure in its entirety. Similarly, a person who believes that even the most minor and inoffensive skin-to-skin contact with a member of the opposite sex causes ritual pollution will certainly feel and behave somewhat differently from someone who believes it permissible to kiss his or her spouse on the way to prayer. Internalized as components of a daily praxis, acceptance or avoidance of such contact could yield subtly yet significantly varying ways of being and feeling in a Muslim body.

Notes

Introduction

1. See A. Kevin Reinhart, "Impurity/No Danger," *History of Religions* 30 (1990–91):1–2.

2. The Anṣār are residents of Medina who, with the emigrants (Muhājirūn) from Mecca, constituted the Muslim community following the Hijra.

3. ʿAbd al-Razzāq al-Ṣanʿānī, *al-Muṣannaf*, ed. Ḥabībarraḥmān al-Aʿẓamī (Simlak, Dahbel/Beirut, A.H. 1391/1972 C.E.), #1208. The *Muṣannaf* of ʿAbd al-Razzāq will henceforth appear in the notes as AR, with the number of the tradition.

4. There is some disagreement about the last two items, which will be discussed in detail in chapter 2.

5. As suggested by the quotation at the beginning of this introduction, believers are required to cleanse themselves of urine or feces (either with stones or similar substances or, as came to be considered preferable, with water) after elimination. This cleansing is known as *istinjā*ʾ. I will not be dealing with *istinjā*ʾ in this study because I do not consider it to be a form of ritual purity. It is an act of physical cleansing required for the preservation of the believer's ordinary state of good hygiene, rather than a ritual performed to produce a state of purity in preparation for ritual activity. It does, of course, fit into the overall system of ritual purity in the sense that one is required to remove all impure substances from one's body and clothing as a prerequisite for ritual purification.

6. In rare cases, an impure substance can undergo a qualitative transformation that renders it pure; thus, wine (which is substantively impure) can change into vinegar (which is pure). However, this is not because the wine has become pure but because it has ceased to be wine. Similar transformations were perceived by some jurists in the biological processes by which such impure substances as menstrual blood and semen (regarded as impure by all schools except the Shāfiʿites) were supposedly transformed into human embryos and mother's milk.

7. It is possible for an object or substance to become secondarily impure (*mutanajjis*) as a result of contact with an impure substance. However, this is not because the pollution of the impure substance involved is communicated to the pure substance; it is, rather, because the impure substance remains physically present.

Thus, if blood is mixed into a pure liquid it may become impure (unless there is a large amount of liquid and admixture of blood is not discernible by color, smell, or taste). It is true that contact with an impure substance will render a small amount of water impure even if no perceptible quantity of the impure substance enters the water. However, this is still based on the assumption that some residue of the impure substance must remain in the water.

8. Robert Parker, *Miasma: Pollution and Purification in Early Greek Religion* (Oxford: Clarendon Press, 1983), pp. 1–143.

9. *Encyclopaedia Judaica* (Jerusalem, Israel: Keter, 1971), s.v. "Purity and impurity, ritual."

10. Jamsheed Choksy, *Purity and Pollution in Zoroastrianism* (Austin: University of Texas Press, 1989), p. 55.

11. Ibid., p. 78.

12. Ibid., p. 92.

13. Ibid., p. 91.

14. Ibid., p. 14.

15. Ibid., pp. 14, 103–4.

16. Cf. Matthew 15:1–7, 23:23–26; Acts 10:9–16; Romans 14:14–23; I Corinthians 10:23–33.

17. John T. MacNeill and Helena M. Gamer, *Medieval Handbooks of Penance: A Translation of the Principal* libri poenitentiales *and Selections from Related Documents* (New York: Columbia Unversity Press, 1938), p. 197.

18. Ibid., pp. 208, 211.

19. Ibid., p. 207.

20. Ibid., p. 206.

21. Ibid., p. 208.

22. Suzanne Pinckney Stetkevych, *The Mute Immortals Speak: Pre-Islamic Poetry and the Poetics of Ritual* (Ithaca and London: Cornell University Press, 1993), pp. 66, 193–96.

23. Hishām ibn-al-Kalbi, *The Book of Idols*, trans. Nabih Amin Faris (Princeton, N.J.: Princeton University Press, 1952), p. 27. Ibn al-Kalbī supports this report, p. 28, with a line of poetry by Balʿā' ibn Qays ibn ʿAbd Allāh ibn Yaʿmar.

24. Stetkevych, *Mute Immortals*, p. 194 (citing al-Tibrīzī, d. A.H. 502/1109 C.E.).

25. In Ibn Isḥāq's biography of the Prophet, a Meccan polytheist vows that he "will not wash his head from sexual impurity (*janāba*)" until he has done battle

against Muḥammad—that is, he will abstain from sexual intercourse (Abū Muḥammad ʿAbd al-Malik ibn Hishām ibn Ayyūb al-Ḥimyarī al-Maʿāfirī al-Baṣrī, *al-Sīra al-Nabawīya li-Ibn Hishām*, ed. Ṭāhā ʿAbd al-Raʾūf Saʿd (Beirut: Dār al-Jīl, A.H. 1411/ A.D. 1991), 3:310; A. Guillaume, *The Life of Muhammad, A Translation of Ibn Ishaq's Sirat Rasul Allah* [Karachi: Oxford University Press, 1967], p. 361.

26. Ibn Hishām, *Sīra*, 1:138, 163, 2:301; Guillaume, *Life of Muhammad*, pp. 11, 207–8.

27. G. Ryckmans, "La confession publique des péchés," *Le Muséon* 58 (1945): 9, 10.

28. A. J. Wensinck, "Die Entstehung der muslimischen Reinheitsgesetzgebung," *Der Islam* 5 (1914):62–80.

29. A more striking example is cited by Wensinck himself, although he dismisses it as merely "merkwürdig." This is a passage describing the rules governing the purity status of water, drawn from the works of a Christian of the Islamic period, Bar Hebräus (*Ethicon*, ed. Bedjan, p. 169, cited in Wensinck, "Enstehung," p. 67). Bar Hebräus's rendition of the rules of water purity parallels Islamic rulings precisely, with a single exception (the specific quantity specified as the minimum not rendered impure by small amounts of polluting matter); it could easily be translated into Arabic and interpolated into a work of Islamic law. Given that it dates from well within the Islamic period, it presumably indicates Islamic influence on Christian practice rather than the opposite; however, it strikingly demonstrates that conceptions of purity and pollution are not necessarily confined by confessional boundaries.

30. I. Goldziher, "Islamisme et parsisme," *Révue de l'histoire des religions* 43 (1901):9.

31. Ibid., p. 10.

32. Cited in Mary Boyce, "*Pādyāb* and *Nērang*: Two Pahlavi Terms Further Considered," *Bulletin of the School of Oriental and African Studies* 54 (1991):287. See also Choksy, *Purity and Pollution*, p. 56.

33. Choksy, *Purity and Pollution*, p. 55.

34. See Boyce, "*Pādyāb* and *Nērang*," pp. 286–87.

35. Ibid., p. 290 n. 53.

36. Ibid., p. 288.

37. In an earlier work, Boyce writes that "clearly most of what the two communities have in common stems from what was general usage for all Zoroastrians in Iran at the time when the Parsis left," in the tenth century C.E. However, she also notes that the two communities remained in contact and that both Arabic vocabulary and such distinctive practices as the building of funerary towers passed from the Iranian Zoroastrians to their coreligionists in Gujarat in the Islamic period (Mary Boyce, *Zoroastrians: Their Religious Beliefs and Practices* [London: Routledge & Kegan Paul, 1979], pp. 157–58).

38. Ibn Hishām, *Sīra*, 2:53 (Guillaume, *Life of Muhammad*, p. 99). This minimal, yet symbolically potent, list of avoidances is somewhat reminiscent of the Christian example in Acts 21:25, which prescribes abstinence "from what has been sacrificed to idols and from blood and from what is strangled and from unchastity."

39. Ibn Hishām, *Sīra*, 3:43. Some of the practices mentioned here seem to have been elements of pagan Arabian practice as well; thus, one should perhaps infer that it was Abū Qays's punctiliousness in the performance of ablutions after sexual pollution—or, alternatively, the fact that he washed his entire body rather than "touching his head with water" like the pagan mentioned above—rather than that the practice itself was novel. Similarly, the statement that he "avoided pollution through contact with menstruating women (*taṭahhara min al-ḥāʾiḍ min al-nisāʾ*)" may mean that he avoided contact of all kinds with any woman who was menstruating, not merely that he refrained from intercourse with his wife during her menstrual period.

40. Ibn Ḥajar al-Haytamī, *Tuḥfat al-muḥtāj bi-sharḥ al-minhāj*, printed in the margin of al-Shirwānī, *Ḥawāshī al-ʿShirwānī wa Aḥmad ibn Qāsim al-ʿAbādī ʿalā tuḥfat al-muḥtāj bi-sharḥ al-minhāj* (n.p., n.d.), 1:185–86.

41. al-Thaʿālibī, whose death date is unknown, dedicated his *Ghurar akhbār mulūk al-furs wa-siyarihim* to a brother of Maḥmūd of Ghazna who died in A.H. 412/1021 C.E. (*EI*[1], s.v. "al-Thaʿālibī").

42. ʿAbd al-Malik ibn Muḥammad al-Thaʿālibī, *Ghurar akhbār mulūk al-furs wa-siyarihim*, ed. H. Zotenberg (Paris: Imprimerie Nationale, 1900), pp. 258–60. Mary Boyce notes that "washing the hands and face" was a phrase used by Zoroastrian scholars to refer to the *kustī/pādyāb* ablutions (which, of course, included more than merely the hands and face) until the modern period (Boyce, "*Pādyāb* and *Nērang*," pp. 286–87). Presumably al-Thaʿālibī is relying on a written source, rather than observing actual behavior.

43. Muslim, ibn al-Ḥajjaj, *Ṣaḥīḥ Muslim bi-sharḥ al-imām Muhyiʾl-Dīn al-Nawawī*, vol. 3, ed. Khalīl Maʾmūn Shīḥā (Beirut: Dār al-Maʿrifa), 3:202–3. Parallels in Aḥmad ʿAbd al-Raḥmān al-Bannā, known as al-Sāʿātī, *al-Fatḥ al-rabbānī li-tartīb musnad al-imām Aḥmad ibn Ḥanbal al-Shaybānī* (n.p.: Maṭbaʿat al-Ikhwān al-Muslimīn, n.d.), 2:152–53; Abū Dāwūd Sulaymān ibn al-Ashʿath al-Sijistānī, *Sunan Abī Dāwūd*, ed. Muḥammad Muḥyiʾl-Dīn ʿAbd al-Ḥamīd (n.p.: Dār Iḥyāʾ al-Sunna al-Nabawīya, n.d.), 1:177–78; Muḥammad ibn Yazīd ibn Māja, *Sunan*, ed. Muḥammad Fuʾād ʿAbd al-Bāqī (n.p.: ʿĪsā al-Bābī al-Ḥalabī wa-Shurakāʾuhu, n.d.), 1:211; Aḥmad ibn Shuʿayb al-Nasāʾī, *al-Sunan al-kubrā*, ed. Muḥammad Ḥabīb Allāh Amīr al-Dīn al-Atharī (Bombay: al-Dār al-Qayyima, A.H. 1405/1985 C.E.), 1:78.

44. Choksy, *Purity and Pollution*, p. 97.

45. Jalāl al-Dīn al-Suyūṭī, *al-Durr al-manthūr fīʾl-tafsīr biʾl-maʾthūr* (Tehran, 1377/[1957]), 1:258. Emphasis mine.

46. It is thus no surprise that most versions of the tradition which do not explicitly mention the Jews leave the people in question anonymous, merely remark-

ing that "they" used to refuse to share a house with a menstruating woman. See Muḥammad ibn Jarīr al-Ṭabarī, *Jāmiʿ al-bayān ʿan taʾwīl āy al-qurʾān* (Beirut: Dār al-Fikr, A.H. 1408/1988 C.E.), 2:380–81.

47. *Archiv für Religionswissenschaft* 13 (1910): 20–46.

48. J. Wellhausen, *Reste arabischen Heidentums*, 2d ed. (Berlin: Druck und Verlag von Georg Reimer, 1897), p. 150.

49. Ibid., p. 158.

50. Thus, he interprets the pious wish that a grave be richly watered with rain in terms of the belief cherished by "many primitive people (*Naturvölkern*)" that water offers protection agains demons, yet remarks that "already in the pre-Islamic period the original meaning was no longer known to the poets who used it" (Goldziher, "Wasser als Dämonen abwehrendes Mittel," *Archiv für Religionswissenschaft* 13 (1919): pp. 21, 27).

51. Muḥammad ibn Ismāʿīl al-Bukhārī, *Ṣaḥīḥ al-Bukhārī*, ed. ʿAbd al-ʿAzīz ibn ʿAbd Allāh ibn Bāz (n.p.: Dār al-Fikr, A.H. 1411/1991 C.E.), 1:51.

52. Abūʾl-ʿAbbās Shihāb al-Dīn Aḥmad ibn Muḥammad al-Qasṭallānī, *Irshād al-sārī li-sharḥ ṣaḥīḥ al-Bukhārī* (Baghdād: Maktabat al-Muthannā; facsimile of Būlāq, A.H. 1403), 1:233.

53. Cf. Qurʾān 2:267, 4:2, 5:100, 7:157, 8:37, 14:26, 21:74, 24:26.

54. Louis Dumont, *Homo Hierarchicus: The Caste System and Its Implications*, trans. Mark Sainsbury (Chicago: University of Chicago Press, 1970), pp. 50–51.

55. Parker, *Miasma*, p. 63. Parker, basing his comments on early Greek belief and practice, may be too general in his comments regarding marriage. Practices such as the seclusion of the newly-wed couple and the avoidance of the "dangerous" glance of brides, attested for various cultures, suggest that some contagious "danger" does surround the marriage rites—even if, to the best of my knowledge, this dangerous state is not counteracted with ritual ablutions. These data demand either that we question Parker's evalution of marriage as being "not an intrusion that requires sealing off, but . . . itself a harness set upon the rebellious body" (in favor, perhaps, of a dual view in which marriage both unleashes the dangerous power of sexuality by licensing intercourse and attempts to constrain it by proscribing adultery) or that we reconsider his basic premise that events are polluting if and only if they involve an uncontrollable irruption of the natural into human life.

56. Mary Douglas, *Purity and Danger: An Analysis of the Concepts of Pollution and Taboo* (London: Routledge, 1966), pp. 42–58.

57. E. Leach, "Anthropological Aspects of Language: Animal Categories and Verbal Abuse," in *Mythology*, ed. P. Maranda (Baltimore: Penguin, 1972), pp. 49–50; quoted in Anna S. Meigs, "A Papuan Perspective on Pollution," *Man*, N.S. 13 (1978), p. 312.

58. Parker, *Miasma*, p. 62.

59. Ibid., p. 62.

60. Jack Goody, *The Domestication of the Savage Mind* (Cambridge: Cambridge University Press, 1977), pp. 45–46.

61. Ibid., pp. 45–46.

62. P. Hershman, "Hair, Sex and Dirt," *Man*, n.s., 9 (1974): 292–93.

63. Mary Douglas, *Natural Symbols: Explorations in Cosmology* (New York: Pantheon Books, 1970), pp. 38–41.

64. Hershman, "Hair, Sex and Dirt," p. 293.

65. John W. Burton, "Some Nuer Notions of Purity and Danger," *Anthropos* 69 (1974): 525.

66. A. Kevin Reinhart, "Impurity/No Danger," pp. 1–24.

67. Ibid., pp. 7–8. Reinhart's discussion of pure and impure bodily secretions, based on the comments of the Muslim jurist and theologian al-Ghazālī (d. A.H. 505/1111 C.E.), may be amplified by noting that the *same* substances categorized as polluting when they exit the body have no polluting effect while they remain within the body. Thus a Muslim jurist writes,

> That which does not exit is not legally classified as substantively impure, because it is in its place (*ghayr al-khārij lā yuʿṭā lahu ḥukm al-najāsa li-kawnihi fī maḥallihi*). [For instance,] if [someone] were to pray while holding a lamb or an egg whose yolk had turned to blood his prayer would be valid; the fact that [the substance in question, i.e., the blood in the lamb or in the egg] has not exited entails that it is not substantively impure.

(Muḥammad ibn Maḥmūd al-Bābartī, *Sharḥ al-ʿināya ʿalāʾl-hidāya*, printed with Ibn Humām, *Sharḥ fatḥ al-qadīr* [Sharikat Maktaba wa-Maṭbaʿat Muṣṭafā al-Bābī al-Ḥalabī, A.H. 1389/1970 C.E.], 1:45.)

68. Julie Marcus, "Islam, Women and Pollution in Turkey," *Journal of the Anthropological Society of Oxford* 15 (1984): 313.

69. A category of spirit beings believed to include black dogs (see Ibn Manẓūr, *Lisān al-ʿarab*, s.v. ḥ-n-n).

70. ʿAmr ibn Baḥr al-Jāḥiẓ, *al-Ḥayawān*, Book One, ed. ʿAbd al-Salām Muḥammad Hārūn ([Cairo]: Maktabat Muṣṭafā al-Bābī al-Ḥalabī wa-awlādihi bi-Miṣr, A.H. 1356/1937–38), 1:222.

71. Cf. ʿAbd al-Raḥmān al-Jazīrī, *Kitāb al-fiqh ʿalāʾl-madhāhib al-arbaʿa* (n.p.: Dār Iḥyāʾ al-Turāth al-ʿArabī, A.H. 1406/1986 C.E.), 2:1.

72. Cf. AR 247, 250, 252, 253.

73. Douglas, *Purity and Danger*, p. 55.

74. Verse 5:4 states that "all good things (*ṭayyibāt*) are lawful to you, as well as that which you have taught the birds and beasts of prey (*al-jawāriḥ*) to catch, training them as God has taught you." It is significant that human control over trained animals is here traced directly back to God.

75. Cf. al-Ṭabarī, *Jāmiʿ al-bayān*, 6:92–93; al-Jazīrī, *al-Fiqh ʿalāʾl-madhāhib al-arbaʿa*, 2:30–31.

76. Qurʾānic usage would suggest the intepretation of "al-ṭawwāfūn ʿalaykum" either as "those who serve you" (cf. Qurʾān 52:24, 56:17, 76:19) or "those who frequent your home" (cf. Qurʾān 24:58). The literal meaning is "those who go around to you."

77. AR 348, 350, 352, 353, 355, 358, 359, 360.

78. al-Bābartī, *Sharḥ al-ʿināya*, published with Ibn Humām, *Fatḥ al-qadīr*, 1:43.

79. Marcus, "Islam, Women and Pollution in Turkey," p. 213.

80. Howard Eilberg-Schwartz, *The Savage in Judaism: An Anthropology of Israelite Religion and Ancient Judaism* (Bloomington: Indiana University Press, 1990), p. 187.

81. Joseph Schacht, *The Origins of Muhammadan Jurisprudence* (Oxford: Clarendon Press, 1950).

82. Norman Calder, *Studies in Early Muslim Jurisprudence* (Oxford: Clarendon Press, 1993).

83. For a thorough survey of the available critiques of Schacht's theses, see Harald Motzki, *Die Anfänge der islamischen Jurisprudenz* (Stuttgart: Deutsche Morgenländische Gesellschaft, 1991), pp. 22–49.

84. Having adopted the methodological stance that "every legal tradition from the Prophet, until the contrary is proved, must be taken . . . as the fictitious expression of a legal doctrine formulated at a later date," Schacht proposes that "its date can be ascertained from its first appearance in legal discussion, *from its relative position in the history of the problem with which it is concerned*, and from certain indications in text and *isnād*" (*Origins of Muhammadan Jurisprudence*, p. 149; emphasis mine).

85. Harald Motzki, *Die Anfänge der islamischen Jurisprudenz, ihre Entwicklung in Mekka bis zur mitte des 2./8. Jahrhunderts* (Stuttgart: Deutsche Morgenländische Gesellschaft, 1991), passim.

86. Schacht, *Origins*, p. 139.

Chapter 1. Qur'anic Rules of Purity and the Covenantal Community

1. Douglas, *Purity and Danger*, p. 42.

2. Of course, the effort to identify the origins and significance of individual biblical food prohibitions stretches back at least to the beginning of the Christian era (see Douglas, *Purity and Danger*, pp. 48–49). However, Douglas was the first to attempt to relate the overall structure of the list of food prohibitions to the overarching symbolic structures of the biblical text.

3. Douglas, *Purity and Danger*, p. 50.

4. Mary Douglas, *Implicit Meanings: Essays in Anthropology* (London: Routledge & Kegan Paul, 1975), p. 267–68.

5. Jacob Milgrom, "Ethics and Ritual: The Foundations of Biblical Dietary Laws," in *Religion and Law: Biblical-Judaic and Islamic Perspectives*, ed. Edwin B. Firmage et al. (Winona Lake, Ind.: Eisenbrauns, 1990), p. 179.

6. Ibid., pp. 177–78, 183–86.

7. See Howard Eilberg-Schwartz, "Creation and Classification in Judaism: From Priestly to Rabbinic Conceptions," *History of Religions* 26 (1987): 361–62. Eilberg-Schwartz's thesis in this article is that Mishnaic purity categories differ substantially from those reflected in the Priestly source of Genesis, and are consciously grounded in the Yahwist rather than the Priestly version of the creation narrative.

8. Douglas, *Purity and Danger*, p. 47.

9. Edwin Firmage, "The Biblical Dietary Laws," in *Studies in the Pentateuch*, ed. J. A. Emerton (Leiden the Netherlands: E.J. Brill, 1990), p. 197.

10. Douglas, *Purity and Danger*, p. 125.

11. That this linkage should emerge from the Qur'ānic text is significant in light of Douglas's apparent ambivalence about the absolute status of her sociological insights into the significance of systems of ritual purity. In one place in her study, despite her vigorous disparagement of psychological interpretations of the same phenomena elsewhere in the book, she explicitly argues that the nature of her own interpretations is basically dictated by her disciplinary commitments; after all, "the sociologists have the duty of meeting one kind of reductionism with their own" (p. 123). As we will see, concern for community boundaries does not seem to be the primary motivating consideration for Islamic jurists as they elaborate the law; however, the thematic linkages within the text of the Qur'ān suggest that a concern with community boundaries, coalescing around the motif of the covenant, is prominent at the most foundational level.

12. The second half of this verse is paralleled by verse 4:43, as discussed on page 47. Longer Qur'anic translations are my own; some shorter references are adapted from N. J. Dawood (*The Koran*, 5th rev. ed. [London: Penguin Books, 1993]). I have referred to a number of different translations in preparing my own. While no trans-

lation of the Qur'ānic text can be fully adequate, I hope that these suffice to serve their purpose within this discussion.

13. I have chosen to use the masculine pronoun here and elsewhere because it seems to me that, as will emerge in various parts of this study, the paradigmatic body in the Islamic discourse of ritual purity is male. Thus, for instance, the Qur'ānic verse under discussion refers to erotic contact as "touching women," a formulation that seems to imply a male listener. Such verses stand in contrast to the many Qur'ānic passages that explicitly address female and male believers, and it should be remembered that, although formulated in male-oriented terms, the rules of purity are equally applicable to women.

14. Cf. Toshihiko Izutsu, *Ethico-Religious Concepts in the Qur'ān* (Montreal: McGill Institute of Islamic Studies, McGill University Press, 1966), pp. 26, 120–24.

15. A third set of Qur'ānic usages of the word "*ni'ma*" seems to identify God's "benefaction" specifically with revelation. This linkage is made explicit in verse 2: 231, which admonishes, "Remember the *favors God has bestowed upon you* (*udkhkurū ni'mat allāh 'alaykum*), and the *Book and the wisdom He has revealed* for your instruction. Fear God and know that God has knowledge of all things." (Here I would again argue that we are dealing less with two completely distinct items than with a rough parallelism.) This close association between *ni'ma* and revelation is reinforced in the passages that speak of the "*tabdīl*," alteration, of God's *ni'ma*. Clearly, this connotation is so closely linked with the theme of the covenant that it is difficult to determine whether these passages should be considered separately at all. Thus, the motif of *tabdīl* is associated with the Israelites' violation of their covenant by the alteration of God's revelation; compare verse 2:59 (narrative of Moses and the Israelites wandering in the wilderness) and its parallel in verse 7:162. Here the reference to alteration of "words" (*qawl*) may suggest a corruption of the text of revelation (parallel to *taḥrīf*); however, the passage also describes a rupture in the covenant. This ambiguity is reflected in a passage such as 2:11 ("Ask the Israelites how many veritable signs We have given them. He that alters (*yubaddil*) God's favor (*ni'ma*) after it has been bestowed on him shall be severely punished"), which may be interpreted to refer to the violation of the covenant or to the alteration of scripture.

16. Also see verse 14:6: "Moses said to his people: 'Remember God's favor to you (*ni'mat allāh 'alaykum*) when He delivered you from Pharaoh's nation, who had oppressed you cruelly . . . "

17. Here it is interesting to compare verse 8:53, which states that "God does not alter a blessing/favor (*ni'ma*) He has bestowed on a people until they alter what is in their hearts." This verse draws the moral of a parallel between the hypocrites in in the Muslim community, who betray the cause of God, and Pharaoh's people in the story of the Exodus: "Like Pharaoh's people and those that have gone before them, they disbelieved God's revelations. Therefore God will smite them for their sins" (8:52; compare 8:54). Although there is naturally no warrant in the Hebrew Bible for the idea that God had a covenantal relationship with the Egyptians, within the Qur'ānic schema in which each people receives its own apostle it is quite reasonable to interpret

8:53 as meaning that God does not rupture His relationship or agreement with a people unless they have already ruptured it themselves.

18. This pattern cannot be mechanically equated with covenantal language, however; compare verse 16:81, where the reference is to the wonders of creation; 27:19 (in which Sulaymān prays, "Inspire me, Lord, to render thanks for the favours You have bestowed on me (*niʿmataka llatī anʿamta ʿalayya*) and on my parents, and to do good works that will please You"); and verse 46:15, where the believer is enjoined to pronounce the same prayer.

19. For a useful summary of both traditional and academic attempts to define the chronology of revelation, see Neal Robinson, *Discovering the Qurʾan, A Contemporary Approach to a Veiled Text* (London: SCM Press Ltd, 1996), chapters 4 and 5.

20. See Jalāl al-Dīn al-Suyūṭī, *al-Itqān fī ʿulūm al-Qurʾān* (Beirut: Dār al-Fikr, A.H. 1408/1988 C.E.), 1:39–40, 56–67.

21. This argument has been applied particularly to the narrative material, known as *asbāb al-nuzūl* ("occasions of revelation"), that purports to recount the situation in which individual verses or passages were revealed. John Wansbrough has argued in his *Quranic Studies: Sources and Methods of Scriptural Interpretation* (Oxford, 1977) that this material was generated largely by the need to define the sequence of revelation in order to establish that verses regarded as abrogating were later than those they supposedly abrogated. Critiquing Wansbrough's work, A. Rippin has contended that the *asbāb* traditions generally neglect issues of chronology, and that "the arguments found in the *naskh* texts are . . . based on logic [i.e., the assumption that the verse laying down the law presently understood to be valid must necessarily be latest] not chronology" ("*Asbāb al-nuzūl* in Qurʾānic Exegesis," *BSOAS* 51 (1988): 18). While Wansbrough's focus on the question of abrogation may be exaggerated, it seems obvious that traditions about the revelation of individual Qurʾānic passages are often molded by both halakhic and haggadic (legal and narrative, in Wansbrough's terminology) considerations.

22. For an extended discussion of the question of continuity in the Qurʾānic text, covering both medieval and modern sources, see Mustansir Mir, *Coherence in the Qurʾan, a Study of Iṣlāḥī's Concept of Naẓm in Tadabbur-i Qurʾan* (Indianapolis: American Trust Publications, 1406/1986).

23. Although I have attempted to frame this chapter as an unmediated encounter with the text of the Qurʾān rather than as a survey of the relevant exegetical material (and did not use exegetical sources in developing my argument), it is interesting to note that more than one of the most prominent modern interpreters of the Qurʾān has reached the same conclusion as I have regarding the cohesiveness and thematic focus of the first part of Sūrat al-Māʾida. Abul Aʿla Maududi writes in his commentary *The Meaning of the Qurān*, "The continuity of the subject shows that most probably the whole of the Sūrah was revealed as a single discourse at one and the same time" (Maududi, *The Meaning of the Qurān*, 8th ed., trans. Muhammad

Akbar [Lahore: Islamic Publications Ltd.], 3:3–4). Mir notes that the exegete Iṣlāḥī "points out that the notion of covenant runs through not only these [first fifty verses of al-Mā'ida] but the rest of the verses of the sūrah as well," although Mir himself finds the passage highly digressive (Mir, *Coherence*, p. 56).

24. Interestingly, one strand of early exegetical opinion holds that the "*'uqūd*" of verse 5:1 are "the oath which God took from His servants to believe in Him and obey Him in what he permitted and forbid for them" (al-Ṭabarī, *Jāmi' al-bayān*, 6:48). For this opinion Ṭabarī cites both Ibn 'Abbās and al-Mujāhid. Ibn 'Abbās is said to have explicated the verse by citing verse 13:25: "As for those who break God's covenant after confirming it, who put asunder what God has bidden to be united and perpetrate corruption in the land, a curse shall be laid on them, and they shall have an evil end." Thus, according to a strong minority interpretation which is probably quite early, a covenantal context is established from the first verse of al-Mā'ida. This is also the interpretation implicitly adopted by Sayyid Quṭb, who includes the first verse of the sūra in a list of verses treating the theme of the covenant and its obligations (*Fī ẓilāl al-qur'ān*, 5th ed. (n.p., 1967 C.E./A.H. 1386), 6:57–58).

25. *Old Testament Theology*, trans. D. M. G. Stalker (New York: Harper & Row, 1962), 1:192.

26. For instance, Sūrat al-Tawba (chapter 9) is supposed to have been promulgated at the ḥajj by 'Alī ibn abī Ṭālib; however, according to some traditions he merely announced the underlying principles (that no nonbeliever would perform the pilgrimage after that year, etc.) rather than reciting the actual text of the sūra. See al-Ṭabarī, *Jāmi' al-bayān*, 10:61–64.

27. This position is particularly associated with John Wansbrough, who suggests that the text of the Qur'ān and the narrative materials associated with the life of the Prophet emerged from the same body of lore. In his *Quranic Studies* (Oxford: Oxford University Press, 1977, pp. 38–42) he examines the text of a narrative describing an encounter between the Prophet's cousin Ja'far ibn abī Ṭālib and the ruler of Ethiopia. Wansbrough points out that the speech attributed to Ja'far in the *Sīra* of Ibn Hishām includes language found in (and thus, according to traditional conceptions, presumably drawn from) Qur'ānic passages attributed to both the Meccan and the Medinian periods, a fact apparently in conflict with the early date of Ja'far's sojourn in Ethiopia. Rather than using traditional ideas about the chronology of the revelation of the Qur'ān to throw doubt on the authenticity of Ja'far's supposed speech, Wansbrough suggests, we should radically rethink the interrelationship between Qur'ān and prophetic biography, "interpret[ing] Ja'far's recital as a report of prophetic logia exhibiting a stage of transmission prior to their incorporation into the Quranic canon."

28. Cf. al-Ṭabarī, *Jāmi' al-bayān*, 6:79–84; Abū'l-Ḥasan 'Alī ibn Aḥmad al-Wāḥidī, *Asbāb nuzūl al-qur'ān*, ed. al-Sayyid Aḥmad Ṣaqr ([Cairo]: Dār al-Kitāb al-Jadīd, A.H. 1389/ 1969 C.E.), pp. 182–83; al-Suyūṭī, *al-Durr al-manthūr*, 2: 257–259.

29. Ibn Hishām, *Sīra*, 6:8–10; Guillaume, *Life of Muhammad*, p. 651.

30. The repetition of the phrase "O people" is a documented convention of early oratory; see Aḥmad Zakī Ṣafwat, *Jamharat khuṭab al-ʿarab fī ʿuṣūr al-ʿarabīya al-zāhira* ([Cairo]: Muṣṭafā al-Bābī al-Ḥalabī, 1962–.), vol. 1, passim.

31. Cf. Qurʾān 48:18, "God was well pleased (*raḍiya*) with the faithful when they swore allegiance to you under the tree; He knew what was in their hearts, and therefore sent down tranquillity (*al-sakīna*) upon them and rewarded them with a speedy victory . . ."

32. Sūrat al-Fatḥ is said to have "been revealed between Mecca and Madīna on the subject of al-Ḥudaybīya, from start to finish" (al-Suyūṭī, *al-Durr al-manthūr*, 6:67; cf. al-Ṭabarī, *Jāmiʿ al-bayān*, 26:68–71; Muḥammad ibn Aḥmad al-Qurṭubī, *al-Jāmiʿ li-aḥkām al-Qurʾān* (Cairo: Dār al-Kitāb al-ʿArabī liʾl-Ṭabāʿa waʾl-Nashr, A.H. 1387/1968 C.E.), 16:259–61; al-Wāḥidī, *Asbāb*, pp. 403–5).

33. Ibn Hishām, *Sīra*, 4:276–77; Guillaume, *Life of Muhammad*, pp. 500–1.

34. The dominant interpretation is that the word is derived from the verb *ḥ-ṭ-ṭ*, "to alleviate, reduce, remove"; the command to "say *ḥiṭṭa*" thus means either that the Israelites should request God's alleviation (i.e., forgiveness) of their sins or that they should say something (perhaps, some exegetes suggested, "There is no god but God") that would induce Him to do so. Another interpretation is that *ḥiṭṭa* is the name of one of the gates of Jerusalem. See al-Ṭabarī, *Jāmiʿ al-bayān*, 1:299–301. With regard to the miracle of the springs, cf. Exodus 17:1–7.

35. Compare 7:160–61, a close parallel despite a change in the order of the two motifs. Interestingly, the narrative of the Farewell Pilgrimage also has a covenantal dimension. At the end of the address as transmitted by Ibn Isḥāq, the Prophet asks the assembled believers: "O God, have I not told you?" The people reply, "O God, yes," and the Prophet concludes: "O God, bear witness" (Ibn Hishām, *Sīra*, 6:10; Guillaume, *Life of Muhammad*, pp. 651–52).

36. See al-Suyūṭī, *Asbāb al-nuzūl* ([Cairo]: Maktabat Nuṣayr, n.d.), p. 99. The prominent modern exegete Abul Aʿla Maududi reaches the same conclusion, writing: "The theme of this Sūra indicates, and traditions support it, that it was revealed after the treaty of Ḥudaybiyah at the end of 6 A.H. or in the beginning of 7 A.H. That is why it deals with those problems that arose from this treaty" (1:3).

37. There is an interesting parallel between the oratorical form and narrative context of this passage and the Book of Deuteronomy in the Hebrew Bible, which similarly uses a piece of oratory in the mouth of Moses to re-evoke a key moment in the history of the Israelites. Just as Moses is supposed to have delivered this address as the community stood at the brink of the conquest of the Land of Canaan, Muḥammad here addresses the Muslim community in the words of revelation at the moment when the reclamation of their holy places has been assured. In both cases, the reclamation of the holy ground has been delayed (in the case of Moses, by the wandering in the desert; in the case of Muḥammad, by the terms of the truce). In both cases, the prophet uses the occasion to evoke the community's covenantal obligations. Thus, Moses reminds the Israelites that "The Lord our God made a covenant with us in Horeb"

(Deut. 5:2) and recounts the story, culminating in the people's statement that "we will hear it, and do it" (Deut. 5:27); Muḥammad, more tersely, enjoins the Muslims to "Remember God's favour to you, and the covenant with which He bound you when you said: 'We hear and obey' " (Qur'ān 5:7).

38. Here I am excluding verse 4 of Sūrat al-Mudaththir (chapter 74), which begins: "You that are wrapped up in your cloak, arise and give warning. Magnify your Lord, purify your garments, and keep away from uncleanness." The injunction to "purify your garments" would seem to qualify for this category in that it enjoins an act of purification; however, it is addressed to a masculine singular listener in a specific situation (traditionally, and plausibly, interpreted to be the Prophet Muḥammad in the throes of revelation) rather than to the community for all time. Furthermore, it was usually interpreted as metaphorical rather than legal. Some early interpreters cited by al-Ṭabarī, appealing to linguistic usage, held that it referred to purification from sin; others argued that that it referred to clothes bought with licit money. A minority (two early authorities) held that it referred to cleansing with water (al-Ṭabarī, *Jāmi' al-bayān*, 29:144–47).

39. This is an Arabic-Hebrew pun; in Arabic it means "watch over us," while in Hebrew it is phonetically similar to "our wicked one."

40. See lists in Theodor Nöldeke, *Geschichte des Qorâns* (Göttingen, 1860), p. 47.

41. The *asbāb al-nuzūl* genre is a body of traditional material in which verse fragments, verses, or whole chapters of the Qur'ān are associated with specific situations in the career of the Prophet that supposedly formed the occasion of their revelation.

42. "There is no God but God; Muḥammad is the Messenger of God."

43. In contrast, references to *al-muslimūn* (the Muslims/submitters) are distributed widely through the Qur'ān, in Meccan and Medinian chapters alike.

44. The word appears three times in the sense of a pact between tribes (4:90, 92; 8:72).

45. Nöldeke, *Geschichte*, p. 50.

46. Here it is unclear whether the reference is to purity of faith or of body; the exegetical tradition would have it that the verse refers to physical ablutions.

47. Ṭabarī, *Jāmi' al-bayān*, 9:196; with several different versions, pp. 195–96; see also al-Suyūṭī, *al-Durr al-manthūr*, 3:169.

48. Douglas, *Purity and Danger*, p. 126.

49. Ibid., p. 124.

50. Mikhail Bakhtin, *Rabelais and His World* (Bloomington, Indiana University Press, 1984), p. 15.

51. Ibid., p. 26.

52. Douglas, *Purity and Danger*, p. 125.

53. This recovered context also sheds light on one aspect of the ritual of ablution which is not legally required but regarded as *sunna*, that is, a laudable practice based on the precedent of the Prophet. This is the custom of beginning one's ablutions by thanking God for the religion of Islam and ending them by pronouncing the *shahāda*: "I testify that there is no God but God, and that Muḥammad is the Apostle of God." In following this practice, the believer renews the covenant binding him to God by evoking his original act of commitment.

Chapter 2. Interpreting the Qur'anic Text

1. Cf. Schacht, *Origins*, pp. 224–27.

2. The problems raised by the "*wuḍū'* verse" (5:6) have been examined in detail by John Burton in his article "The Qur'ān and the Islamic Practice of Wuḍū'," *BSOAS* 51 (1988): 21–58. However, Burton does not address the question of the role of the Qur'ān in the early development of Islamic law; he simply assumes that the ultimate origin of all of the relevant opinions and practices must be exegetical. While he cites some opinions attributed to early jurists, his interest is in examining the opinions of the classical Qur'ān commentors rather than in reconstructing the dynamics of the preclassical period. Thus, although we cover some of the same substantive questions, this discussion should prove complementary to his.

3. The second half of this verse is paralleled by verse 4:43:

> O believers, do not approach prayer when you are intoxicated, until you know what you are saying; or when you are sexually polluted, unless passing on the way, until you wash yourselves. If you are sick or traveling, or one of you has relieved himself (lit., "come from the privy") or you have touched women, and you cannot find water, go to clean sand/dust and wipe your faces and hands with it. Indeed, God is forgiving and clement.

4. Burton suggests that this inference is not completely unavoidable; alternatively, "the intention may be that all four classes could be equally governed by the non-availability of water when they need it to purify themselves for the ritual prayer" ("The Qur'ān and the Islamic Practice of Wuḍū'," p. 21).

5. al-Ṭabarī, *Jāmi' al-Bayān*, 6:112 (note that al-Suddī is also credited with the statement that the phrase refers to rising from sleep; this could indicate either that the attribution is false or that al-Suddī, like al-Zajjāj (see below), required the phrase to do double duty).

6. AR 157–70.

7. Abū Bakr ʿAbd Allāh ibn Muḥammad ibn abī Shayba, *al-Kitāb al-muṣannaf fī'l-aḥādīth wa'l-āthār* (Beirut: Dār al-Tāj, A.H. 1409/1989 C.E.), #284–303. Ibn abī Shayba's *Muṣannaf* will henceforth be cited as IAS, with the number of the tradition.

8. al-Ṭabarī, *Jāmiʿ al-bayān*, 6:110–13.

9. AR 165.

10. Motzki, *Anfänge*, pp. 107, 128–34.

11. Ibid., pp. 241–42.

12. AR 160.

13. Ibn Ḥajar al-ʿAsqalānī, *Tahdhīb al-tahdhīb* ([Beirut]: Dār Ṣādir, n.d. [facsimile of Haidarabad, A.H. 1325–27/(1907–10 C.E.)]), 5:68.

14. AR 161.

15. Ibn Ḥajar, *Tahdhīb al-Tahdhīb*, 8:355.

16. IAS 290.

17. AR 163; IAS 289. See also AR 164, which also implies that Ibrāhīm performed *wuḍūʾ* only for a *ḥadath*.

18. Ibn Ḥajar, *Tahdhīb al-tahdhīb*, 1:178.

19. IAS 295; al-Ṭabarī, *Jāmiʿ al-bayān*, 6:111.

20. AR 164.

21. Ibn Ḥajar, *Tahdhīb al-tahdhīb,*11:168, 1:187.

22. Ibid., 11:167.

23. Ibid., 7:421–22.

24. AR 166.

25. Ibn Ḥajar, *Tahdhīb al-tahdhīb*, 1:342–43.

26. Ibid., 4:222–26.

27. IAS 291. But see discussion of ʿAbd Allāh ibn ʿUmar, p. 69.

28. IAS 287.

29. Ibn Ḥajar, *Tahdhīb al-tahdhīb*, 4:150–52.

30. Ibid., 11:349.

31. IAS 302; al-Ṭabarī, *Jāmiʿ al-bayān*, 6:112.

32. IAS 293.

33. IAS 296. Here I am interpreting "al-nās" to mean "people" in general, since the context gives no indication that only jurists (another common acceptation of the word) are intended.

34. Ibn Ḥajar, *Tahdhīb al-tahdhīb*, 7:276–78.

35. IAS 301; Ṭabarī, *Jāmi' al-bayān*, 6:110 (report about Sa'd's practice), 111 (statement by Sa'd). For Sa'd, see Ibn Ḥajar, *Tahdhīb al-tahdhīb*, 3:483–84.

36. AR 159; al-Ṭabarī, *Jāmi' al-bayān*, 6:111.

37. Harald Motzki, analyzing the section on marriage and divorce from the *Muṣannaf* of 'Abd al-Razzāq, has documented that 'Aṭā's responses to questions from Ibn Jurayj show an intimate knowledge of a Qur'ānic text that seems to correspond in great detail to the one known to later generations (*Anfänge*, pp. 98–106). 'Aṭā''s remarks also reflect a fairly sophisticated level of juristic interpretation of the Qur'ānic text, in the sense that they sometimes presuppose analysis of the interrelation of different passages dealing with the same subject. However, 'Aṭā''s interest in the Qur'ān seems to have been pragmatic rather than theoretical; he does not engage in textual analysis for its own sake, and sometimes does not explicitly state the Qur'ānic basis for an opinion unless questioned by a student. Thus, based on a broad survey of 'Aṭā' material in a quite different subject area, it would not be surprising that 'Aṭā' seems to be aware of the relevant Qur'ānic verse (and probably convinced that his own opinion is generally consistent with it), but does not hint at any technical analysis of the verse's problematic syntax.

38. *EI²*, s.v. "'Abd Allāh ibn al-'Abbās."

39. AR 167.

40. al-Bukhārī, *Ṣaḥīḥ*, 1:68; al-Bannā, *al-Fatḥ al-rabbānī*, 2:54; Abū Dāwud, *Sunan*, 1:120; Ibn Māja, *Sunan*, 1:170. AR 162 has Anas's report that "we" used to perform *wuḍū'* only for a *ḥadath*, without the reference to the practice of the Prophet.

41. Ibn Ḥajar, *Tahdhīb al-tahdhīb*, 1:376–79.

42. The death date of the Kūfan 'Amr ibn 'Āmir appears to be unknown; see Ibn Ḥajar, *Tahdhīb al-tahdhīb*, 8:60.

43. AR 157, 158; IAS 298; al-Dārimī, *Sunan*, 1:169; Muslim, *Ṣaḥīḥ*, 3:168–69; *al-Fatḥ al-rabbānī*, 2:55; Abū Dāwūd, *Sunan*, 1:120; al-Nasā'ī, *Sunan*, 1:40; al-Tirmidhī, *Ṣaḥīḥ*, 1:79; Ibn Mājah, *Sunan*, 1:170; al-Ṭabarī, *Jāmi' al-bayān*, 6:113–14.

44. Muḥammad ibn Idrīs al-Shāfi'ī, *al-Risāla*, ed. Aḥmad Muḥammad Shākir (n.p., n.d.), p. 108.

45. al-Bannā, *al-Fatḥ al-rabbānī*, 2:54; al-Dārimī, *Sunan*, 1:168–69; Abū Dāwūd, *Sunan*, 1:41; al-Ṭabarī, *Jāmi' al-bayān*, 6:113.

46. This report may be quite early, as the requirement to cleanse the mouth with a toothpick before every prayer was ultimately itself rejected as excessively onerous. See Abū Dāwūd, *Sunan*, 1:40.

47. AR 170 states that Ibn ʿUmar performed *wuḍūʾ* for every prayer. However, this was not undisputed; IAS 291 claims that he performed several prayers with the same *wuḍūʾ*.

48. Ibn Māja, *Sunan*, 1:170–71.

49. The reasons for arguing that this interpretation of the verse corresponded to the practice, rather than that the practice was generated by this interpretation of the verse, will be discussed below.

50. Whether the category of "contact with women" included minimal forms of contact requiring *wuḍūʾ* or only sexual contact requiring *ghusl* was a matter of controversy and will be discussed below.

51. al-Zajjāj (attributed), *Iʿrāb al-Qurʾān*, part 2, ed. Ibrāhīm al-Abyārī ([Cairo], A.H. 1383/1963 C.E.), 2:693.

52. Mālik ibn Anas, *al-Muwaṭṭa*; 1:23–4. Zayd ibn Aslam al-ʿAdawī was a Medinian jurist. He was known for his knowledge of Qurʾānic exegesis, although he was accused of interpreting the Qurʾān according to his own opinions. Ibn Ḥajar, *Tahdīb al-tahdhīb*, 3:395–97.

53. Cf. al-Ṭabarī, *Jāmiʿ al-bayān*, 5:334–35.

54. Muḥammad ibn Idrīs al-Shāfiʿī, *al-Umm* (Beirut: Dār al-Maʿrifa, n.d.), 1:12.

55. al-Shaybānī, *Kitāb al-Āthār* (Karachi, A.H. 1385/1965 C.E.), 1:434–36 (#165). The same dilemma is reflected in a tradition cited by al-Bukhārī (*Ṣaḥīḥ*, 1:234):

> Ibn ʿAbbās said: I slept one night at the house of my maternal aunt Maymūna. The Prophet went to sleep; during the night (*fī baʿḍ al-layl*), the Messenger of God got up and performed a light *wuḍūʾ* from a waterskin that was hanging up—ʿAmr said that it was very light and scanty—then got up to pray. I performed *wuḍūʾ* the same way he did and came and stood to his left. He moved me to his right, and prayed as long as God willed him to. Then he lay down and slept so deeply that he snored (*ḥattā nafakha*). The crier (*al-munādī*) came to call him to prayer, and he got up and went with him to pray (*qāma maʿahu ilāʾl-ṣalāt*) and prayed without performing *wuḍūʾ*. We said to ʿAmr, "Some people say that the Prophet's eyes sleep and his heart does not sleep." ʿAmr said, "I heard ʿUbayd ibn ʿUmayr say, 'The Prophets' dreams are [a kind of] revelation'; then he recited, {I dreamt that I slaughtered you [Qurʾan 37:102]}."

This anecdote represents a debate set in the generation after Ibrāhīm in which a prominent Meccan traditionist cites a *ḥadīth* report clearly intended to document that the Prophet did not perform *wuḍūʾ* after sleep, then accepts an argument about the exceptional nature of this practice that would seem to have been in the air at the time ("some people say"). ʿAmr then supplies his own support for this argument by citing another report referring to the exceptional nature of the prophets' experience in sleep: their dreams, far from rendering them oblivious to reality, are privileged glimpses into reality. It is unclear whether the Qur'ānic citation, referring to Ibrāhīm's premonitory dream of slaughering Ismāʿīl, is part of the quotation from ʿUbayd ibn ʿUmayr or a piece of corroborating evidence supplied by ʿAmr.

56. Ibn Hishām, *Sīra*, 2:246; Guillaume, *Life of Muhammad*, p. 183.

57. It is an index of the Islamic juristic tradition's commitment to the image of the Prophet as a human being subject to all the constraints of nature that the tradition generally does not flinch at associating him with all of the normal bodily functions. Devotional sources, on the other hand, frequently suggest that the Prophet produced no wastes or that they instantly evaporated with a smell of musk.

58. al-Shāfiʿī, *al-Umm*, 1:12.

59. Bukhārī, *Ṣaḥīḥ*, 1:68.

60. Muslim, *Ṣaḥīḥ*, 4:294–96.

61. Ibn Ḥazm grounds the requirement for *wuḍū'* from sleep in a tradition in which Zirr ibn Ḥubaysh reports that "the Prophet used to order us, when we were traveling, to wipe our boots and not to take them off for three days from defecation, urination, or sleep—anything but sexual pollution." However, this report is a paraphrase rather than an exact reproduction of words attributed to the Prophet. It seems likely that sleep is included in the list as a result of the transmitters' understanding it as a source of minor impurity, rather than vice versa (al-*Muḥallā* [Beirut, n.d.], 1:223).

62. al-Dārimī, *Sunan*, 1:184; al-Bannā, *al-Fatḥ al-rabbānī*, 2:83–84; Abū Dāwud, *Sunan*, 1:52: Ibn Māja, *Sunan*, 1:161.

63. IAS 1415. This is probably also the meaning of ʿAbīda al-Salmānī's cryptic comment, "He knows best about himself" (AR 490, 491; IAS 1405)—in other words, no one knows better than the individual involved whether he has passed gas.

64. IAS 1417 (Ṭāwūs was asked about a man who slept sitting up; he said, "It is a drawstring; if you loosen it . . . "—meaning, "He should perform *wuḍū'*"); 1418 (ʿIkrima said, "It is a drawstring; if someone sleeps, he should perform *wuḍū'*").

65. See al-Jazīrī, *Kitāb al-fiqh ʿalā'l-madhāhib al-arbaʿa*, 1:80. Although the Ḥanafīs are the only school flatly to deny that sleep cancels *wuḍū'*, the detailed rules developed by the Shāfiʿī school suggest the same conclusion. Thus, they hold that it is not necessary to perform *wuḍū'* after sleep if one slept sitting up with one's anus pressed against the floor (ibid., p. 81). Interestingly, another important function of the formula that "the eyes are the drawstring of the anus" seems to have been to refute the argument that *wuḍū'* was required only after recumbent sleep. By asserting that it was "the eyes" (i.e., consciousness) that mattered, the formula implicitly denied that the position of the rest of the body was decisive. Thus, al-Dārimī follows the tradition with the remark, "Abū Muḥammad ʿAbd Allāh was asked, 'Do you follow [this *ḥadīth*]?'; he said, 'No; if someone sleeps standing up, he need not perform *wuḍū'*'" (*Sunan*, 1:184).

66. See AR 491 (ʿAbīda [al-Salmānī]; report 490 inserts "while prostrate [in prayer]" (*sājidan*), which changes the force of the report; IAS 1415 (Abū Mūsā al-Ashʿarī); Badr al-Dīn al-ʿAynī, *ʿUmdat al-qārī sharḥ ṣaḥīḥ al-Bukhārī* (Beirut: Muḥammad Amīn Damj, n.d.), 1:109–10; Ibn Ḥazm, *al-Muḥallā*, 1:224. al-ʿAynī also mentions a Ḥumayd ibn ʿAbd al-Raḥmān and an al-Aʿraj; it is not clear to which person of either name he is referring. There are two scholars by the name of Ḥumayd ibn ʿAbd al-Raḥmān, a Meccan who died in either A.H. 95 or 105 (Ibn Ḥajar, *Tahdhīb al-tahdhīb*, 3:45–46) and a Baṣran of unknown death date who transmitted from several Companions of the Prophet (*Tahdhīb al-tahdhīb*, 3:46).

67. Ibn Ḥajar, *Tahdhīb al-tahdhīb*, 5:362–63.

68. Ibid., 7:84.

69. Ibid., 4:84–88.

70. Lāḥiq ibn Ḥumayd al-Sadūsī, Abū Mijlaz al-Baṣrī al-Aʿwar (ibid., 11:171–72).

71. Ibid., 10:289–93.

72. ʿAbd al-Raḥmān ibn ʿAmr ibn abī ʿAmr al-Shāmī, Abū ʿAmr al-Awzāʿī (ibid., 6:238–42).

73. Shuʿba ibn al-Ḥajjāj al-Azdī, Abū Bisṭām al-Wāsiṭī (ibid., 4:338–46).

74. For instance, al-ʿAynī (*ʿUmdat al-qārī*) lists Saʿīd ibn al-Musayyab as holding this opinion; however, IAS presents a report (1422, from Qatāda) that he endorsed al-Ḥasan [al-Baṣrī]'s opinion that *wuḍūʾ* was necessitated by sleep in any position. Similarly, Ibn Ḥazm states that this is a well-authenticated opinion of Ibn ʿUmar's yet himself states on the same page that Ibn ʿUmar required *wuḍūʾ* for recumbent sleep (*nawm al-muḍṭajiʿ*); this is the opinion ascribed to him in AR (484, 485) and IAS (1402).

75. AR 53; IAS 178, 180.

76. AR 54, 55.

77. AR 54.

78. IAS 181.

79. AR 56; IAS 185. Compare the statement, attributed by Ibn Māja to Ibn ʿAbbās, that "people refuse to do anything but wash [their feet], [but] all I find in the Book of God is wiping" (*Sunan*, 1:156).

80. IAS 182.

81. AR 58.

82. AR 54.

83. Ibn Ḥajar, *Tahdhīb al-tahdhīb*, 10:168.

84. IAS 56 (ʿUthmān) and 57 (ʿAbd Allāh ibn Zayd) report that the Prophet wiped his feet. Interestingly, however, other versions of the ʿUthmān tradition specify

that he washed his feet (see below, note 87). Either an early reference to the wiping of the feet in IAS 56 was "corrected" elsewhere to reflect the practice of washing, or the reference to wiping was inserted by a Qur'ānic literalist.

85. AR 123; al-Nasā'ī, *Sunan*, 1:29.

86. AR 120; see also AR 122, IAS 54 ("I merely wanted to show you the Prophet's ablutions (*ṭuhūr*)"); IAS 55 ("This is the *wuḍū'* of your (pl.) Prophet (*nabīyikum*)"); al-Bannā, *al-Fatḥ al-rabbānī*, 2:7–10; al-Nasā'ī, *Sunan*, 1:24, 30.

87. AR 119 (ʿAbd Allāh ibn Muḥammad ibn ʿAqīl ibn abī Ṭālib - Maʿmar - ʿAbd al-Razzāq).

88. ʿAbd Allāh ibn Muḥammad ibn ʿAqīl ibn abī Ṭālib died before the revolt of Muḥammad ibn ʿAbd Allāh ibn al-Ḥasan (A.H. 145), according to one report in 142 (Ibn Ḥajar, *Tahdhīb al-tahdhīb*, 6:13–16). His informant, Rubayyiʿ bint Muʿawwidh ibn ʿAfrā', although no death date is available for her, is said to have participated in the "*bayʿa* under the tree" (Ibn Ḥajar, *Tahdhīb al-tahdhīb*, 12:418). This seems to imply a somewhat improbable age gap between her and her alleged visitor, which would tend to throw doubt on the authenticity of this tradition. However, it is not completely implausible if we assume that she lived to an advanced age.

89. See al-Kulaynī, *al-Furūʿ min al-Kāfī*, 3:24–26. The form of these reports is also significant; Abū Jaʿfar (i.e., the Fifth Imām of the Twelver line) offers to show those present "the Prophet's [way of performing] *wuḍū'*."

90. Cf. al-Kulaynī, *al-Furūʿ min al-Kāfī*, 3:27.

91. Schacht, *Origins*, p. 242.

92. AR 139, 140; al-Dārimī, *Sunan*, 1:176; al-Bukhārī, *Ṣaḥīḥ*, 1:55; Muslim, *Ṣaḥīḥ*, 1:100–4; al-Bannā, *al-Fatḥ al-rabbānī*, 2:6; Abū Dāwud, *Sunan*, 1:78–79; al-Nasā'ī, *Sunan*, 1:30. A similar text that merely states that one must "perform *wuḍū'* well" to achieve this effect (cf. AR 141).

93. IAS 80 (also 62, without final comment; even more abbreviated versions 63, 65). A similar point about ʿUthmān's privileged access to the *sunna* of the Prophet is suggested by IAS 56:

> ʿUthmān called for water and performed *wuḍū'*, then laughed and said, "Why don't you (pl.) ask me why I'm laughing?" They said, "O Commander of the Faithful, what made you laugh?" He said, "I saw the Prophet perform *wuḍū'* as I [just] performed *wuḍū'*; he washed out his mouth and blew water out of his nose, washed his face three times and his hands three times, and wiped his head and the tops of his feet."

94. Muslim, *Ṣaḥīḥ*, 3:103.

95. AR 133.

96. AR 61; also in al-Ṭabarī, *Jāmiʿ al-bayān*, 6:126. Aḥmad ibn Ḥanbal (al-Bannā, *al-Fatḥ al-rabbānī*, 2:41) records another tradition in which the washing of the feet is associated with the authority of the founder of the Umayyad line: "Muʿāwiya showed them how the Prophet performed *wuḍūʾ*; he repeated his washings three times, and washed his feet." Here again, the preservation of the Prophet's distinctive mode of performing *wuḍūʾ* is represented as a specifically caliphal prerogative.

97. Ibn al-ʿArabī, *Aḥkām al-qurʾān*, ed. ʿAlī Muḥammad al-Bijāwī (N.p: Dār Iḥyāʾ al-Kutub al-ʿArabīya, A.H. 1376/1957 C.E.), 2:574–75.

98. A Baṣran who died "when Bishr ibn Marwān was governor of ʿIrāq (A.H. 72–74; see *EI*², s.v. "Bishr ibn Marwān")" (Ibn Ḥajar, *Tahdhīb al-tahdhīb*, 2:396).

99. A Companion of the Prophet who served as a military commander and as governor of Baṣra and Kūfa at various times during the reigns of ʿUmar and ʿUthmān. *EI*², s.v. "al-Ashʿarī, Abū Mūsā"; Ibn Ḥajar, *Tahdhīb al-tahdhīb*, 5:362–63.

100. AR 159.

101. See *EI*², s.v. "Khārijites."

102. AR 1277.

103. In this passage, a band of *jinn* report that they went to (*lamasnā*) the heavens; al-Ṭabarī glosses the phrase as "*ṭalabnāʾl-samāʾa wa-aradnāhā*" (we sought the heavens and desired to go there) (al-Ṭabarī, *Jāmiʿ al-bayān*, 29:110).

104. AR 499, 500; see also al-Ṭabarī, *Jāmiʿ al-bayān*, 5:105.

105. AR 496, 497; IAS 491, 492; *Muwaṭṭaʾ*, 1:49; al-Ṭabarī, *Jāmiʿ al-bayān*, 5:104. Al-Ṭabarī's report, like AR 497, adds an explicitly exegetical exegetical remark: "It (i.e., kissing) is touching (*hiya min al-limās*)."

106. AR 505, 507.

107. al-Ṭabarī, *Jāmiʿ al-bayān*, 5:101–3.

108. Ibid., 5:102.

109. Ibn Ḥajar, *Tahdhīb al-tahdhīb*, 8:351–56.

110. AR 506; al-Ṭabarī, *Jāmiʿ al-bayān*, 5:101–3.

111. AR 509, 510, 511; IAS 485, 489; al-Bannā, *al-Fatḥ al-rabbānī*, 2:89–90; Abū Dāwūd, *Sunan*, 1:123–25; Ibn Māja, *Sunan*, 1:168; al-Nasāʾī, *Sunan*, 1:46; al-Ṭabarī, *Jāmiʿ al-bayān*, 5:105–6.

112. IAS 510 (for biographical data, see Ibn Ḥajar, *Tahdhīb al-tahdhīb*, 6: 260–62).

113. al-Shaybānī, *Āthār*, #21; AR 501; IAS 500, 505, 507.

114. IAS 494, 495. Muḥammad ibn al-Ḥasan al-Shaybānī, who is interested in establishing that the true Kūfan position is that kissing does not require *wuḍūʾ*, reports that al-Shaʿbī did not require *wuḍūʾ* for kissing (*Kitāb al-Ḥujja ʿalā ahl al-Madīna*, ed.

Mahdī Ḥasan al-Kaylānī al-Qādirī [Beirut: ʿĀlam al-Kutub, A.H. 1403/1983 C.E.], 1:65–66). (For al-Shaʿbī's biographical data, see Ibn Ḥajar, *Tahdhīb al-tahdhīb*, 5:65–69.)

115. IAS 497 (for biographical data, see Ibn Ḥajar, *Tahdhīb al-tahdhīb*, 2:432–34).

116. IAS 497 (for biographical data, see Ibn Ḥajar, *Tahdhīb al-tahdhīb*, 3:16–18).

117. AR 504.

118. AR 513.

119. AR 514; al-Bannā, *al-Fatḥ al-rabbānī*, 2:91; al-Nasāʾī, *Sunan*, 1:46–47.

120. al-Shaybānī, *Ḥujja*, 1:65–66.

121. al-Shaybānī, *Āthār*, #21.

122. Later elaborations of this doctrine and its significance for the underlying gender ideology of the law of ritual purity will be discussed in chapter 4.

123. AR 922.

124. IAS 1667.

125. IAS 1668, 1669 (which speaks of ʿAbd Allāh's having recanted the opinion). Ibn Abī Shayba offers another view of the controversy in the following anecdote: "Zubayd said: I became sexually impure and did not find water, so I asked Abū ʿAṭīya and he said, 'Don't pray.' I asked Saʿīd ibn Jubayr, and he said, 'Perform *tayammum* and pray' " (IAS 1668). Zubayd ibn al-Ḥārith, a Kūfan who transmitted to Sufyān al-Thawrī, died in A.H. 122–24/739–42 C.E. (Ibn Ḥajar, *Tahdhīb al-tahdhīb*, 3:310–11).

126. AR 917.

127. AR 922.

128. AR 923; IAS 1669.

129. Cf. AR 1613–15; IAS 1552–54; Saḥnūn ibn Saʿīd al-Tanūkhī, *al-Mudawwana al-kubrā* (n.p., A.H. 1324/[1906–1907 C.E.]), 1:37 (the interpretation is attributed to Zayd [ibn Aslam, d. A.H. 136/753–54 C.E.], but rejected by Mālik).

130. Probably al-Ḥasan ibn Muslim ibn Yannāq, a Meccan who died "before Ṭāwūs [ibn Kaysān]" (*Tahdhīb al-tahdhīb*, 2:322), that is, in or before A.H. 106/724–25 C.E.

131. IAS 1664.

132. IAS 1663.

133. IAS 1665.

134. IAS 1666. For biographical data on Sulaymān ibn Mūsā, see *Tahdhīb al-tahdhīb*, 4:226–27.

135. AR 911–24; IAS 1659–62; al-Bukhārī, *Ṣaḥīḥ*, 1:101–4; Muslim, *Ṣaḥīḥ*, 4:279–85; al-Bannā, *al-Fatḥ al-rabbānī*, 2:189–90; Abū Dāwūd, *Sunan*, 1:235–238; Ibn Māja, *Sunan*, 1:188–89; al-Nasāʾī, *Sunan*, 1:88.

136. AR 915. Al-Bukhārī transmits a version without the final exchange between ʿAmmār and ʿUmar (*Ṣaḥīḥ*, 1:101); nevertheless, he also includes in his section on *tayammum* the dialogue cited below, which makes reference to this exchange. See also Ibn Māja, *Sunan*, 1:188.

137. Al-Bukhārī, *Ṣaḥīḥ*, 1:104. Al-Bukhārī includes two versions of this anecdote, both of them transmitted from al-Aʿmash, a Kūfan who died in the 140s A.H. See also al-Bannā, *al-Fatḥ al-rabbānī*, 2:182–83; al-Nasāʾī, *Sunan*, 88.

138. Al-Bukhārī, *Ṣaḥīḥ*, 1:104.

139. As we have already seen, Qurʾānic interpretation was also informed and constrained by a related but independently powerful tradition of practice. Thus, at least one truly anomalous syntactical possibility was completely ignored. As noted by later Qurʾānic commentators, on a purely syntactical level "travel" and "sickness" appear parallel to "touching women" and "coming from the privy" in verse 5:6. There is no purely textual reason not to assume that illness and travel, like elimination and contact with the opposite sex, are sources of pollution. It would be perfectly possible to imagine a system in which such conditions would be considered defiling. Sickness, in the loss of bodily control that it entails and the shadow of death that it implies, could easily be understood to cause a loss of purity. Traveling, the abandonment of the domesticated order of the settlement for the liminal fluidity of the road, is also subject to such an interpretation—at least from the point of view of modern western purity theory. For early Muslims, however, neither possibility seems to have been conceivable. "Touching women" and "coming from the privy" were sources of pollution, while traveling and illness were possible conditions under which normal ablutions might be impossible or harmful. The reading of the text was, here, limited by the pre-understanding of a practicing community. (Cf. al-Nawawī's comment that "the order (*naẓm*) of the verse implies that illness and travel are causes of impurity (*ḥadathān*)—but no one holds this (*lā yaqūluhu aḥad*)." (*al-Majmūʿ sharḥ al-Muhadhdhab* [n.p.: Zakarīyā ʿAlī Yūsuf, n.d.], 2:3.)

140. Al-Bukhārī, *Ṣaḥīḥ*, 1:99; see also AR 879, 880; al-Bannā, *al-Fatḥ al-rabbānī*, 2:181–83; Ibn Māja, *Sunan*, 1:187, 188; al-Nasāʾī, *Sunan*, 1:89.

141. Ibn Ḥajar al-ʿAsqalānī, *Fatḥ al-bārī bi-sharḥ ṣaḥīḥ al-Bukhārī*, ed. Ṭāhā ʿAbd al-Raʾūf Saʿd et al. ([Cairo]: Maktabat al-Kullīyāt biʾl-Azhar, A.H. 1398/[1907–10 C.E.), 2:252.

142. Ibn Hishām, *Sīra*, 2:83; Guillaume, *Life of Muhammad*, p. 112.

Chapter 3. "Cancelers of *Wuḍuʾ*" and the Boundaries of the Body

1. Michael Cook, "Magian Cheese: An Archaic Problem in Islamic Law," *BSOAS* 47 (1984), pp. 449–67.

2. See al-Jazīrī, *Kitāb al-fiqh ʿalāʾl-madhāhib al-arbaʿa*, 1:568–69.

3. This conceptualization of fasting also illuminates another major homology between the rules of fasting and those relating to ritual purity: the fact that sexual

activity ruptures both a fast and a state of ritual purity. In both cases, there are two different criteria for the consequences (respectively, repetition of the fast or *ghusl* ablutions) to be incurred: ejaculation (even without penetration) and penetration (even without ejaculation). Both criteria, of course, can be understood from the point of view of transgression of the frontier of the body. In the Islamic system, one is pure only so long as one is *continent*—self-*contained*—in both senses of the word: that of sexual restraint and that of withholding bodily discharges. The ideal of a perfectly nonporous body implicit in both sets of rules is carried to an extreme in ascetic practice, where sexual abstinence and fasting are transformed into constant states.

4. AR 658.

5. Qur'ān 21:69, 38:42, 78:24 (references to coolness).

6. Qur'ān 2:80, 11:113. The phrase is also used once in a neutral context, meaning "to burn" (Qur'ān 24:35).

7. Abū Ghānim al-Khurāsānī al-Ibāḍī, *al-Mudawwana al-Kubrā*, (n.p.: Dār al-Yaqẓa al-ʿArabīya, n.d.), p. 14. The reference is to a slogan used by the pro-washing party in the controversy over wiping or washing the feet, "Woe to the heels from the Fire" (*wayl li'l-aʿqāb min al-nār*).

8. Abd Allāh ibn Aḥmad ibn Qudāma, *al-Mughnī*, ed. Muḥammad Khalīl Harās ([Cairo]: n.d.), 1:180.

9. Abū'l-Walīd Sulaymān ibn Khalaf ibn Saʿd al-Bājī, *al-Muntaqā sharḥ al-Muwaṭṭa'*, vol. 1, ed. Muḥammad ʿAbd al-Qādir Aḥmad ʿAṭā (Beirut: Dār al-Kutub al-ʿIlmīya, A.H. 1420/1999 A.D.), p. 332.

10. AR 665; IAS 550, 551. See also AR 666 (without anecdote); al-Bannā, *al-Fatḥ al-rabbānī*, 2:97–98; Abū Dāwūd, *Sunan*, 1:134–35; al-Nasā'ī, *Sunan*, 1:54–55.

11. *Aqiṭ* is "milk which [has been churned and cooked until it] has become congealed and hard as stone." Edward William Lane, *Arabic-English Lexicon* (Beirut: Librairie du Liban, 1968; facsimile of London: Williams and Norgate, 1863), s.v. "thawr."

12. AR 667. See also AR 668, IAS 549, Muslim, *Ṣaḥīḥ,* 4:266 (without the question); al-Bannā, *al-Fatḥ al-rabbānī*, 2:95–96; Abū Dāwūd, *Sunan*, 1:134 ("al-wuḍū' mimmā anḍajat al-nār"); al-Nasā'ī, *Sunan*, 1:53–54 (without the question).

13. al-Dārimī, *Sunan*, 1:185; Muslim, *Ṣaḥīḥ*, 4:265; al-Nasā'ī, *Sunan*, 1:54.

14. al-Bannā, *al-Fatḥ al-rabbānī*, 2:97.

15. Cf. al-Bannā, *al-Fatḥ al-rabbānī*, 2:96–97; al-Nasā'ī, *Sunan*, 1:54.

16. IAS 522.

17. AR 635.

18. IAS 523.

19. Ibn Ḥajar, *Tahdhīb al-tahdīb*, 2:42–43.

20. al-ʿAynī, *ʿUmdat al-Qāri,* 3:105; Abū Dāwūd, *Sunan*, 1:133; al-Nasāʾī, *Sunan*, 1:55. al-ʿAynī notes that this report is also to be found in the compilations of al-Ṭaḥāwī and Ibn Ḥibbān.

21. Abū ʿAmr ʿUthmān ibn ʿAbd al-Raḥmān ibn al-Falāḥ, *ʿUlūm al-ḥadīth* (Damascus, A.H. 1406/1986 C.E.), pp. 277–78.

22. Ibn Ḥajar, *Tahdhīb al-tahdhīb*, 2:42–43.

23. Ibid., 4:280–81.

24. Mālik ibn Anas, *Muwaṭṭaʾ*, 1:28–29; IAS 527, 528.

25. Badr al-Dīn al-ʿAynī, *ʿUmdat al-qāriʾ sharḥ Ṣaḥīḥ al-Bukhārī* (Beirut: Muḥammad Amīn Damj, n.d.), 3:105.

26. al-Shaybānī, *Āthār*, #19.

27. Ibid., p. 32.

28. The major ablutions (entailing bathing of the entire body) that must be performed in cases of sexual impurity).

29. AR 653.

30. AR 655.

31. IAS 548.

32. IAS 535, 539; see also AR 653 and IAS 538, AR 658 (from Ibn Masʿūd).

33. Ibn Māja, *Sunan*, 1:163.

34. His death date is unkown (see Ibn Ḥajar, *Tahdhīb al-tahdhīb*, 12:112), so it is difficult to estimate the time period in which the anecdote is supposed to be set.

35. Mālik ibn Anas, the eponymous authority of the Mālikī school, emphasized the authoritative status of the "practice of the people of Madīna" as an authentic continuous tradition deriving from the practice of the Prophet. In contrast, al-Shāfiʿī demanded that practices attributed to the Prophet be documented by concrete *ḥadīth* reports authenticated with chains of transmission.

36. See Abū Ghānim al-Khurāsānī, *al-Mudawwana al-kubrā*, 1:8.

37. AR 665, 666, 667, 668, 671, 673.

38. AR 665, 666.

39. AR 672.

40. AR 665, 666; IAS 550, 551; Muslim, *Ṣaḥīḥ*, 4:266; al-Bannā, *al-Fatḥ al-rabbānī*, 2:98; al-Nasāʾī, *Sunan*, 1:115; al-Ṭaḥāwī, *Maʿānī al-āthār*, 1:63.

41. al-Bannā, *al-Fatḥ al-rabbānī*, 2:97; Abū Dāwud, *Sunan*, #195; al-Ṭaḥāwī, *Maʿānī al-āthār*, 1:62–63. The various versions seem to converge on Yaḥyā ibn abī

Kathīr, d. 129/132 (Ibn Ḥajar, *Tahdhīb al-tahdhīb*, 11:268–70), although there are not enough versions for this pattern to be particularly pronounced.

42. Chains of transmission running through al-Zuhrī: AR 667, 668; IAS 549; Muslim, *Ṣaḥīḥ*, 4:266; al-Nasāʾī, *Sunan*, 1:53–54 (two versions); al-Ṭaḥāwī, *Maʿānī al-āthār*, 1:63. Chains of transmission that do not run through al-Zuhrī: al-Bannā, *al-Fatḥ al-rabbānī*, 2:96; Abū Dāwud, *Sunan*, 1:134; al-Tirmidhī, *Sunan*, 1:108; al-Ṭaḥāwī, *Maʿānī al-āthār*, 1:63. Interestingly, Ibn Abī Shayba records a version of the Abū Hurayra report (IAS 562) that does not run through Ibn Shihāb—and also does not attribute the formula to the Prophet.

43. AR 665, 671; IAS 553, 560. Sometimes ʿĀʾisha and Zayd ibn Thābit appear as links to the Prophet himself, rather than as independent exemplars of the practice. AR 665 merely states that they both performed *wuḍūʾ* from cooked food; AR 666 cites them as sources for a statement to this effect by the Prophet, although with an incomplete chain of transmission (*qāla al-Zuhrī: wa-balaghanī dhālika ʿan Zayd ibn Thābit wa-ʿan ʿĀʾisha ʿan al-nabī* . . .), while both Muslim (*Ṣaḥīḥ*, #785, #787) and Ṭaḥāwī (*Maʿānī al-āthār*, 1:62) have complete *isnād*s.

44. Schacht, *Origins*, pp. 171–72.

45. ʿAbd Allāh ibn Zayd ibn ʿAmr / ʿĀmir ibn Nābil ibn Mālik, Abū Qilāba al-Jarmī al-Baṣrī. He died in Syria between 104 and 107, reportedly having fled there from an unwanted judicial appointment. Ibn Ḥajar, *Tahdhīb al-tahdhīb*, 5:224–26.

46. IAS 563: "I performed *wuḍūʾ* (*tawaḍḍaʾtu*) from cooked food."

47. AR 669: "Abū Mūsā al-Ashʿarī said: It makes no difference to me whether I plunge my hand into excrement and blood (*farth wa-dam*) or eat cooked food (lit: food that has been touched by fire), then pray without performing *wuḍūʾ*. al-Ḥasan said: We follow this opinion"; IAS 554: "Abū Mūsā used to perform *wuḍūʾ* from cooked food."

48. Ibn Ḥajar, *Tahdhīb al-tahdhīb*, 10:167–69. There is significant uncertainty about the date of his death; Ibn Ḥajar also records reports that he died in A.H. 125/742–43 C.E. and that he survived until the reign of the ʿAbbāsid caliph al-Manṣūr (A.H. 136–58/754–75 C.E.).

49. IAS 552; also Ṭaḥāwī, *Maʿānī al-āthār*, 1:62. Anas ibn Mālik was the personal servant of the Prophet from an early age.

50. Ibn Saʿd, *Kitāb al-Ṭabaqāt al-kubrā*, ed. Bruno Meissner (Leiden the Netherlands: E. J. Brill, 1915), 7:115.

51. AR 670, IAS 555 (with slight divergences in wording). The two chains of transmission converge at the link after Abū Qilāba, Ayyūb [ibn abī Tamīma al-Sakhtiyānī]. The anecdote would presumably be set in the period when al-Ḥajjāj was governor of ʿIrāq, between A.H. 75/694 C.E. and his death in A.H. 95/714 C.E. Relations between the two men are supposed to have been extremely strained, due to Anas's perceived support for challengers to the regime (see EI^2, s.v. "Anas b. Mālik"). Ibn

ʿAbd Rabbih records an exchange in which the Umayyad caliph ʿAbd al-Malik upbraids al-Ḥajjāj for his treatment of Anas and reminds him of the latter's exalted status as a Companion of the Prophet (*al-ʿIqd al-farīd*, vol. 5, ed. Aḥmad Amīn et al. [Cairo: Maṭbaʿat Lajnat al-Taʾlīf waʾl-Tarjama waʾl-Nashr, A.H. 1385/1965 C.E.], pp. 36–41). For the biography of al-Ḥajjāj, see *EI*², s.v. "al-Ḥadjdjāj b. Yūsuf."

52. IAS 561: "Abū Qilāba reported from a man of the [tribe of] Hudhayl—I believe that he mentioned that he was a Companion—[that] he said: One must perform *wuḍūʾ* (*yutawaḍḍaʾ*) from cooked food"; IAS, 558: "Abū Qilāba used to order *wuḍūʾ* from cooked food; one time he gave them *nabīdh* to drink and ordered them to perform *wuḍūʾ*, and they performed *wuḍūʾ*."

53. Ibn Ḥajar, *Tahdhīb al-tahdhīb*, 2:266.

54. Ibid., 9:450.

55. Ibid., 9:451.

56. Abūʾl-Qāsim ʿAlī ibn al-Ḥusayn Ibn ʿAsākir, *Taʾrīkh madīnat dimashq* (Beirut: Dār al-Fikr, A.H. 1417/1997 A.D.), 45:297–305, 322–24.

57. For a full exposition of the conspiracy theory connected to this incident, see *EI*¹, s.v. "al-Zuhrī." For criticism of the anecdote, see Oleg Grabar, "The Omayyad Done of the Rock in Jerusalem," *Ars Orientalis* 3 (1959): 36, and A. A. al-Dūrī, "al-Zuhrī," *BSOAS* 19 (1957): 10–11.

58. *EI*¹, s.v. "al-Zuhrī." The caliph involved is supposed to have been either Walīd I (ruled 86/705–96/715) or Hishām (ruled 105/724–125/743). This was apparently a question of abiding interest to the Marwānid house; al-Ṭabarī preserves a letter in which ʿUrwa ibn al-Zubayr responds to a query from ʿAbd al-Malik ibn Marwān regarding the identity of the slanderers (al-Ṭabarī, *Jāmiʿ al-Bayān*, 18:86–87).

59. *EI*¹, s.v. "al-Zuhrī." In a report cited by Ibn Ḥajar, Hishām ibn ʿAbd al-Malik requests that al-Zuhrī dictate *ḥadīth* to one of his sons (*Tahdhīb al-tahdhīb*, 9:449).

60. Ibn Ḥajar, *Tahdhīb al-tahdhīb*, 4:351–52.

61. al-Dūrī, "al-Zuhrī," pp. 11–12.

62. Ibn Ḥajar, *Tahdhīb al-tahdhīb*, 9:449.

63. Ibn Saʿd, *al-Ṭabaqāt al-kubrā*, 5:284.

64. For al-Ḥasan's letters admonishing ʿUmar ibn al-ʿAzīz (mainly with the remembrance of death), see Aḥmad Zakī Ṣafwat, ed., *Jamharat rasāʾil al-ʿarab fī ʿuṣūr al-ʿarabīya al-zāhira*, vol. 2: al-ʿAṣr al-umawī (Beirut: al-Maktaba al-ʿIlmīya, n.d.), pp. 324–33.

65. Ibid., 7:119–20. One wonders how this attitude, documented in several different reports, relates to al-Ḥasan's *qadarī* theological position. The attitude that the iniquitous rule of the Umayyads was imposed by God seems more akin to the

predestinarian views allegedly promulgated by the dynasty itself than to al-Ḥasan's own free-will tenets. However, the general sentiment that "God transforms through repentance, not through the sword" (cf. Qur'ān 13:11) seems to be in consonance with al-Ḥasan's austere and moralistic message. al-Ḥasan's general attitude towards the Umayyad dynasty is probably best expressed in the oration he is supposed to have given to the mobilizing populace on the occasion of Yazīd ibn al-Muhallab's revolt in A.H. 101/719–20 C.E.: after delivering a scathing denunciation of Yazīd, al-Ḥasan is accused by the mob of being a partisan of the Umayyads, upon which he retorts with an even more blistering critique of the ruling house (al-Ṭabarī, *Ta'rīkh al-umam wa'l-mulūk,* ed. Muḥammad Abū'l-Faḍl Ibrāhīm [Beirut, n.d.]), 6:587–88).

66. Ibn Sa'd, *Ṭabaqāt*, 5:251.

67. Ibid., 5:256.

68. Tilman Nagel, *Rechtleitung und Kalifat: Versuch über eine Grundfrage der Islamischen Geschichte,* Studien zum Minderheitenproblem im Islam 2 (Bonn: Selbstverlag des orientalischen Seminars der Universität Bonn, 1975), pp. 70–81. Nagel's argument is largely based on the texts of epistles attributed to al-Ḥasan.

69. Ibn Ḥajar, *Tahdhīb al-tahdhīb*, 7:475–78.

70. Ibn Sa'd, *Ṭabaqāt*, 5:294.

71. Ibn Ḥajar, *Tahdhīb al-tahdhīb*, 5:225.

72. Ibn Sa'd, *Ṭabaqāt*, 7:134.

73. Ibid., p. 134.

74. Ibid.

75. Ibid., p. 135.

76. *EI*[2], s.v. "Anas b. Mālik."

77. Ibn Ḥajar, *Tahdhīb al-tahdhīb*, 7:477.

78. Ibn Ḥajar, *Tahdhīb al-tahdhīb*, 5:67–68.

79. IAS 543.

80. AR 642. The highly contrived form of the report, in which Abū Hurayra cites his Prophetic *ḥadīth* and is directly confronted by Ibn 'Abbās with testimony to the contrary, would tend to raise doubts about its accuracy.

81. Ibn Sa'd, *Ṭabaqāt*, 5:130.

82. Ibid., 5:246.

83. 'Abīda ibn 'Amr / ibn Qays ibn 'Amr al-Salmānī al-Murādī, Abū 'Amr al-Kūfī (d. 72–74). He was considered a Follower (*tābi'ī*), i.e., a member of the generation following that which had known the Prophet—he converted two years before the death of the Prophet, but never saw him. He transmitted from 'Alī, Ibn Mas'ūd, and

Ibn al-Zubayr, and was also known for his *fiqh*. Ibn Sīrīn had a great regard for him (Ibn Ḥajar, *Tahdhīb al-tahdhīb*, 7:84).

84. AR 660; parallel report, IAS 545. The chains of transmission diverge after Ibn Sīrīn.

85. Ibn Sa'd, *Ṭabaqāt*, 7:147. Like Ibn Sīrīn, he is supposed to have disdained the financial support of the government. One story recounts that thirty-some thousand (*dīnārs*?) of his *'aṭā'* stipend accumulated in the treasury; when urged to collect he refused, saying, "I have no need for it until God judges between me and Banū Marwān" (p. 128).

86. AR 639, 640, 651; IAS 521.

87. Ibn Ḥajar, *Tahdhīb al-tahdhīb*, 9:473–75.

88. AR 635, 638.

89. Ibn Ḥajar, *Tahdhīb al-tahdhīb*, 7:217–18.

90. Ibid., 4:84–88.

91. AR 643.

92. Although it seems that the dimensions of his conflict with the Marwānids may have been inflated by posterity through conflation with the story of his conflict with 'Abd Allāh ibn al-Zubayr, which had less lasting relevance to the political passions of the Muslims.

93. AR 633.

94. IAS 524.

95. AR 641.

96. IAS 544.

97. See Ibn Ḥajar, *Tahdhīb al-tahdhīb*, 6:94–95 ('Abd al-A'lā ibn 'Āmr al-Tha'labī al-Kūfī).

98. Aḥmad ibn Ḥanbal, *Musnad al-Imām Aḥmad ibn Ḥanbal*, ed. Shu'ayb al-Arna'ūṭ et al (Beirut, Mu'assassat al-Risāla, A.H. 1419/1998 A.D.), 23:186–87 (*ḥadīth* #14920). al-Bannā's *al-Fatḥ al-rabbānī* does not include this report in its section on *wuḍū'* from cooked food. The same report is also found in al-Ṭaḥāwī's *Sharḥ ma'ānī al-āthār*, vol. 1, ed. Muḥammad Zahrī al-Najjār et al. (Beirut: 'Ālam al-Kutub, A.H. 1414/1994 C.E.), p. 67. That 'Aṭā' transmitted this report from Jābir is independently reported through the *isnāds* Ibn Jurayj - 'Abd al-Razzāq and Yaḥyā ibn Rabī'a - 'Abd al-Razzāq (AR 647, 664).

99. Shams al-Dīn Muḥammad ibn Aḥmad ibn 'Uthmān al-Dhahabī, *Ta'rīkh al-islām wa-wafayāt al-mashāhīr wa' l-a'lām*, ṭabaqa 14, ed. 'Umar 'Abd al-Salām Tadmurī (Beirut: Dār al-Kitāb al-'Arabī, A.H. 1408/1988 C.E.), pp. 446–47; *Das Biographische Lexikon des Ṣalāḥaddīn Ḫalīl ibn Aibak aṣ-Ṣafadī*, Bibliotheca Islamica vol. 6, part

15, ed. Bernd Radtke (Wiesbaden: in Kommission bei Franz Steiner Verlag, 1979), p. 439.

100. Ibn ʿAsākir, *Taʾrīkh madīnat Dimashq*, 22:399; 22:400.

101. AR 644, IAS 525; Ṭaḥāwī, *Maʿānī al-āthār*, 1:65. The *ḥadīth* is also cited from Umm Salama without the anecdote about Marwān and ʿAbd Allāh ibn Shaddād, AR 638. A Medinian who made trips to Kūfa, ʿAbd Allāh ibn Shaddād was reputed to be a Shīʿite and (as has already been noted) took part in the rebellion of Ibn al-Ashʿath. His political background suggests a pointed use of the name of Marwān, cf. Ibn Ḥajar, *Tahdhīb al-tahdhīb*, 5:351–52.

102. Ibn Saʿd, *Ṭabaqāt*, 5:253; Ibn ʿAsākir, 45:200.

103. Ibn Saʿd, *Ṭabaqāt*, 5:265 (compare AR 671, stating the same of Ibn ʿUmar).

104. Ibid., 5:265.

105. Ibn Saʿd, *Ṭabaqāt*, 5:265.

106. Ibid., 5:265.

107. AR 61: "Wiping the feet was mentioned to ʿUmar ibn ʿAbd al-ʿAzīz; he said, 'I have heard it reported from (*balaghanī ʿan*) three Companions of the Prophet, the least authoritative (*adnā*) of whom is your cousin al-Mughīra ibn Shuʿba, that the Prophet washed his feet.' "

108. AR 797b: "ʿUmar ibn ʿAbd al-ʿAzīz wrote to the people of Miṣṣīṣa, 'Remove your foot coverings every three days.' "

109. Ibn Saʿd, *Ṭabaqāt*, 5:293; Ibn ʿAsākir, 45:215.

110. Ibn Saʿd, 5: 263, 265.

111. Ibid., 5:270.

112. Ibid., 5:385, 399; Ibn ʿAsākir, 45:214–15.

113. Ibid., 5:399.

114. *Tazakkā* means "to be pure"; *zakāt*, from the same root means "[purification of one's income through] alms tax."

115. Ibn Saʿd, *Ṭabaqāt*, 5:363.

116. IAS 28. A more common wording is, "God does not accept prayers without purification or alms from misappropriated/falsely seized booty (*innaʾllāh lā yaqbalu ṣalāt bi-ghayr ṭuhūr wa-lā ṣadaqa min ghulūl*)" (26, 27, 29).

117. Cf. Ibn Saʿd, *Ṭabaqāt*, 5:360.

118. See Q 6:70, 10:4, 22:19, 37:67, 38:57, 40:72, 44:46, 44:48, 56:42, 56:54, 78:25, etc. The hyphothesis that this stricture is derived from Qurʾānic associations between certain substances and the punishments of Hell may also explain another odd

rule that seems to have been disputed by early Muslim thinkers. This was the question of whether it was permissible to perform one's *wuḍū*ʾ with water from a brass (*nuḥās*, *ṣufr*) vessel (cf. AR 171–80, IAS 395–404); according to some early thinkers, brass is also a component of the scene in Hell. Qurʾān 55:35 states that God will send flames of fire and "*al-nuḥās*" against the damned. While some early interpreters argued that "*nuḥās*" in this context meant smoke, others held that the denizens of the Fire would be tortured with molten brass (see al-Ṭabarī, *Jāmiʿ al-bayān*, 27:140–41). While ʿUmar ibn ʿAbd al-ʿAzīz (as has already been mentioned) did not himself observe this particular practice, the debate on this point fits into the paradigm that ʿUmar seems to have followed.

119. Qurʾān 38:42.

120. Ibn Saʿd, *Ṭabaqāt*, 5:373. With respect to the foundation of ʿUmar's purity practices in close adherence to the Qurʾān, it is also relevant to mention his apparent adherence to the doctrine that unbelievers were impure (*najas*), which is based on a literal interpretation of Qurʾān 9:28; see chapter 4.

121. When considering this theme we should keep in mind that some people in this period probably did not have their own ovens; where communal ovens were used, ʿUmar's worries about whether the fuel was *ḥalāl* in the financial sense would have been relevant even for ordinary people of pious inclinations. Another custom that may be relevant is the use of dung as fuel.

122. Ibn Saʿd, *Ṭabaqāt*, 5:345. It should be noted that abstinence from cooked food was a form of austerity familiar to the Christian ascetic tradition from before the Islamic period. Particularly in vogue among hermits, it was also known in monastic rules, especially as a form of self-denial during Lent. Interestingly, scruples about cooking food were also entertained by the Manichaeans. See F. Mugnier, "Abstinence," *Dictionnaire de Spiritualité, ascétique et mystique*, ed. M. Viller et al. (Paris: Beauchesne, 1932), col. 122, 123, 126. I thank Professor Fred Donner for drawing my attention to cases of this practice in the Christian tradition.

123. This does not necessarily imply that the relevant *ḥadīth* are spurious. From the point of view of a secular historian, the Prophet's actual words and practice with regard to this issue are simply irrecoverable; the available evidence is so tenuous and contradictory that no firm conclusions are possible at this remove.

124. AR 659.

125. Shāfiʿī, *al-Umm*, 1:19.

126. Cf. AR 449: ʿAṭāʾ states that it is necessary to perform *wuḍū*ʾ after touching a donkey's genitals but not after touching a camel's genitals. His rationale is that the donkey is impure; the same rule applies to any animal whose meat cannot be eaten.

127. al-Shaybānī, *Āthār*, #22; AR 429, 431, 433, 435; IAS 1740, 1741, 1744.

128. al-Shaybānī, *Āthār*, #23; AR 430; IAS 1738, 1739.

129. AR 425, 426; IAS 1745.

130. AR 423, reading "rijl" in the final sentence and "rajul" in the one preceding.

131. AR 439.

132. AR 417, 418, 419–22; IAS 1726, 1732, 1733.

133. AR 420, 422, 423, 424, 432; IAS 1734.

134. IAS 1734.

135. IAS 1737.

136. AR 439.

137. IAS 1728, 1729.

138. AR 437, IAS 1730 (both *isnād*s run through ʿAbd al-Raḥmān ibn Ḥarmala).

139. al-Shaybānī, *Āthār*, #23; AR 430, 431, 436; IAS 1738, 1741, 1742, 1752.

140. IAS 1749.

141. AR 436; IAS 1749, 1740. The opinion is also attributed to Ḥudhayfa through a pair of Baṣran *isnād*s.

142. IAS 1743.

143. IAS 1747, 1750.

144. AR 434: A man asked Saʿd ibn abī Waqqāṣ whether touching the penis necessitated *wuḍūʾ*. He said: "If there is a part of you that is unclean (*najis*), cut it off." AR 414 (same text with slight variations, AR 415, IAS 1731): One of the sons of Saʿd ibn abī Waqqāṣ said: One time I was holding the Qurʾān (*muṣḥaf*) for Saʿd ibn abī Waqqāṣ while he studied (*yastadhkiru*), until my penis began to itch and I scratched it. When he saw me put my hand in there, he said: "Did you touch it?" I said: "Yes." He said: "Get up and perform *wuḍūʾ*."

145. al-Shaybānī, *Āthār*, #23; IAS 1749.

146. IAS 1748.

147. al-Shaybānī, *Āthār*, #22; *Ḥujja*, 1:59.

148. AR 439.

149. AR 433; IAS 1744.

150. AR 438.

151. AR 438.

152. AR 433, IAS 1744. Also see AR 427, where al-Ḥasan is represented as transmitting a similar report from a person or persons speaking in an assembled "group (*rahṭ*) of the Companions of the Prophet."

153. AR 411. In the text in the *Muwaṭṭa'* (1:47) ʿUrwa says, "I didn't know that (*mā ʿalimtu dhālika*)." Mālik's version is also reported by al-Shāfiʿī (*al-Umm*, 1:19), Abū Dāwūd (*Sunan*, 1:125–26), and al-Nasā'ī (*Sunan*, 1:37). Cf. AR 411; IAS 1725; al-Dārimī, *Sunan*, 1:184–85; al-Bannā, *al-Fatḥ al-rabbānī*, 2:86–87; al-Tirmidhī, *Sunan*, 1:113–114; Ibn Māja, *Sunan*, 1:161.

154. Ibn Saʿd, *Ṭabaqāt*, 5:43.

155. Ibn Ḥajar, *Tahdhīb al-tahdhīb*, 10:92.

156. Ibid., 12:404.

157. al-Mizzī, *Tahdhīb al-Kamāl*, (Beirut, A.H. 1413/1992 C.E.), 35:137.

158. IAS 1724.

159. Calder, *Studies*, p. 63.

160. The crux of the problem lies in the proviso so casually inserted by Calder: the line of reasoning assumes that the *ḥadīth* is from the beginning "allied to a theory advocating the sufficiency of Prophetic hadith as legal authority." The existence of a Prophetic *ḥadīth* renders other exempla obsolete if, and only if, the people carrying on the debate agree that such a *ḥadīth* is a uniquely binding form of evidence. This may seem self-evident to us; however, we should remember that we have read the works of al-Shāfiʿī and later Islamic scholars, while first- and second-century Muslim thinkers had not. Without the rigorous standards that developed in the third century A.H./ninth century C.E., the citation (and, indeed, the generation) of lesser forms of validation could continue even in the presence of a Prophetic *ḥadīth*. This might be either on substantive grounds (the practice of eminent figures other than the Prophet being accorded a validity of their own) or on formal ones (Companion and other testimony being considered as indirect evidence of the true practice of the Prophet). The argument that the early Muslim community—and particularly its most prominent and pious members—could not have been ignorant of the practice of the Prophet is, after all, not at all irrational. I would not deny that in many individual cases Prophetic *ḥadīth* are posterior to the theory of the supremacy of Prophetic *ḥadīth*, because they were generated by the demand it created; the better established the supremacy of Prophetic *ḥadīth* in legal reasoning, the better the market for Prophetic *ḥadīth*. This does not prove that all Prophetic *ḥadīth* postdate all reports about later figures.

161. See Ibn Ḥajar, *Tahdhīb al-tahdhīb*, 7:84. ʿAbīda is considered a *tābiʿī*; he converted two years before the death of the Prophet, but never saw him.

162. IAS 1726: "Ibn Sīrīn [said], 'I asked ʿAbīda about God's statement, {*aw lāmastum al-nisā'* }; he made a gesture with his hand (*qāla bi-yadihi*), and I inferred what he meant and did not ask him.' " Several parallel reports, all through Muḥammad [ibn Sīrīn], are found in al-Ṭabarī, *Jāmiʿ al-Bayān*, 5:104–5.

163. See Ibn Manẓūr, *Lisān al-ʿArab*, s.v. *n-s-w*.

164. IAS 1726.

165. Since we know of ʿAbīda's supposed opinion only through Muḥammad ibn Sīrīn, we could also infer that the opinion was actually Muḥammad's own. ʿAbīda seems to have been a pet authority of Muḥammad ibn Sīrīn's; in the previous section we saw that he was the latter's model in the matter of *wuḍūʾ* from cooked food as well.

166. Motzki, *Anfänge*, pp. 97–98.

167. AR 422.

168. AR 405.

169. Calder, *Studies*, p. 58.

170. Of course, even this logic is not compelling. The fact that a passage matching the text of the *Muwaṭṭaʾ* as we know it was inserted into the *Ḥujja* does not mean that other changes in the text of the *Muwaṭṭaʾ* did not occur after that time.

171. Calder, *Studies*, p. 65.

172. al-Shaybānī, *al-Ḥujja*, 1:59–64.

173. Calder, *Studies*, p. 62.

174. Ibid., p. 62.

175. Ibid., p. 63.

176. Ibid., p.62.

177. The incongruity may indeed be very slight, since companions were often regarded as witnesses of an implicitly Prophetic practice. (Of course, this argument may be regarded as an ex post facto defense of cherished Companion traditions in the face of the emergent supremacy of the example of the Prophet.)

178. Ibid., p. 62.

179. "Followers," i.e., members of the generation following the contemporaries of the Prophet.

180. See AR 516–25, 545–81; IAS 432–43, 1249–53, 1458–81; al-Shaybānī, *Ḥujja,* 1:66–71.

181. al-Shaybānī, *Ḥujja*, 1:66–67.

182. Ibid., pp. 67, 69.

183. Ibid., p. 68.

184. al-Shāfiʿī, *al-Umm*, 1:17–18.

185. AR 547; IAS 1458, 1461.

186. IAS 1463.

187. AR 549.

188. IAS 1454, 1459.

189. IAS 1466.

190. IAS 1468.

191. AR 545, 546, 548, 555; IAS 1462.

192. AR 558, 559. Perhaps as a corollary of the classical view that this was originally a regional controversy between the Iraqīs and the Ḥijāzīs, later authors occasionally claim that ʿAṭāʾ taught that there was no *wuḍūʾ* for bleeding. Cf. Bahāʾ al-Dīn Abūʾl-Maḥāsin Yūsuf ibn Rāfiʿ ibn Shaddād, *Dalāʾil al-aḥkām* (Beirut, A.H. 1413/1992 C.E.), 1:118.

193. AR 548: "I [i.e., Ibn Abī Najīḥ, a Meccan who died in A.H. 131–32] asked ʿAṭāʾ and Mujāhid about a wound in someone's hand in which there is blood that is visible but does not flow. Mujāhid said, 'He performs *wuḍūʾ*.' ʿAṭāʾ said, '[He does not have to perform *wuḍūʾ*] unless it flows.' "

194. IAS 1460: "Mujāhid was asked about a man whose hand bleeds without the blood spreading (*yakhruju min yadihi al-dam wa-lā yujāwizuʾl-dam makānahu*); he said, 'He does not perform *wuḍūʾ*.' "

195. IAS 1465.

196. IAS 1466.

197. The people whose behavior relevant to this issue is described in reports by witnesses include Ibn ʿUmar (d. 73–74), Abū Hurayra (d. 57–59), Saʿīd ibn al-Musayyab (d. 93–100), Jābir ibn ʿAbd Allāh (d. 61–78), and Abūʾl-Sawwār al-Baṣrī (death date unknown; transmitted from ʿAlī and al-Ḥasan). While there are not enough *isnād*s for these traditions to make any educated guess about their authenticity or provenance, it is notable that the approximate period to which they belong would be very logical in the context of the chronological convergence noted above. If the generation that died around the turn of the first/second century theorized about and developed a consensus on this particular issue—which may not have seemed pressing to earlier Muslims—it would make sense for them to collect and transmit their own generation's memories of the behavior of the preceding generation. This second set of reference figures would thus be people who probably never thought to develop or state explicit opinions of their own on this issue, but whose example became relevant to their successors who did.

198. Based on either the report stating that he was fifty-five at the time of his death (combined with the death date 118) or the report stating that he was born in 61 (Ibn Ḥajar, *Tahdhīb al-tahdhīb*, 8:355).

199. Ibid., 8:351–52.

200. ʿUrwa died in the early 90s of the first century A.H. (Ibn Ḥajar, *Tahdhīb al-tahdhīb*, 7:184).

201. AR 578.

202. Mālik, *Muwaṭṭa'*, # 101; cf. AR 579, 580, 581.

203. Ibn Hishām, *Sīra*, 4:163–64 (Guillaume, *Life of Muhammad*, pp. 446–47); al-Ṭabarī, *Ta'rīkh*, 2:558–59; Abū Dāwūd, *Sunan*, 1:136. Abbreviated version, al-Bukhārī, *Ṣaḥīḥ*, 1:59.

204. Schacht, *Origins*, p. 190.

205. G.H.A. Juynboll, *Muslim Tradition, Studies in Chronology, Provenance and Authorship of Early Ḥadīth* (Cambridge: Cambridge University Press, 1983), pp. 6–7.

206. Ibid., pp. 198–213.

207. "Rerences to ʿUmar b. ʿAbdalʿazīz are generally spurious," *Origins*, p. 101 n. 2; cf. also p. 119 ("the reference to ʿUmar b. ʿAbdalʿazīz is in any case spurious"); p. 183 ("This is no doubt later than the Caliphate of ʿUmar b. ʿAbdalʿazīz"); p. 199; p. 201 ("no reliance can be placed on the individual reference to ʿUmar b. ʿAbdalʿazīz"); p. 206 ("typical of the fictitious character of the frequent references to ʿUmar b. ʿAbdalʿazīz").

208. Ibid., p. 192.

209. Patricia Crone and Martin Hinds, *God's Caliph, Religious Authority in the First Centuries of Islam* (Cambridge: Cambridge University Press, 1986), ch. 4 (pp. 43–57). For a specific example in which Crone rejects the possibility of a legal precedent's genuinely originating in Umayyad administrative practice (casting particular doubt on the welter of opinions alleging to derive from ʿUmar ibn ʿAbd al-ʿAzīz), see "Jāhilī and Jewish law: the *qasāma*," *Jerusalem Studies in Arabic and Islam* 4 (1984): 187–89.

210. Ibn ʿAsākir, *Ta'rīkh madīnat Dimashq*, 22:396–97. In the *Musnad* of Aḥmad ibn Ḥanbal only the initial question and answer on *al-ʿumrā* are reported.

211. Juynboll, *Muslim Tradition*, pp. 5, 32.

212. Crone and Hinds, *God's Caliph*, p. 53. Interestingly, despite his apparent assumption that Umayyad "administrative practice" was essentially secular in nature, Schacht also argues that "the Umaiyads and their governors were responsible for the elaboration of some of the . . . basic features" of ritual law; however, despite providing footnote references to the work of two of his predecessors in the field, Schacht (unusually) provides no examples at all of his own. (*Origins*, pp. 192–93)

213. Ibid., pp. 53–54.

214. Abū Ghānim al-Khurāsānī, *al-Mudawwana al-kubrā*, 1:7.

Chapter 4. Substantive Impurity and the Boundaries of Society

1. Baber Johansen, *The Islamic Law on Land Tax and Rent: The Peasants' Loss of Property Rights as Interpreted in The Hanafite Legal Literature of the Mamluk and Ottoman Periods* (London, New York: Croom Helm; New York: Methuen, c. 1988).

2. The term used is *rijs*, considered by lexicographers to be equivalent to *najis*; see Qur'ān, verses 5:90 and 6:145. Verse 5:90 states, "O believers, wine and games of chance, idols and divining arrows, are abominations (or "filth": *rijs*) devised by Satan; avoid them, that you may prosper." Some difficulty was posed by the fact that 5:90 parallels substances that could be categorized with impure with *activities* (games of chance, the use of divining arrows) that were understood to be forbidden but not literally polluting. Thus, Ibn Ḥajar al-Haytamī remarks that liquid wine is substantively impure "because God called it unclean (*rijs*), which in technical legal terminology means 'substantively impure' (*wa-huwa shar'an al-najis*); this does not necessarily entail that the things mentioned after [wine] in the Qur'ānic verse are ritually impure, because 'unclean' (*rijs*) can be either metaphorical or literal and it is possible for the literal and the metaphorical meaning to be combined [in one usage], even though it is inadvisable [*'alā imtinā'ihi*]" (*Tuḥfat al-muḥtāj*, 1:288) The difficulty indicated by Ibn Ḥajar al-Haythamī is a significant one, and one which other commentators did not dismiss so lightly (see the comments of Ibn Qāsimabādī at the bottom of the same page, where he notes the need for some evidence [*qarīna*] on which to base the allegation that *rijs* when applied to wine should be interpreted as "substantively impure"). It is a possibility worth consideration that the usage should be interpretated to refer to metaphorical "filth" throughout. For a discussion of this issue in Qur'ānic interpretation, see Kueny, *A Drink of Many Colors*, chapter 1, passim.

3. AR 375–87.

4. IAS 346–60, 368–84. Reports 361–67 deal specifically with water from which a menstruating woman has drunk.

5. The possibility that direct physical contact with women might be polluting to men is also suggested by the avoidance of such contact (outisde of the marital context) by the Prophet. Ibn Isḥāq writes:

> The apostle never used to take the women's hands [when they gave their oath of allegiance to him]; he did not touch a woman nor did one touch him except one whom God had made lawful to him or was one of his wives.

When receiving the oath of allegiance from women, the Prophet and the woman are each supposed to have plunged one hand into a vessel of water. (Guillaume, *Life of Muhammad*, pp. 553–54; also see Ibn Hishām, *Sīra*, 2:312; Guillaume, p. 212) The practice of sealing a pact by jointly dipping the hands into a bowl of liquid may have existed in other contexts as well; Ibn Isḥāq recounts how a clan "pledged themselves to the death" in the *jāhilīya* and solemnized their oath by dipping their hands into a bowl of blood (*Sīra*, 2:19; Guillaume, *Life of Muhammad*, p. 86). This practice, as indicated by the use of blood, cannot have originally been motivated by considerations of ritual purity; indeed, even water would (in the context of later understandings of the mechanics of pollution) function as a medium transmitting pollution. However, the adaptation of the practice to avoid skin-to-skin contact with women suggests that some stigma or danger must have attached to such touching. The danger may or may not have been considered reciprocal; this practice is expressed exclusively from the male point of view and thus is always articulated as an avoidance of women.

6. A number of traditions claimed that the Prophet had forbidden men to purify themselves with water first used by women; see AR 375–78; IAS 354–60; al-Bannā, *al-Fatḥ al-rabbānī*, 1:210–11; Abū Dāwūd, *Sunan*, 1:63; Ibn Māja, *Sunan*, 1:132. However, other traditions reported that the Prophet and his wife ʿĀʾisha (or another wife) had simultaneously performed *ghusl* by scooping water from the same vessel and that, more generally, men and women had done so during the lifetime of the Prophet (cf. IAS 346, 368–83; Abū Dāwūd, *Sunan*, 1:61–62; Ibn Māja, *Sunan*, 1:133–35; al-Nasāʾī, *Sunan*, 1:21). These traditions were often interpreted to indicate that it was permissible for men and women to use the same water simultaneously, while it was forbidden for men to use water previously utilized by women. Interestingly, some forms of the tradition (Abū Dāwūd, *Sunan*, 1:63; al-Bannā, *al-Fatḥ al-rabbānī*, 1:210; Ibn Māja, *Sunan*, 1:133) make the prohibition mutual: "The Prophet forbid women to perform *ghusl* with water already used by men, and men to perform *ghusl* with water already used by women." This anticipates the symmetrical understanding of the polluting quality of heterosexual contact discussed below. Yet other traditions, however, stated that the Prophet had performed ablutions with water from which one of his wives had already performed *ghusl* (al-Bannā, *al-Fatḥ al-rabbānī*, 1:211–13; Ibn Māja, *Sunan*, 1:132).

7. AR 379.

8. Water, vessels, and other items can be rendered secondarily impure (*mutanajjis*) by contact or intermixture with an impure substance (*najāsa*); this is a temporary condition and can be reversed by washing or, in the case of water, by dilution with pure water. Nevertheless, it is distinct from the states of impurity attributed to the human person. It is counteracted, not by ritual ablutions, but by physical removal of the offending substance. Conversely, a human being is never considered to be *mutanajjis*.

9. Al-Ṭabarī, *Jāmiʿ al-bayān*, 10:105. Interestingly, Ibn Manẓūr transmits a report in which the verb *anjasa* is used, precisely like *ajnaba*, to mean "have intercourse with (a woman)"; clearly, the two shared the connotation of sexual impurity. (*Lisān al-ʿArab*, s.v. *n-j-s*)

10. IAS 1825–27; al-Bukhārī, *Ṣaḥīḥ*, 1:85; Muslim, *Ṣaḥīḥ*, 4:288–90; al-Bannā, *al-Fatḥ al-rabbānī*, 1:252–54; Abū Dāwūd, *Sunan*, 1:156–57; Ibn Māja, *Sunan*, 1:178; al-Nasāʾī, *Sunan*, 1:73–74.

11. Shāfiʿī, *Al-Umm*, 1:8.

12. al-Bukhārī, *Ṣaḥīḥ*, 1:85.

13. AR 309; see also IAS 1828.

14. al-Bannā, *al-Fatḥ al-rabbānī*, 1:205. See also IAS 353; al-Bannā, *al-Fatḥ al-rabbānī*, 1:211–12; Ibn Māja, *Sunan*, 1:132; al-Dārimī, *Sunan*, 1:187.

15. Ḥammād ibn abī Sulaymān Muslim al-Ashʿarī mawlāhum, a Kūfan (Ibn Ḥajar, *Tahdhīd al-Tahdhīb*, 2:16–18).

16. IAS 499.

17. al-Shāfiʿī, *al-Umm*, 1:15–16. Compare Saḥnūn, *al-Mudawwana*, 1:13, where it is flatly stated that "a woman is equivalent to (*bi-manzilat*) a man in this."

18. Both al-Shāfiʿī and Aḥmad ibn Ḥanbal are alleged to have taken both sides on this issue, according to Ibn Qudāma (*al-Mughnī*, 1:184). However, the opinion that a woman's *wuḍūʾ* was not canceled by contact with a man remained a marginal minority opinion in the classical tradition.

19. The following account is based on al-Jazīrī, *al-Fiqh ʿalāʾl-madhāhib al-ʿarbaʿa*, 1:81–84, and *al-Mawsūʿa al-fiqhīya* (Kuwayt: Wizārat al-Awqāf waʾl-Shuʾūn al-Islāmīya, A.H. 1416/1995 A.D.), 35:331–33.

20. The Ḥanbalīs follow the same approach as the Shāfiʿīs, with a few differences of detail.

21. This is not to say that Shāfiʿīs ignored or denied the possibility of homoerotic pleasure; rather, they were more interested in the construction of normative sexual categories and less interested in the vagaries of individual desire than their Mālikī counterparts. al-Māwardī records the opinion of Abū Saʿīd al-Iṣṭakhrī, who argues that (a man's) touching an attractive boy should cancel *wuḍūʾ* just as touching a woman does, because "many people's desires incline towards [such youths]." al-Māwardī counters this argument with the majority opinion of the school, which is that deviant cases should be referred to the norm. Otherwise, one would have to accept Mālik's argument that one's *wuḍūʾ* could be cancelled by touching an animal, if one felt pleasure—and this, al-Māwardī states, is an opinion rejected by consensus (al-Māwardī, *al-Ḥāwī al-kabīr*, vol. 1 (Beirut: Dār al-Fikr, A.H. 1414/1994 C.E.), p. 229).

22. Thus, for instance, the nineteenth-century Shāfiʿī jurist ʿAbd al-Ḥamīd al-Shirwānī:

> [We also know that the corpse of a human being is pure] because if it were impure, we would not have been commanded to wash it, as is the case with all other impure things—I mean, things that are substantively impure. It should not be objected that if it were pure we would not be commanded to wash it, as is the case with all other substantively pure things, because we say that the washing of a pure [body] is established (*maʿhūd*) in the case of minor pollution (*al-ḥadath*) and other [situations], in contrast to things that are [substantively] impure [which are never washed]. [This is] assuming that the purpose of [washing a corpse] is to honor it (*takrīmuhu*) and remove dirt from it.

(al-Shirwānī, *Ḥawāshī al-ʿShirwānī wa Aḥmad ibn Qāsim al-ʿAbādī ʿalā tuḥfat al-muḥtāj bi-sharḥ al-minhāj* [n.p., n.d.], 1:293)

23. AR 6108–11; IAS 11147–154; al-Bannā, *al-Fatḥ al-rabbānī*, 2:145–146.

24. Mālik, *Muwaṭṭa'*, 1:398.

25. Another objection to the practice lay in the systematic consideration that states of personal pollution were incurred through one's own bodily functions, not through contagion. This argument was, however, not completely distinct from the objection that a dead believer could not be defiling. Muḥammad al-Shaybānī's *Kitāb al-Aṣl*, after denying that someone who prepares or washes a dead body must perform any ablutions beyond the removal of any substantive impurity that may have onto his body, presents the following exchange *(Kitāb al-Aṣl*, ed. Abū'l-Wafā' al-Afghānī [Beirut: ʿĀlam al-Kutub, A.H. 1410/1990 C.E.], 1:77):

> Q: Why isn't [someone who has washed or prepared a corpse] obligated to perform *wuḍū'*, given that he has touched a corpse? A: Because touching a corpse is not a polluting bodily function (*ḥadath*) requiring him to perform *wuḍū'*. Don't you see (*a-lā tarā*) that if a man performs *wuḍū'*, then touches a dog, a pig, or carrion (*jīfa*), this does not cancel his *wuḍū'*—and these [things] are substantively impure! A dead Muslim is purer and cleaner (*aṭhar wa-anẓaf*) than these [things].

26. See AR 6101–7; IAS 11134, 11137–39, 11145–46.

27. AR 6105.

28. AR 6103.

29. al-Bukhārī, *Ṣaḥīḥ*, 2:91; IAS 11134.

30. al-Bukhārī, *Ṣaḥīḥ*, 2:91.

31. al-Shāfiʿī, *al-Umm*, 1:266.

32. In addition to verse 9:28, which is the focus of the juristic discussion, the Qur'ānic text links the issue of (sincere) belief with the theme of purity in verses 6:125, 7:71, 9:95, 9:125, and 10:100. (All of these verses use the term *rijs*, also sometimes interpreted to mean "punishment.")

33. This is clearly the understanding of al-Ṭabarī, who cites the *ḥadīth* "A believer is never substantively impure (*inna'l-mu'min lā yanjasu*)" in the context of his commentary on verse 9:28 (*Jāmiʿ al-bayān*, 10:105).

34. AR 6106. Nevertheless, early jurists transmitted that the Prophet commanded ʿAlī to wash Abū Ṭālib, who died as a nonbeliever and used the precedent to demonstrate that Muslims could wash the corpses of nonbelieving relatives (cf. al-Shāfiʿī, *al-Umm*, 1:266).

35. Ibn Hishām, *Sīra*, 4:124 (Guillaume, *Life of Muhammad*, p. 377).

36. Ibn Hishām, *Sīra*, 5:50 (Guillaume, *Life of Muhammad*, p. 543).

37. Ibn Hishām, *Sīra*, 1:137 ((Guillaume, *Life of Muhammad*, pp. 8–9). The Arabic wording is "*hum najas, ahl shirk*."

38. *Innaka najis ʿalā shirkika, wa-lā yamassuhā illāʾl-ṭāhir.*

39. Ibn Hishām, *Sīra*, 2:189 (Guillaume, *Life of Muhammad*, p. 157).

40. The idea that the impurity of nonbelievers is contingent on their failure to perform ablutions is also suggested by the occasional report that refers to them in one category with Muslims in a state of major pollution. Thus, for instance, Ibn Abī Shayba transmits a report from ʿĀmir stating that "There is nothing wrong with (*lā ba's bi*) water from which a menstruating woman, a person in a state of sexual pollution (*al-junub*), or a polytheist (*al-mushrik*) has drunk" (IAS 366). ʿĀmir is probably ʿĀmir ibn Sharāḥīl al-Shaʿbī, d. A.H. 103–10; Jābir is probably Jābir ibn Yazīd al-Juʿfī, who died between A.H. 127 and 132.

41. Cf. Ibn Qudāma, *al-Mughnī*, 1:193.

42. Ibn Hishām, *Sīra*, 2:227, 2:284–85 (Guillaume, *Life of Muhammad*, pp. 176, 200). ʿAbd al-Razzāq reports two instances in which the Prophet instructed a new convert to wash himself, as well as an opinion to the same effect from al-Zuhrī (9833, 9834, 9836, 6:9–10). See also al-Bannā, *al-Fatḥ al-rabbānī*, 2:147–48; al-Nasāʾī, *Sunan*, 1:56–57.

43. AR 8935. Probably because shaving of the head did not fit into the Qurʾānic/*fiqh* paradigm in which water and dust were the only purificants, it completely lost its role in the developing *fiqh* (except as it related to the rules for *iḥrām*, which escaped such systematization). Thus, some early *fuqahāʾ* were even moved to ask whether shaving of the head caused impurity and thus required a major ablution. See AR 696, 702; in both cases, however, the suggestion is rejected.

44. AR 9835.

45. *Lisān al-ʿArab*, *"ṭ-h-r."* According to *EI*[2], s.v. "khitān," the current Meccan word for "circumcision" is still "ṭahār" (purity).

46. Ibn Qudāma, *al-Mughnī*, 1:19–194.

47. These traditions, with references to earlier collections, appear in al-Suyūṭī, *al-Durr al-manthūr*, 3:226–27. Also see al-Ṭabarī, *Jāmiʿ al-bayān*, 10:108.

48.The chronological order suggested here is, of course, an inference based on ambiguous evidence. As in the case of the admission of nonbelieving slaves and People of the Book to the Meccan sanctuary, I am making this inference on the assumption that narratives or opinions that are *oblivious* to a given issue should, all other things being equal, be considered chronologically prior to opinions that explicitly address it. This assumption applies, of course, only in cases where the narrative or opinion raises a pressing question in the light of doctrines that came to be important in the eyes of Muslims. This is, obviously, an argument from silence, and should thus be treated with caution. It is broader, and thus somewhat less risky, than the equivalent Schachtian argument that if a given individual *text* (particularly that of an alleged statement by the Prophet) is not cited in a context that would be expected to elicit it, then it did not exist at the date of the composition in question.

Using the chains of transmission to date the opinions making exceptions to the exclusion of nonbelievers from the Meccan sanctuary is difficult. It is, of course, notoriously difficult to date an individual *ḥadīth*. The attribution of the opinion to Qatāda neither supports nor destabilizes the general chronological schema presented below. Qatāda died in A.H. 117–18/735–37 C.E. (*Tahdhīb al-tahdhīb*, 8:355). While he thus lived longer than ʿUmar ibn ʿAbd al-ʿAzīz or the other main figures in the developments I suggest below, this does not mean that his opinion chronologically follows the beginning of the controversy initiated by the dissemination of the doctrine that nonbelievers were ritually impure. Qatāda was these figures' contemporary; not only did he live much of his life before the reign of ʿUmar ibn ʿAbd al-ʿAzīz, but it is unneccessary to assume that ʿUmar's policy immediately changed everyone's attitudes towards the interpretation of verse 9:28; many people presumably would have continued to adhere to the doctrines they had known earlier. It is also interesting to note that Qatāda is supposed to have explicitly addressed the question of the ritual purity status of nonbelievers outside of this context, stating that they were "*najas*" in the sense that they were suffering from sexual impurity (*ajnāb*), presumably as a result of their failure to peform the proper ablutions. See al-Ṭabarī, *Jāmiʿ al-bayān*, 10:105.

49. Ibn Hishām, *Sīra*, 5:225.

50. Another factor contributing to the early lack of concern with the purity implications of this anecdote (illustrated by the absence of any reference to the issue in the text of the *Sīra*) relates to the gradual emergence of Muslim conceptions of sacred space. The Prophet's mosque in Medina was a multifunctional space accommodating a number of domestic and practical activities that later Muslims would exclude from their more elaborate and exclusive places of worship.

51. AR 1620–22; IAS 8773, 8775.

52. IAS 8773; see also IAS 8775, AR 1620.

53. Yet another version of the story may be understood to reverse its implications once again. Here, the Prophet's Companions object, "O Prophet, they are impure people (*qawm anjās*)" and the Prophet replies, "None of the people's filthiness/defilements (*anjās*) is upon the earth; the people's filthiness is only upon themselves (*laysa ʿalāʾl-arḍ min anjās al-nās shayʾ; innamā anjās al-nās ʿalā anfusihim*)." (Abū Bakr Aḥmad ibn ʿAlī al-Rāzī al-Jaṣṣāṣ, *Aḥkām al-qurʾān*, vol. 3 [Cairo, A.H. 1347]), p. 109; al-Ṭaḥāwī, *Sharḥ maʿānī al-āthār*, 1:13) This wording, as pointed out by al-Shawkānī (*Nayl al-awṭār*, n.p., n.d., 1:21) tends to imply that the "impurity" or "filth" involved is spiritual rather than physical (*ḥissī*).

54. al-Ṭabarī, *Jāmiʿ al-bayān*, 10:105; Al-Suyūṭī, *al-Durr al-manthūr*, 3:227. Interestingly, ʿUmar ibn ʿAbd al-ʿAzīz's letter barring non-Muslims from mosques is presented by neither ʿAbd al-Razzāq nor Ibn abī Shayba. Ibn abī Shayba attributes a similar directive, although without an explicit exegetical link, to ʿUmar : "ʿUmar ibn ʿAbd al-ʿAzīz wrote, 'No judge should sit in a mosque and have Jews and Christians come to him there' " (IAS 8778).

55. It is interesting to note that in a version reported by al-Suyuṭī (*Durr*, 3:227) ʿUmar's directive seems to have been associated with the drive to expel Christians and Jews from the Arabian Peninsula. The expulsion of non-Muslims from Arabia is more traditionally attributed to ʿUmar ibn al-Khaṭṭāb. However, ʿUmar ibn ʿAbd al-ʿAzīz does seem to have been involved in the dissemination of the idea that the Arabian Peninsula should be exclusively Muslim. An interesting passage in Muḥammad al-Shaybānī's recension of Mālik's *Muwaṭṭa*ʾ (pp. 311–12) begins with a report stating that ʿUmar [ibn al-Khaṭṭāb] expelled Jews, Christians, and Magians from Mecca and Medina. al-Shaybānī then inserts an editorial note that ʿUmar actually expelled non-Muslims from the entire region, based on a *ḥadīth* of the Prophet stating that "two religions should not remain in the Arabian Peninsula." He then presents an *isnād* ending with ʿUmar ibn ʿAbd al-ʿAzīz, who states: "I have heard (*balaghanī*) that the Prophet said, "Two religions should not remain in the Arabian Peninsula." al-Shaybānī then reiterates that it was actually ʿUmar *ibn al-Khaṭṭāb* who expelled non-Muslims from the peninsula. The whole passage seems oddly forced in its effort to identify the *ḥadīth* and the expulsion with ʿUmar ibn al-Khaṭṭāb rather than ʿUmar ibn ʿAbd al-ʿAzīz. It seems likely either that the precedent of the first ʿUmar was elaborated and linked with a *ḥadīth* text by ʿUmar ibn ʿAbd al-ʿAzīz, or that ʿUmar found it necessary to revive the memory of ʿUmar's supposed action for practical or ideological reasons.

56. IAS 25727 (al-Ḥasan al-Baṣrī; 25726 reports that he disapproved of such contact, without mentioning the possibility of handshaking followed by *wuḍū*ʾ); al-Ṭabarī, *Jāmi*ʿ *al-bayān*, 10:106; al-Suyūṭī, *al-Durr al-manthūr*, 3:227.

57. IAS 8776.

58. Ibn Ḥajar, *Tahdhīb al-tahdhīb*, 6:22–23.

59. Ibid., 10:42–44.

60. It should be noted that, although (as noted above) there is a stream of opinion seeking to exempt protected People of the Book from the strictures of verse 9:28, the line of thought associated with the name of ʿUmar ibn ʿAbd al-ʿAzīz makes Jews and Christians the prime referents of the term "polytheists" as used in the verse. This may be because this understanding of verse 9:28 was associated with ʿUmar's expulsion of Jews and Christians from the Ḥijāz; see above, n. 54. al-Dārimī (d. A.H. 255/868–69 C.E.) preserves a report from Ḥammād [probably Ḥammād ibn abī Sulaymān, d. A.H. 119–20] that "I asked Ibrāhīm about shaking hands with Jews, Christians, Magians and menstruating women; he did not think that it necessitated *wuḍū*ʾ" (al-Dārimī, *Sunan*, 1:247). This report, if authentic, suggests that interest in the question was arising among the younger generation before the death of Ibrāhīm in A.H. 95; interestingly, the inclusion of menstruating women in the list suggests that Ḥammād equated the possible impurity of nonbelievers with that of Muslims.

61. Norman Calder has recently argued that *Kitāb al-Umm*, like all of the early texts attributed to early authors who were taken as founding figures by the various schools of Islamic law, is not an authored text at all but a series of "sedimentary layers" of school opinion that developed over an extended period of time and, even in its earliest

nucleus, cannot be traced back to the figure of al-Shāfiʿī or the time in which he lived. Having examined the section of the text of *al-Umm* dealing with ritual purity in detail, I have reached the conclusion that Calder's inferences about the process that produced the text as we know it are untenable as they stand. Of course, it is impossible to demonstrate affirmatively that the text was in fact authored by the individual known to the history of Islamic law under the name of Muḥammad ibn Idrīs al-Shāfiʿī. It is difficult even to imagine what type of evidence would suffice to establish this definitively. However, I believe that it can be demonstrated that the traditional conception of this text as a more or less unitary composition consisting primarily of opinions attributable to one person (whether or not that person was named al-Shāfiʿī) corresponds to the internal evidence of the text more closely than Calder's alternative narrative.

62. al-Shāfiʿī, *al-Umm*, 1:8.

63. Ibid., 1:54.

64. Ibid., 1:54. This statement is not completely logical, as the inclusion of the dead body of a polytheist in the list of beings that can pass over ground without polluting it does not fit with the final statement of principle, that "no *living* human being is ever substantively impure" (emphasis mine). My hypothesis is that the words "*wa-lā maytatuhu*" ("or the corpse [of a polytheist]") represent either a logical slip in the original text—a phenomenon that is not unknown in our era or in times past—or a later addition to the original text. It is also, of course, possible that the concluding principle that "no living human being is ever substantively impure" is itself an interpolated inference by a later reader. I find this somewhat less likely than the other hypothesis, given that it fits the general content of the passage far better than the isolated reference to dead bodies; however, the assumption that "no living human being is ever substantively impure" is a later interpolation would have little effect on my general argument.

As far as I have been able to determine, al-Shāfiʿī does not make any direct statement regarding the purity status of dead bodies, believing or polytheist, in *al-Umm*. At several points in the text, he seems to equate decomposed human corpses with *najāsa*. Thus, he states that it is not permissible to perform *tayammum* with graveyard dust because it is mixed with the bones and flesh of the dead and it is not possible to wash these substances out of the dust without washing away the dust itself; "the same applies," he concludes, "to any substantive impurities (*anjās*) that mix with dust and themselves becomes like dust." Similarly, he argues that "if particles (*ajsād*) [of an impure substance] dissolve in (*dhahaba fī*) dust and mix with it so that they can no longer be distinguished from it, they are like [the dust of] graveyards, where one may not pray and which cannot be purified, because the dust is indistinguishable from the forbidden substance (*al-muḥarram*) mixed with it (*al-Umm*, p. 53). Similarly, al-Shāfiʿī counsels that it is not advisable to pray on graves because of the *ḥadīth* to this effect and because "earth where the dead are interred is not the cleanest (*anẓaf*) earth" (*al-Umm*, 1:278). One interpretation of this material is that al-Shāfiʿī considered not dead human bodies per se, but *decomposed* corpses to be substantively impure. This idea is supported by al-Shāfiʿī's frequent references to the possibility of the corpse beginning to decompose and the necessity to perform the final rites quickly enough to avert it. This assumption is supported by the term al-Shāfiʿī uses to refer to decomposition: *taghayyur*, "change," which is a key concept in the law of ritual purity as a whole. Another interpretation of al-Shāfiʿī's oblique comments about the purity status of corpses is also possible. It is notable that in this passage al-Shāfiʿī associates the dust of human corpses with substantive purity but never directly refers to it as *najis*; instead, he uses the term *muḥarram*, literally "forbidden [substance]," which for him is functionally synonymous to *najis*. Assuming, as I do, that the text is essentially a unitary composition presenting a coherent understanding of the law, one can infer that al-Shāfiʿī is inclined to regard dead human bodies in general as impure—hence, for instance, his reluctance to abandon the practice of performing *ghusl* after washing a corpse—but is constrained by his familiarity with the *ḥadīth* "do not deem your dead impure."

65. al-Shāfiʿī incorporates the requirement to remove substantive impurities (*najāsa*) from one's body and clothing before worship into this schema by stating that, although the impurities themselves are physical and discernible, the *obligation to remove them* is *taʿabbud*—that is, purely a matter of obedience to a divine command. Al-Shāfiʿī classifies this as *taʿabbud li-maʿnan maʿlūm*, "*taʿabbud* for a known cause" (*al-Umm*, 1:44–45).

66. al-Shāfiʿī, *al-Umm*, 1:18.

67. Ibid., pp. 29–30.

68. Ibid., 1:29.

69. Ibid., 1:34.

70. Ibid., 1:55.

71. Qur'ān 6:2, 7:12, 23:12, 32:7, 37:11, 38:71, 38:76, and 17:61 refer to Adam's creation from mud (*ṭīn*).

72. Qur'ān 15:26, 15:28, 15:33.

73. al-Ṭabarī, *Jāmiʿ al-Bayān*, 14:28–29.

74. Qur'ān 7:12, 38:17; see also 17:61.

75. Qur'ān 22:5; 23:12–16; 40:67–68; 75:36–40.

76. It should be emphasized that, as I discuss throughout this study, Islamic legal thinkers continued to differ not only in points of detail but in their understanding of the overall symbolic logic of the system of purity as a whole. The preservation and authority of reports dating from various stages in a given controversy always provided the opportunity for later jurists to embrace a doctrine that had at one point been rejected. Thus, the line of thought discussed here is only one of those pursued by later Islamic jurists. The preferred (but not exclusive) opinion of the Mālikī, Shāfiʿī, and Ḥanbalī schools is that death does not render human beings substantively impure. The teaching attributed to Abū Ḥanīfa is that death does render the corpse impure, but it is then purified by the required washing. There is also a difference of opinion, even among members of a single school, about the purity status of dead nonbelievers. See

Ibn Qudāma, *al-Mughnī*, 1:60; Ibn Taymīya, *al-Akhbār al-ʿilmīya min al-ikhtiyārāt al-fiqhīya*, ed. Aḥmad ibn Muḥammad ibn Ḥasan al-Khalīl (Riyad: Dār al-ʿĀṣima, A.H. 1418/1998 C.E.), p. 38.

77. al-Qurṭubī, *al-Jāmiʿ li-aḥkām al-qurʾān*, 10:293–94. See also Maḥmūd ibn ʿUmar al-Zamakhsharī, *al-Kashshāf ʿan ghawāmiḍ al-tanzīl*, vol. 2 (Beirut: Dār al-Kutub al-ʿArabī, [no date]), p. 680.

78. ʿAlāʾ al-Dīn Abū Bakr ibn Masʿūd al-Kāsānī, *Kitāb Badāʾiʿ al-ṣanāʾiʿ* ([Cairo]: Sharikat al-Maṭbūʿāt al-ʿIlmīya, A.H. 1327), 1:299.

79. Al-Haytamī, *Tuḥfat al-muḥtāj*, in margin of *Ḥāshiyat al-Shirwānī*, 1:292. See also Aḥmad ibn Yaḥyā ibn al-Murtaḍā (d. A.H. 840), *Kitāb al-Baḥr al-zakhkhār al-jāmiʿ li-madhāhib ʿulamāʾ al-amṣār*, 2nd ed. (Beirut: Muʾassassat al-Risāla, A.H. 1394/1975 C.E.), 1:14.

80. Ibid., 1:292. Muḥammad ibn Muḥammad al-Ruʿaynī al-Ḥaṭṭāb similarly states that a human corpse is pure "regardless of whether [the deceased was] a believer or a nonbeliever, because of the inviolability and dignity of humanity (*ḥurmat al-ādamīya wa-karāmatihi*) and God's exaltation (*tafḍīl*) of humanity." (*Mawāhib al-Jalīl*, vol. 1 [(Cairo), A.H. 1328], p. 99.) Here again, without any explicit Qurʾānic citation, the wording of verse 17:70 is reproduced precisely.

81. Abūʾl-Ṭayyib Ṣiddīq ibn Ḥasan ibn ʿAlī al-Ḥasīn al-Qinūjī al-Bukhārī, *Fatḥ al-barayān fī maqāṣid al-qurʾān*, vol. 7 (Ṣaydā and Beirut: al-Maktaba al-ʿAṣrīya, A.H. 1412/1992 C.E.), p. 424.

82. See al-Zamakhsharī, *al-Kashshāf*, 2:680–82; al-Fakhr al-Rāzī, *al-Tafsīr al-kabīr*, vol. 11, 3d ed. [no city, no date], pp. 16–17; al-Qurṭubī, *al-Jāmiʿ li-aḥkām al-qurʾān*, 10:294–95.

83. al-Shirwānī, 1:292–93.

84. al-Haytamī, *Tuḥfat al-muḥtāj*, 1:287.

85. al-Shirwānī, *Ḥāshiya*, 1:287–88.

86. al-Haytamī, *Tuḥfat al-muḥtāj*, 1:294–95.

87. Fakhr al-Dīn ʿUthmān ibn ʿAlī al-Zaylaʿī, *Tabyīn al-ḥaqāʾiq sharḥ kanz al-daqāʾiq* (Cairo: Būlāq, A.H. 1313/[1895 C.E.]), 1:9. Emphases mine.

88. al-Thaʿlabī, *Qiṣaṣ al-anbiyāʾ al-musammā bi-ʿarāʾis al-majālis* ([Cairo: Maktabat al-Kullīyāt al-Azharīya, n.d.), p. 17; shorter version, Ibn Kathīr, *Qiṣaṣ al-anbiyāʾ* (Cairo: Dār al-Kutub al-Ḥadītha, A.H. 1388/1968 C.E.), 1:41. Compare al-Kisāʾī: "This is a weak creature: it has been made of clay and is hollow. And what is hollow must have food" (*The Tales of the Prophets of al-Kisaʾi*, trans. W. M. Thackston, Jr. [Boston: Twayne Publishers, 1978], p. 25.)

89. Ibn Manẓūr, *Lisān al-ʿArab*, s.v. *b-ṭ-n*.

90. al-Ṭabarī, *Jāmiʿ al-Bayān*, 27:125.

91. Ibid., 30:344–45.

92. al-Ṭabarī, *Ta'rīkh*, 1:92; parallel, Ibn Kathīr, *Qiṣaṣ al-anbiyā'*, 1:40.

93. al-Ṭabarī, *Ta'rīkh*, 1:93.

94. See also al-Ṭabarī, *Ta'rīkh*, 1:94.

95. al-Thaʿlabī, p. 17; parallel, Ibn Kathīr, *Qiṣaṣ al-anbiyā'*, 1:40–41.

96. al-Ṭabarī, *Ta'rīkh*, 1:108; also Ṭabarī, *Jāmiʿ al-Bayān*, 1:235.

97. al-Ṭabarī, *Ta'rīkh*, 1:110; also Ṭabarī, *Jāmiʿ al-Bayān*, 1:236.

98. Ibn Kathīr reports this as the opinion of Mujāhid, Ibn Jurayj, and Qatāda, citing the reasoning of an Abū'l-ʿĀliya that "it was a tree that made anyone who ate from it have a polluting bodily function (*aḥdatha*), and there can be no polluting bodily functions in paradise" (*Qiṣaṣ al-anbiyā'*, 1:14). See also al-Ṭabarī, *Jāmiʿ al-bayān*, 1:232–33.

99. al-Thaʿlabī, p. 20.

100. Ibid., p. 21.

101. Ibid., pp. 23–24.

102. Cf. Qur'ān 9:120, addressed to Adam. Some of the lore surrounding the Qur'ānic image of heaven suggests that the blessed will have *appetite* (in the sense of a relish for food and drink, an ability to enjoy them), but no *hunger* in the sense of biological need. Cf. the comment, attributed to Ibrāhīm al-Taymī, that "each man in Paradise is given a hundred earthly men's share of desire (*shahwa*), their appetite/capacity for eating (*akl*) and their ardor (*himma*)." See al-Ṭabarī, *Jāmiʿ al-bayān*, 29:222–23.

103. For several versions of this statement, presented as interpretations of Qur'ān 76:21 ("Their Lord will give them pure nectar to drink"), see al-Ṭabarī, *Jāmiʿ al-bayān*, 29:222–23.

104. al-Ṭabarī, *Jāmiʿ al-bayān*, 29:222–23.

105. al-Ṭabarī, *Ta'rīkh*, 1:127; also al-Ṭabarī, *Jāmiʿ al-bayān*, 1:175.

106. al-Ṭabarī, *Jāmiʿ al-bayān*, 29:220.

107. This is the pattern proprosed by Carol Delaney on the basis of her fieldwork in a modern Turkish village ("Mortal Flow: Menstruation in Turkish Village Society," in *Blood Magic: The Anthropology of Menstruation*, ed. Thomas Buckley and Alma Gottlieb [Berkeley/Los Angeles/London: University of California Press], p. 76). However, Delaney sees the contrast between the heavenly and earthly spheres in terms of a gender dichotomy in which women are associated with the impurity of the natural world. The significance of gender to the classical sources' understanding of the law of purity is discussed in the final section of this chapter.

108. Jalāl al-Dīn al-Suyūṭī, *al-Itqān fī ʿulūm al-Qur'ān*, ed. Muḥammad Abū'l-Faḍl Ibrāhīm (n.p.: Manshūrāt al-Riḍā, A.H. 1343/[1924–25 C.E.], 3:83; for the various reports about the possible Qur'ānic status of this passage, see John Burton, *The Sources*

of Islamic law: Islamic Theories of Abrogation (Edinburgh: Edinburgh University Press, 1990), pp. 50–51.

109. Ibn Hishām, *Sīra*, 2:15 (Guillaume, *Life of Muhammad*, p. 84).

110. The three leading candidates for the identity of the Forbidden Tree were wheat, the grapevine, and the fig tree (al-Ṭabarī, *Jāmiʿ al-bayān*, 1:231–33; Ibn Kathīr, *Qiṣaṣ al-anbiyāʾ*, 1:14. The centrality of the motif of wheat is reflected in reports like the following:

> It is said that one of the things that Adam brought out of paradise with him was a sack of wheat. It is also said that Gabriel only brought Adam wheat when he got hungry and asked his Lord for food. God sent Gabriel to him with seven grains of wheat. He put them in Adam's hand, and Adam said to Gabriel, "What is this?" Gabriel said, "This is what caused you to be expelled from paradise (*hādhā mā akhrajaka min al-janna*)" (al-Ṭabarī, *Taʾrīkh*, 1:128).

111. Cf. al-Jazīrī, *Fiqh*, 2:248 (the *ḥadīth* most often cited in the juristic debate on interest, listing gold, silver, wheat, barley, dates, and salt); al-Bukhārī, 3:31 (gold, wheat, dates, barley).

112. Note that in some parts of the Islamic Middle East, grain was used as a medium of exchange into the modern period for such transactions as paying a village imām.

113. Reinhold Loeffler, *Islam in Practice: Religious Beliefs in a Persian Village* (Albany: State University of New York Press, 1988), pp. 44–45. Emphasis mine.

114. al-Kisāʾī, *Tales*, pp. 30–31.

115. An interesting aspect of the narrative about sleep cited above is that, in this case, the condition of the people of paradise transcends Adam's original state rather than merely restoring it.

116. AR 152; see also AR 151, 153–56.

117. Al-Shirwānī, *Ḥāshiya*, 1:186.

118. Peter Brown, *The Body and Society* (New York: Columbia University Press, 1988), pp. 220–21. Emphases mine.

119. A striking exception to this trend, from a North African scholar inspired by psychoanalytic theory, is Abdelwahab Bouhdiba's *Sexuality in Islam* (London, Boston, Melbourne and Henley: Routledge & Kegan Paul, 1985), passim. Although Bouhdiba's interpretations of statements relating to female sexuality from the classical tradition are sometimes unconvincingly benign (cf., for instance, his argument that the Qur'ān expresses "tender emotions" towards the sexual scheming of Joseph's would-be seducer, p. 25), his overall discussion is refreshing in its refusal to regard the Islamic tradition as fundamentally misogynistic.

120. Sherry B. Ortner, "Is Female to Male as Nature is to Culture?" reprinted in *Woman, Culture, and Society*, ed. Michelle Zimbalist Rosaldo and Louise Lamphere (Stanford, Calif.: Stanford University Press, 1974), p. 73.

121. Ibid., p. 72.

122. Ibid.

123. See Alma Gottlieb, "Menstrual Cosmology among the Beng of Ivory Coast," in Buckley and Gottlieb, *Blood Magic*, pp. 55–74.

124. D. A. Spellberg, *Politics, Gender, and the Islamic Past: The Legacy of 'A'isha bint Abi Bakr* (New York: Columbia University Press, 1994), pp. 138–39.

125. Lila Abu-Lughod, *Veiled Sentiments* (Berkeley: University of California Press, 1986), pp. 132–33.

126. Julie Marcus, *A World of Difference* (London; Atlantic Highlands, N.J.: Zed, 1992), pp. 87–88.

127. Ibid., p. 83.

128. Ibid., p. 84.

129. Italics mine.

130. "covered."

131. Carol Delaney, "Mortal Flow: Menstruation in a Turkish Village Society," p. 82.

132. Geraldine Brooks, *Nine Parts of Desire* (New York: Anchor Books, Doubleday, 1995), p. 172.

133. Marjo Buitelaar, *Fasting and Feasting in Morocco: Women's Participation in Ramadan* (Oxford/Providence: Berg, 1993), p. 115.

134. Ibid., pp. 114–15. Although I do not know how many women actually made use of the practice, I also heard several women bringing up the possibility of using medical means to prevent menstruation during Ramadan when I was in Jordan in 1992–93.

135. Ibid., pp. 112–15.

136. al-Suyūṭī, *al-Durr al-manthūr fī'l-tafsīr bi'l-ma'thūr*, 4:260. For an interesting treatment of this interpretation of the story from a psychoanalytic perspective, see Bouhdiba, *Sexuality in Islam*, pp. 25–26.

137. Muslim, *Ṣaḥīḥ*, 2:253–56; al-Bukhārī, *Ṣaḥīḥ*, 1:90; Ibn Māja, *Sunan*, 2:1326–27.

138. al-ʿAynī, *ʿUmdat al-Qārī'*, 3:270.

139. al-Ṭabarī, *Ta'rīkh*, 1:109; also see 1:111, al-Ṭabarī, *Jāmiʿ al-bayān*, 1:237.

140. al-ʿAynī, *ʿUmdat al-qārī'*, 3:255.

141. al-Bukhārī, *Ṣaḥīḥ*, 6:293; al-Bannā, *al-Fatḥ al-rabbānī*, 11:128–31; Ibn Māja, *Sunan*, 2:988.

142. al-Bukhārī, *Ṣaḥīḥ*, 1:88.

143. Cited by Muḥammad ibn Khalīfa al-Washtānī al-Ubbī (*Ikmāl ikmāl al-mu'allim*, printed with *Ṣaḥīḥ Muslim*, ed. Muḥammad Salīm Hāshim [Beirut: Dār al-Kutub al-ʿIlmīya, 1994), 1:307. al-Washtānī retorts to this that "[The distinction] does not break down because of this, because the Imām did not base the distinction on her being excluded from all forms of worship—in which case it could be countered that she is permitted to engage in many of them—but on her being excluded from prayer, which is the most noble act of worship and the one in which the worshiper is closest to God." The opinion that menstruating women should engage in some sort of religious meditation at prayer times seems to have been relatively well represented in early times; al-ʿAynī writes,

> There were some early Muslim authorities (*al-salaf*) who instructed menstruating women to perform *wuḍū'* at prayer time and to recollect God, facing the *qibla* while they sat doing so; this has been transmitted from ʿUqba ibn ʿĀmir and Makḥūl, who said, "That was one of the customs of the Muslim women when they were menstruating" (*kāna dhālika min hady nisā' al-muslimīn fī ḥayḍihinna*). ʿAbd al-Razzāq said, "I heard that menstruating women were instructed to do this at every prayer time; ʿAṭā' said, 'I have not heard about that, but it is a good [practice].' " Abū ʿAmr said, "It is something that is rejected by the majority of the religious scholars (*huwa amr matrūk ʿinda jamāʿat al-fuqahā'*); indeed, they consider it objectionable (*yakrahūnahu*)." Abū Qilāba said, "We asked about that, and we found no basis for it (*lam najid lahu aṣlan*)." Saʿīd ibn ʿAbd al-ʿAzīz said, "We are not familiar with it (*lā naʿrifuhu*), and I consider it objectionable (*akrahuhu*)." The Ḥanafī [manual] *Munyat al-muftī* says, "It is desireable (*yustaḥabbu*) for her to perform *wuḍū'* at the time of each prayer and to sit in the area in her house that is set aside for prayer (*masjid baytihā*) glorifying God and declaring His unicity (*tusabbiḥu wa-tuhallilu*) for as long as it takes her to perform her prayers when she is in a state of purity, so that her habit [of prayer] is not destroyed." The *Dirāya* says, "She is credited with the reward for the best prayers that she used to perform [when she was in a state of purity]" (al-ʿAynī, *ʿUmdat al-Qārī'*, 3:301).

144. Ibid., p. 307.

145. For opposite positions on this question, see al-ʿAynī, *ʿUmdat al-Qāri*, 3:301, and Muḥyī al-Dīn al-Nawawī, *al-Minhāj*, in margin of *Ṣaḥīḥ Muslim*, 1:255.

146. Delaney, "Mortal Flow," p. 76.

147. Ibid., p. 79.

148. al-Ṭabarī, *Jāmiʿ al-bayān*, 1:175–76.

149. Victor Turner, *The Ritual Process* (Chicago: Aldine Publishing Company, 1969), p. 41.

150. Mircea Eliade, *The Myth of the Eternal Return*, trans. Willard R. Trask ([New York]: Pantheon Books, 1954), pp. 5–6.

151. Anna S. Meigs, "A Papuan Perspective on Pollution," *Man*, n.s., 13 (1978): 312–13.

152. Cf. Qur᾿ān 7:172; for a discussion of universalist interpretations of the covenant, see Bernard G. Weiss, "Covenant and Law in Islam," in *Religion and Law: Biblical-Judaic and Islamic Perspectives*, ed. Edwin B. Firmage et al. Winona Lake: Eisenbrauns, 1990, pp. 49–83, passim.

153. Cf. Dru C. Gladney, *Muslim Chinese: Ethnic Nationalism in the People's Republic* (Cambridge, Mass.: published by the Council on East Asian Studies and distributed by Harvard University Press, 1991), pp. 7–15.

154. Choksy, *Purity and Pollution*, p. 78.

155. Numbers 12:12.

156. Leviticus 17:11, 14.

157. *Encyclopaedia Judaica*, s.v. "Ablution."

158. *Encyclopaedia Judaica*, s.v. "Purity and Impurity."

159. Philippe Ariès, *The Hour of Our Death*, trans. Helen Weaver (New York: Alfred A. Knopf, 1981), pp. 29–30.

160. Peter Brown, *The Cult of the Saints: Its Rise and Function in Latin Christianity* (Chicago: University of Chicago Press, 1981), p. 4.

161. Ariès, *Hour*, p. 31. Also see Byron R. McCane, "Is a Corpse Contagious? Early Jewish and Christian Attitudes toward the Dead," *Society of Biblical Literature 1992 Seminar Papers*, ed. Eugene H. Lovering, Jr., pp. 378–88.

Bibliography

Abū Dāwūd, Sulaymān ibn al-Ashʿath al-Sijistānī. *Sunan Abī Dāwūd*. Ed. Muḥammad Muḥyi'l-Dīn ʿAbd al-Ḥamīd. Dār Iḥyā' al-Sunna al-Nabawīya. N.p., n.d.

Abu-Lughod, Lila. *Veiled Sentiments*. Berkeley: University of California Press, 1986.

Aries, Philippe. *The Hour of Our Death*. Trans. Helen Weaver. New York: Alfred A. Knopf, 1981.

AR See al-Ṣanʿānī, ʿAbd al-Razzāq.

al-ʿAynī, Badr al-Dīn Abū Muḥammad Maḥmūd b. Aḥmad. *ʿUmdat al-qāri sharḥ Ṣaḥīḥ al-Bukhārī*. 25 volumes in 12. Beirut: Muḥammad Amīn Damj, n.d.

Bakhtin, Mikhail. *Rabelais and His World*. Bloomington: Indiana University Press, 1984.

al-Bannā, Aḥmad ʿAbd al-Raḥmān, known as al-Sāʿātī. *al-Fatḥ al-rabbānī li-tartīb musnad al-imām Aḥmad ibn Ḥanbal al-Shaybānī*. 13 vols. in 6. N.p.: Maṭbaʿat al-Ikhwān al-Muslimīn, [1934?–39].

Bouhdiba, Abdelwahab. *Sexuality in Islam*. London, Boston, Melbourne, and Henley: Routledge & Kegan Paul, 1985.

Bousquet, G.-H. "La pureté rituelle en Islâm (Étude de fiqh et de sociologie religieuse)." *Revue de l'histoire des religions* 138 (1950): 53–71.

Boyce, Mary. "*Pādyāb* and *nērang*: Two Pahlavi Terms Further Considered." *Bulletin of the School of Oriental and African Studies* 54 (1991): 281–91.

———. *Zoroastrians: Their Religious Beliefs and Practices*. London: Routledge & Kegan Paul, 1979.

Brooks, Geraldine. *Nine Parts of Desire*. New York: Anchor Books, Doubleday, 1995.

Brown, Peter. *The Body and Society*. New York: Columbia University Press, 1988.

———. *The Cult of the Saints: Its Rise and Function in Latin Christianity*. Chicago: University of Chicago Press, 1981.

Büchler, A. "The Levitical Impurity of the Gentile in Palestine before the Year 70." *Jewish Quarterly Review* 17 (1926–27): 1–81.

Buitelaar, Marjo. *Fasting and Feasting in Morocco: Women's Participation in Ramadan*. Oxford/Providence: Berg, 1993.

al-Bukhārī, Muḥammad ibn Ismāʿīl. *Ṣaḥīḥ al-Bukhārī*. 8 vols. in 4. Ed. ʿAbd al-ʿAzīz ibn ʿAbd Allāh ibn Bāz. N.p.: Dār al-Fikr, A.H. 1411/1991 C.E.

Bulliet, Richard W. *Islam, the View from the Edge*. New York: Columbia University Press, 1994.

Burton, John. "The Qurʾān and the Islamic Practice of Wuḍūʾ." *BSOAS* 51 (1988): 21–58.

———. *The Sources of Islamic Law: Islamic Theories of Abrogation*. Edinburgh: Edinburgh University Press, 1990.

Burton, John W. "Some Nuer Notions of Purity and Danger." *Anthropos* 69 (1974): 517–36.

Calder, Norman. *Studies in Early Muslim Jurisprudence*. Oxford: Clarendon Press, 1993.

Choksy, Jamshīd. *Purity and Pollution in Zoroastrianism*. Austin: University of Texas Press, 1989.

Cook, Michael. "Magian Cheese: An Archaic Problem in Islamic Law." *BSOAS* 47 (1984): 449–67.

Crone, Patricia. "Jāhilī and Jewish Law: the *qasāma*." *Jerusalem Studies in Arabic and Islam* 4 (1984): 153–200.

Crone, Patricia, and Martin Hinds. *God's Caliph: Religious Authority in the First Centuries of Islam*. Cambridge: Cambridge University Press, 1986.

al-Dārimī, ʿAbd Allāh ibn ʿAbd al-Raḥmān. *Sunan al-Dārimī*. 2 vols. in 1. Dār Iḥyāʾ al-Sunna al-Nabawīya, n.d.

Dawood, N. J. *The Koran*. 5th rev. ed. London: Penguin Books, 1993.

Delaney, Carol. "Mortal Flow: Menstruation in Turkish Village Society," in *Blood Magic: The Anthropology of Menstruation*, ed. Thomas Buckley and Alma Gottlieb, 75–93. Berkeley/Los Angeles/London: University of California Press, (c) The Regents of the University of California, 1988.

Douglas, Mary. *Implicit Meanings: Essays in Anthropology*. London: Routledge & Kegan Paul, 1975.

———. *Natural Symbols: Explorations in Cosmology*. New York: Pantheon Books, 1970.

———. *Purity and Danger*. London and New York: Routledge, 1966.

Dumont, Louis. *Homo Hierarchicus: The Caste System and its Implications*. Trans. Mark Sainsbury. Chicago: University of Chicago Press, 1970.

al-Dūrī, A. A. "al-Zuhrī." *BSOAS* 19 (1957): 1–12.

EI[1] = *Encyclopaedia of Islam*. 1st ed. 10 vols. Leiden, the Netherlands: E. J. Brill, 1913–38, reprinted 1987.

EI[2] = *Encyclopaedia of Islam*. New Edition. Nine vols. to date. Leiden, the Netherlands: E. J. Brill, 1986–.

Eilberg-Schwartz, Howard. "Creation and Classification in Judaism: From Priestly to Rabbinic Conceptions." *History of Religions* 26 (1987): 357–81.

———. *The Savage in Judaism*. Bloomington and Indianapolis: Indiana University Press, 1990.

Eliade, Mircea. *The Myth of the Eternal Return*. Trans. Willard R. Trask. [New York]: Pantheon Books, 1954.

al-Farrā', Abū Zakariyā' Yaḥyā b. Ziyād. *Maʿānī al-Qur'ān*. Vol. 1. Cairo, 1980.

Firmage, E. "The Biblical Dietary Laws and the Concept of Holiness," in *Studies in the Pentateuch*, ed. J. A. Emerton, 177–208. Leiden: E. J. Brill, 1990.

Goldziher, I. "Islamisme et parsisme." *Révue de l'histoire des religions* 43 (1901): 1–29.

———. "Wasser als Dämonen abwehrendes Mittel." *Archiv für Religionswissenschaft* 13 (1910): 20–46.

Goody, Jack. *The Domestication of the Savage Mind*. Cambridge: Cambridge University Press, 1977.

Grabar, Oleg. "The Omayyad Done of the Rock in Jerusalem." *Ars Orientalis* 3 (1959): 33–62.

Guillaume, A. *The Life of Muhammad, A Translation of Ibn Ishaq's Sirat Rasul Allah*. Karachi: Oxford University Press, 1967.

Halverson, John. "Animal Categories and Terms of Abuse." *Man*, n.s., 11 (1976): 505–16.

al-Haytamī, Ibn Ḥajar. *Tuḥfat al-muḥtāj bi-sharḥ al-minhāj*, printed in the margins of al-Shirwānī, ʿAbd al-Ḥamīd. *Ḥawāshī al-ʿShirwānī wa Aḥmad ibn Qāsim al-ʿAbādī ʿalā tuḥfat al-muḥtāj bi-sharḥ al-minhāj*. 10 vols. n.p., n.d.

Hershman, P. "Hair, Sex and Dirt." *Man*, n.s., 9 (1974): 274–98.

Hutchinson, Sharon. " 'Dangerous to Eat': Rethinking Pollution States among the Nuer of Sudan." *Africa* 62, no. 4 (1992): 490–504.

IAS See Ibn Abī Shayba.

al-Ibāḍī, Abū Ghānim al-Khurāsānī. *al-Mudawwana al-kubrā*. 2 vols. Dār al-Yaqẓa al-ʿArabīya, n.d.

Ibn Abī Shayba, Abū Bakr ʿAbd Allāh ibn Muḥammad. *al-Kitāb al-Muṣannaf fī'l-aḥādīth wa'l-āthār*. 7 vols. Beirut: Dār al-Tāj, A.H. 1409/1989 C.E.

Ibn al-ʿArabī. *Aḥkām al-qurʾān*. 4 vols. Ed. ʿAlī Muḥammad al-Bijāwī. N.p.: Dār Iḥyāʾ al-Kutub al-ʿArabīya, A.H. 1376/1957 C.E.

Ibn ʿAsākir, Abūʾl-Qāsim ʿAlī ibn al-Ḥusayn ibn Hibat Allāh ibn ʿAbd Allāh al-Shāfiʿī. *Taʾrīkh madīnat Dimashq*. 69 vols. to date. Beirut: Dār al-Fikr, A.H. 1407/1987 C.E.–.

Ibn al-Falāḥ, Abū ʿAmr ʿUthmān ibn ʿAbd al-Raḥmān. *ʿUlūm al-ḥadīth*. Damascus, A.H. 1406/1986 C.E.

Ibn Ḥajar al-ʿAsqalānī, Aḥmad ibn ʿAlī. *Fatḥ al-bārī bi-sharḥ ṣaḥīḥ al-Bukhārī*. 28 vols. in 14. Ed. Ṭāhā ʿAbd al-Raʾūf Saʿd et al. [Cairo]: Maktabat al-Kullīyāt biʾl-Azhar, A.H. 1398/1978 C.E.

———. *Tahdhīb al-tahdhīb*. 12 vols. [Beirut]: Dār Ṣādir, n.d. (facsimile of Haidarabad, A.H. 1325–27/[1907–10 C.E.]).

Ibn Ḥazm. *al-Muḥallā*. Beirut, n.d.

Ibn Hishām. *al-Sīra al-nabawīya li-Ibn Hishām*. Ed. Ṭāhā ʿAbd al-Raʾūf Saʿd. 6 vols. in 3. Beirut: Dār al-Jīl, A.H. 1411/1991 C.E.

Ibn Humām, Kamāl al-Dīn ibn ʿAbd al-Wāḥid al-Sīwāsī. *Sharḥ fatḥ al-qadīr*. 10 vols. [Cairo]: Sharikat Maktabat wa-Maṭbaʿat Muṣṭafā al-Bābī al-Ḥalabī, A.H. 1389/1970 C.E.

Ibn al-Kalbī, Hishām. *The Book of Idols*. Trans. Nabih Amin Faris. Princeton, N.J.: Princeton University Press, 1952.

Ibn Kathīr, Abūʾl-Fidāʾ Ismāʿīl. *Qiṣaṣ al-anbiyāʾ*. Ed. Muṣṭafā ʿAbd al-Wāḥid. Cairo: Dār al-Kutub al-Ḥadītha, A.H. 1388/1968 C.E.

Ibn Māja, Muḥammad ibn Yazīd al-Qazwīnī. *Sunan*. 2 vols. Ed. Muḥammad Fuʾād ʿAbd al-Bāqī. ʿĪsā al-Bābī al-Ḥalabī wa-Shurakāʾuhu. n.p., n.d.

Ibn Qudāma, ʿAbd Allāh ibn Aḥmad. *al-Mughnī*. Ed. Muḥammad Khalīl Harās. [Cairo]: n.d.

Ibn Qutayba. *Kitāb al-Maʿārif*. Ed. Ferdinand Wüstenfeld. Göttingen, 1850.

Ibn Saʿd. *al-Ṭabaqāt al-kubrā*. 9 vols. Leiden, the Netherlands: E. J. Brill, 1905–40.

Ibn Shaddād, Bahāʾ al-Dīn Abūʾl-Maḥāsin Yūsuf b. Rāfiʿ. *Dalāʾil al-aḥkām*. Beirut, A.H. 1413/1992 C.E.

Izutsu, Toshihiko. *Ethico-Religious Concepts in the Qurʾān*. Montreal: McGill University Institute of Islamic Studies, McGill University Press, 1966.

al-Jāḥiẓ, ʿAmr ibn Baḥr. *al-Ḥayawān*. 7 vols. Ed. ʿAbd al-Salām Muḥammad Hārūn. [Cairo: Maktabat Muṣṭafā al-Bābī al-Ḥalabī wa-Awlādihi bi-Miṣr, A.H. 1356/1937–38 C.E.].

al-Jazīrī, ʿAbd al-Raḥmān. *Kitāb al-Fiqh ʿalāʾl-madhāhib al-arbaʿa*. Vol. 1. N.p.: Dār Iḥyāʾ al-Turāth al-ʿArabī, A.H. 1406/1986 C.E.

[al-Kisāʾī, Muḥammad ibn ʿAbd Allāh]. *The Tales of the Prophets of al-Kisaʾi.* Trans. W. M. Thackston, Jr. Boston: Twayne Publishers, 1978.

Kueny, Kathryn Mary. *A Drink of Many Colors: Altered States of Wine in Islam.* Doctoral dissertation submitted to the Divinity School of the University of Chicago, Chicago, Illinois, August 1995.

Lane, Edward William. *Arabic-English Lexicon.* 1863; facsimile, Beirut: Librairie du Liban, 1968.

Loeffler, Reinhold. *Islam in Practice: Religious Beliefs in a Persian Village.* Albany: State University of New York Press, 1988.

Mālik ibn Anas. *al-Muwaṭṭaʾ.* 2 vols. Ed. Bashshār ʿAwād Maʿrūf and Maḥmūd Muḥammad Khalīl. Beirut: Muʾassassat al-Risāla, A.H. 1412/1991 C.E.

Marcus, Julie. "Islam, Women and Pollution in Turkey." *Journal of the Anthropological Society of Oxford* 15, no. 3 (1984): 204–18.

———. *A World of Difference.* London; Atlantic Highlands, N.J.: Zed, 1992.

Maududi, Abul Aʿla. *The Meaning of the Qurān.* 8th ed. Trans. Muhammad Akbar. Lahore: Islamic Publications Ltd., 1988.

al-Mawsūʿa al-fiqhīya. 38 vols. to date. Dawlat al-Kuwayt: Wizārat al-Awqāf waʾl-Shuʾūn al-Islāmīya, 1987–.

McCane, Byron R. "Is a Corpse Contagious? Early Jewish and Christian Attitudes toward the Dead." *Society of Biblical Literature 1992 Seminar Papers.* Ed. Eugene H. Lovering, Jr. pp. 378–88.

McNeill, John T., and Helena M. Gamer. *Medieval Handbooks of Penance: A Translation of the Principal* libri poenitentiales *and Selections from Related Documents.* New York: Columbia University Press, 1938.

Meigs, Anna S. "A Papuan Perspective on Pollution." *Man* n.s., 13 (1978): 304–18.

Milgrom, Jacob. "Ethics and Ritual: The Foundations of the Biblical Dietary Laws," in *Religion and Law: Biblical-Judaic and Islamic Perspectives*, ed. Edwin B. Firmage et al., 159–91. Winona Lake, Ind.: Eisenbrauns, 1990.

Mir, Mustansir. *Coherence in the Qurʾan, a Study of Iṣlāḥī's Concept of Naẓm in Tadabbur-i Qurʾan.* Indianapolis: American Trust Publications, 1406/1986.

al-Mizzī. *Tahdhīb al-Kamāl.* Beirut, A.H. 1413/1992 C.E.

Morony, Michael G. *Iraq after the Muslim Conquest.* Princeton, N.J.: Princeton University Press, 1984.

Motzki, Harald. *Die Anfänge der islamischen Jurisprudenz.* Stuttgart: Deutsche Morgenländische Gesellschaft, 1991.

Mugnier, F. "Abstinence." *Dictionnaire de Spiritualité, ascétique et mystique,* ed. M. Viller et al. Paris: Beauchesne, 1932– .

Muslim ibn al-Ḥajjāj. *Ṣaḥīḥ Muslim bi-sharḥ al-imām Muḥyi'l-Dīn al-Nawawī al-musammā'l-Minhāj*. 18 vols. in 9. Ed. Khalīl Ma'mūn Shīḥā. Beirut: Dār al-Ma'rifa, A.H. 1414/1994 C.E.

Nagel, Tilman. *Rechtleitung und Kalifat: Versuch über eine Grundfrage der Islamischen Geschichte*. Studien zum Minderheitenproblem im Islam 2. Bonn: Selbstverlag des orientalischen Seminars der Universität Bonn, 1975.

al-Nasā'ī, Aḥmad ibn Shu'ayb. *al-Sunan al-kubrā*. Ed. Muḥammad Ḥabīb Allāh Amīr al-Dīn al-Atharī. Bombay: al-Dār al-Qayyima, A.H. 1405/1985 C.E.

Neusner, Jacob. *The Idea of Purity in Ancient Judaism*. Leiden: E. J. Brill, 1973.

Nöldeke, Theodor. *Geschichte des Qorâns*. Göttingen, 1860.

Ortner, Sherry B. "Is Female to Male as Nature is to Culture?" Reprinted in *Woman, Culture, and Society*, ed. Michelle Zimbalist Rosaldo and Louise Lamphere, 67–87. Stanford, Calif.: Stanford University Press, 1974, (c) 1974 by the Board of Trustees of the Leland Stanford Junior University.

Parker, Robert. *Miasma: Pollution and Purification in Early Greek Religion*. Oxford: Clarendon Press, 1983.

al-Qasṭallānī, Aḥmad ibn Muḥammad. *Irshād al-sārī li-sharḥ ṣaḥīḥ al-Bukhārī*. 10 vols. A.H. 1304/[1886–87 C.E.]; facsimile Baghdad: Maktabat al-Muthannā, n.d.

al-Qinūjī, Abū'l-Ṭayyib Ṣiddīq ibn Ḥasan ibn 'Alī. *Fatḥ al-barayān fī maqāṣid al-qur'ān*. Vol. 7. Ṣaydā and Beirut: al-Maktaba al-'Aṣrīya, A.H. 1412/1992 C.E.

al-Qurṭubī, Muḥammad ibn Aḥmad. *al-Jāmi' li-aḥkām al-qur'ān*. 20 vols. Cairo: Dār al-Kātib al-'Arabī li'l-Ṭabā'a wa'l-Nashr, A.H. 1967/1387 C.E.

Quṭb, Sayyid. *Fī ẓilāl al-qur'ān*. 8 vols. 5th ed. n.p. A.H. 1386/1967 C.E.

al-Rāzī, al-Fakhr. *al-Tafsīr al-kabīr*. 32 vols. in 16. 3d ed. N.p, n.d.

Reinhart, A. Kevin. "Impurity/No Danger." *History of Religions* 30 (1990–91): 1–24.

Ricoeur, Paul. *The Symbolism of Evil*. Boston: Beacon Press, 1967.

Rippin, Andrew. "The Function of *Asbāb al-Nuzūl* in Qur'ānic Exegesis." *BSOAS* 51 (1988): 1–20.

Robinson, Neal. *Discovering the Qur'an: A Contemporary Approach to a Veiled Text*. London: SCM Press Ltd, 1996.

Ryckmans, G. "La confession publique des péchés en Arabie méridionale préislamique." *Le Museon* 58 (1945): 1–14.

al-Ṣafadī, Khalīl ibn Aybak. *Das Biographische Lexikon des Ṣalāḥaddīn Ḥalīl ibn Aibak aṣ-Ṣafadī*. Bibliotheca Islamica, vol. 6. part 15. Ed. Bernd Radtke. Wiesbaden: in Kommission bei Franz Steiner Verlag, 1979.

Ṣafwat, Aḥmad Zakī. *Jamharat khuṭab al-'arab fī 'uṣūr al-'arabīya al-zāhira*. [Cairo]: Muṣṭafā al-Bābī al-Ḥalabī, 1962–.

Saḥnūn ibn Saʿīd al-Tanūkhī. *al-Mudawwana al-kubrā.* 4 vols. N.p., A.H. 1324/[1906–7 C.E.].

al-Ṣanʿānī, ʿAbd al-Razzāq. *al-Muṣannaf.* 11 vols. Ed. Ḥabībarraḥmān al-Aʿẓamī. Simlak, Dabhel/Beirut, A.H. 1391/1972 C.E.

Schacht, Joseph. *The Origins of Muhammadan Jurisprudence.* Oxford: Clarendon Press, 1950.

al-Shāfiʿī, Muḥammad ibn Idrīs. *al-Umm.* 8 vols. in 4. Beirut: Dār al-Maʿrifa, n.d.

al-Shaybānī, Muḥammad b. al-Ḥasan. *Kitāb al-Aṣl.* 5 vols. Ed. Abū'l-Wafā' al-Afghānī. Beirut: ʿĀlam al-Kutub, A.H. 1410/1990 C.E.

———. *Kitāb al-Āthār.* Karachi, A.H. 1385/1965 C.E.

———. *Kitāb al-Ḥujja ʿalā ahl al-Madīna.* 4 vols. Ed. Mahdī Ḥasan al-Kaylānī al-Qādirī. Beirut: ʿĀlam al-Kutub, A.H. 1403/1983 C.E.

———. *Muwaṭṭa' al-imām Mālik.* Ed. ʿAbd al-Wahhāb ʿAbd al-Laṭīf. Beirut: Dār al-Qalam, n.d.

al-Shirwānī, ʿAbd al-Ḥamīd. *Ḥawāshī al-ʿShirwānī wa Aḥmad ibn Qāsim al-ʿAbādī ʿalā tuḥfat al-muḥtāj bi-sharḥ al-minhāj.* 10 vols. N.p., n.d.

Spellberg, D. A. *Politics, Gender, and the Islamic Past: The Legacy of ʿA'isha bint Abi Bakr.* New York: Columbia University Press, 1994.

Stetkevych, Suzanne Pinckney. *The Mute Immortals Speak: Pre-Islamic Poetry and the Poetics of Ritual.* Ithaca and London: Cornell University Press, 1993.

al-Suyūṭī, Jalāl al-Dīn. *Asbāb al-nuzūl.* [Cairo]: Maktabat Nuṣayr, n.d.

———. *al-Durr al-manthūr fī'l-tafsīr bi'l-ma'thūr.* 6 vols. Tehran: al-Maṭbaʿa al-Islāmīya, A.H. 1377/[1957 C.E.]

———. *al-Itqān fī ʿulūm al-Qur'ān.* 4 vols. in 2. Ed. Muḥammad Abū'l-Faḍl Ibrāhīm. Manshūrāt al-Riḍā, A.H. 1343 Sh.

al-Ṭabarī, Muḥammad ibn Jarīr. *Jāmiʿ al-bayān ta'wīl āy al-qur'ān.* 30 vols. in 15. Beirut: Dār al-Fikr, A.H. 1408/1988 C.E.

———. *Tārīkh al-umam wa'l-mulūk.* 11 vols. Ed. Muḥammad Abū'l-Faḍl Ibrāhīm. Beirut, n.d.

al-Ṭaḥāwī, Abū Jaʿfar Aḥmad ibn Muḥammad. *Sharḥ maʿānī al-āthār.* Vol. 1. Ed. Muḥammad Zahrā al-Najjār and Muḥammad Sayyid Jādd al-Ḥaqq. Beirut: ʿĀlam al-Kutub, A.H. 1414/1994 C.E.

al-Thaʿālibī, ʿAbd al-Malik ibn Muḥammad. *Ghurar akhbār mulūk al-furs wa-siyarihim.* Ed. H. Zotenberg. Paris: Imprimerie Nationale, 1900.

al-Thaʿlabī. *Qiṣaṣ al-anbiyā' al-musammā bi-ʿarā'is al-majālis.* [Cairo]: Maktabat al-Kullīyāt al-Azharīya, n.d.

al-Tirmidhī. *Ṣaḥīḥ al-Tirmidhī.* [Cairo]: al-Maṭbaʿa al-Miṣrīya biʾl-Azhar, A.H. 1350/ 1931 C.E.

Von Rad, Gerhard. *Old Testament Theology.* Vol. I. Trans. D.M.G. Stalker. New York: Harper & Row, 1962.

Wansbrough, John. *Quranic Studies: Sources and Methods of Scriptural Interpretation.* Oxford: Oxford University Press, 1977.

———. *The Sectarian Milieu: Content and Composition of Islamic Salvation History.* Oxford; New York: Oxford University Press, 1978.

al-Washtānī, Muḥammad ibn Khalīfa. *Ikmāl ikmāl al-muʿallim.* Printed with Muslim ibn al-Ḥajjāj, *Ṣaḥīḥ Muslim.* 9 vols. Ed. Muḥammad Salīm Hāshim. Beirut: Dār al-Kutub al-ʿIlmīya, 1994.

Weiss, Bernard G. "Covenant and Law in Islam," in *Religion and Law: Biblical-Judaic and Islamic Perspectives,* ed. Edwin B. Firmage et al. 49–83. Winona Lake, Ind.: Eisenbrauns, 1990.

Wellhausen, J. *Reste arabischen Heidentums.* 2d ed. Berlin: Druck und Verlag von Georg Reimer, 1897.

Wensinck, A. J. "Die Entstehung der muslimischen Reinheitsgesetzgebung." *Der Islam* 5 (1914): 62–80.

al-Zajjāj (attributed). *Iʿrāb al-Qurʾān.* 3 vols. Ed. Ibrāhīm al-Ibyārī. [Cairo], A.H. 1383/1963 C.E.

al-Zamakhsharī, Maḥmūd ibn ʿUmar. *al-Kashshāf ʿan ghawāmiḍ al-tanzīl.* Vol. 2. Beirut: Dār al-Kutub al-ʿArabī, n.d.

al-Zarkashī, Badr al-Dīn Muḥammad ibn ʿAbd Allāh. *al-Burhān fī ʿulūm al-qurʾān.* 4 vols. N.p.: Dār Iḥyāʾ al-Kutub al-ʿArabīya, A.H. 1376/1957 C.E.

al-Zaylaʿī, Fakhr al-Dīn ʿUthmān ibn ʿAlī. *Tabyīn al-ḥaqāʾiq sharḥ kanz al-daqāʾiq.* 6 vols. Būlāq, A.H. 1313/[1895 C.E.].

Index

25322984R00153

Made in the USA
Lexington, KY
22 August 2013